FIFTY [KEY]

CLASSIC[...]

Ranging from Homer to Cassius Dio, *Fifty Key Classical Authors* is the essential introduction to the most significant writers and texts from the ancient world. Entries include:

- Aristotle
- Caesar
- Catullus
- Horace
- Lucan

- Ovid
- Quintilian
- Sappho
- Tacitus
- Virgil

With suggestions for further reading and a concise timeline, this chronological guide to influential Greek and Roman writers is an invaluable tool for anyone with an interest in classical civilisation.

Alison Sharrock is Reader in the Department of Classics and Ancient History at the University of Manchester.

Rhiannon Ash is a Lecturer in the Department of Greek and Latin at University College London.

ROUTLEDGE KEY GUIDES

Routledge Key Guides are accessible, informative and lucid handbooks, which define and discuss the central concepts, thinkers and debates in a broad range of academic disciplines. All are written by noted experts in their respective subjects. Clear, concise exposition of complex and stimulating issues and ideas makes *Routledge Key Guides* the ultimate reference resource for students, teachers, researchers and the interested lay person.

FIFTY KEY CLASSICAL AUTHORS

Alison Sharrock and Rhiannon Ash

London and New York

First published 2002
by Routledge
11 New Fetter Lane, London EC4P 4EE

Simultaneously published in the USA and Canada
by Routledge
29 West 35th Street, New York, NY 10001

Routledge is an imprint of the Taylor & Francis Group

© 2002 Alison Sharrock and Rhiannon Ash

Typeset in Times by Taylor & Francis Books Ltd
Printed and bound in Great Britain by TJ International Ltd, Padstow, Cornwall

British Library Cataloguing in Publication Data
A catalogue record for this book is available from the British Library

Library of Congress Cataloging in Publication Data
Sharrock, Alison.
Fifty key Classical authors / Alison Sharrock and Rhiannon Ash.
p.cm. – (Routledge key guides)
Includes bibliographical references (p.) and index.
1. Classical literature–History and criticism–Handbooks, manuals, etc.
2. Classical literature–Chronology–Handbooks, manuals, etc. 3. Civilization,
Classical–Handbooks, manuals etc. I. Title: 50 key Classical authors. II. Ash,
Rhiannon. III. Title. IV. Series.

PA3002.Z5 S53 2001
880′.09–dc21   2001048305

ISBN 0–415–16510–5 (hbk)
ISBN 0–415–16511–3 (pbk)

CHRONOLOGICAL LIST OF CONTENTS

ALPHABETICAL LIST
OF CONTENTS

PREFACE

This book is for students, of all sorts. We hope they will derive some profit and pleasure from it, and that they will come to outgrow it.

In consideration of our intended audience, we have tried to keep footnotes to a minimum. We beg the indulgence of those many scholars from whose learning we have profited, but whose names don't appear in the notes. We ask forgiveness also of those whose favourite author didn't quite make it into our list of fifty, for there are bound to be omissions that seem odd to some readers. We apologise particularly to students of the later centuries of 'antiquity', whose authors aren't represented here. That would be another book.

We acknowledge with gratitude the support and help of many friends and colleagues: Margaret Atkins, Susanna Braund, Sergio Casali, Andy Fear, Monica Gale, John Henderson, Jon Hesk, Stephen Instone, David Mackie, Chris Pelling, Tim Sharrock, Mathilde Skoie, Diana Spencer, Effie Spentzou, Richard Steadman-Jones, Richard Stoneman, Stephen Todd and Margaret Williamson. A special word of thanks should go to Sharon Smith, who gave service beyond the call of duty. The editorial staff at Routledge provided invaluable help and guidance. Finally, we would both like publicly to thank each other for a very happy collaboration.

This book is dedicated to the memory of the journalist Kerem Lawson, and to all his family and friends.

INTRODUCTION

When the Roman poet Horace dedicated his *Odes* to his patron Maecenas and, in the same act, presented them to the world, he did so with a poem in which he expressed the sentiment that 'if you insert me among the lyric bards, I shall touch the stars with my head' (*Odes* 1.1.35–6). Ancient literary theorists loved creating canons of authors in a given genre – comic dramatists, tragedians, lyric poets, epic poets, even women poets – partly because they liked categorising things and putting them into lists and partly because ancient Greek and (still more) Roman culture had a very strong sense of the authoritative power of the past, and of the ethical and aesthetic value of its heritage. In Roman society, this finds expression in the honour paid to *mos maiorum* ('the ways of our ancestors'). The notion applies in social *mores*, in politics, in religion and in literary culture. Horace, then, wanted to join the canon of lyric poets; he has undoubtedly succeeded in joining the canon of Classical authors that has had so much influence over the development of Western literary culture.

There are problems with canons. The primary problem is that a canon necessarily excludes, and this process tends to affect those who are otherwise already in some way socially excluded – the poor, women, foreigners, anyone who isn't a member of the dominant culture. By excluding, it also occludes, hides. Moreover, given that written texts, even once they are printed, aren't invulnerable to the ravages of time, the formation of a canon tends to encourage the survival of certain voices and the loss of others. If books aren't read, they cease to exist. So how do we justify the creation of our own canon? In some ways, this project of ours might look a bit reactionary, since the notion that history consists in the celebration of Great Men is associated with traditionalist approaches both to the past and to contemporary culture. Well, our 'Fifty Great Men' are actually 'Forty-Eight Great Men and Two Great Women'. Better than nothing.

A crucial thing about this book is that it is *not* a canon. It is very consciously not a codification of 'the best' Classical authors in isolation from other works of literature and literary criticism; rather, it is an introduction to some of the people and texts which make ancient Greco-Roman culture exciting, in the opinion of two people who work with ancient texts and modern students. Still, readers may take issue with some of the decisions we have made about who's in and who's out. In some cases, we have included representatives of genres: in Greek lyric, we have Sappho and Pindar, leaving out Alcaeus, Bacchylides and many others; in Greek oratory we have Demosthenes and Lysias, but not Isaeus or Isocrates; we have Juvenal but not Persius, Propertius but not Tibullus (except in so far as he gets a piggy-back from Sulpicia, which reverses 2,000 years of history). But our offerings are only a beginning. They seek to set readers on the path towards reading the Classics, from which they can branch out into other readings and other texts.

The survival of ancient texts is crucially bound up in the issue of the canon: partly because the canon promotes survival and partly because accidents of preservation feed into later canons. It is worth remembering that vastly more ancient literature has been lost than survives. How different would the ancient world look if we had a complete play of Middle Comedy, the prosecution speech in the murder-and-adultery case presented in Lysias 1, the second book of Aristotle's *Poetics* (as Eco fantasises in *The Name of the Rose*), Ennius' mid-Republican *Annals* in their entirety, the later books of Livy which dealt with Augustus, the poems of Gallus, Ovid's tragedy *Medea*, the autobiography of the younger Agrippina (the mother of Nero), Tacitus' *Book of Jokes* which is referred to by Fulgentius – not to mention all those works whose loss is so complete that we don't even know we are missing them. Before we go on to look at our selection of texts, then, a brief word about how we know anything at all about ancient authors.

Because most of us read our texts today in easy, clear modern editions, and in translations based on those editions, it is tempting to forget that these books are just the twenty-first–century manifestation of a complex and continuing process of survival, discovery and transmission. In brief, the main ways through which the words of ancient authors are knowable by modern editors are through manuscript tradition, through finds of papyrus, inscriptions and other direct ancient evidence, and through quotation. The last of these is itself dependent on one or other of the first two.

The beginning of the manuscript tradition is the process whereby literary works were disseminated in the ancient world. Copies were made, by hand. Works survived if more copies were made, and copies of the copies, and so on right up until the invention of printing in the fifteenth century (in the West). Indeed, the process continues beyond that time, although once the copies are no longer produced by hand the risk of getting things wrong and losing things is much reduced. Some ancient works reached the end of antiquity but not beyond; others survived the Middle Ages in only one or two manuscripts, or not at all; others have a huge and complex manuscript tradition. Sometimes the range of available manuscripts of a work will show a large number of variants. (Scribes make mistakes, which late scribes copy, and so on.) Or, perhaps worse, it may be that none of the existing versions in the extant manuscripts makes any sense, because the right one has been lost and nobody can make head nor tail of what is left. This is sometimes called a *locus desperatus* (hopeless case) – and is thankfully quite rare. It is a task requiring great skill and erudition to sift through the remains and come to plausible proposals for a text.

Some stages in the Chinese whispers can be cut through, and some losses of manuscripts overcome, by gifts of archaeology over the last couple of centuries. Even today, new pieces of papyrus, new inscriptions on stone, new graffiti on buildings, and so on, still come to light. But we shouldn't be too romantic or optimistic about this. The vast majority of such finds are yet more texts of Homer, or financial accounts, or laundry lists. And even if it does turn out to be something interesting, the ancient papyrus could easily be 500 years or more newer than the original author, so epigraphic evidence isn't a direct window onto the ancient world. The final means, quotation, is dependent on the other two, since the text in which something is quoted is itself subject to the same process, but it is worth mentioning as a separate category because it affects the way we read so many fragmentary texts. The fragments in these cases aren't broken manuscripts, or bits of papyrus which have been burnt or smudged or rotted or whatever. Rather, they are quotations in later authors, who might be preserving a juicy bit of an otherwise lost ancient text for us because of a metrical or philological oddity, or because the quoter thought the quotation proved his point about something else.[1]

Okay, so we've got our text. Why *Classical* texts? Let's go back to that 500 years between the papyrus find and the original author, and remember that the ancient Greek and Roman worlds, which we are inclined to think of as a single unit (a Greco-Roman mishmash), covered a vast range of time and space and cultural difference, as well as having a lot in common. This book ranges over some 1,000 years and could have gone further: we have made the conscious decision to stop before 'late antiquity' because of the enormous number of important authors from the third and fourth centuries AD and on. Even if we allow for the fact (or, rather, the impression) that time has speeded up with technological advances, it would still be worth remembering that the difference between Homer and Apuleius is nearly as great as the difference between the present day and William the Conqueror. One scholar put the point this way: writing in America in the 1960s, Otis suggested that the world of Virgil was closer to his own society than it was to the world of Homer, not in actual years but in certain kinds of cultural development, such as literacy, government, education and roads.[2] At the same time, it seems to me possible that Virgil might have said the opposite, and that both Virgil and Otis would be right.

This question about what we mean by Classical authors raises another issue on which this book might seem traditional – periodisation. We have chosen to present our authors in chronological order, and in groups, to which we even give names like 'Hellenistic' and 'Neronian'. It is now commonly recognised that the perceived 'periods' of ancient history (and indeed of any history) are products of ways of thinking about the past. They are useful tools for making sense of the world, but they are not themselves objective realities. This isn't to say that they are just inventions and that 'really' democratic Athens is just the same as imperial Rome – indeed, the point of our chronological ordering is to emphasise the senses in which that is *not* true – but rather it is to say that historical periods are nebulous and loose terms that we use to give us a structure and vocabulary for talking about the past, and which ought constantly to be questioned even as they are also utilised. Simple points to keep in mind: periods have fuzzy edges; periods reflect trends not absolutes; periods look different depending on how you look at them.[3]

For example, it is possible to see a great flowering of cultural activity during what we call the fifth century BC, centred on Athens: an exciting time, with the democratic reforms, Pericles, Thucydides, the Peloponnesian War, the Parthenon and tragedy. Classical Athens, the golden age. And then we could see another great outburst of activity in the Roman golden age: as the Republic dies and the new imperial system comes into action, we have Cicero and

Virgil, who between them constituted the staple diet for learning the Latin language and European social *mores* for nearly two millennia to come (I'm exaggerating only very slightly), and we have the Palatine library, the Ara Pacis (altar of peace), Catullus, Horace, Ovid, Livy and many more. Between these two great outpourings, we have something we call the 'Hellenistic' age, when, in the years after Alexander the Great, the library at his Egyptian city of Alexandria became an important focus for intellectual activity. This was a period of scholar-poets, in which there was a high premium on erudition and abstruse learning. There were poets like Aratus, who wrote a long poem on the constellations which was hailed by Callimachus as the sweetest of poetry (*Epigram* 27); Nicander, writing didactic poems on such exciting topics as cures for snake bites; a flourishing trade in epigrams, short poems on a range of topics, including erotically charged love poems addressed to both women and boys. It was also a time of interest in the emotions, in children, in the bizarre.[4] Or, after the great Augustan age at Rome, we are tempted – by a long history of scholarship and by the authors' own self-posturing – to see Decline: the imperial system corrupted, Latin turning silver. Finally (or, rather, first) the part of the story which is most of all subject to the effects of periodisation is the start. 'In the beginning, there was Homer.'

Well, no: the Homeric poems are themselves the products of a dynamic intertextual tradition which reaches back beyond our sight. And although it is true that in some ways the likes of Tacitus and Statius saw their own culture as in decline, as deteriorating from a greater past, so too did Catullus and Virgil – and even Homer. The simple stories of Rise and Fall, then, need to be used with caution and to be nuanced by a more dynamic, intertextual view of literary history.

Using this book

This book is designed primarily for undergraduates studying some form of Classics, although we hope it will be useful to students of other literatures, to school teachers and their most advanced pupils, and to the general reader. We have aimed to offer a brief introduction to the life and works of each author, but this isn't an encyclopedia or a dictionary: we have concentrated most of our efforts on producing literary essays, readings which try to capture something of what might be interesting or important or just fun in each author. Our primary aim is to encourage people to read the texts themselves. We would recommend that one useful exercise for the reader would be to test out our readings yourself, trying to find more examples from the texts which illustrate the points we raise. We would also hope to encourage readers to make connections, and it is with this in mind that we have devised the index in such a way as to point out some of the links which bind together the parts of the Classical canon.

At the end of each essay, we have directed the reader towards some of the main texts and translations, and made some suggestions for further reading. We have restricted our suggestions to works in English, on the grounds that this book is primarily designed for English-speaking students. We have tried not to fill too much space with bibliographical details and long lists of books because, in this Internet age, finding secondary material is an easier task than it has ever been and finding information about new books even easier. Here we offer suggestions about some of the main suppliers of Classical editions. The aim is for readers to be able to make judgements about the kind of edition they want and to know how to look for it. We give website addresses here because, although they won't remain stable, they are likely to continue to be the best way of finding the most up-to-date information about the editions available.

Oxford Classical Texts   The real thing, as far as it exists today. We refer to them frequently, abbreviating to OCT. These are Latin and Greek texts with *apparatus criticus* (listing of variant readings). All except a few of the most recent have introductions in Latin, discussing the process of editing the text. There are some surprising omissions (Ovid's *Metamorphoses* still awaits its OCT), and some editions are old and awaiting replacement. But still generally the best choice for a basic Greek or Latin text.

http://www.oup.co.uk/search/?view=searchresults&field-6556= Oxford+Classical+Texts

Teubner   When there isn't an OCT, try a Teubner: also excellent texts and sometimes better or more complete than the Oxford version.

http://www.teubner.de/

Loeb Classical Library   These editions have English translation with facing Greek text (green covers) or Latin text (red covers), introductions and brief notes. Some of the newest are excellent, and also good for ancient testimonies to our authors. Some of the translations, particularly older ones, are dated and/or idiosyncratic. An excellent standby and all-rounder.

http://www.hup.harvard.edu/Web_Loeb/Loeb.home.page.html

Penguin Classics Penguin publish translations of very many Greek and Roman authors. Modern ones in particular are generally both readable and accurate, with useful introductions and a few notes.

http://www.penguinclassics.com/

World's Classics These editions, published by Oxford University Press, are the obvious alternative to Penguin translations. They are more scholarly than their rival, particularly in the introductions which can be quite technical in places, and their notes are more extensive (although still small). They are generally extremely reliable translations, and since most books have been produced recently by leading scholars in the field they are in general a very safe bet.

http://www.worldsclassics.co.uk/

When we move into commentaries, it is harder to recommend a series which comes anywhere near being complete. Nonetheless, two are worthy of mention.

Cambridge Greek and Latin Classics According to its own statement:

> This series was conceived to meet the demand for classical texts with commentaries aimed at student level that say more about works as literature and concentrate less exclusively on textual and syntactical matters.

Introduction, text, commentary. Excellent for study of set books.

http://uk.cambridge.org/classics/cglc/author/

Aris and Phillips The 'Classical Texts' series from this publisher offers editions aimed at undergraduates, containing introduction, Greek or Latin text, facing translation and notes, mostly keyed to the translation. Less advanced than the Cambridge series.

http://www.arisandphillips.com/cat98011.htm

A few other books are worth drawing to the reader's attention. The Classical Association publishes a series of pamphlets called *Greece and Rome New Surveys in the Classics*, which are in general good basic introductions to ancient authors and to the contemporary debates about them. For this reason, the New Surveys are good sources of bibliographical information.

Cambridge University Press's *Landmarks of World Literature* doesn't as yet have many Classical works (Homer, Virgil, Aeschylus), but it will be worth watching. Short, very readable books by experts in the field.

http://uk.cambridge.org/series/lwl/default.htm

The Cambridge University Press *Companions* are another general literary series with some Classical examples and more to come. Already in existence are *Aristotle*, *Virgil*, *Plato* and *Greek Tragedy*; *Ovid* will appear soon after this book, and there are plans for several more. These are substantial multi-authored books, which are both accessible and challenging.

http://uk.cambridge.org/series/ccl/default.htm

General further reading

There are several large reference works which should be found in any good university library.

Conte, G.B., *Latin Literature: A History*, trans. J. Solodow, Princeton, NJ: Princeton University Press, 1994.

Dihle, A., *A History of Greek Literature from Homer to the Hellenistic Period*, London: Routledge, 1994.

Easterling, P.E. (ed.), *Cambridge History of Classical Literature: vol. I (Greek Literature)*, Cambridge: Cambridge University Press, 1985.

Fantham, E., *Roman Literary Culture from Cicero to Apuleius*, Baltimore, MD: Johns Hopkins University Press, 1996.

Hornblower, S. and Spawforth, A. (eds), *Oxford Classical Dictionary*, 3rd edn, Oxford: Oxford University Press, 1996.

Howatson, M.C. (ed.), *Oxford Companion to Classical Literature*, 2nd edn, Oxford: Oxford University Press, 1989 (also available in abridged form).

Kenney, E.J. (ed.), *Cambridge History of Classical Literature: vol. II (Latin Literature)*, Cambridge: Cambridge University Press, 1982.

A few technical terms

Throughout this book, a number of critical terms are used, which are in common use among literary critics but may need some explanation for the reader new to such matters.

Intertextuality   There is a great deal of theory around this important critical idea. The crucial point is to understand that no work of literature is an island, that all texts come into being through interaction with other texts and that the production of meaning isn't isolated but interactive. Excellent discussions of such matters in Classical literature can be found in: L. Edmunds, 'Intertextuality today', *Lexis*, 13, 1995, pp. 3–22; D.P. Fowler, 'On the shoulders of giants: Intertextuality and Classical Studies', *Materiali e Discussioni per l'analisi dei testi classici*, 39, 1997, pp. 13–34; S. Hinds, *Allusion and Intertext: Dynamics of Appropriation in Roman Poetry*, Cambridge: Cambridge University Press, 1998.

Teleology   The 'telos' of something is its end or goal. This applies in the literal sense of the final limit, but also in the symbolic sense of 'purpose' or, in modern jargon, 'outcome'. If we speak of a narrative being strongly teleological, we mean that it has a strong narrative line which drives the story forward and also that it has a big purpose towards which its values, as well as its narrative, are directed. Epic is teleological.

Programmatic   Ancient authors liked to tell their audiences what the work was about. They often did this not directly through a prologue or an introduction (like this one) but more symbolically through self-reflexive language, which hints at the essentiality of the text itself while also speaking the content of the text. For example, 'arms and the man' (the famous opening of Virgil's *Aeneid*) tells us that this is an epic, that this epic is interactive with the two great Homeric epics and that we ought to take it seriously. Likewise, the song of the locked-out lover is programmatic for elegy; the quarrels with critics in Terence and Aristophanes are programmatic for comedy (highly antagonistic in the ancient world); the Republican-style annalistic opening of Tacitus' *Annals* is a programmatic statement about the senatorial position of the historian.

Genre   Ancient authors had a very strong sense of genre and generic appropriateness, which can work as well in the breaking as in the making. Genre, in this sense, means epic, tragedy, elegy, lyric, oratory, diatribe, biography, and so on. Here, if anywhere, is a set of categories with fuzzy edges, for the authors will often deliberately push back the boundaries of the genre, as Juvenal does in giving lowly satire epic proportions or Ovid does in inventing a mixture of elegy and didactic for his *Ars Amatoria*.

Literary life The writers of ancient *Lives* of literary figures are themselves constrained by the demands of their genre. This is an important point, which we shall make several times in this book. Much of what we know (or, rather, what we repeat) about the lives of Classical authors comes from guess-work based on the literary works themselves and on ancient biographers' ideas about what would be appropriate, what would make a good story for their subject, what would sound plausible because it has sounded plausible before. Be suspicious, then, if the dates of a watershed in a writer's life happen to coincide with some major historical event; if it is said that a practitioner of a given genre was taught by the most famous immediate predecessor in the same genre; if a motif keeps recurring ... in fact, be suspicious of anything you are told about an author's life! This isn't to say that everything is wrong, for indeed, apart from anything else, the poets themselves may well have modelled their lives on those of earlier practitioners. It is simply to say that 'life' is a 'genre'.[5]

Persona A 'persona' in Latin is a mask. Ancient drama usually (perhaps always – it is disputed) used masked actors, their masks designating individual characters and character-types. In literary criticism, the term has come to mean the projections of themselves that authors display in their works. It isn't only authors who do this, however: the term can also be used for any role or self-image or projected image which a character may present within a literary work – or indeed in life. It is specially important to think about persona in literature which makes extensive use of first-person presentation ('I did this'), but it isn't only by saying 'I am' that authors can create images of themselves.

Nachleben How writers are received by later generations, and how their work is imitated, used and interpreted, has a significant effect on how still later readers respond to them. This 'afterlife' is referred to as 'Nachleben'.

Notes

1 On this, see M.P. Brown, *A Guide to Western Historical Scripts from Antiquity to 1600*, London: British Library, 1990; L. Reynolds and N. Wilson, *Scribes and Scholars: A Guide to the Transmission of Greek and Latin Literature*, 3rd edn, Oxford: Oxford University Press, 1991.
2 B. Otis, *Virgil: A Study in Civilised Poetry*, Oxford: Oxford University Press, 1964, p. 3. What he actually says is:

> What did [Virgil] do that Homer did not do, so that in the doing an obvious 'imitation' of Homer could become the true epic of a metropolis that has vastly more in common with contemporary New York than with Mycenae or Tiryns?

While I think there is a great deal to question in Otis's progressivist story of literature and culture, he makes a valuable point. Maybe we should also remember that Otis was writing that book before either of the authors of this book were born.
3 On this whole topic, see M. Golden and P. Toohey (eds), *Inventing Ancient Culture: Historicism, Periodization and the Ancient World*, London: Routledge, 1997.
4 We should probably think of these differences as primarily changes of emphasis or of artistic fashion, rather than as real differences in the valuation of children, the bizarre or anything else.
5 See M.R. Lefkowitz, *Lives of the Greek Poets*, London: Duckworth, 1981, which will be mentioned several times in this book.

IN THE BEGINNING

HOMER

Modern scholars have probably written more about Homer's epics and their reception than about any other surviving works of literature by any Classical author. Yet we still don't know for sure who Homer was, nor even whether the epics were the work of a single author. The *Iliad* and the *Odyssey* are the first (and arguably the greatest) extant works of Greek literature, created perhaps at some point between 750 and 700 BC by a poet (or poets) working against the backdrop of the oral tradition. This creative environment had a fundamental impact on the nature of Homeric poetry, which is so distinctive because of its repeated epithets and vivid formulae. Homer's epics were composed at a pivotal time, not least of all because the Greek alphabet had recently been created via a Phoenician original, perhaps early in the eighth century BC.[1] Although the emergence of the Greek alphabet would ultimately sound the death-knell for true oral poetry, Homer's epics preserve aspects of an oral culture which flourished in the so-called 'Dark Ages' of Greece (*c.* 1100–776 BC).

Any number of theories have been put forward to explain the process by which the *Iliad* and the *Odyssey* were written down.[2] Either the poet himself (or an interested party) exploited the new medium of writing to preserve the epics within his own lifetime or else the epics survived and continued to flourish within the oral tradition after the poet's death, only being written down much later towards the end of the sixth century BC during the reign of the Athenian tyrant Pisistratus, who died in 527 BC.[3] Perhaps a combination of both versions is most likely: Pisistratus could certainly have assembled different versions of Homer's epics which were in circulation in order to preserve the best for posterity (or, in the short term, for performance at the Panathenea festival). Indeed, scholars have suggested that portions of the epics were either added later (*Iliad* 10) or were work-in-progress in need of a final polish (*Odyssey* 23.297–24.548). At any rate, analysts of the epic language, in which different dialects from different periods are mixed together, suggest that the *Iliad* was composed first, and then the *Odyssey*. Both poems are written in dactylic hexameters and each contains twenty-four books.[4]

The *Iliad* is a poem about war and (as the title suggests) about Troy, although the final destruction of the city is conspicuously not narrated in the poem itself. Other poets, such as Virgil in *Aeneid* 2 and Quintus Smyrnaeus in the third century AD, subsequently composed epics which filled the gap, but Homer himself only foreshadowed the final cataclysm with increasing insistence. So Zeus tells Hera that he will prolong the fighting 'until the Achaians capture tall Ilium through the schemes of Athene' (*Iliad* 15.70–1) and Andromache addresses her husband Hector's corpse, lamenting the likely fate of their young son, Astyanax: 'I think he will never reach manhood, for before then this city will be sacked utterly. For you, its guardian, have perished ... ' (*Iliad* 24.727–30). These are only two instances of a pervasive device, which means that the end of the narrative does not, in effect, coincide with the end of the story. Virgil would later use this same technique on an even grander scale, politicising and extending the predictions so that they looked forward to his own contemporary world. Homer's foreshadowing is enacted on both the divine and human levels, but operates within a more confined sphere.

Many of the events which we consider to be absolutely central to the Trojan war, such as the infiltration of the city by the wooden horse, the slaughter of the defenceless Astyanax (such a dominant event in Euripides' *Women of Troy*) and the murder of the old king Priam, don't feature directly in the design of the *Iliad*, but the art of good storytelling involves knowing what to include and what to leave out. The *Odyssey* fills in a few gaps retrospectively, as the bard Demodocus sings of the fall of Troy (*Odyssey* 8.499–520) and Odysseus, summoning ghosts from the underworld, tells the dead Achilles about the exploits of his son Neoptolemus (*Odyssey* 11.523–37). Yet this comes later: the *Iliad*'s central theme is relatively circumscribed and springs from the anger of Achilles, the greatest warrior fighting for the besieging Greek forces. His outraged withdrawal from the battlefield is triggered when Agamemnon deprives him of his prize of war, a woman called Briseis. Achilles has urged Agamemnon to give back his trophy, Chryseis, the daughter of a priest of Apollo, because the god is angry with the Greeks after the king's refusal to return the girl to her father.

While the *Odyssey* revolves around one man's fate, the *Iliad* presents two complex groups: the Greek army, with its hierarchy of heroes, and the city of Troy, with its distinctive female and familial elements. Achilles and Hector certainly dominate the action, but they are depicted against the broad backdrop of a heroic community. Certain features are common to both sides, such as the presence of wise old men who cannot fight, but whose long experience of life allows them to act as advisers: on the Greek side, there are Nestor and Phoenix, while on the Trojan side, there is Priam.

Yet there are also differences, especially at the start. When the two sides march into battle, they are sharply differentiated:

> the Trojans advanced with clamour and shouting, like wildfowl, as when the clamour of cranes goes high to the heavens, when the cranes escape the winter time and the unceasing rains and clamorously fly to the streaming Ocean, bringing to the Pygmaian men bloodshed and destruction: at daybreak they bring on the baleful battle against them. But the Achaian men went silently, breathing strength, stubbornly resolved each in his heart to stand by the others.
>
> (*Iliad* 3.2–9)

Trojan cacophony is contrasted with ominous Greek silence.

These collective differences are reinforced by distinctive individuals. Paris, the cause of all the trouble, who is decked out in a colourful leopard-skin (*Iliad* 3.17), is taken from the battle by Aphrodite to indulge in love-making with Helen (*Iliad* 3.373–447). His articulation of his passion for Helen (*Iliad* 3.441–6) foreshadows a similar speech by Zeus to Hera before they go to bed (*Iliad* 14.314–28), but Paris isn't a god. Both Paris' dress and his hedonistic nature cohere with stereotypical images of gaudy, lascivious easterners.

Another difference between the Greeks and the Trojans emerges when we see Hector talking to his wife Andromache and, after removing his frightening helmet, playing with his baby son Astyanax (*Iliad* 6.390–493). Trojan identity is so wrapped up in the family, which marks them off from the Greeks whose families are far away in Greece. Indeed, even Helen's flight from Menelaus underscores the fragmentation of the family unit. Achilles is the only Greek who has any contact with his family, but his mother Thetis is a goddess and his encounters with her symbolically take place away from the Greek camp.

However, as the epic progresses, these initial differences between the two sides are elided. Greeks and Trojans undergo common experiences in battle, death and bereavement. We watch helplessly as individuals on both sides are locked into a downward spiral of destruction by their desire for honour, revenge and victory. When Hector kills Patroclus, the young warrior in his last words predicts that the Trojan will be killed in turn by Achilles (*Iliad* 16.851–4). Hector rejects this as a possibility, but, on the point of being slaughtered by Achilles, similarly foretells death for his killer (*Iliad* 22.356–60). Achilles recognises that his death may be imminent, but he is prepared to accept it, whenever Zeus and the other immortal gods determine. The appearance of the adjective 'immortal' (*Iliad* 22.366) in a context where mortality is the main issue seems particularly poignant, standard epithet for the gods though this is.

Above all it is in the final book that the notion of common humanity transcending the different sides is played out. After the funeral games for Patroclus in Book 23, where the Greek heroes take their final bow, the focus shifts to the extraordinary journey of the old man Priam to the Greek camp to ask for the return of his son's corpse from the man who killed him. All in all, the prognosis for this mission isn't good, as the book opens with the distraught Achilles dragging Hector's body around Patroclus' tomb (*Iliad* 24.11–18). However, Apollo, whose displeasure with the Greeks began the epic, expresses pity for Hector, which prompts Zeus to intervene. Sending Thetis to Achilles and Iris to Priam, the king of the gods engineers the payment of a ransom to secure the return of Hector's body to his grieving family. Even as Priam is about to set out on the journey which will do most to elide the differences between Greeks and Trojans, it is significant that he reminds us of the Trojan stereotype, angrily denouncing his surviving sons as 'liars, dancers and champions at beating the floor in dances' (*Iliad* 24.261). Hector, he suggests, was different, but we can speculate that this was probably why he died.

Although Priam's confrontation with Achilles was precipitated by the gods, at the moment of their face-to-face encounter, the divine architects fade into the background as the old man kisses the hands of the man who had killed so many of his sons and appeals to him, urging him to remember his own father, Peleus, and to take pity accordingly. The impact of this speech on both men is devastating:

> He [Achilles], having taken the old man's hands, pushed him away gently, and the two remembered, as Priam, having sunk to the ground at Achilles' feet, wept vehemently for manslaughtering Hector and Achilles wept now for his own father, now again for Patroclus.

> (*Iliad* 24.508–12)

This is perhaps the finest moment in a poem filled with fine moments. The sheer power of Achilles' emotions prompts him to

push away the old man, but he does so gently. He isn't rejecting
Priam's supplication, but is trying to soften the intensity of the pain
by creating a modicum of physical distance between them. Yet the
pair are intertwined from the very start of this passage by the use of
a verb in the dual form. This is an archaic usage which can only be
introduced when two protagonists are the subject of a particular
verb, and naturally it suggests a particularly strong connection
between the two subjects. This moment is intensified by a gap in
Priam's knowledge of the situation. Priam has tried to stir up
Achilles' feelings of pity by asking the hero to identify him with his
own father, Peleus, who is also an old man, albeit one who has a
living son. However, Achilles knows that his own death is imminent
and that, before too long, Peleus will be undergoing the same
agonies of outliving his child as Priam is experiencing before
Achilles' very eyes.[5] Here too there is a moment of foreshadowing,
one which Achilles understandably finds hard to bear.

It is one of the paradoxes of the poem that such intensely painful
moments generate a kind of aesthetic pleasure, which would have been
especially acute for the original listeners, who were hearing the story
as a group surrounded by their own parents and children. Today, we
tend to do our reading alone and in silence, which is a far cry from the
atmosphere in which the epics were originally performed.

The *Iliad* sets a precedent to which all subsequent epic poets had
to respond. Homer uses so many devices which are replicated and
refined subsequently within the genre, even when the creative
medium of oral poetry had long disappeared. No doubt Homer
himself was to some extent passing on techniques which others had
deployed before him, but it is through his poetry that they become
famous. The most notable are the *teichoskopia* (*Iliad* 3.161–242,
Helen and Priam), that is the scene whereby characters look down
from a city wall at the figures below and discuss them; the epic
catalogue (*Iliad* 2.484–779); the use of extended similes, the
ekphrasis, that is the device whereby the poet stops the action to
describe in detail a particular object (for example, *Iliad* 18.483–608,
the extended description of Achilles' shield);[6] the stylised fighting;
the use of set epithets; and, above all, the creation of a divine
pantheon, whose originality is highlighted by Herodotus:

> It is they [Homer and Hesiod] who gave the Greeks a
> theogony and gave the gods their titles; they who assigned

them their statuses and skills and gave an indication of their appearance.

(Histories 2.53)

The inclusion of anthropomorphic gods, who regularly involve themselves in human affairs, is perhaps one of Homer's most important legacies to the genre.[7] The *Iliad* presents various partisan gods and goddesses, who lend their support to one side or the other, and whose immortal status brings into sharp relief the suffering and fleeting nature of mortal lives. As Rutherford has observed, 'The most important aspect of the gods in the *Iliad* is the way in which they help to define the human condition'.[8] Even Zeus, the king of the gods, is said to have a soft spot for Troy (*Iliad* 4.44–52), a city which has loyally made sacrifices at his altars (although ultimately this piety will do her citizens no good). Other pro-Trojan divinities are Apollo and Aphrodite, while the Greeks are supported by Athena, Poseidon and Hera.

It is particularly disturbing that the gods are often gripped by all too human emotions, such as anger, jealousy or love. These are 'warts and all' gods who sulk, cry, make love and have family quarrels, but who also have power and immortality. Of course, the gulf between what we, the external audience, witness and what the protagonists of the poem themselves see is a powerful narrative device. Sometimes an individual will catch a glimpse of a divinity, such as when Achilles sees Athena, who has grabbed him from behind by the hair (*Iliad* 1.194–200), but the audience has the privileged viewpoint, as when we observe memorable scenes such as the seduction of Zeus by Hera (*Iliad* 14.153–351) or the council of the gods (*Iliad* 4.1–72) when Zeus and Hera refer to cities of men rather as if they were bargaining chips in some kind of game.

Homer's second epic, the *Odyssey*, is rather a different kind of work from the *Iliad*. It traces the homeward journey of the Greek hero, Odysseus, after the war has finished, and explores the chaos (emotional and practical) caused by his prolonged absence from Ithaca. Here his loyal wife Penelope is under siege from various suitors and his son Telemachus has grown up without knowing his father. Where the action of the *Iliad* was restricted to Troy and the Greek camp (with various interludes in heaven), the *Odyssey* is much more panoramic, both in time and in space, as Odysseus travels through various magical lands over the Aegean in his effort to return home. The poem's narrative framework is more ambitious than that of its predecessor, as we are presented with a 'split-screen' structure focusing both on the roving Odysseus and on his family in Ithaca. Each screen has its own distinct set of protagonists, who are physically separate, but who remain emotionally interconnected, even after twenty years have passed.

Only when Odysseus finally returns to Ithaca in *Odyssey* 13 do the two worlds start to become reintegrated, but it is an expression of his long absence that he fails to recognise his homeland once he arrives. His patron goddess Athena has to intervene to tell him where he is. Moreover, just as it takes Odysseus some time to realise that he is home, the complex process of reintegration between individuals after twenty years requires more than a simple recognition scene (of which there are many in the second half of the poem: Telemachus, Argus, Eurycleia, Eumaeus, Philoetius, Penelope and Laertes all have their recognition scenes with Odysseus). Odysseus and Penelope naturally need plenty of time to tell each other what has happened to them over their twenty-year separation (*Odyssey* 23.300–9).

One reason why the *Odyssey* has such a different tone from the *Iliad* is the presence of vivid, carefully constructed female characters throughout the narrative. Since the *Iliad* was a poem of war, there was perhaps not so much scope for depicting female characters, but Homer has certainly made up for lost time in the *Odyssey*. Indeed, at the end of the nineteenth century, Samuel Butler once came up with the contentious (but engaging) theory that the poem was actually composed by a woman,[9] but this idea rests on the dubious basis that only people of a particular gender or race can write meaningfully about their own set of experiences.

Among the more memorable female characters in the *Odyssey* are the divine sorceress Circe, the nymph Calypso, Helen (who gets to tell her side of the story in *Odyssey* 4), the beautiful princess Nausicaa, Odysseus' guardian goddess Athena, his old nurse Eurycleia and, above all, his loyal wife Penelope. Penelope is presented as a worthy wife for Odysseus, since she mirrors his cunning in so many ways. Not only does she put off the suitors for four years by pretending that she cannot marry until she has finished weaving a funeral shroud for Laertes, which she carefully unpicks every night (*Odyssey* 2.93–110, 19.137–56 and 24.128–46), but she also checks that Odysseus is really Odysseus by ordering their marriage-bed to be moved. Only Odysseus can know that the bedpost consists of an olive tree, so his expression of disbelief confirms his identity (*Odyssey* 23.174–206).

Penelope is certainly an enigmatic figure, but she is also unusual. Despite the extent to which she is portrayed as cunning, even deceitful, nevertheless she still emerges from Homer's story as an ideal wife. Elsewhere in Greek literature, cunning women tend to signal trouble for men and, indeed, after Homer there developed 'a subordinate tradition that competed with the "vulgate" of a chaste and faithful Penelope'.[10] Not every reader of Homer was prepared to overlook Penelope's crafty ways, despite the unusual circumstances.

In structural terms, the loving relationship which Penelope and Odysseus share with one another binds the epic together even when the story ranges very far afield. On the island of Ogygia, for instance, the alluring nymph Calypso marvels at the longing Odysseus feels for the absent Penelope (*Odyssey* 5.206–13), despite the gilded cage in which Calypso has placed him. Odysseus diplomatically reassures Calypso that Penelope is far less attractive than she is, but we don't believe him: he is simply trying to spare Calypso's feelings.

Female characters also allow scope for humour within the epic. One of the nicest examples is the encounter between Odysseus and the beautiful young princess Nausicaa on Phaeacia (*Odyssey* 6). Odysseus, caked in salt and totally naked after his narrow escape from the sea, emerges from the bushes clutching nothing but a branch and approaches Nausicaa and her friends, who are washing some clothes. The friends run away, leaving Nausicaa to stand her ground. In the circumstances, Odysseus wisely decides not to supplicate the princess by falling at her knees in case this causes alarm, and against all the odds, he wins her over with a charming speech in which he compares her with Artemis. The gulf between his extraordinary appearance and his captivating words creates a wonderful comic moment, which shows off Odysseus' natural intelligence at its best and wins him a warm welcome in the palace of Nausicaa's father, Alcinous. The poise with which Odysseus handles this situation can be contrasted strongly with the way in which the less competent Aeneas handles the chance meeting with his mother Venus disguised as a huntress in *Aeneid* 1.

There is so much more that we would like to know about Homer and his world. For example, why is there such a close relationship between his epics and themes which appear in Near Eastern texts such as the Epic of Gilgamesh? How closely can the events of the *Iliad* be related to the thirteenth century BC, the period when the Trojan war is assumed to have happened? When and where were these unusually long epics first performed? How and why were the epics preserved in the first place? In the absence of clear answers to these questions, we can at least enjoy Homer's epics for their own sake. If modern critical techniques, such as narratology, are continuing to shed new light on these rich texts,[11] that is a mark of the extraordinary creativity of the mind (or minds) which originally produced them.

Notes

1   The first surviving Greek inscriptions are usually dated to *c*. 770–50 BC.
2   See R. Thomas, *Literacy and Orality in the Ancient World*, Cambridge: Cambridge University Press, 1992, pp. 44–50.
3   On Pisistratus, see H. Shapiro, *Art and Cult under the Tyrants in Athens*, Mainz am Rhein: Philipp von Zabern, 1989, pp. 1–5.
4   The book divisions were probably not created by the poet, but were added in the Hellenistic era. See R. Janko, *The Iliad: A Commentary*, vol. 4, books 13–16, Cambridge: Cambridge University Press, 1992, p. 31.
5   See O. Taplin, *Homeric Soundings: The Shaping of the Iliad*, Oxford: Oxford University Press, 1992, p. 270.
6   This device wasn't restricted to epic. See J.A.W. Heffernan, *The Museum of Words: The Poetics of Ekphrasis from Homer to Ashbery*, Chicago, IL, and London: University of Chicago Press, 1993.
7   On how later epic writers responded to Homer in this area, see D. Feeney, *The Gods in Epic*, Oxford: Oxford University Press, 1991.
8   R. Rutherford, *Homer*, Greece and Rome New Surveys in the Classics 26, Oxford: Oxford University Press, 1996, p. 44.
9   See Rutherford, *op. cit.*, p. 69.
10 M.A. Katz, *Penelope's Renown: Meaning and Indeterminacy in the Odyssey*, Princeton, NJ: Princeton University Press, 1991, p. 77.
11 See I.J.F. de Jong, *Narrators and Focalizers: The Presentation of the Story in the Iliad*, Amsterdam: Grüner, 1987, and de Jong in I. Morris and B. Powell (eds), *A New Companion to Homer*, Leiden, New York and Cologne: Brill, 1997, pp. 305–25.

See also in this book

Apollonius Rhodius, Callimachus, Hesiod, Lucan, Statius, Virgil

Texts, translations and commentaries

The Greek text is available in OCT, Teubner and Loeb.

The Penguin translations of the *Iliad* and *Odyssey* by E.V. Rieu have now been superseded by those of R. Fagles (together with the Penguin translation of the *Iliad* by M. Hammond), but there are also Oxford World's Classics translations of the *Iliad* by R. Fitzgerald and of the *Odyssey* by W. Shrewring, and University of Chicago translations of the *Iliad* and *Odyssey* by R. Lattimore.

There are commentaries on *Iliad* 24 by C. MacLeod and on *Odyssey* 19–20 by R. Rutherford in the Cambridge Greek and Latin Classics Series, and on *Iliad* 8–9 by C.H. Wilson and on *Odyssey* 1–2 by P.V. Jones in the Aris and Phillips Series. There are also multi-volume commentaries on the *Iliad* by G.S. Kirk, J.B. Hainsworth, R. Janko, M.W. Edwards and N. Richardson published by Cambridge University Press, and on the *Odyssey* by A. Heubeck, S. West, J.B. Hainsworth, A. Hoekstra, J. Russo and M. Fernandez-Galiano published by Oxford University Press.

Further reading

Bowra, C.M., *Homer*, London: Duckworth, 1972.

Cohen, B., *The Distaff Side: Representing the Female in Homer's Odyssey*, Oxford and New York: Oxford University Press, 1995.

Griffin, J., *Homer on Life and Death*, Oxford: Oxford University Press, 1980.

Heffernan, J.A.W., *The Museum of Words: The Poetics of Ekphrasis from Homer to Ashbery*, Chicago, IL, and London: University of Chicago Press, 1993.

Jong, I.J.F. de, *Narrators and Focalizers: The Presentation of the Story in the Iliad*, Amsterdam: Grüner, 1987.

Katz, M.A., *Penelope's Renown: Meaning and Indeterminacy in the Odyssey*, Princeton, NJ: Princeton University Press, 1991.

Morris, I. and Powell, B. (eds), *A New Companion to Homer*, Leiden, New York and Cologne: Brill, 1997.

Parry, A. (ed.), *The Making of Homeric Verse: The Collected Papers of Milman Parry*, Oxford: Oxford University Press, 1971.

Rutherford, R., *Homer*, Greece and Rome New Surveys in the Classics 26, Oxford: Oxford University Press, 1996.

Segal, C., *Singers, Heroes and Gods in the Odyssey*, Ithaca, NY, and London: Cornell University Press, 1995.

Taplin, O., *Homeric Soundings: The Shaping of the Iliad*, Oxford: Oxford University Press, 1992.

Thomas, R., *Literacy and Orality in the Ancient World*, Cambridge: Cambridge University Press, 1992.

HESIOD

Mount Helicon is famous throughout Western literature as the sacred haunt of the Muses. At the opening of the *Theogony*, Hesiod relates how he met these nine musical goddesses while he was tending his sheep on Helicon, and received from them instructions to sing of the generations of the gods. A long progeny of poetic imagery derives from this meeting: in the form both of allusions by later poets to the scene and of actual cultic practices connected with the Muses in the area. Helicon signifies poetry and is 'sacred to the

Muses' largely because Hesiod lived there and talked about it.[1] The local river Permessos and the spring Hippocrene (supposedly created when the ground was struck by the hoof of the mythical horse Pegasus), which also feature in the scene, share in the poetic symbolism.

Although Hesiod was admired throughout antiquity as a great poet, he belongs to a world which is fundamentally different not only from the modern world, but even from the later Classical world. He lived at probably around the same time as the Homeric poems were taking their present shape.[2] The eighth to fifth centuries were a time when the world was alive with myth, with gods in the wind, in the mountains, in the emotions and in all people's actions, with a mythic past alive in the present, but also unknowable.[3] The mythic expression of poetic inspiration (the meeting with the Muses) would probably have been understood by Hesiod and his audience both as a 'real vision of the divine' and as a 'metaphor for thinking of poetry': indeed, they probably wouldn't have made that distinction at all.

What is crucial about Hesiod isn't just that he was a very early poet, but that he spoke in his poetry about his experiences as a poet, thus providing us with the first surviving ancient 'poet's voice', in the sense of a developed, self-aware personality presented as a first-person character in poetry. This isn't to say, however, that he wrote autobiography. Everything we know about Hesiod we learn from his own work, so the details are as subject to poetic embellishment as are those of a sophisticated liar like Ovid. Later scholars' and poets' comments or inventions, such as the 'Contest of Homer and Hesiod',[4] have more value in telling us how Hesiod was regarded in later antiquity than they have for any factual accuracy about his life. But here is what he tells us. Hesiod lived in a town called Ascra, in Boeotia (central Greece), near the foot of Mount Helicon. His father had been a seaman from Cyme on the coast of Asia Minor, but had settled on the land in Ascra because of 'poverty'. Poverty was no doubt endemic in Hesiod's society, but it is also something of a leitmotif in the *Works and Days* (on which more in a moment) and so particularly suspect as a biographical detail. After their father's death, Hesiod and his brother Perses had divided up his property, but Perses had bribed certain local nobles into supporting him in attempts to get more than his share. The details are obscure and may well be poetic fiction, or at least exaggeration.

Hesiod tended the land and his flocks – and sang poetry. The only time he had been anywhere by sea was when he competed in a poetry competition at the funeral games for a local notable at Chalcis in Euboea. He sailed from Aulis to do so, in the poetically appropriate path of the Greeks heading for Troy. Hesiod reports (*Works and Days* 650–60) that he won a tripod. Hesiod clearly played an active role in the communal poetic life of central Greece. Given the fame which must have come quickly (otherwise we should know nothing of him), the victory at Chalcis was probably not the only one.

Of the works that have come down to us under Hesiod's name, it is likely that only two were in fact by him. Both are hexameter poems in elevated language (like epic), but short (unlike epic): one, the *Theogony*, tells a creation story of how the gods came to be; the other, the *Works and Days*, gives advice on how to live well, particularly in working a farm. The poems were greatly admired and imitated by the poets of the Hellenistic age and their Roman followers. They were attracted to Hesiod's otherness from the inimitable Homer, his 'shortness', his sense of himself as poet, of the craft of poetry and the imagery of poetics.

The poems show considerable Oriental influence, both in content (for example, the cycle of races, the conflicts between generations of the gods) and in form, for the didactic advice in the *Works and Days* is much indebted to Middle Eastern Wisdom literature.[5] Both poems are marvellous sources for Greek myth. It is important, however, to remember that 'Greek myth' wasn't a coherent, consistent, or developed system, but a vast web of interrelating and sometimes conflicting stories.

The *Theogony* tells the story of the ancestries and births of the gods. First of all, along with primeval 'chaos'[6] and Earth and Tartarus (the hollow region below the earth), there came the most beautiful of the immortals – Eros. Not the cuddly boy with arrow and wings, but a god of terrible and essential power, necessary because the generation of all the gods is represented as very physical and sexual. From 'Chaos' came Erebos (another 'hell') and Night: from Night came Day, through intercourse with Erebos. The creation is told as if it were a series of physical births: Earth bore Heaven, then the mountains and the sea. These she bore by autoconception (*Theogony* 132). Thereafter she bears many through intercourse with Heaven, who is her son. Greek and Oriental stories of the gods often involve incest – it is part of the definition of their non-human status. This union is the archetypal *hieros gamos*, the holy marriage of Heaven (Ouranos) and Earth (Gaia) celebrated in myth and ritual as a fertility rite for the cosmos. And so it goes on.

A cycle of power and its overthrow is set in motion when Heaven tries to shut up his and Earth's children in a cave. Earth persuades her son Kronos to castrate his father. He throws Ouranos' genitals into the sea and, from the foam which froths around them, Aphrodite is born. Kronos, now in power, swallows all his children as they are born, but is tricked into swallowing a stone in place of the youngest, Zeus, who grows up to overthrow him. With Zeus, the cycle stops. He fights the Titan gods of the previous generation and overthrows them, establishing the reign of the Olympian gods, still active in Hesiod's day.

One fascinating aspect of the poem is the way in which the beautiful and the monstrous are juxtaposed, for in succession a very physical Divine Abstraction bears beautiful children and terrifying monsters with a hundred arms. Interesting also is the slippage from concrete to abstract – Earth conceives through drops of blood from Heaven's severed genitals; the river Styx is both a goddess with a house, roofed with long rocks, and able to be taken as a jug of water when required for the gods to swear by (*Theogony* 775–89). Such apparently surreal multi-representations are only possible because of the mythic world-view.

The *Works and Days* is the ancestor in the Western tradition of the type of literature called 'didactic', the self-declared aim of which is to impart some body of knowledge or set of precepts to the reader. Such poems exhibit an extreme case of the general tendency in ancient literature towards some sort of message or teaching, and it is more extreme in part because it is more explicit. (The *Theogony* is in a sense also a didactic poem, of the 'body of knowledge' type.) Usually a named addressee will be the recipient of the advice, with other readers also involved, with varying degrees of directness. In Hesiod's case, his addressee is his brother: in the eastern Wisdom tradition, the addressee is often a son, but Hesiod has chosen a relationship with a less threatening, less authoritarian pose. Whether or not the real Perses (if so there was) was in fact a lazy good-for-nothing and a cheat, the character in the poem is constructed as one who is particularly in need of Hesiod's most important precept – the value of hard work.

Work isn't only necessary for subsistence and so happiness: it is also both morally good, since it engenders the good citizen and neighbour, and it is ordained by the gods. In Hesiod's rather pessimistic theology, Zeus has arranged things so that mankind doesn't get what he needs easily but has to work. To be human is to eat cultivated grain, cooked into bread; to cook the meat usually of farmed animals, sacrificing it first to the gods who receive the smoke

15

and scent of the burnt bones.[7] It is also to live under the shadow of poverty and death. To work, then, is part of what it is to be human and is therefore also, in a sense, a religious obligation.

The poem is wide-ranging in its short scope: there are myths told as lessons; general injunctions to work (ἐργάςευ, νήπιε Πέρση, 'work, foolish Perses' – *Works and Days* 397); quite complex instructions such as the passage on how to make a plough (you should have two ready in case one breaks – 432–3); advice on the right time to perform various activities, be it sowing the seed, marrying or buying a slave; and general advice of a proverbial nature, such as the injunctions against urinating facing the sun (727) or cutting your nails at a feast of the gods (742–3). With all the caution necessary in dealing with a poem, it is possible to use Hesiod as an important source for the social history of eighth/seventh-century Greece, and for contributions to the mythic world-view of that time, although one must remember the eclectic nature of Greek myth.

There are several features in the poems which are archetypal for Western culture, but also paralleled in other cultures. One such feature is the cycle of ages.[8] This is a myth, of Eastern origin, in which the world has been through a series of ages: Gold, Silver, Bronze, Heroic and Iron, in which Hesiod (and all his later imitators) now live.[9] It is a story of deterioration from the paradisial beginning to the present age of toil and wickedness. The exception to the serial degeneration is the Heroic Age, which is probably an intrusion of Greek heroic myth (Heracles, Troy, Theseus, and so on) into this mostly Near Eastern creation myth. It is possible that the Bronze Age reflects memories of the historical Bronze Age, which features also in Homeric epic, while the Gold is the kind of 'perfect beginning' which occurs in many myths, and which has poetic and political 'children' throughout antiquity and beyond. The Silver is an odd one: during this time, people have a hundred-year-long childhood but only a short life thereafter. This may indicate a degeneration from the long lives of the Golden men (who never grew old, but eventually fell asleep and became 'good spirits') and perhaps also a symbolic representation of the youthfulness of mankind as a race.

Hesiod might reasonably be described as the father of Western misogyny. In both poems, he tells versions of the story of Pandora, which is a story of how human life came to be as it is. Pandora was the first woman. Previous to her existence, *man*kind had lived a blessed life, free from work, suffering, illness and women, dying like falling asleep (*Works and Days* 116), but when men received the fire from Prometheus, Zeus punished them by sending a 'lovely evil' (*Theogony* 585). She was made by all the gods (her name means 'all gift'), with a beautiful body and a 'bitch-like' mind. Now she sits in man's house, devouring his substance. Man must work to fill her belly with food, and with his seed so that she may produce children, without which he faces the final extinction. 'Woman', then, is part of the human condition. The famous 'Pandora's box' is an error. Hesiod's Pandora had a jar, which she opened and so allowed plagues and other toils and evils out into the world, while only hope remained inside (*Works and Days* 94–8). The meaning of this jar has been debated, but many people would now accept that at least one of its functions is as a metaphor for the womb, which was thought by the ancients to be like an upturned jar. The 'hope' hidden inside is the unborn child. If this is right, then the myth is laying the blame for the evils of the world not only on woman, but specifically on woman's sexuality.[10]

Notes

1 See W.G. Thalmann, *Conventions of Form and Thought in Early Greek Epic Poetry*, Baltimore, MD: Johns Hopkins University Press, 1984, and A. Schachter, *Cults of Boiotia 2*, London: Institute of Classical Studies, 1986.

2 On the dating of Hesiod, see M.L. West, *Hesiod: Works and Days*, Oxford: Oxford University Press, 1978, pp. 30–1. It is generally thought that Hesiod lived around, probably a little before, 700 BC.

3 See J.P. Vernant and P. Vidal-Naquet, *Myth and Tragedy in Ancient Greece*, New York: Zone Books, 1988, pp. 23–9, for a related argument to do with the historical moment of Greek tragedy. In brief, it dies when society lost touch with the mythic world-view. This shouldn't be taken to suggest that people in the fourth or the first century didn't believe in the supernatural or magic, or that they weren't superstitious – they were. A good place to follow up this issue is R. Buxton (ed.), *From Myth to Reason? Studies in the Development of Greek Thought*, Oxford: Oxford University Press, 1999.

4 This story may have been the invention of the fourth-century BC Sophist Alcidamas. The text can be found in the fifth volume of the OCT of the works of Homer.

5 See West, *op. cit.*, pp. 3–15, 27; also P. Walcot, *Hesiod and the Near East*, Cardiff: Cardiff University Press, 1966, pp. 80–103.

6 West translates this word as 'chasm' because the Greek word χάος doesn't have quite the modern connotations of disorder.

7 Hesiod tells us this through the myth of Prometheus, who stole fire from the gods to give it to men, and who invented the sacrificial customs whereby the gods receive scented but inedible parts (it was 'a trick'). The work of the French anthropologists is crucial to the understanding of Hesiod and the anthropology of early Greek society

and myth. See especially J.P. Vernant, *Myth and Society in Ancient Greece*, Brighton: Harvester Press, 1980, pp. 168–85.
8   The most famous Hesiodic offspring here is the cycle of ages enigmatically presented in Virgil's great hymn to the new age: *Eclogue* 4.
9   See West, *op. cit.*, pp. 28–9, 172–7.
10 For a valuable (if difficult) discussion of Pandora, see P. Pucci, *Hesiod and the Language of Poetry*, Baltimore, MD: Johns Hopkins University Press, 1977, ch. 4.

See also in this book

Callimachus, Lucretius, Ovid, Virgil

Texts, translations and commentaries

The OCT has gone through a third edition in 1990 (ed. R. Merkelbach and M.L. West).

West has produced a very useful translation in the World's Classics Series, reissued in 1999. There is also a Penguin edition, by Dorothea Wender, in which Hesiod shares space with the early elegiac poet Theognis (Harmondsworth, 1996).

The Loeb edition, which contains also the *Homeric Hymns* and other works attributed to the early poets, is old: second edition, 1936.

The standard scholarly editions are M.L. West, the *Hesiod: Theogony*, Oxford: Oxford University Press, 1966, and his *Hesiod: Works and Days*, Oxford: Oxford University Press, 1978. Each volume contains a substantial introduction, the Greek text and an excellent commentary.

Further reading

Hamilton, R., *The Architecture of Hesiodic Poetry*, Baltimore, MD: Johns Hopkins University Press, 1989.
Walcot, P., *Hesiod and the Near East*, Cardiff: Cardiff University Press, 1966.
West, M.L., *The East Face of Helicon: West Asiatic Elements in Greek Poetry and Myth*, Oxford: Oxford University Press, 1997.

ARCHILOCHUS

The ancient Greeks were in no doubt about the power of words to hurt, whether it was a matter of curses, magic, entertainment, or political and legal rhetoric. Just as the role of the praise poet was to affirm society's sense of the heroic, so it was that of the blame poet to abuse abuses, and thus to reinforce approved behaviour. Ancient literary theory likes inventors, and for the poetry of blame it found one in Archilochus of Paros, who was credited with the invention of the iambic metre (the one most associated with the poetry of blame) and with being the father of the invective tradition. There are many later ancient testimonies to the virulent tongue of Archilochus (for example, Horace *Epistles* 1.19.23ff., *Ars Poetica* 79; the *Palatine Anthology* 7.69, 9.185; Plutarch *Cato the Younger* 7): the poet's own programme can perhaps be taken from fragment 23:[1] 'I know the art of loving him that loves me, hating my hater and foulmouthing him with an ant's venom.'

Archilochus is justly seen as the father of carping satire, but he is more than that: a poet of cult songs, particularly to Dionysus, Demeter and Heracles; a poet of political engagement, who sang his city out to war and back again, while harbouring no grand illusions about the glories of war; a poet of love, friendship and drinking, as well as of hate and blame. Archilochus has an important place in the development of the lyric voice, as well as in invective. But interpreting the meagre fragments which survive out of his huge output is a daunting task. There is no complete poem.

The ancient testimonies are expansive on the subject of Archilochus' life. Although, as is so often the case, much of what they tell us is inference from the poems themselves, the biographical tradition remains an important part of the reception of his poetry, especially since much of what we know of the poetry comes from the tradition rather than from the fragments themselves. Biographical information in the Lives is supported (and sometimes refuted) by some fairly extensive inscriptional evidence.[2] Archilochus was born into an aristocratic Parian family in the seventh century BC. He mentions a total eclipse of the sun in fr. 122 (an unkind father suggests that this wasn't more amazing than that someone would want to marry his daughter!), the date of which is almost certainly 6 April 648 BC. The story that Archilochus was the bastard son of a noble and a slave-girl is no longer universally accepted, nor is the tradition that he was a mercenary soldier and something of a rebel. He seems to have contributed to the founding of a Parian colony on Thasos, in which his family was involved. The Lives give Archilochus a poetic initiation, in the form of a meeting with some women who turned out to be the Muses, and a poetic death – he was killed by a man named Corax. This 'crow' name is almost too good to be true, since it is a traditional designation for an unfriendly critic (Plutarch and the *Suda* call it a nickname). Corax was forced to expiate this crime against Apollo by honouring the 'cicada', symbol of the poet.[3] Archilochus was worshipped as a hero in his native Paros from at least the third century BC. The most famous event in his life is told as biography, but is just as much a piece of literary criticism. The story goes that he was engaged to marry a girl called Neoboule, but that her father Lycambes reneged on the promise. Archilochus hounded father and daughter (and a few sisters for good measure) with his virulent poetry, to the point where they were driven to suicide. The power of the invective voice to hurt is thus given the ultimate affirmation.

Earlier scholars hailed Archilochus as the inventor of the self and as the first to express his personal self-consciousness in Western literature and thought.[4] Recent criticism suggests, however, (a) that Archilochus is writing in an established tradition of oral poetry which exhibits these subjective features and is at least as old as Homer, and (b) that a lot of what looks intimately, self-revealingly personal may in fact be conventional. The poet performs as a representative of the wider community, channelling common concerns through a first-person speaking voice, not as a lone individual self expressing the true details of his own life and inner being. This view is now largely accepted; yet most people would probably agree that there is something very different from Homeric objectivity here, however much it may share traditional features, in the kind of voice and pose in the persona who speaks these poems. The difference is perhaps best thought of as one of genre, rather than of historical development.

Ancient testimonies present Lycambes as the arch-enemy of Archilochus (for example, Horace *Epode* 6.13, *Epistles* 1.19.23–5). Only one fragment (172) actually names him, although others are often assumed to be referring to the same story. Fr. 172 may introduce a poem of which we have quite a lot of fragments. It begins by accosting Lycambes with his crime and proclaiming him the laughing-stock of the city (thus enacting what it proclaims). Of the crime itself, we hear only an accusation of a generalised betrayal of friendship (fr. 173) before the poem turns to an animal fable. The fable could, with a bit of stretching, refer to the famous broken engagement. It could also (or instead) be more generally active as a conventional way of directing appropriate behaviour. Many critics (including all those mentioned in the 'Further reading') have noted recently that much of the abuse of Lycambes seems to be traditional, and that the name itself suggests a kind of bogeyman ('Wolf-walker', as West puts it) from popular entertainment. Whether or not there is any real individual behind the character, he undoubtedly serves as a conventional enemy onto whom the blame-poet's societally deter-mined anger can be focused. Such scapegoating reinforces not only the approved behaviour but also the in-group's sense of its communal identity. Lycambes' daughter Neoboule ('Newcounsel') also suggests a traditional figure, while the sexual terms of the abuse of her are conventional in the bawdy first-person narratives of iambic poetry.

A number of critics have noticed ways in which Archilochus models himself (and Lycambes) on Homeric precedent, particularly Odysseus (and Autolycus).[5] But it has also seemed to critics that Archilochus opposes the aristocratic values of the Homeric world, especially as they relate to the glorifying of the heroic warrior code. Much has been made of a few fragments which seem to express disillusionment with war (which, let it be said, isn't entirely absent from Homer) and a scornful attitude to heroic greatness. On the other side, however, are poems which affirm military values and incite courage in war. Songs about drinking on duty (Elegiac fragments 2 and 4, West) may not be the most obvious affirmations of military discipline, but they might be rather effective at fostering the ordinary comradeship which is essential to military success.

The most famous fragment in this area is one in which the speaker announces that he has dropped his shield and run away from the battle to save his life (Elegiac fragment 5, West). It is a good heroic shield, what is more, which is now being worn by a barbarian; but the speaker's attitude is 'I don't care – I'll get another just as good'. Does this reflect a rebellion against the heroic code of 'death rather than dishonour'? Perhaps, but dropping the shield is a motif which crops up frequently, famously in the lying Cretan tale told by Odysseus to Eumaeus (*Odyssey* 14) and in the repeated Aristophanic joke against Cleonymus, who supposedly did the same thing. Critics now suspect that there is some kind of literary *topos* going on here, rather than a personal confession of cowardice. One might note that the speaker of Archilochus' poem plans to get another and fight again. Not much of an anti-heroic rebellion, then.

Another fragment (114) looks like it might be expressing just the opposite of the Homeric celebration of the warrior, as beautiful as he is brave. The speaker rejects the good-looking commander in favour of a short, bandy-legged man (who must remind us of the Homeric Thersites) – as long as he is brave. If there is a rejection of Homeric heroism here (and the fragment is hardly sufficient for us to be sure), then it is replaced by a more 'realistic' heroism which isn't very different.

Many of the political poems encourage patriotism and scourge anti-social behaviour. Fr. 93 complains about some 'sons of Pisistratus' who did something bad with 'a cargo of pure gold for bribing Thracian dogs' (3–4). What their crime was remains a mystery, but 'for sake of private gain they did a public harm' (4–5). That is bad. Sometimes Archilochus' patriotism is tinged by his satiric style, as when he calls the colony Thasos 'the spine of a donkey, wreathed with unkempt forest' (fr. 21). It isn't a beautiful or lovely place, or charming like the Siris riverlands (fr. 22), while Paros is negatively (if we can tell from so tiny a fragment) portrayed by 'figs and life at sea' (fr. 116). But these jibes don't imply disillusionment with his society. Archilochus can be rude about friends, as well as enemies.

Obscenity is crucial to invective. It has a ritual, apotropaic function (warding off evil), as well as an insulting, demeaning one. Fr. 25 comes from an iambic poem satirising the *priamel*, which is a form of expression in which the speaker says something along the lines of 'some people prefer [seafaring], others prefer [soldiering], others [farming], but I prefer [to be a poet and lie in the shade of a tree]'. Fr. 25 says:

> There is no single kind of human nature, but different things warm different people's hearts. For instance, Melesandros favours prick, Phalangios the cowherd is for … .

Unfortunately there is a gap here in the fragment, but probably some word for 'bottom' filled the gap. It is hard to tell whether other examples of obscenity are meant to be insulting: 'And his dong [*sic*] … flooded over like a Prienian stall-fed donkey's' (fr. 43). Probably so!

Other sexually explicit poems may have been insulting if the named characters are real, but for the audience they are likely also to have been ritual affirmations of fertility. Frr. 118–20 compare the speaker's sexual prowess (which he also thereby relates) with his skill in leading the dithyramb (which he thereby enacts):

> I wish I had as sure a chance of fingering Neoboule – the workman falling to his flask – and pressing tum to tummy and thighs to thighs … as sure as I know how to start the lovely round of singing lord Dionysus' dithyramb when the wine has blitzed my brains in.

The longest fragment (196a) comes from an epode in which the speaker relates his seduction of a young girl. The nervous girl tries to suggest that the man might pay these attentions to another in her family, who is longing for a man – Neoboule again, whom the speaker rejects as 'past ripe' (24) and promiscuous. The girl's body is metaphorically equated with the flowery field in which the seduction takes place. The poet promises to 'dock at the grass borders' (21), which probably means avoid penetration, as indeed happens. Is this a personal testimony or a ritual (or stylised but not formally ritual) performance? Probably the latter, but that doesn't make the poem any less erotic (or, perhaps, exploitative).

Poetry in this period has no modern aesthetic of sincerity – it doesn't have to reflect the poet's own feelings and personal life in order to be good poetry, and real. That isn't to say, however, that real feelings aren't expressed in archaic poetry. Among the most moving of Archilochus' poems are the laments about men lost at sea, including the poet's brother-in-law (so we are told – it doesn't matter whether it is true). One of the longer fragments is 13, an elegiac poem encouraging a friend to 'spend no more time in womanish lament' (12), but at the same time giving expression to the grief and so helping to heal it. There is a striking image of grief: 'swollen are our lungs with piercing pain' (5). It should be the shipwrecked men's lungs which would be swollen, whereas the grieving usually have swollen eyes, but the enormity of the image allows the violence of grief to have its way. Even if we know that the shipwreck is a *topos*, that there are many such poems about shipwrecks, we shouldn't doubt that these poems reflect the anguish of this island community.

Whether it is blame for anti-social behaviour, courage and suffering in war, life-affirming sexuality, or grief for loss, what Archilochus does is to channel society's joys, hopes and fears into an 'I' who is a representative of the group.

Notes

1 I am using the translations and designations of fragments as in West's World's Classics edition.
2 For details, see A.P. Burnett, *Three Archaic Poets: Archilochus, Alcaeus, Sappho*, London: Duckworth, 1983, pp. 16–17. See also, importantly, M. Lefkowitz, *The Lives of the Greek Poets*, London: Duckworth, 1981, pp. 26–7.
3 For these stories, see the *testimonia* 12–18 in the Loeb edition.
4 See B. Snell, *The Discovery of the Mind: The Greek Origins of European Thought*, Oxford: Basil Blackwell, 1953, pp. 46ff.
5 See especially P.A. Miller, *Lyric Texts and Lyric Consciousness: The Birth of a Genre from Archaic Greece to Augustan Rome*, London: Routledge, 1994.

See also in this book

Horace, Juvenal, Pindar

Text and translation

The Greek text is available in M.L. West, *Iambi et Elegi Graeci* (2nd edn, vol. 1, Oxford: Oxford University Press, 1989).

M.L. West, *Greek Lyric Poetry* (World's Classics Series, Oxford: Oxford University Press, 1994), contains translations of all the early Greek lyric, iambic and elegiac poets except Pindar and Bacchylides.

There is a recent Loeb edition by D.E. Gerber (*Greek Iambic Poetry*, 1999) which contains lots of *testimonia*.

Further reading

Burnett, A.P., *Three Archaic Poets: Archilochus, Alcaeus, Sappho*, London: Duckworth, 1983 (republished in Bristol Classical Paperbacks, 1998).

Miller, P.A., *Lyric Texts and Lyric Consciousness: The Birth of a Genre from Archaic Greece to Augustan Rome*, London: Routledge, 1994.

Rankin, H.D., *Archilochus of Paros*, Park Ridge, NJ: Noyes Press, 1977.

West, M.L., *Studies in Greek Elegy and Iambus*, Berlin and New York: de Gruyter, 1974.

SAPPHO

Greek and Roman antiquity, that patriarchal world, speaks to us in overwhelmingly male voices, with the result that the late twentieth-century flowering of critical interest in 'women in antiquity' has had to rely almost exclusively on male representations of and responses to women. But not quite exclusively. There were female authors in the ancient world, although much of their work is lost and otherwise obscured, like that of the Latin poet Sulpicia, whose elegiac poetry is transmitted under the name of a cognate male poet. It may come as a surprise to some readers that the ancient woman's voice which we hear most clearly is from the archaic period of Greek literature, not from a more recent time. This may be, in part, because women (at least upper-class women) had more opportunities for poetic production in aristocratic archaic Lesbos than in democratic Classical Athens, from which most of our Greek sources stem.

Sappho lived on the island of Lesbos, in the later part of the seventh and the beginning of the sixth centuries BC. Apart from that, almost nothing is reliably known about her life, which more than for any other poet of antiquity has been fictionalised and appropriated by later writers and myth-makers. Some of the values expressed in her poetry are clearly those of the aristocratic society (joy to friends and grief to enemies) to which she presumably belonged, and may reflect her family's (and her own) involvement in the power struggles among the great families of archaic Lesbos, as do those of her contemporary Alcaeus, also a great lyric poet. The story that she suffered a period of exile in Sicily would be consonant with such a political background. There is no hint of a husband for Sappho in the poems, but a daughter, Cleis, is apparently mentioned, as is a brother Charaxus. The husband, parents and two other brothers are supplied later, and reproduced by the late antique biographers (*Suda*).

Sappho wrote lyric poetry (that is, poetry to be sung to the accompaniment of the lyre), in a variety of styles and metres, but it is for the metre named after her that she is best known.[1] A 'Sapphic' poem is made up of stanzas each consisting of three lines of eleven syllables followed by a single line of five syllables, the syllables following a formal pattern of 'longs' and 'shorts'.[2] Both the metre and the substance of Sappho's poetry were influential over poets of later antiquity, the most famous case being the close imitation by the Roman poet Catullus of fragment 31 (Catullus 51).[3] Sappho's dialect of Greek was literary Aeolic. Her poems were collected and arranged into nine books in the Hellenistic period. They are now highly fragmentary, however, with only one poem surviving complete, together with many fragments ranging from several stanzas to single words.

Alongside this respectable tradition of literary appreciation, Sappho's life and work spawned a prodigious mythology. She is credited with a heterosexual lover, Phaon, for love of whom she is said to have leaped to her death from the rocks of Leucas: the story is perhaps partially transferred from a myth of Aphrodite. She is also made into the heterosexual beloved of her fellow Lesbian poet Alcaeus.[4] She was the subject of comic plays in the fourth century BC (bawdy and heterosexual). Ovid (or less likely an imitator) places her among his mythical heroines abandoned by their lovers and writing appealing letters to them (*Heroides* 15). On a more poetic but not unconnected track, she is hailed as the 'tenth muse' from at least Hellenistic times, and frequently thereafter (see Williamson 1995: 14). The tendency to see Sappho as a muse isn't the happiest part of the literary community's response to this great female poet, for it tends to reflect an inability to see her as an active, creative poet rather than an object of poetic desire. The breaking down of boundaries between subject and object, singer and addressee, desirer and desired, which many modern readers have discerned in Sappho's own poetry, has been inappropriately applied in the response to her and to other women poets. So often, throughout the history of Western literature, women who write, and especially those who write in the learned languages of Latin and Greek, are celebrated as 'the tenth muse' or 'another Sappho', instead of being criticised and admired as poets in their own right.

For whom, and about whom, were these poems written?[5] Because Sappho's audience clearly includes young girls (words like *parthenos*, 'virgin', and *kore*, 'girl', occur frequently), one common way of conceptualising the social context of her performance has been to see her as a teacher running a kind of finishing school for aristocratic young girls in the period leading up to their marriage. It is very likely that many of her poems are written for choruses of girls, both in ritual and less formal situations, and that the girls learned music and dancing, as well as aristocratic socialisation and preparation for marriage, from their association with Sappho. It is an interesting aspect of her poetry that the audience are themselves also singers, sometimes the singers of the poem itself. It would seem likely, also, that her songs were not confined to this narrow circle, but included also poems for other occasions when women might be together, such as weddings and religious rituals. There is no overwhelming reason to suppose that the only audience was girls in their early to mid-teens. Since it is possible in Greek to express gender without indicating age, it is often not possible to tell whether a girl or a woman is addressed. Some of the poems are overtly ritual, whether or not they were actually performed at ceremonies.

Sappho is, of course, the original lesbian, but although she has been an important symbolic figure for modern lesbians, the ancient response to her doesn't explicitly see her as what we would call a 'lesbian' writer. This isn't simply a matter of separating the poet herself from the first-person speaker of the poem (important and complex though that is), nor is it simply a case of refusal to acknowledge female homoerotic love, but rather it is a matter of different ways of conceptualising sexuality. Suffice it to say here, first, that ancient peoples didn't categorise people according to choice of sexual partner and, second, that the gorgeously sensuous and erotic language addressed to girls by Sappho is also conven-tional, public and directed towards the furthering of societal norms. It undoubtedly also celebrates the love between women. Williamson shows how Sapphic sexuality is communal, aristocratic and institutionalised, but also a lived experience; not necessarily directed towards penetration and so on, but rather towards erotic tenderness and passionate friendship; expressing admiration for a lovely girl as object of desire in erotic terms, both for the female speaker and for a heterosexual lover (usually bridegroom):

> the challenge of reading Sappho is not to separate the individual from the collective, or (especially) the sexual from the social and religious, but to reunite them in ways our culture has all but forgotten.
>
> (Williamson 1995: 132)[6]

The homoerotic sensuality expressed in the poems is integrated into a heterosexual and monogamous structure of society, for one of its functions is as a marker of that odd 'in-between' moment on the threshold of adult sexuality, a moment which so fascinated the ancient world.

The recurrent features of Sappho's poetry are a delicate and sensuous beauty, and tenderness touched with varying intensity of eroticism. Romantic sentiment is tinged with irony and playfulness, however, and even the occasional bite of invective, as when (if the reconstruction is correct) a girl friend has left Sappho's friendship to associate with a rival, perhaps artistic, perhaps also political.[7]

Many of the poems are clearly marriage hymns, or other poetic celebrations of marriages. There is a fragment of a poem (44) which describes the arrival of Hector bringing his bride Andromache to Troy. The thirty-five mutilated lines of this fragment probably contain the end of the poem: if so, the couple don't actually arrive, and the emphasis is all on creating the mood of joyous anticipation. The passionate emotional intensity of Sappho's circle is fully in harmony with the societal emphasis on the desirability of the virgin bride. One fragment compares the bride to a sweet ripe apple which is out of reach of the harvesters (105), while another consists of a dialogue between the bride and her departing virginity (114). The element of grief in the marriage hymn is both a conventional requirement to uphold the bride's purity and also, no doubt, a reality for girls undergoing a massive upheaval in their lives.

One of the better-known fragments (94) shows this delicate balance of grief and joy at marriage. A girl is leaving Sappho's society, almost certainly in order to marry. She expresses her grief at parting, and leaves with tears. Either the girl herself or Sappho speaks the first line of our fragment: 'and honestly I wish I were dead'. Sappho reminds the girl of the many happy times they have spent together: the flowers (perhaps metaphorical also for poems), the togetherness, the perfume, the soft beds on which 'you would satisfy your longing', the shrines, groves and dances. Fragment 96, in calmer vein, both celebrates the bride who 'stands out among Lydian women like the rosy-fingered moon after sunset, surpassing all the stars, and its light spreads alike over the salt sea and the flowery fields', and also gives expression to her tender memory of the friends she has left behind.

Sometimes the poetry's homoeroticism is almost indistinguishable from the transferred eroticism of marriage.[8] The 'delicate grove of apple-trees' into which Aphrodite is invited in the hymn which is fr. 2 is probably metaphorically the erotic circle of Sappho and her friends. It is a garden of homoerotic love, but one in which the 'apple-trees' can be seen as waiting for the harvester, the groom.

I mentioned above that the poetry seems to dissolve the rigid oppositions of singer and audience, desirer and object of desire. In one poem (fr. 22), Sappho urges her friend Abanthis to sing about Gongyla, another member of the group – 'while desire once again flies around you, the lovely one – for her dress excited you when you saw it: and I rejoice'. All three women seem bound up in a circle of love and song. We can see here a kind of celebration of female charms which avoids the objectification that besets so much male-authored love poetry, however well intentioned.

The most famous fragment of Sappho is by no means the easiest to interpret. It is fr. 31, in which the speaker sees the beauty and charm of a loved one and is overwhelmed. The man who sits opposite her and hears her sweetly talking and laughing seems like a god. This man has caused many readers to see the poem as a wedding song, with the man as groom. The suffering incurred by the speaker may be a result of jealousy at the man who takes her beloved's attention away, or it may be simply the effect of the beloved's charms on Sappho, to which the man himself is remarkably immune. It isn't necessary to decide on the exact imagined context in order to appreciate the power with which the effects of love are described. As the ancient critic Longinus, helpfully quoting the passage, said:

> are you not amazed how at one and the same moment she seeks out soul, body, hearing, tongue, sight, complexion as though they had all left her and were external, and how in contradiction she both freezes [there is a textual difficulty here, but the point remains] and burns, is irrational and

sane, is afraid and nearly dead, so that we observe in her not one single emotion but a concourse of emotions?

(*On the Sublime* 10.1–3)

This fragment contains one of those wonderfully incomprehensible descriptions of colour from the ancient world: 'I am paler than grass'. It is true, but not an adequate explanation, to point out that the grass got rather burnt – and so pale – in the Lesbian summer. This striking image must reflect quality as well as hue of colour.

The one fully extant poem of Sappho that we possess is a hymn to Aphrodite. It is placed first in modern editions and probably in the Hellenistic collection. The poem is a cletic hymn: the speaker calls on the goddess with several epithets, reminds her of past services and asks for her aid again. The poem almost enacts its own epiphany for, in the section reminding the deity of past services, Sappho remembers how Aphrodite came to her and asked who she wanted brought into her love – just exactly as Sappho now wants Aphrodite to ask and fulfil. The poem ends with a prayer that Aphrodite will be the poet's 'fellow-fighter' (28). The word playfully uses and parodies the epic language of divine invocation for help in battle.

Finally, for me the most remarkable and precious accent of a woman's voice that we may be hearing in the poetry of Sappho is the voice of a mother celebrating her relationship with her little daughter: 'I have a beautiful child who looks like golden flowers, my darling Cleis, for whom I would not [take] all Lydia or lovely ... ' (fr. 132). The fragment is preserved in a technical comment on a metrical nicety.

Notes

1 One ancient scholar, Marius Victorinus, claims that the Sapphic metre was invented by Alcaeus (*testimonium* 33). Sappho is also credited with the invention of the plectrum for plucking the lyre's strings, with a particular kind of lyre (the *pectis*) and with a musical mode known as the 'Mixolydian'. See the *testimonia* to Sappho in the Loeb edition (*testimonia* 37 and 38). It is clear that ancient writers on poetry, metre and music, regarded her as a major figure in the development of their subjects.

2 See M.L. West, *Introduction to Greek Metre*, Oxford: Oxford University Press, 1987, pp. 33–4.

3 I am using the designation of fragments in West's World's Classics translation.

4 See *testimonium* 8 in the Loeb edition for other lovers, including poets.

See also M. Williamson, *Sappho's Immortal Daughters*, Cambridge, MA: Harvard University Press, 1995, pp. 7–11.
5 See L.H. Wilson, *Sappho's Sweetbitter Songs: Configurations of Female and Male in Ancient Greek Lyric*, London: Routledge, 1996, ch. 6.
6 Williamson, *op. cit.*, pp. 28ff., also has a good discussion of this difference in the construction of sexuality and the whole issue of sexuality in Sappho's poetry, while there is more flowery and romantic but still useful consideration in A.P. Burnett, *Three Archaic Poets: Archilochus, Alcaeus, Sappho*, London: Duckworth, 1983. See also Wilson, *op. cit.*, p. 70.
7 See for example fr. 57, where the rival Andromeda is portrayed as a country bumpkin.
8 So often, in fact, that some commentators over the years have argued that the apparent homosexuality of the poems is in fact entirely directed towards a conventional way of meditating on heterosexual desire, by transference. Most scholars would now consider that some kind of lived homoerotic experience is implied by the poems.

See also in this book

Archilochus, Catullus, Pindar, Sulpicia

Texts and translations

D.L. Page's OCT of selected lyric, *Lyrica Graeca Selecta*, 1968, unfortunately numbers the fragments differently from most editions and translations. The edition with commentary of E. Lobel and D.L. Page, *Poetarum Lesbiorum Fragmenta*, Oxford: Oxford University Press, 1955, is therefore preferable. In the World's Classics translation, West has used the numbering as in E.-M. Voigt, *Sappho et Alcaeus*, Amsterdam: Athenaeum-Polak & Van Gennep, 1971, which is nearly all the same as in Lobel–Page.

The Loeb edition is by D.A. Campbell, *Greek Lyric*, vol. 1, 1983 (reprinted with corrections, 1990). It also contains numerous ancient testimonies to Sappho.

M.L. West, *Greek Lyric Poetry*, Oxford World's Classics, Oxford: Oxford University Press, 1994, contains translations of all the early Greek lyric, iambic and elegiac poets except Pindar and Bacchylides.

Further reading

Sappho is well served with modern critical literature. This is a selection of the most recent.

Burnett, A.P., *Three Archaic Poets: Archilochus, Alcaeus, Sappho*, London: Duckworth, 1983 (republished in Bristol Classical Paperbacks 1998).
Du Bois, P., *Sappho is Burning*, Chicago, IL: University of Chicago Press, 1995.
McIntosh Snyder, J., *Lesbian Desire in the Lyrics of Sappho*, New York: Columbia University Press, 1997.

Williamson, M., *Sappho's Immortal Daughters*, Cambridge, MA: Harvard University Press, 1995.

Wilson, L.H., *Sappho's Sweetbitter Songs: Configurations of Female and Male in Ancient Greek Lyric*, London: Routledge, 1996.

The collection edited by E. Greene, *Reading Sappho: Contemporary Approaches*, Berkeley and Los Angeles, CA: University of California Press, 1996, contains an excellent range of studies by leading critics of early lyric. For Sappho's eventful *nachleben*, there is a second volume, also edited by Greene: *Re-Reading Sappho: Reception and Transmission*, Berkeley and Los Angeles, CA: University of California Press, 1996.

ATHENIAN HEGEMONY

AESCHYLUS

Aeschylus practically invented drama. There had been dramatic presentations before, but these were limited to the performances of a chorus and a single actor, with very limited scope for interaction. Aeschylus introduced a second actor (so says Aristotle, *Poetics* 1449a.15–17) and in doing so opened up a vista of potential for representation of 'people doing things': 'drama' is derived from the Greek word *dran*, meaning 'to do' (see Aristotle *Poetics* 1448a.28–9, 1448b.1–2). Sophocles later added a third actor, three remaining the limit for Athenian tragedy. Aeschylus followed Sophocles in this further innovation, in his own majestic way, but it was Aeschylus' developments in dramatic art which started the whole movement. Actors, whether one, two or three, played more than one role.

Aeschylus was born, probably in 525 BC, at Eleusis, a village west of Athens. He died, probably in Sicily, where he was a frequent visitor, at the age of around 69, the shortest-lived of the three great tragedians. He wrote some ninety plays, of which a mere seven survive,[1] and was victorious in the dramatic competition on probably about half of the times he entered (that is, thirteen times according to one ancient source).[2] Aeschylus' life spanned an era in which Athens rose to dominance, leading the Greeks against the Persian invasions. Aeschylus himself fought at the Battle of Marathon in 490, and possibly at Salamis and Plataea as well. During his life also, the system of radical democracy at Athens developed and flourished, the key democratic reforms of Ephialtes coming during the height of Aeschylus' career. This information is not just 'scene-painting': Aeschylus' activities as a citizen of Athens are integral to the understanding of his drama.

The main occasion for tragedy at this time was the City Dionysia, a spring festival in honour of the god Dionysus, which was also a celebration and affirmation of the life of Athens. On three successive days, three tragedians produced their offerings: three tragedies, followed by a satyr play. The three playwrights were in competition with each other, the prize being a crown of ivy and a great deal of kudos. In most of his entries, Aeschylus produced connected trilogies, rather than three plays on different material as was more common with Sophocles and Euripides. Drama in Aeschylus' day was a crucially important forum for the communal working through of issues central to the life of the community. If we call Aeschylus the 'poet of the democracy', that doesn't mean that he was driven by party politics (a misleading notion for antiquity anyway), nor that he was simply a propagandist, in the modern sense, for the democratic government, but rather that he wrote plays which explored, subverted, reinforced and contributed to the development of issues at the heart of his community: the precious and precarious relationships of humans and the gods, of men and women, of parents and children, of the household (*oikos*) and the city (*polis*); the nature of persuasion, of force and of power, and most of all of 'justice', in a world where a structured legal system was developing, but was tied up in conflicting rights and responsibilities.

The primary subject matter for Aeschylus was myth, specifically heroic and human myth. Although the gods pervade the plays, as they pervaded the lives of contemporaries, of the extant plays only two have gods as central characters. This is because the primary concern of tragedy is the human condition, conceived and defined by the Greeks in opposition to and relationship with the gods on the one hand, and the beasts on the other. In *Prometheus Bound*,[3] the central protagonist, Prometheus, is a Titan (or, in Hesiod *Theogony* 510, the son of the Titan Japetus), one of the primeval divine beings who were generally in conflict with the Olympian gods (Zeus, Apollo, and so on). Although there is almost no fully human character in the play (the human woman Io, who had been turned into a cow, may well have been represented horned, as she often is in ancient art), the play is nonetheless about the human condition: close to its heart is the work of Prometheus in bringing mankind to a state of civilisation, in defiance of the orders of Zeus, who in this play looks like the embodiment of tyranny. This may seem odd, especially since people generally see Aeschylus as a 'religious' poet. In *Prometheus Bound*, Zeus is a force of strength, but lacks *metis*, the cunning intelligence which will ensure his omnipotence.[4] Prometheus, on the other hand, represents that quality. When eventually the two are reconciled, if that is indeed how the trilogy developed, Zeus is able to incorporate both strength and *metis* and so ensure that he isn't overthrown. We might, therefore, see the play as a kind of 'hymn to Zeus', in that it explains how the god came to be the way he is, which is a common feature of hymns. We should also remember that ancient Greek religion isn't primarily about love and goodness.

This concentration on human matters, even when it is the gods who speak and act, is seen also in the *Eumenides*, where Orestes is the only human character, apart from a brief appearance by a priestess and a group of silent Jurors, and most of the action is driven by the gods, Athene, Apollo, the Furies. But the issues about which the gods are contending are human issues – retribution, relationships, gender, justice. The play opens with Orestes at the *omphalos*, the navel stone in Delphi, at the centre of the world and, in a sense, his own mother.

The other exception to the rule of heroic mythic subject matter is the one 'historical' play of Aeschylus, the *Persians*, which dramatises the reaction at the Persian court to their king Xerxes' defeat at the hands of the Greeks. Aeschylus succeeds in elevating recent history to the status of myth, making a tragedy out of real life, while avoiding either Greek triumphalism or simplistic self-criticism. Real history as subject matter for tragedy is unusual: Aeschylus generally wrote plays in which the big issues of his day were central, but he did so not by representing those issues directly or by using anything like modern realism. His drama is symbolic, its mythic subject matter endowed with a significance beyond the ordinary. This is part of what makes it tragic.

Aeschylus' style, like his subject matter, is dense, complex, allusive, highly poetic, full of structuring imagery, at times as dark and threatening as the awful events his plays present. Aeschylus is a master of metaphor and a creative inventor of words, particularly compounds, manipulating the semantic range in the service of his art. Let one example suffice. In the *Agamemnon*, when the chorus is relating the story of Helen's flight to Troy (from which Agamemnon is about to return victorious), she is described 'sailing out from her bedchamber on the disappearing tracks of the sea'.

> ἐκ τῶν ἁβροπήνων
> προκαλυμμάτων ἔπλευσεν
> ςεφύρου γίγαντος αὖραι,
> πολύανδροί τε φεράσπιδες κυναγοὶ
>   κατ' ἴχνος πλατᾶν ἄφαντον
> κελσάντων Σιμόεντος ἀκ-
>   τὰς ἐπ' ἀεξιφύλλους
> δι' Ἔριν αἱματόεσσαν.

she came out of her luxuriously woven chamber-curtains and sailed forth, before the blast of giant Zephyrus, and [after her] many men, shield-bearers, hunters upon the vanished trail of oars, the trail of those who had landed on the leafy shores at the mouth of Simois, by the will of bloody Strife.

(*Agamemnon* 690–7)[5]

Helen and her ship are imagistically combined, momentarily hinting at the thousand ships which famously followed her. She is for a split second a hunted animal, but already she has escaped and landed on the shore. She seems to move from curtained bed sailing straight out over the sea, with the notoriously disappearing trace on the water acting both literally and symbolically as an image of loss and desire. Aeschylus' language isn't easy, but it is enormously powerful.

We have one connected trilogy extant from Athenian tragedy: Aeschylus' *Oresteia*, which took the victory in 458 BC. The subject matter comes from the Trojan mythic world, with Homer always in the background, but the treatment is fundamentally different and fundamentally tragic. A recurrent feature of tragedy is that the sufferings it depicts come in cycles, that evil in one generation begets evil in another. In the house of Atreus (father of Agamemnon and Menelaus, Greek leaders in the Trojan war), there is a long history of horrors within the family, right from the start when Tantalus fed his own son Pelops to the gods. This act is repeated when Atreus tricks his brother Thyestes into eating his own (Thyestes') sons. There is a feud in this great family – and both greatness and families are crucial elements in tragedy – but it is endowed with greater tragic significance by the way in which a kind of dark destructive force seems to drive the action, each act of which is surrounded by a complex web of symbolism.

The cycles in this trilogy are not just recurrent motifs; they are also cycles of revenge. With Aeschylus begins the revenge tragedy which was to flourish so powerfully in Renaissance Europe. The principle is the *lex talionis*: that 'he who acts is acted on'. It is important to understand that this isn't simply a moral judgement (as in 'the doer *shall* suffer') but a statement of tragic necessity – evil breeds evil ('the doer suffers'). So it is that as each act of revenge takes place, the avenger becomes polluted by the action even while *also* being an 'agent of Zeus'. Don't look for comfort, or for a coherent and kindly theology, from the gods of ancient Greece.

The first play, *Agamemnon*, presents the return of the victorious king from the war at Troy – to suffer death in the bath at the hands of his wife. From the start, joy and foreboding are anxiously intertwined, when the last in a string of beacon-fires is sighted. The fires which signify victory also reflect the destruction of Troy, which will end in Agamemnon's own destruction; they symbolise both the light of knowledge and also the funeral fire, the fire of dangerous passion. Anxiety too colours the reaction of the chorus, who remember the beginning of the Trojan expedition, when Agamemnon sacrificed his daughter Iphigenia ('glory of the house', 208) to appease the goddess Artemis and allow the fleet to sail to Troy. In killing her husband, Clytemnestra avenges her daughter's death. She is a magnificent and terrifying woman, to whom we will return. But why is the death of Agamemnon tragic? It is because he is a great hero, for that is what tragedy is about; because he doesn't die gloriously on the battlefield, but ignominiously, naked and disarmed (and so unmanned) in the bath, and a sacrificial bath at that (rather than just a good wash), which makes him into a sacrificial victim (to 'answer' Iphigenia); because he is killed by a woman and a member of his own family – for in tragedy we see the great heroes *on the inside*, and the great families tearing themselves apart; because his death is driven by the force of the hereditary curse. By comparison, the death of Achilles foreshadowed in the *Iliad*, even if we want to see some tragic elements in it (such as his 'fated' foreknowledge), isn't fundamentally tragic, but epic.

The second play, the *Libation Bearers* (*Choephoroe*), begins with Clytemnestra and her lover Aegisthus, a surviving son of Thyestes, in possession of the palace and the rule of Argos. The situation is deeply disordered. Orestes, son of Agamemnon and Clytemnestra, had been sent away many years previously, for safekeeping by another king. He returns now to avenge the death of his father, to claim his patrimony and so to set right the disorder of the house. In the version of this story in Homer's *Odyssey* (1.29–43, 298–300; 3.303–10), he has no difficulty in doing so, for there the role of Clytemnestra in the murder and the adultery are played down almost to invisibility, whereas in Aeschylus all the emphasis is on her. What is the difference? Here we must introduce two crucial tragic elements: the conflicts in an ancient ethic and *aporia*. It was commonplace in ancient morality that you should do good to your friends and harm to your and their enemies. For Orestes to kill Aegisthus to avenge Agamemnon is, relatively speaking, no problem at all. But whatever she may do, your mother doesn't cease to be your 'friend' – the Greek word *philos* ('friend') is a statement about obligations and relationship rather than personal affection or friendship in our sense. In order to help his friend (Agamemnon) by avenging him, therefore, Orestes has to harm another 'friend', his mother. No amount of pleading can remove the pollution of matricide; nor will the fear of pollution allow him to shirk his duty to avenge his father. Orestes has no way out: that is tragic *aporia*, where a choice must be made but all choices are bad.

Orestes dispatches Aegisthus without a thought, and then faces his mother in a confrontation which mirrors that between Clytemnestra and Agamemnon in the first play. In each case, the killer must force the victim to submit to her/his will and enter the house. This entry dramatises the killing itself, which is by convention not shown on the ancient Greek stage. The climax of *aporia* comes when Orestes hesitates. He asks his companion Pylades 'what shall I do?' (τί δράσω, 899) – you can hear the weakness, the anxiety – *ti* ('what') is such a tiny word for such an enormous deed. Pylades speaks his only lines (three) in the play and seals Clytemnestra's fate.[6] No justification from Apollo, the instigator of Orestes' deed, can stop the pollution, however, and Orestes is sent mad by the Furies and chased off the stage – a graphic scene in which they are visible only to him.

In the final play, the Furies themselves form the chorus. It is called the *Eumenides*, or 'kindly ones', for this positive side is another name and aspect of the Furies. These divine beings, chthonic deities rather than Olympian (although sometimes working for Zeus), at their most horrific are terrifying monsters who pursue those who have committed crimes, particularly the shedding of the blood of blood-relatives.[7] By the end of the play, their positive aspect is prominent, and they are made guardians of familial morality and so protectresses of the fertility and stability of the society. After its opening scene at Apollo's oracle at Delphi, the play soon moves to Athens (a scene-change very unusual in tragedy at this period) where Apollo has sent Orestes to stand trial. The Furies are his accusers, Apollo his defence; a panel of Athenian citizens sit in judgement, with Athene herself as their president. Orestes is acquitted. Why?

A court for homicide is instituted for the trial, on the hill of the Areopagus in Athens, making this the founding moment of the Athenian legal system. Some four years before the play was produced, as part of the reforms of Ephialtes, the functions of the Areopagus court had been reduced from major general legislation to being a court for homicide. (It is impossible to make simple distinctions between the 'legal' and the 'political' in fifth-century Athens.) This move was a democratic one, because the court, in its legislative form, had been dominated by the aristocracy. The democratic assembly gains in political power as a result. Aeschylus projects the new status of the court onto distant antiquity: what is more, he increases the authority of the court's juridical role by having it instituted by the patron goddess Athene. The more legislative functions, he suggests (with others), were accretions not in the original conception of the court. The play, then, becomes a celebration of the Athenian legal and political system.[8]

It has been a common interpretation to see the trilogy as charting a process of developing civilisation, from the chaos and destruction of private vendetta enforced by violence to the establishment of societal justice enforced by law. In this way, the cycle of vengeance is broken and Orestes is freed from fear. At one level, the trilogy certainly ends with a powerful resolution and sense of ending, not only from the trial and acquittal itself, but also from the integration of the Furies/Eumenides into Athens. The play ends with a procession in the manner of the great Athenian religious celebrations, as the Eumenides are escorted to their place of worship. We should note, in this, that a 'sad ending' in a straightforward sense is *not* a necessary feature of ancient tragedy. But however much the play may be a celebration of the Athenian legal system and of Athenian democracy, it is still also a place for playing out anxieties about the tensions and ambiguities underlying that system.[9]

One of those tensions, and one of the answers to the many-sided question of why Orestes is acquitted, has to do with the relationships of male and female, a crucial aspect of the trilogy which I have skirted round up to now. The *Eumenides* represents a beginning-story, an *aetion*, not only for the Athenian legal system, but also for Athenian patriarchy. In the acquittal of Orestes, the male defeats the female *because that is how it should be* according to the norms of Athenian patriarchy. The role of Athene in this is crucial – a female deity who 'supports the male in all things', as she says, 'except to give me in marriage' (736–8), a daughter with no mother, who sprang fully formed and armed from the head (note the significance of the head, as opposed to the belly/womb) of her father Zeus. That is why she gives Orestes her casting vote. Apollo's argument (657–66) that the father is the true parent, the mother being only a receptacle for the father's seed, is no joke. The transformation of the Furies into their positive, and submissive, aspect is part of this reordering of society along patriarchal lines.

Let's return to Clytemnestra. Here is an extraordinarily powerful woman, who takes vengeance into her own hands and who chooses her own sexual partner; one who rules the house and disrupts the transmission of its property and reputation from its expected patriarchal order. She is also by far the most powerful speaker in the play. In probably the most famous scene of the trilogy (855ff.), she welcomes the returning Agamemnon with deceitful words of praise and devotion, foreboding his death (for those who know), almost challenging him to understand, but denying him the possibility of understanding. She lays out for him a path of purple cloth, to walk on in triumphant entry to his home (905ff.). Agamemnon knows that to do so would be an act of hubris and would expose him to the jealousy of the gods. Nonetheless, in the end he submits, because Clytemnestra is the more powerful. What he doesn't know is that the cloth makes a metaphorical path of blood, flowing from the past of the family curse into the future of his death – and eventually Clytemnestra's. After her moment of awful glory, Clytemnestra becomes victim in the second play, where again the conflict is set up along the lines of gender. Orestes needs to kill his mother in order to grow up: a terrible thing, but in a metaphorical way only an exaggerated and dramatised form of what every Greek boy had to do. A boy didn't become his mother's equal as an adult, but rather her superior. The 'righting' of the social order as patriarchy at the end of the trilogy doesn't resolve, but perhaps papers over, the tensions among the genders from which such tragic force flows.

Notes

1 *Agamemnon, Libation Bearers, Eumenides, Persians, Prometheus Bound* (of questionable authenticity), *Seven against Thebes* and *Suppliants.*
2 For a list of reasonably reliable facts about the life of Aeschylus, see A.H. Sommerstein, *Aeschylus: Eumenides*, Greek and Latin Classics Series, Cambridge: Cambridge University Press, 1989, pp. 17–18.
3 There is dispute as to whether this play was indeed by Aeschylus. See M. Griffin (ed.), *Aeschylus, Prometheus Bound*, Cambridge: Cambridge University Press, 1983, pp. 31–5.
4 See M. Detienne and J.P. Vernant, *Cunning Intelligence in Greek Culture and Society*, Hassocks: Harvester Press, 1978, esp. p. 59.
5 I have used the text and translation of E. Fraenkel, in his edition of and commentary on the *Agamemnon.*
6 See B.M.W. Knox, *Word and Action: Essays on the Ancient Theater*, Baltimore, MD, and London: Johns Hopkins University Press, 1979, ch. 3.
7 On the connection of blood ties with the female in Aeschylus, see S. Goldhill, *Aeschylus, the Oresteia*, Landmarks of World Literature, Cambridge: Cambridge University Press, 1992, p. 42.
8 There are other views on what Aeschylus is doing here. See A.J. Podlecki, *The Political Background of Aeschylean Tragedy*, Ann Arbor, MI: University of Michigan Press, 1966. For a succinct and persuasive account of Aeschylus' innovations in the myth of Orestes and the Areopagus court, see Sommerstein, *op. cit.*, pp. 4–6.
9 Goldhill 1992, p. 21.

See also in this book

Euripides, Seneca the Younger, Sophocles

Texts, translations and commentaries

The plays are available in OCT, Teubner, Loeb and Penguin Classics versions, but not as yet World's Classics.

There are commentaries on various individual plays, including the all-time classic: E. Fraenkel's monumental commentary on the *Agamemnon*, first published in 1950 and still in print with Oxford University Press for a mere £131. The same publisher offers a commentary on the *Libation Bearers* by A.F. Garvie. *Eumenides* and *Prometheus Bound* have editions in the Cambridge Greek and Latin Classics Series, while *Persians* and *Eumenides* (again) have Aris and Phillips volumes.

Further reading

Easterling, P.E. (ed.), *The Cambridge Companion to Greek Tragedy*, Cambridge: Cambridge University Press, 1997.
Goldhill, S., *Reading Greek Tragedy*, Cambridge: Cambridge University Press, 1986.
Goldhill, S., *Aeschylus, the Oresteia*, Landmarks of World Literature, Cambridge: Cambridge University Press, 1992.
McAuslan, I. and Walcot, P. (eds), *Greek Tragedy*, Greece and Rome Studies, Oxford: Oxford University Press for the Classical Association, 1993.
Podlecki, A.J., *The Political Background of Aeschylean Tragedy*, Ann Arbor, MI: University of Michigan Press, 1966 (2nd edn with new preface and updated bibliography in Bristol Classical Press paperbacks, 1999).
Segal, E. (ed.), *Oxford Readings in Greek Tragedy*, Oxford: Oxford University Press, 1983.
Taplin, O., *Greek Tragedy in Action*, London: Methuen, 1978.
Winnington-Ingram, R.P., *Studies in Aeschylus*, Cambridge: Cambridge University Press, 1983.
Zeitlin, F., 'The dynamics of misogyny in the *Oresteia*', *Arethusa*, 11, 1978, pp. 149–84.

PINDAR

When he was a boy, so the story goes, Pindar fell asleep in a field and was visited by some bees who left traces of honey on his lips: that honey came out as poetry. Some of the most complex, most difficult, most *poetic* poetry of antiquity was written to celebrate victories in the major athletic contests of the Greek world. Why was so much made of winning a race, and why in so apparently non-populist a way? First, it is because these contests – which are also religious festivals – go to the heart of the society: the extent of their significance was recognised in the Hellenistic age by the development of a universal Greek system of dating by reference to the greatest of the games, the Olympics.[1] Second, Pindar's poetry celebrates not just successful athletes, but the whole world of late archaic aristocratic society. It is important to remember the crucial value placed on success in that highly competitive society. Sporting victories are successes not only for individuals, but for their families and for their whole communities.[2] The performance of a victory ode actually enacts the significance of the victor's success within his community. It is a performance, not a sports commentary.

Pindar was born in a small town near Thebes, probably in 518 BC. As usual, we know almost nothing about his life, and what we know is dependent on apparently autobiographical material in his own poems, the conventions of which we may be failing to understand.[3] It is likely that his family was aristocratic – the persona he projects in his poetry is that of a rather conservative aristocrat – and that he travelled widely in the Greek world. We do know that he was commissioned to write poems for individuals and states all over the Greek world over a period of fifty or sixty years. His first commissioned work (*Pythian* 10) was written when he was only twenty, while his last work for which a reasonably secure date is known is from 446 (*Pythian* 8). The date of 438 is sometimes given for his death, although the round number of his years may look suspiciously like a conventional guess to indicate 'a very old man'. Since it is clear that he lived and composed into the time during which the great Athenian tragedians were active, while remaining almost immune to influence from them, it is tempting to see Pindar's death as a significant moment for the end of the 'archaic' period of ancient Greek literature.

In later antiquity, Pindar was ranked greatest of the 'canon' of nine lyric poets: Alcman, Alcaeus, Anacreon, Bacchylides, Ibycus, Pindar, Sappho, Simonides, Stesichorus. It is interesting to see the words Quintilian uses:

> Pindar is by a long way the greatest of the nine lyric poets
> for his spirit, magnificence, wise sayings, poetic figures, most
> fertile/fortunate abundance of ideas and words, and a kind
> of eloquence like some river.

> (*Training in Oratory* 10.1.61)

On the last point, he follows Horace, who called Pindar 'a great rushing river' (*Odes* 4.2). Hellenistic scholars arranged Pindar's works into seventeen books: the four books of victory (epinician) odes, comprising Olympian, Pythian, Nemean and Isthmian, plus paeans (hymns to Apollo), dithyrambs (for Dionysus), other hymns, partheneia (songs for choruses of virgin girls, probably performed as part of initiation rites for girls reaching womanhood), dance-songs, laments, and encomia (another kind of praise-song). The epinician odes have survived complete; fragments of the others survive, the most substantial being from the paeans.

All Pindar's poetry was written for specific occasions, often commissioned, probably for payment, although it isn't certain how the process of remuneration works for archaic praise-poets. The opening of *Isthmian* 2 seems to suggest an attack on a rival (perhaps Simonides?) for the level (or the fact?) of his fees, or for introducing fees, but it is unlikely that there was no transaction involved between Pindar and his patrons. Pindar speaks of 'owing' the song to the victor's success, because greatness deserves praise, but he also implies that the song deserves reward. It is probably best to think of the relationship in terms of archaic and aristocratic gift-giving rather than in terms of strict financial contract. Some critics have argued that the odes may usually have been performed by a single individual (who would sometimes but not always be the poet himself), but the received view is that they were performed by a chorus, under the leadership either of the poet himself or of a chorus leader.

The odes were performed in celebration of victory, usually on or after the victor's return home from the festival. There are many lesser local festivals, some of which are mentioned as auxiliary subject matter for praise in the poems, but it is the four pan-Hellenic meetings which really mattered.[4] This is more than just sport (if sport is ever 'just' anything): the athlete encapsulates the heroic ideals of archaic society, displaying the endurance, strength, skill and drive to succeed which win wars and raise mankind nearer to the gods – but not too near. The anxiety of hubristic excess lurks behind every epinician poem, for without that risk of being *too* great there is no possibility of *being* great. The encomiand (person praised) is celebrated at least in part because of the risks he takes. One of the greatest risks is of not winning, for this society isn't tolerant of losers nor generous to the defeated. Even if we allow something for the conventions of praise, we should probably believe Pindar when he talks (in celebration, not sympathy) of the defeated slinking home by sidestreets, unable to face their compatriots (*Pythian* 8.81–7, *Olympian* 8.67–9).

On the surface, Pindar's epinician odes all seem quite similar. After all, if a victor wants a victory ode, he wants it to do certain traditional things that everyone will recognise. It should normally include praise of the victor, his family, perhaps his trainer and his city; mention of previous victories; and hopes for further success. *Nemean* 6, for example, lists twenty-five victories by members of the encomiand's family. Pedigree and glory are mutually reinforcing in archaic thought. The ode will probably include a story from myth and then end with further praise of the encomiand (ring composition). Most of the odes are structured in triads of stanzas: strophe, antistrophe, epode. These terms relate to the movement of the chorus in dance: turn, counter-turn, aftersong, as they are sometimes called. Some odes are made up entirely of strophes, which suggests that they were intended for performance in procession. All the strophes and antistrophes in an ode are 'in responsion', which means that they are metrically identical, while the epodes are different (giving a structure AAB AAB, and so on). No two odes use exactly the same metre. Given the importance of metre in ancient poetry, and given the fact that these poems we have are only the *words* of the song, this great variety of complex metrical patterning should warn us against any simplistic assessment of the odes as 'all the same'.

Pindar isn't the best source for the details of athletic competition in the early fifth century. This is not to deny the possibility of using him as a historical source, but rather to stress that this isn't the sports page. He has little to say about the contest itself – there is, for example, no account of the ancient equivalent of a 'golden goal' or the nanosecond by which a runner might beat a world record. Indeed, a description of an athletic contest is more likely to be of a mythic competition, not the contemporary one being celebrated, as in *Isthmian* 1 (for a victory in the chariot race by Herodotus of Thebes), where the competitive exploits of the heroes Castor and Iolaus are expanded at greater length than that of the encomiand. Once you have got used to Pindar's manner, this apparent disproportion isn't really surprising. One of the things Pindar is doing in his use of mythic colouring is to merge the victor, his family and the heroes of myth into a nexus of celebration.

Pindar's myths have elicited massive critical interest: What are they for? Often the connection between the encomiand and the mythological *exemplum* seems tenuous to modern readers (and indeed later ancient ones) who expect narrative linearity and transparent poetic unity. There are connections, of course, and it is rightly in the nature of reading that critics will look for (and find) connections, but we should note also that what matters is setting the encomiand within the traditional mythic ideal of heroism, not clear connections which might themselves independently justify that setting. It is the poet, in his ceremonial act of performance, who enacts the interaction between present and mythic past.

Seen within this broader framework of the celebration of heroic ideals, the myths are deeply appropriate. Favourites include not just Pelops the charioteer and Castor the boxer, but also Heracles, greatest of heroes and founder of the Olympian games; the legendary first king of Aegina, Aeacus, who helped Apollo and Poseidon build the walls of Troy, and from whom were descended other favourite heroes, such as Peleus, who married a goddess; Jason before his heroic stature was undermined by Euripides in *Medea* (*Pythian* 4 tells at length the story of Jason and the golden fleece).

These heroes pushed back the boundaries of humankind, as (it is implied) do their descendants the victors. But when Heracles reached the Pillars of Heracles, which bound the world in early Greek geography, he turned back (see *Nemean* 3.20–3, *Isthmian* 4.11.13, *Olympian* 3.43.5). Even Heracles, who was to transcend his human nature and – exceptionally for a hero – actually became a god, even he didn't transgress too far. In praising human success, epinician poetry also preaches the need to acknowledge the power of the gods and the limits of human activity. The encomiand's success comes from the gods: when Pindar stresses this, it is both an encouragement to cultivate right attitude towards the gods and itself a form of praise, for it implies that the victor is exactly the sort of man whom the gods support. To owe the victory to the gods, then, is better than owing it to oneself. In the archaic and aristocratic dynamics of success as displayed by the odes, in-born talent is crucial, as is the support of the gods and hard toil. *Olympian* 10.20–1 is a good example of these features, including in-born worth, training, the support of the gods and the need for toil, in two lines. The poet 'finds the mark' for his praise (the metaphor, like many Pindaric metaphors for poetry, resonates with the subject matter), but fears to 'overshoot the mark' (for example, *Olympian* 13.94, *Nemean* 8.20–2), since to do so (to praise excessively) would be to expose the encomiand to the evil eye of envy. Envy, it could be said, is both the guarantor of greatness and the greatest risk it incurs.

For greatness to be realized, it also needs to be celebrated. The poet's offering is (metaphorically?) the fulfilment of a debt (for example, *Isthmian* 1.41–5) and a ritual libation (for example, *Isthmian* 6). It is also intimately tied up in the greatness of the victor, for the poet's glory often shares illustrations, metaphors and vocabulary with the victor's own fame. For example, the paths of song and paths of victorious glory are combined in *Isthmian* 6.22. Pindaric odes are extraordinarily fertile ground for the imagery of poetics: archery, javelin-throwing, long jump, the flight and song of birds, journey, sculpting, weaving, chariot-racing, wine, honey (this list isn't exhaustive). It is because of this sharing of imagery with the encomiand and the heroic *exemplum* that there can be an argument about the referent of the 'eagle' in Pindar's poetry (*Nemean* 5.21, 6.48–9): most critics have taken it to refer to the poet, soaring high above his rivals and ordinary speech, but it could also suggest the high-soaring glory of the encomiand. The point, I think, is that the one carries the other.

This shifting, complex interaction of referents (where the same vocabulary is referring to different things) is one of the features which make Pindar's poetry hard, together with the allusiveness of many of the mythic narratives, the lack of linear chronology and the sudden transitions in grammatical structure. For the richness of his poetic language, we need look no further than the opening words of our collection, put there by the Hellenistic scholars who presumably saw the programmatic possibilities of the ode. *Olympian* 1, for the tyrant Hieron of Syracuse's victory in the single-horse race,[5] opens like this:

> Best of all things is water; but gold, like a gleaming fire by night, outshines all pride of wealth beside. But, my heart, would you chant the glory of games, look no further than the sun by day for any star shining brighter through the deserted air, nor shall we sing games greater than the Olympian.
>
> (1–7, in the translation by Lattimore)

Immediately we are bombarded by images of excellence: water without which life cannot exist; the fire of the sun (and fire itself, the two of which must be suggested in the opening line), which is the other essential element in human life; gold, the standard of greatness, shining, holiness. All these things build up to the Olympic games, which outshine the world. The implication is that victory in these games isn't only great and famous, but also has an inherent quality which is both essential to human civilisation and links the hero to the divine. That very first word ἄριστον (*ariston*, 'best') sums it all up – epinician poetry is the celebration of archaic, aristocratic, heroic aristeia (heroic deeds, done by *aristo*crats).

Notes

1 The system involved counted years in 'Olympiads', series of four years corresponding to the dating of the games, starting from the institution of the games in 776 BC. There were many other ways of reckoning time as well.
2 I happen to be writing this chapter during the 1998 World Cup. The social and political valuation of sporting success seems surprisingly familiar.
3 See, especially here, M.R. Lefkowitz, *The Lives of the Greek Poets*, London: Duckworth, 1981, and her *First-Person Fictions: Pindar's Poetic 'I'*, Oxford: Oxford University Press, 1991.
4 For description of the games, see V. Olivova, *Sports and Games in the Ancient World*, London: Orbis, 1984, and M.M. Willcock, *Pindar: Victory Odes*, Greek and Latin Classics Series, Cambridge: Cambridge University Press, 1995, pp. 4–9.
5 This is a chariot pulled by one horse, not horseback riding. Hieron, like most rulers, didn't drive himself but merely owned the horse, as in modern horse-racing.

See also in this book

Callimachus, Catullus, Horace, Sappho

Texts, translations and commentaries

A second edition of his earlier OCT was produced by Sir Maurice Bowra in 1963. There is a more recent Teubner edition by H. Maehler.

The Penguin translation is also Bowra's (originally 1969), with the Odes arranged in his best estimate of chronological order.

A new Loeb edition, in two volumes, has been produced by W.H. Race (1997).

Two other translations worth noting are G.S. Conway and R. Stoneman, *The Odes and Selected Fragments of Pindar*, London: Dent, 1997, and R. Lattimore, *The Odes of Pindar*, 2nd edn, Chicago, IL: University of Chicago Press, 1976.

M.M. Willcock, *Pindar: Victory Odes*, Cambridge: Cambridge University Press, 1995, is in the Greek and Latin Classics Series, and contains edition and commentary of *Olympians* 2, 7 and 11; *Nemean* 4; *Isthmians* 3, 4 and 7. There is also an Aris and Phillips edition of a selection (*Olympian* 1; *Pythian* 9; *Nemeans* 2 and 3; *Isthmian* 1) by S. Instone (1996).

Further reading

Bowra, C.M., *Pindar*, Oxford: Oxford University Press, 1964.

Carne-Ross, D.S., *Pindar*, New Haven, CT, and London: Hermes Books, 1985.

Kurke, L., *The Traffic in Praise: Pindar and the Poetics of Social Economy*, Ithaca, NY, and London: Cornell University Press, 1991.

Lefkowitz, M.R., *First-Person Fictions: Pindar's Poetic 'I'*, Oxford: Oxford University Press, 1991.

Nagy, G., *Pindar's Homer: The Lyric Possession of an Epic Past*, Baltimore, MD, and London: Johns Hopkins University Press, 1990.

Steiner, D., *The Crown of Song: Metaphor in Pindar*, London: Duckworth, 1986.

SOPHOCLES

Sophocles has earned almost universal critical admiration. The younger contemporary of Aeschylus, older contemporary of Euripides, he creates the perfect balance (so it has seemed to critics ancient and modern) between those two extremes. Sophocles seems almost to be the embodiment of the cultural achievements of the fifth century, which his long life nearly spanned (about 496 to 406/5 BC).

For so important a figure, we have surprisingly little direct evidence: just seven plays[1] (out of probably 123), plus some fragments and ninety titles, together with ancient biographical testimonies of variable reliability. As well as being a successful and popular dramatist, who may have won as many as twenty-four times out of about thirty entries, Sophocles was also an active citizen of Athens, for which he regularly fulfilled civic offices, even as late as his 80s. His strange and beautiful last play, *Oedipus at Colonus*, was written shortly before his death at the age of 93, but was not performed until 401, after the destruction and restoration of the Athenian democracy in the aftermath of the Peloponnesian War. That play about mystery, death and rebirth contains an ode in celebration of Colonus, the birthplace of Sophocles and the last resting place of his greatest creation, Oedipus. But we shouldn't get too romantic about this. Oedipus 'rests' as a demonic power, whose driving force is the desire to harm enemies (and so 'help friends') – and the supernatural ability to do so.

All seven tragedies take their subject matter from heroic myth. Because the audience can be expected – in general terms – to know the story and to recognise the mythic world, the tragedian can play with their expectations, both fulfilling and surprising them. In the *Philoctetes* (409), it looks for one awful (or wonderful) moment that an event will be staged which will cause Troy not to fall, and if there is one 'given' in Greek myth it is the fall of Troy. The title character, suffering a supernatural sickness, had been abandoned on the island of Lemnos by the Greeks on their way to Troy. They now receive a prophecy which states that only with Philoctetes and the bow of Heracles (which is in his possession) can they defeat Troy. Odysseus and Neoptolemus (son of the now-dead Achilles) go to fetch him. But Philoctetes is adamant in his refusal, for the Greeks are now his enemies whom he must seek to harm, in accordance with the norms of the Greek ethic that you 'help friends and harm enemies'. Neoptolemus is won over by Philoctetes and is persuaded to take him home to Oeta in Thessaly, instead of Troy. They move to go. It looks for a moment as if Troy will not fall. There is a further development which leads eventually to the play ending with the necessary departure to Troy, but Sophocles has already held up to us the alternative possibility.

In *Philoctetes*, Odysseus is the paradigmatic opportunist, a manipulative, deceptive schemer who seeks to win at all costs. Frequently his portrayal in Greek tragedy is a negative one, but the playwrights don't just trot out fifty Odysseuses all the same. In Sophocles' *Ajax* (earlier than *Philoctetes*), we see a noble Odysseus, who tries to help his dead enemy. The plays aren't sealed units; representations of 'the same material' can be significantly different.

Sophocles' most important technical innovation was the intro-duction of the third actor,[2] which allowed him to represent complex relationships and dynamic three-way interactions. His plays tend to be dominated by one central, heroic protagonist. The 'hero' dominates not because the play is only interested in him/her (although the *hero* may be so); not because other characters are trivial (they are not); not even because the hero speaks or is present for a high proportion of the play (which is by no means always the case): it is because the play is interested in the events surrounding the ramifications from the activity, personality and situation of one extraordinary person. Take the case of Oedipus in *Oedipus at Colonus*. Oedipus dominates the play, because he is a huge and fascinating character, but to ignore his sons Polynices and Eteocles, his daughters Antigone and Ismene, and what is happening to them all as children of Oedipus, is to misunderstand the play and the cyclic nature of tragedy, and the tragic nature of cycles in families. The story is set at the moment when Oedipus arrives at a grove of the Eumenides, near Athens, and in fulfilment of a prophecy that this will be his resting place. So he will soon die: various people, including his sons, want to gain possession of his body, which will have the power of an avenging spirit. He curses his sons, who will eventually kill each other. Antigone will be buried alive for ritually burying Polynices. That story had already been told by Sophocles in another play, the *Antigone*, written some forty years before *Oedipus at Colonus*. Polynices' and Eteocles' role in *Oedipus at Colonus* is precisely *as* sons of Oedipus – cursed in his parentage, cursing his sons. The daughters also are under the curse of the perverted intergenerational and incestuous relationships of this family.

The Sophoclean hero is marked out from the ordinary, in greatness and in suffering. The 'heroic temper' is one which drives a person towards an inevitable end, despite pleas, despite consequences. Ajax, in his play, is a paradigm case. Ajax had been in competition with Odysseus for the arms of the dead Achilles and killed himself after he was maddened by Athene into killing some sheep, thinking he was killing the Greek leaders. He is ashamed over his failure to kill his enemies and his humiliation at the hands of Athene. The action revolves first around his determination to kill himself, despite the pleas of his friends, and then around the debate over whether to give him honourable burial. The concentration of this highly centripetal play is all on Ajax, first alive then dead.

By contrast, the *Women of Trachis* is a play split down the middle. Deinaira seeks to return to herself the love of her husband, the great hero Heracles. She sends him a cloak soaked in what she believes to be a love potion but is in fact poison, which had been given to her deceitfully many years previously by the centaur Nessus, whom Heracles killed when he tried to rape Deinaira. Husband and wife never meet in the play: the split is the message, bridged as it is by the poisoned communication of the fatal potion. Around the split, also, revolve a series of oppositions, such as those between civilisation and barbarism, city and wilderness, male and female, god and man, man and beast. But these polarities are unstable, for at the centre of the civilised house is hidden the monstrous, bestial poison.

The interactions of civilisation and barbarism are active also in the *Philoctetes*, where we see perhaps the most extreme form of heroic isolation. Philoctetes is alone on the island, with only the bow of Heracles to keep him anywhere near humanity. The hero's exceptionality can risk leading him right out of human society altogether. He may become a hero in the religious sense – not a deified mortal (if Heracles is deified at the end of the *Women of Trachis*, that is another matter, another element in his myth), but one whose dead body has a kind of demonic power which arises, at least in part, from his heroic excess, as in *Oedipus at Colonus*. Moral goodness, it should be noted, isn't the point.

A different kind of 'hero' is presented in the *Antigone*. The play revolves around the clash between Antigone's desire to bury her brother, Polynices, and the ruling of her uncle, Creon, now king of Thebes, that Polynices was a public enemy and therefore should not be buried. Antigone has all the stubbornness of an Ajax or a Philoctetes – or her own father. She will die for her belief, and Creon will lose his son and his wife to sympathetic suicide. It is easy for modern readers to give the moral high-ground to Antigone and condemn Creon as a selfish tyrant (as his son, Antigone's lover, calls him). But tragic morality is more complex, more grey. Antigone's heroic devotion is troubled by her treatment of her sister Ismene (whom she rejects), by the uncomfortably erotic undertones in her language about Polynices (it should be remembered that they are the children of incest) and by the fact of her opposition to her legal *kyrios*, the uncle who is now head of her family. If she claims 'the gods' for her side, she forgets that others call on the gods to protect the laws of cities. The play refuses to give a definitive judgement between the claims of family and of city, refuses even to allow the clear distinctions between the two which Antigone and Creon both seek to impose for their own purposes.

One extraordinary play has dominated tragedy. It is worthwhile to consider, when making generalisations about Greek tragedy, whether one is really saying something about *Oedipus the King* and extrapolating from that basis. This would be a mistake, because although the play is hugely important and has rightly been admired, it isn't simply a paradigm beside which all others must be judged. Greek tragedy is more creative and dynamic than that, even though *Oedipus the King* is an almost overwhelmingly powerful intertext. But why is the play so powerful, so compelling?[3]

One reason is the ferociously logical and teleological plot, where every action – self-referentially – brings the audience inexorably closer to disaster. By comparison with many ancient tragedies, an unusually large amount *happens* within the 'single action' – which is the discovery by Oedipus that he has unknowingly killed his father and married his mother. Both plot and play are structured around questions, starting with the riddle of the Sphinx, which haunts the present of the play, although it belongs to the past. What goes on four legs in the morning, two at noon and three in the evening, and is weakest when it has most? The answer is man – and Oedipus, a baby with pinned legs in the morning (crawling – not that Oedipus could crawl at the time of his exposure, of course, because he was too young); a man standing tall in the middle of the play; and an old man, prematurely aged by his blindness and feeling his way with a stick (the third foot), at the end. Past, present and future are intertwined and vividly portrayed in this play which so tidily obeys the 'law' of unity of time.

The first question, 'How do we stop the plague?', soon becomes 'Who killed Laius?', which itself slips almost unnoticed into 'Who is Oedipus?' The answer to all the questions is, of course, horribly the same. Oedipus is the son of Laius; Laius was killed by Oedipus; we stop the plague by getting rid of the killer of Laius. The one apparently unmotivated event, the arrival of the Corinthian messenger at line 924, not only injects new life into the play and takes it up a gear towards the climax, but also turns out to have been motivated directly by the previous scene: it is an answer to the prayer of Jocasta for deliverance. The messenger indeed brings 'deliverance' and a solution, but not the one Jocasta sought.

This remorselessness of the plot is a narrative representation of that sense of human helplessness in the face of the future, which people have wanted to call 'fate'; for the crucial actions of Oedipus' life evolve in accordance with the destiny apparently assigned to him before his conception and foretold through oracles. While to call the play a 'tragedy of fate', as was traditional, is fraught with difficulty, it must be part of its power that people respond in fear and fascination to the complex issues of free will and determinism (does the fact that the gods foretell the future *cause* it to happen?); of the nature of choice and the meaning of action; of the questions these raise about the place of humanity in the universe.

This is why it is important to be as clear as possible (although after clarity comes further complexity) that what happens to Oedipus is *not* a just reward for some great sin. In the days when the 'tragic flaw' was popular, various attempts were made to find one for Oedipus, but the point of the play, the point of tragedy, is that this is a man who did nothing wrong but who turned out to have done the most awful wrongs.[4] If it were straightforwardly a matter of 'justice' that Oedipus should suffer as he does, it wouldn't be tragic.

This isn't to say, however, that he isn't *guilty*, for it is the guilt of the action, not the knowledge or intention of the agent, that pollutes the tragic world. Moreover, although it would be wrong to say that 'Oedipus is punished for his pride' (particularly because the punishment would have to precede the crime), it is nonetheless dramatically and thematically crucial that Oedipus should start the play as an embodiment of heroic greatness: a brilliant intellect, a forceful personality, happy, wise, resourceful, powerful – and proud of it. The greater the height, the greater the fall, but this reversal of fortune is dramatic more than it is moral. If we try to make any sense of it all in terms of the gods, we might say that the play is a lesson in the truth of prophecy, however unfair that may be to Oedipus; that the audience may be reminded of the weakness of humanity (but also of its strength?); that Greek religion isn't so much about justice and morality as about power and the maintenance of the status quo; that the Greek gods are jealous of good fortune (a common ancient idea).

Aristotle regarded *peripeteia* ('reversal of fortune') as a desirable feature of tragedy, and likewise *anagnorisis* ('recognition' – *Poetics* 1452a22–b8). Part of the power of the play stems from its almost overdetermined reversal, integrally linked with its recognition scene, for it is at the moment when he recognises who he is, and what he has done, that Oedipus falls. He stabs out his eyes, in an act of self-mutilation which is the dramatically logical conclusion of his failure to see his situation. Throughout the play, he has been linked in imagery with a series of oppositions – blindness and insight, doctor and disease, curser and thing cursed (he cursed the murderer, and anyone who helped him, not excluding himself, if he should accidentally have protected the man – 249–51); king and outcast (as a baby and as an exile from Corinth): these are only the most obvious instances. It is around the moment of recognition, also, that all these polarities hinge.

I have hinted at irony. Here is another Oedipal overdetermination, for the play positively drips with irony: from the explicit 'I will fight for him as if he were my father' (264), said by Oedipus of his determination to find the murderer of Laius, to the many references to sight and knowledge (integrally linked in Greek, as in English), to eyes and to feet,[5] and the situational irony of the contrast between the sighted Oedipus who doesn't know and the blind prophet Tiresias who does. Oedipus, of course, will become blind when he comes to know. It is a remarkable feature of the play that the tone of foreboding and of seriousness is maintained throughout, the ironies never becoming a sick joke – unless the gods are sick. Here we can see most particularly the effective use of the audience's knowledge of the myth, for much of the play's force would simply be lost if the audience weren't in a position of superior knowledge. Do the audience therefore play god with Oedipus? Perhaps, but they also recognise themselves in him.

Notes

1   *Ajax, Antigone, Women of Trachis, Oedipus the King, Electra, Philoctetes, Oedipus at Colonus.* About 404 lines of the satyr play *Trackers* also survive.
2   According to Aristotle (*Poetics* 1449a.15–17), who says he also invented 'scene-painting'.
3   There are many answers to that: more than ever I am conscious that I am offering only first thoughts, which readers will soon outgrow.
4   See E.R. Dodds, 'On misunderstanding the *Oedipus Rex*', *Greece and Rome*, 13, 1966, pp. 37–49.
5   Oedipus was bound by the ankles as a baby when the shepherd took him supposedly to expose, but in fact gave him to the Corinthian. The name means 'swollen foot'. See S. Goldhill, *Reading Greek Tragedy*, Cambridge: Cambridge University Press, 1986, pp. 216–18, for what else it might mean.

See also in this book

Aeschylus, Euripides, Seneca the Younger

Texts, translations and commentaries

The OCT volume is by H. Lloyd-Jones and N.G. Wilson, while the Teubner is by R. Dawe.

The recent Loeb edition is in three volumes, also by H. Lloyd–Jones.

All the plays are available in Penguin volumes, one for the Oedipus plays and one for the rest. The version by R. Fagles (*Sophocles: The Three Theban Plays*, Harmondsworth: Penguin, 1984) contains an introduction and notes by Bernard Knox, and is an excellent way of getting a quick overview of Knox's extensive work on the Oedipus plays.

A World's Classics volume contains *Antigone, Oedipus the King* and *Electra*, while another Oxford series, Greek Tragedy in New Translations, offers an *Ajax* (called by its Greek title, *Aias*) and an *Electra*.

Antigone (by Griffith), *Electra* (Kells), *Oedipus the King* (called, as it often is, by its Latin title *Oedipus Rex*; Dawe), *Philoctetes* (Webster) and *Women of Trachis* (called *Trachiniae*; Easterling) have editions in the Cambridge Greek and Latin Classics Series.

Aris and Phillips editions exist on *Ajax* (Garvie), *Antigone* (Brown), *Philoctetes* (Ussher), the *Three Theban Plays* (Trypanis) and *Electra* (March).

Further reading

There is a great deal written on Greek tragedy, and Sophocles in particular. The following list represents only a small sample.

Blundell, M.W., *Helping Friends and Harming Enemies: A Study in Sophocles and Greek Ethics*, Cambridge: Cambridge University Press, 1989.

Easterling, P.E. (ed.), *The Cambridge Companion to Greek Tragedy*, Cambridge: Cambridge University Press, 1997.

Goldhill, S., *Reading Greek Tragedy*, Cambridge: Cambridge University Press, 1986.

Knox, B.M.W., *Oedipus at Thebes*, New Haven, CT: Yale University Press, 1957.

Knox, B.M.W., *The Heroic Temper: Studies in Sophoclean Tragedy*, Berkeley and Los Angeles, CA: University of California Press, 1964.

Segal, C.P., *Tragedy and Civilization: An Interpretation of Sophocles*, Cambridge, MA: Harvard University Press, 1981.

Winnington-Ingram, R.P., *Sophocles: An Interpretation*, Cambridge: Cambridge University Press, 1980.

HERODOTUS

Herodotus has been called the 'father of history' (Cicero *On Laws* 1.1.5) – and the 'father of lies' (Plutarch *On the Malice of Herodotus*).[1] He wrote his *Histories* or 'investigations', a great rambling work of narrative, description and comment about the characteristics and past deeds of the Greek world and the non-Greek East, at a time when the influences of oral literature were still very strong, when the author was still a teller of tales and when the mythic world of Homer was the more distant, inscrutable and marvellous continuation back in time of essentially the same project as recent history. The difference wasn't so much between myth and history, although Herodotus certainly 'rationalises' some stories, but between the more recent and the more distant past.[2]

Herodotus' extraordinary sensitivity to cultural difference may stem in part from his upbringing in the frontier world of Halicarnassus, a Greek city on the coast of Asia Minor (in what is now Turkey), a city which was culturally Ionian but with Dorian influences and history, and which was self-consciously Greek but intermingled with non-Greek Carians and even some Persians. Details of Herodotus' life that come down to us from antiquity are very unreliable, since the tendency for biographers to make their subjects' lives fit their works and fit patterns for great men's lives, is almost certainly affecting the picture.

Herodotus lived from probably around the 480s to the 420s BC. He is said to have been exiled by Lygdamis, Persian-backed tyrant of Halicarnassus, to have been involved in the removal of that tyrant, but then to have been forced into permanent exile in the resultant political upheavals; he supposedly spent some time in Athens, where he acquired a lot of information for his *Histories* from members of the influential Alcmaeonid family (so it is inferred from the pro-

Alcmaeonid bias of some of his stories); and finally he joined a new colony (a settlement of Greeks, instigated by Athens) at Thurii in southern Italy. All this information must be treated with the greatest caution, but happily it makes little difference to the interest and value of his great work. Somewhere in all this, he must have travelled widely. The suggestion that he didn't in fact visit most of the places he claims to have seen is not now generally accepted.

Herodotus says that he writes the *Histories* in order to celebrate and commemorate the marvels of the Greeks and the barbarians (that is, non-Greeks), and especially the reasons why they came to fight each other. It may come as a surprise to those who know only the modern historical tradition, of which Herodotus was the father but not a part,[3] to discover that Herodotus and his audience would have seen his project as closely akin to Homer's. Keeping the past alive by telling of it is a debt which the author owes to the past, which would wholly die without the 'teller of tales'.[4] The big *telos* (the goal of both narrative and content) of the work is the Persian Wars of the 490s and 480s, in which the Greeks repelled the invasion of the Persian king Xerxes. The wars involved battles the memory of which resonated down the fifth century, particularly in the dark days of the Peloponnesian War between Athens and Sparta, as symbols of manly courage and Greek success: Artemesium, Thermopylae, Salamis, Plataea and, before them, Marathon, when the Greeks repelled Xerxes' father Darius in 490 BC. The story of the runner, whose dash from the battle to Athens is the supposed origin of the 'marathon' race today, isn't in Herodotus. Interestingly, there is instead the story of a still more remarkable feat of running, in which the messenger runs from Athens to Sparta (some 140 miles) in two days (*Histories* 6.105–6). Herodotus' narrative of all these battles is duly powerful, but in total they make up only a small fraction of the work. He is as much concerned with causes, with cultures and with marvels as he is with the wars themselves. Herodotus offers us not a dry narrative, but a world.

Herodotus writes as a Greek. He is undoubtedly tolerant of cultural difference, and self-consciously so, as is shown by the story he relates to illustrate the dictum that 'custom is king' (3.38). A group of Greeks and a group of Indians from the tribe of the Callatiae are invited by the Persian king Darius to indulge in the funeral practices of the other group. (The Greeks cremate their dead; the Indians consume them.) Each group reacts with horror at the obscenity of the suggestion that they might burn/consume their dead (that is, adopt the practice of the other group). Greekness, nonetheless, remains the norm[5] in all Herodotus' anthropological commentaries, which are many. There is, for example, a long list of Egyptian 'opposite' practices (2.35ff.), which show not only the Greek and Herodotean tendency to see the world as structured by polarities, but also the construction of the distant barbarian as an inversion which defines the normality of its (Greek) opposite.

Despite this Greekness, however, the narrative focalisation is with the barbarians for very much of the time, first Lydian then Median and Persian, even Egyptian, Scythian and Thracian. Only quite rarely is it with Greeks. Part of the reason for this, perhaps, is that it is precisely the non-Greek experience that needs to be described for the Greek audience who wish to understand this great event of the recent past. Herodotus traces the origins of the Persian War back to the conquest of the Lydian kingdom (neither Greek nor Persian) in Asia Minor by the Persian empire in 547 BC. The last Lydian king, Croesus, whose fabulous wealth reached mythic proportions, is a major player in the early parts of the work, first as king himself and then as commentator on the action in the Persian court, where he is kept as an adviser and what we might call an 'honoured slave'. The 'wise adviser' is a recurrent motif in the narrative.

Interwoven with the narrative of increasing Persian power and of cultural and political clashes is a vast wealth of stories about the world. The whole of Book 2 (the book divisions were devised in the Hellenistic age) is devoted to a description of the country and customs of Egypt, while there are excursuses also on the Scythians, Thracians and others: Herodotus sees the world as radiating out from Greece, and the edges of the world as having the most 'things rare and beautiful' (3.116). He is more interested in the Eastern half of the world surrounding the Mediterranean, whereas of the West his knowledge is hazy. With characteristic reticence, he expresses doubt about the existence of a great river called the Eridanus which flows into the northern sea (this river is perhaps best called 'mythical': its myth contains traces of the Rhône, the Rhine and the Po). Nor does he have any confidence about some places called the 'Tin Islands' (3.115–16) – probably the Scilly isles, or perhaps Britain itself.

> In spite of my efforts to do so, I have never found anyone who could give me first-hand information of the existence of a sea beyond Europe to the north and west.

> (*Histories* 3.115)

There are so many fascinating stories told by the teller of tales that this short essay cannot hope to do them justice. There is the account of how the Egyptian pharaoh Psammetichus wanted to discover whether the Egyptians or the Phrygians were the oldest race of humans (2.2). He therefore arranged for two babies to be brought up with animals, with no-one allowed to speak a word in their presence. The first recognisable word which the children repeatedly spoke was *bekos*, which Psammetichus discovered was the Phrygian word for 'bread'. This 'proved' the greater antiquity of the Phrygians, since the language was held to be innate in the children. Or there is the story at 4.42, which Herodotus doesn't himself believe, that a group of Phoenician sailors sailed right round the bottom of Africa. The reason he doesn't believe it is their claim that during their trip the sun was on the wrong side of them – as, of course, it would be if it were true, since they would have gone into the southern hemisphere.

Or there is the story of how Athenian women came to wear Ionian dress: they were so angry at the death of their men in an expedition against Aegina that they killed the one survivor with their brooches (5.87–8). The women had been in the habit of wearing Dorian dress, 'very similar to the fashion at Corinth', but they were now made to wear tunics with no brooches. Actually, Herodotus tells us, this dress wasn't originally Ionian, for at first all Greek women wore the Dorian style, but rather it was Carian. The historical value of this unimportant little story is potentially huge: it reflects on the use of dress as a means of social control; attitudes to women's behaviour and self-control; the Greek (and other) tendency to see women as a group, not individuals; group responsibility; attitudes to Greekness and to the intra-Greek cultural divisions.

Even when the author is wrong, Herodotus' *Histories* are a useful historical source for a variety of reasons including the very fact that he offers alternative explanations. But what sort of a historian was he? How did he collect and evaluate his material, and make sense of the world, particularly the world of the past?[6] Two things above all make Herodotus a historian: his active tracking of sources and his sense of the marvellous. Admiration for great deeds and things is, we might think, more a characteristic of the epic poet than of the detached, objective, rational historian; but it is precisely the ability to be surprised that makes Herodotus into an acute observer of things different from his own experience.

The sources for the *Histories* are legion and often untraceable.[7] There are literary precursors which Herodotus is certainly using, such as the proto-historian and geographer Hecataeus of Miletus, whose work describing a journey around 'the earth' contained a great deal of information about the climate, people and customs of Europe and Asia (including Africa). There is almost certainly also influence from the Ionian philosophers, who, in the generations immediately before Herodotus, tried to explain the world in a variety of ways. There are also the scores, perhaps hundreds, of people he talked to, people who were sometimes themselves eye-witnesses to the events or places they describe, sometimes descendants of those who were and sometimes just repeating a story they had heard from others. Often, they are *polis*-groups, 'the Corinthians say this', 'the Athenians say that'. Sometimes, quite likely, informants were deliberately or accidentally deceiving the enquirer. Often Herodotus will offer more than one version of an event, or explanation of a phenomenon; sometimes he makes a judgement between them, sometimes just lets them all stand.

But he doesn't simply take down everything he happens to hear: he also goes in search of information, as in the well-known case of his investigation into the antiquity of the hero-god Heracles (2.42–4). Herodotus heard from Egyptian priests of a god he thought he recognised as Heracles. This god, according to the Egyptians, came into being 17,000 years before the reign of the Pharaoh Amasis (mid-sixth century BC), whereas Herodotus places the Greek hero only a few hundred years before his own time. In order to investigate the matter, he travels to Tyre to visit one ancient temple of Heracles, and from there follows a lead to Thasos, where he interprets the evidence as showing worship of Heracles five generations before the hero arrived in Greece. His conclusion from all this is that there are two separate Heracleses: one a very ancient god and son of Zeus, the other a much more recent hero and son of Amphitryon.

All these lesser stories make for a highly complex narrative structure. Indeed, Herodotus might also be called the 'father of digression', for his narrative line ranges as widely as his own travels (see Lang 1984). All together, the work has a strong forward movement, from Croesus and Cyrus to Xerxes and the Athenians, but within that linear structure the narrative takes many twists and turns, looping back on itself, dropping a thread and refinding it later, slipping back into the mists of heroic and even geological time (for example when talking about the Nile silting up over 20,000 years – 2.11). It is easy for the structure to seem chaotic, but there are a few things worth noting about this narrative complexity. First, we shouldn't underestimate the appetite of the preliterate and newly literate audience for non-linear narrative. Homeric epic, teleologically driven as it is, nonetheless is full of digressions and disruptions to its narrative line. This may in part relate to the fact of oral performance, for the *Histories* will have been performed, in sections, in public or semi-public contexts. It would be misleading, however, to suggest that the bits performed on any one occasion correspond exactly to the narrative chunks which a modern critic observes. Rather, it isn't in the nature of an oral society, with its (to modern eyes) untidy sense of historical time, to expect what we would call neat narrative direction.

Moreover, Herodotus does have means of structuring his account. One device is what modern critics call 'archaic ring composition', when at the end of a digression the author will redirect his narrative by returning to his starting place:

> So much, then, for the animal life in that part of Libya where the nomads are: I have made it as full and accurate as my extensive enquiries permit. Continuing westward from the Maxyes ...

> (*Histories* 4.192–3)

There is also a sense of rhetorical development at many levels of the narrative. As the story works towards its climax in Xerxes' invasion of Greece, the narrative tension rises accordingly. 'That was the beginning of the evil', says Herodotus (5.97), in true epic style, of the Athenian involvement in the Ionian revolt; then the long sequence at the court of Xerxes (7.12ff.), including the visitation from a divine being who persuades the king to make war on Greece; then the mustering and movement of the army (7.20ff.), which drinks the rivers dry (7.21).

The 'digression' to tell about the hospitality of Pythius the Lydian (7.27ff.) in fact moves the story forward. This very rich man treats the whole army to dinner and offers to pay the expenses of the war. Xerxes is so pleased that not only does he decline the request, he even gives Pythius still greater wealth. But when they are setting off again, a bad omen persuades Pythius to request that the eldest of his five sons be allowed to remain at home, the others going with the army (7.38–9). Xerxes reacts with anger and violence: the unfortunate young man is cut in two and the army marches out between the two halves of his body. Two things (among many) that this story is doing are, first, replaying the Persian–Lydian connection which Herodotus saw as the ultimate beginning of the whole affair and, second, displaying again the capriciousness and cruelty of the Eastern potentate. However generous Herodotus may be towards other customs, there can be no denying his expressed views about absolute rulers.[8] Tyrants are the people given the worst press in his narrative.

Characteristically, however, Herodotus makes room for the airing of different views. One scene is particularly important in this regard, because it is the earliest known example of what later becomes a popular set-piece: the constitutional debate. In Book 3. 80ff., a group of seven conspirators have just overthrown the Magus who is ruling Persia. Before setting up the new government, the conspirators have a debate about what kind of government is the best: monarchy, democracy or oligarchy. Darius argues for monarchy, claiming that since they are talking about all these in their ideal forms, surely nothing could be better than having the best person in the world in charge (3.82)! He wins the debate, by a majority of four out of seven (3.83). He then also wins the kingship, by a trick which seems to gain divine approbation (3.85–6). This Darius will later crush the Ionian revolt, and will be defeated by the Greeks at the Battle of Marathon, but Herodotus still has plenty to say about his achievements (3.89–96).

I end this essay with two points about Herodotus which make him particularly foreign to the modern ideal of the historian. First, I have mentioned that both the performance and much of the source material of the *Histories* is oral. This is the reason, in part, for the extraordinary amount of direct speech in Herodotus, something which modern histories wouldn't contain. How can he know what people said? For one thing, Herodotus rarely claims that he is reporting the exact words but, more importantly, it is likely that there would be little expectation among the audience or in the author that speeches would be produced verbatim. An illiterate or newly literate society has little notion of 'the exact words', since checking is impossible. They do, however, have a very strong notion of the power and importance of speech in human relations and therefore human history. An account of great deeds and events wouldn't be complete without them. Second, Herodotus tends to see the motivation in historical events as stemming largely from personal desires and intentions on the part of individuals, rather than from the social, demographic or more broadly political influences on events which constitute modern historians' explanations of the world. It would be an oversimplification to claim that Herodotus is wrong and naïve in his analysis. Instead, we should see his explanations as signs of how the world looked in the fifth century BC. It was a world dominated by reciprocity, and in particular the desire for revenge. It is this force which drives the opening stories of cycles of outrage, with the rapes of Io, Europa, Medea and Helen, which really started it all.

Notes

1 This designation may stem from Plutarch's disapproval of some of the views Herodotus expressed or implied, especially about his native Boeotia, rather than because he thought it bad history.
2 See T. Luce, *The Greek Historians*, London: Routledge, 1997.
3 J. Gould, *Herodotus*, London: Weidenfeld and Nicolson, 1989, p. 3.
4 Gould, *op. cit.*, pp. 119–20.
5 See P. Cartledge, *The Greeks: A Portrait of Self and Others*, Oxford: Oxford University Press, 1993, p. 77.
6 See especially D. Lateiner, *The Historical Method of Herodotus*, Toronto, Ont., and London: University of Toronto Press, 1989.
7 There are scholars who think that Herodotus' work is largely fictional, that his descriptions of the sources are made up to sound plausible, rather than having any bearing on reality. See particularly for this view, which is now a minority opinion, D. Fehling, *Herodotus and His 'Sources'*, Liverpool: Francis Cairns, 1989. There is a major discussion in W.K. Pritchett, *The Liar School of Herodotus*, Amsterdam: Gieben, 1993.
8 See Cartledge, *op. cit.*, esp. p. 61.

See also in this book

Cassius Dio, Livy, Polybius, Tacitus, Thucydides

Texts, translations and commentaries

The OCT is by K. Hude (3rd edn, 1963). There is a more recent Teubner by H.B. Rose (1987–97).

There are good new translations in World's Classics (1998) and Penguin (revised 1996).

W.W. How and J. Wells, *A Commentary on Herodotus* in two volumes (with introduction and appendixes), Oxford: Oxford University Press, 1912, is an old commentary on the Greek text, reprinted by OUP in 1989. Editions with commentary in the Cambridge Greek and Latin Classics Series are in preparation for Books 3, 4, 7, 8 and 9.

Further reading

Gould, J., *Herodotus*, London: Weidenfeld and Nicolson, 1989.
Harrison, T.E.H., *Divinity and History: The Religion of Herodotus*, Oxford: Oxford University Press, 2000.
Hartog, F., *The Mirror of Herodotus: The Representation of the Other in the Writing of History*, Berkeley and Los Angeles, CA: University of California Press, 1988.
Lang, M.L., *Herodotean Narrative and Discourse*, Cambridge, MA: Harvard University Press, 1984.
Lateiner, D., *The Historical Method of Herodotus*, Toronto, Ont., and London: University of Toronto Press, 1989.
Luce, T., *The Greek Historians*, London: Routledge, 1997.
Thomas, R., *Herodotus in Context: Ethnography, Science and the Art of Persuasion*, Cambridge: Cambridge University Press, 2000.

EURIPIDES

Euripides hasn't always enjoyed universal acclaim. It was said, for example, that he emasculated tragedy, and that he killed it; that he hated women; that he dressed his heroes in rags and made them behave like beggars; that he tied his plots in knots, and equally his characters' tongues and his readers' minds, with his displays of playful sophistry and nihilism.[1] Whether intentionally or not, Euripides was good at shocking people. Two famously outrageous lines are Medea's challenge to misogyny, 'I would rather stand three times by my shield than give birth once' (*Medea* 250–1), and Hippolytus' sophistic attempt to squirm out of a promise, 'My tongue swore, my mind remained unsworn' (*Hippolytus* 612). Aristophanes couldn't be expected to let that one pass (*Frogs* 101–2).

Evaluations like those above partly stem from the fact that Euripides was an innovator in a crowded field (Aeschylus, Sophocles and many others) and partly arose because there were people around at the time to get them started, in particular Aristophanes laughing (appreciatively?) in the wings and Aristotle round the chronological corner. Indeed, much of what Aristophanes and Aristotle say, and the way they say it, is driven by the needs and conventions of their own genre. Aristophanes, in his *Frogs* and *Women at the Thesmophoria* in particular, pokes comic, playful, gender-bending fun at Euripides, in order to show in comic terms much of what I am going to say in this essay in literary critical terms; Aristotle has various philosophical purposes behind his astute literary critical analyses. Although Euripides may not have achieved resounding success in the dramatic competitions (winning the first prize on only four occasions), the critical reception of his work in Aristophanes and in the fourth century BC shows that he was acknowledged as a genius, even if not a conventional one. Success in the competitions isn't an overwhelming sign of the critical standing of a work: Sophocles' *Oedipus the King* didn't win first prize.

Euripides' long life, like that of Sophocles, is one of the hallmarks of the fifth century. He was born sometime in the 480s BC, and died a few months before Sophocles in 406. The last two years of his life were spent at the Macedonian court of King Archelaus, where he went in 408, whether from bitterness, to escape an Athens now ravaged by war, or more likely simply for a visit. Athens itself, cultural developments in the later decades of the fifth century, and the Peloponnesian War all inform Euripides' drama in complex and subtle ways. An accident of textual history has allowed nearly twenty plays of Euripides to survive (out of over ninety which were known in antiquity): the tragedies *Medea, Hippolytus, The Madness of Heracles, The Children of Heracles, The Suppliant Women, The Phoenician Women, Hecabe, Women of Troy, Helen, Electra, Orestes, Andromache, Iphigenia among the Taurians, Iphigenia at Aulis, Ion, Bacchae*; the satyr play[2] *Cyclops*; and the prosatyric play *Alcestis*. This last is formally a tragedy, but was produced fourth in the performance and so in the slot normally occupied by a satyr play, and indeed has many satyr-like features, particularly in its second half. Various fragments of other plays remain. There is also the *Rhesus*, which is attributed to Euripides but probably falsely.

Euripides' plays often attract the adjective 'realistic'. While there are indeed many senses in which this is a useful critical term to apply to Euripides, it needs to be considered alongside and perhaps in tension with another Euripidean feature, his self-consciousness about drama as a sophisticated poetic and artistic discourse. This is arguably the most striking characteristic of Euripides. In the following paragraphs, these two apparently opposed Euripidean traits should be seen each informing and perhaps undercutting the other.

Euripidean realism manifests itself most obviously in attention to everyday details not normally part of the elevated tragic world. The classic example is in the *Electra* (the story of the murder of Clytemnestra and Aegisthus by Orestes, egged on by Electra), which opens with a distortion of the normal myth by having Electra married to a peasant. This innovation constitutes an extreme case of the humility and homeliness which will characterise the play and make the murders so chilling, and also it acts as a symbol for the removal of heroic status from the principals. The internal purpose in having Electra married to a peasant is to ensure that she bears only weak sons, not noble ones who might carry on the feuding cycle which has dogged the house of Atreus since before Atreus' own time. There is a certain irony, therefore, when Orestes makes an impassioned speech about the nobility of spirit in this supposedly inferior man (369–400).

Whereas tragic eating is usually perverted (especially in the house of Atreus, where the eating of children goes back to its foundation and the story of how Tantalus served his son Pelops to the gods as a meal, just as Atreus served his brother Thyestes with his children), in the *Electra* we see preparations for an ordinary meal (408–31); likewise we see an ordinary, everyday sacrifice in which Aegisthus is engaged when Orestes comes to kill him (related in the messenger speech at 774–859), in stark contrast with the various perverted sacrifices which litter tragedy and this cycle in particular, such as the sacrifice of Orestes' eldest sister Iphigenia, killed to appease Artemis and allow Agamemnon's ships to sail to Troy. Electra's trap for her mother, with the false report that she has borne her first child (651–8), is equally homely and equally chilling. Notable also for its everyday details is the *Ion*, a play of great generic complexity which involves the eponymous hero in sweeping out the temple of Apollo (102ff.), where he is a slave. He turns out to be Apollo's son. Both *Ion* and *Electra* are important in the history of the development of comedy, as well as tragedy.

'Realism' is a good term also for the sense many readers and viewers have that Euripides is putting really quite ordinary characters into heroic situations which are beyond them (*Electra, Orestes, Andromache, Ion, Suppliant Women*). 'Realistic', again, are the intense psychological explorations of such characters as Medea (in the play of that name), whose horrific determination to kill her children in revenge for her desertion by Jason is portrayed as the agonised decision of a sane but deeply troubled woman – as well as a strong woman who *will not* be insulted; Phaedra, in the *Hippolytus*, whose guilty love for her stepson is examined with a sensitivity sometimes lacking in those critics (including Aristophanes) who use this example and the previous one to accuse Euripides of misogyny;[3] and Heracles, whose madness in the play of that name is the most developed examination of the mental disturbance which seems to have fascinated tragic writers and audiences (*Bacchae, Orestes*, Sophocles' *Ajax*).

On the question on misogyny, it seems to me that if there is a valid accusation to be made about the negative representation of women in Euripides, it stems not from the Melanippes and Phaedras and Sthenoboeas doing bad things, as Aristophanes would have it (for example, *Women at the Thesmophoria* 547, *Frogs* 1043). If we see these as signs of misogyny, we are simply caught in the misogynistic trap which moves implicitly from the particular to the general because it sees 'women' as a class. No-one calls Aeschylus a misandrist for presenting on stage a man who kills his mother, or one who sacrifices his daughter. More insidiously misogynist is the way that Phaedra is eclipsed from the play after her suicide note condemns Hippolytus: she isn't allowed to join in the general reconciliation among men with which the play ends. We might note also that the only way Euripides and the fifth-century audience can conceive of a strong woman, a woman who won't be insulted without revenge (as any heroic man would not), a woman who harms her enemies (and so, tragically, harms also her friends), is to make her a monster – but many of us would say that however wrong Medea's actions, she is still a powerful and, against the odds, a sympathetic character. Perhaps there is indeed a kind of endemic misogyny here, but not simply because Euripides portrays bad women.

At the same time as Euripides developed these 'realistic' elements in his drama, however, he was also involved in a kind of anti-realism, a self-conscious artistry which denies and perhaps even mocks the kind of 'realism' which, in traditional drama, implies a denial that the play is aware of itself as a play. A simple example of anti-realism is the appearance and escape of Medea at the end of her play, on a chariot sent by her grandfather the Sun. Almost certainly she will have used the machine on which gods customarily appeared in tragic plays. Beyond the spectacle (and that is great enough) she is thus metamorphosed into a demonic force: her tragedy is that she is still human, still a suffering mother.

More significant for the dramatic practice of Euripides and the future of drama is the anti-realism of dramatic form, through which the playwright points to the formal sign-system of his (and the audience's) activity. An example is Euripides' liking for a formal prologue, in the modern sense of a character addressing the audience and filling them in about what is happening and will happen (as opposed to the ancient Aristotelian sense of 'prologue' which is 'all the parts of a play up to the first entry of the chorus' – *Poetics* 1452b.19). With Euripides, the speaker of the prologue moves towards the boundaries of the dramatic illusion, standing part-way between play and not-play. This was to be a move with a long history.

The other end of his plays were still more self-conscious. Euripides quite frequently uses the device of a 'god from the machine' (usually referred to in Latin: *deus ex machina*), who enters the play at a moment of high tension and directs it with varying degrees of comfort to its end. In some cases the god fills out the remainder of the myth or sets the story back on its 'proper' mythic course; in some s/he tells a story of origins which ostensibly makes some better sense of the tragic mess lying between god and audience; sometimes s/he is needed actually to bring about the conclusion of the play. These scenes make for a powerful sense of ending, but they have been much criticised (for example, Aristotle *Poetics* 1454b). A more positive reading would see that they are part of the metatheatrical artfulness of Euripides. By 'metatheatrical', I mean 'theatre about theatre': passages which allude, explicitly or implicitly, to the fact that they are part of a play, and self-referentially reflect on the drama itself. The endings of many Euripidean plays are surreal, almost jokes about the need for tidy endings like the one being presented.[4]

Some endings are self-referential escapes, where the god helps out in an escape from the dramatic narrative as well as the dramatic situation, as in *Helen* or *Iphigenia among the Taurians* or the other 'escape' plays parodied in Aristophanes' *Women at the Thesmophoria*. Some are more sinister, as in *Orestes*, in which Apollo calls a sudden halt to the action when Orestes is about to kill Hermione, with the help of Pylades and a really nasty Electra (the poor girl has a bad press in Euripides – but so does Pylades), and insists that they get back to their proper mythic places. Instead of killing Hermione, Orestes must marry her (see *Andromache* 426 for a bleak version of this marriage); having failed in the Argive court, Orestes should go off to Athens to play through Aeschylus' *Eumenides*. The ironic point of this most negative play is that lawcourts, including the Areopagus, have *already been invented*, so the matricide takes place in a legal, not a pre-legal, society. But Apollo can sort it all out. Or can he? I suggest that this ending is a bleak parody of the need for this kind of ending and that, despite its overdetermined 'sense of ending', it really solves nothing.

In the play just discussed, the relationship with Aeschylus was crucial. This leads to another important element in Euripides' metatheatrical technique: intertextuality, the relationship with other plays. Many Euripidean plays are written with an eye to previous plays: no doubt more would be clearly so if more plays survived. Probably the best-known example is the scene where Electra, in her play, parodies and denies the recognition scene in Aeschylus' *Libation Bearers*. Intertextuality and surreal endings also inform another play from the Atreid cycle, *Iphigenia at Aulis*. This late play (it won posthumously in 405 BC) tells the story of the sacrifice of Iphigenia, with her father's wavering consent and despite Achilles' useless protection (she had been lured to Aulis on the pretext of a planned marriage to Achilles). At the end of the play, a miracle is reported: just as Iphigenia was about to be sacrificed ('willingly', 'heroically' – 1555, 1562), a young deer was substituted as victim at the last moment, the girl being whisked away from sight. The mythic variant must be older than the play, since the plot of the other Iphigenia play[5] depends on it, but the presentation is what the playwright makes of it. The powerful intertextuality with the *Oresteia* (we are meant to remember the 'unripe grape' at *Agamemnon* 970, which stands for Iphigenia, whose crushing led to Clytemnestra's determination to kill Agamemnon) and the disbelief of Clytemnestra, in many ways the most powerful voice in the *Iphigenia at Aulis*, at the story of the substitution, both call into question the stability of the 'happy ending'. Moreover, the good wishes of the chorus for Agamemnon's well-omened voyage to Troy and return to Greece are undermined not only by the story we know (of Agamemnon's pollution both by the death of Iphigenia and by the destruction of Troy) but also by the total absence in this chorus of anything resembling rational thought. They are simply bowled over by the war machine.

In Agamemnon's conflict over whether or not to sacrifice Iphigenia, Euripides is closer than he often is to an uncomplicated tragic *aporia* ('no way out' – although perhaps the true tragedy might be *making you think* that he could be in a state of truly tragic *aporia*). Other plays present a tragedy of pathos and of victims, such as the extremely doleful *Women of Troy* and *Hecabe*. These plays offer a tragedy of victims – and this might be what Aristotle meant by calling Euripides the 'most tragic poet' (*Poetics* 1453a.29–30) – but in some cases the victim turns horribly, as Hecabe does in her play: she takes vengeance on the barbarian king who had killed her youngest son, by blinding him and killing his children.[6] Although it would be simplistic to call Euripides a pacifist, some of his plays are eloquent testimonies to the degrading and dehumanising effect of suffering, and of war in particular, and perhaps the current Peloponnesian war most of all. In the killing of Hector's young son Astyanax, thrown from the battlements of Troy so that he couldn't grow up and avenge his father and city, it would be possible to see a reflection of the suffering imposed by the Athenian state on the people of Melos in 415 BC.

Euripides may have been 'the most tragic of poets', but he was also most responsible, it would seem, for the metamorphosis of the genre, through his challenging developments which stretch the boundaries of generic expectations. The change and reduction in the role of the chorus as an integral part of the dramatic form cannot be attributed to Euripides alone, but the evidence we have would suggest that he played a large part in it. We might look at the chorus of the *Orestes*, told to shut up and go away when they try to engage Electra in mutual wailing in their parodos; or that of *Iphigenia at Aulis*, who don't understand what is going on (although it should be noted that the *Bacchae*, with its highly integrated chorus, was produced at the same time); or that of the *Women of Troy*, whose songs seem to relate very little to the action. A good way to see the development of the chorus is to compare Aeschylus' *Suppliants* with Euripides' play of that name. The stories of the two plays are completely different (Aeschylus' play is about the Danaids, who wanted to avoid marrying their cousins, the sons of Aegyptus; Euripides' play is about how the mothers of heroes who died fighting on Polynices' behalf at Thebes attempted to persuade the Athenians to retrieve their bodies), but the point I want to make here is about the way the chorus functions. In Aeschylus' play, the suppliant women (the Danaids) who form the chorus are a character in their own right; in Euripides' play, the chorus of mothers is quite subservient to their advocate, the disgraced King Adrastus, while another (again individualised) focus of interest is the self-sacrificing Evadne, who leaps onto her husband's pyre. The chorus just wail.

Still more significant for the future of drama are those Euripidean elements out of which new comedy was to grow, for the rather serious comic drama of the fourth and third centuries appears to owe more to late (and not so late) Euripides than it does to Old Comedy. There are babies abandoned with tokens, ready to be discovered at the right moment, disasters narrowly averted, slaves with a role to play, scenes of everyday life. Important plays in this regard are *Iphigenia among the Taurians, Ion, Helen* and *Alcestis*. They are sometimes called 'tragicomedies', but I think it is most appropriate to think of them as tragedies which are pushing back the boundaries of the genre. Nor are they so straightforwardly light as seems to be suggested. The *Helen*, for example, is a play light in tone: the real Helen never went to Troy but spent the whole time safe and chaste (but presumably deadly bored) in Egypt; there Menelaus, shipwrecked on his way home with the phantom which had replaced her, meets her, is forced to realise the truth and escapes with her. But behind the lightness, together with the comic aspects (like the unheroic Menelaus) and the 'happy ending', the play might be seen to express a bleak nihilism: all that destruction at Troy wasn't just for a woman, but the phantom of a woman; the cause of the war, dubious at best, turns out to be completely false. There is a frequent undercurrent in tragedy which would see humanity at the mercy of deathless, so playful, gods. This play, in that sense, is well and truly tragic.

Tragic also, and for all its oddity not a play which suggests that Euripides had pushed the genre into oblivion, is his late masterpiece: the posthumously produced *Bacchae*. This play tells the story of the refusal of Pentheus, King of Thebes, to recognise the divinity of the new god Dionysus, the son of Pentheus' aunt Semele and of Zeus. The Theban women, who also reject the god, are sent mad and are forced to become Bacchants, leaving the city for the wilds of the mountain. Pentheus is enticed by Dionysus, in disguise, into being dressed as a woman and hidden at the top of a pine tree, in order to witness, so he supposes, the illicit practices (particularly sexual) of the Bacchant women. But Pentheus is recognised and is torn to pieces by his own mother, who thinks she has killed a young lion. Thus is Dionysus' godhead affirmed. The play takes on the polarity which was a way of thought for the Greeks: the state and the individual, the city and the wilderness, adult and child, man and woman, creative fertility and destruction, and so on, polarities which inform also the Dionysiac festivals themselves, at which the plays were performed. Although the *Bacchae* is in some ways more formally conventional than other Euripidean plays, for example in the use of the chorus and in the maintenance of a tragic tone, it is perhaps the most metatheatrical of Euripides' plays, a final expression of his view of drama as Dionysiac poetics.

Notes

1 I am using the terminology of 'sophistry' here in something like its modern conventional manner. For a study of Euripides' relationship with the professional teachers of higher education in his day (related but not identical to the modern usage), see D.J. Conacher, *Euripides and the Sophists*, London: Duckworth, 1998.

2 After the three tragedies which made up the bulk of a day's viewing at the City Dionysia, the audience were rewarded with a light play with a chorus of satyrs.

3 Euripides wrote two *Hippolytus* plays, only one of which survives.

Critics have assumed that in the lost play Phaedra was represented in a much more negative light, but the point remains that the supposedly misogynistic Euripides produced some exceptionally sensitive representations of women.

4 On Euripidean endings, see F.M. Dunn, *Tragedy's End: Closure and Innovation in Euripidean Drama*, Oxford: Oxford University Press, 1996.

5 *Iphigenia among the Taurians*, a play of about 413 BC, in which the rescued Iphigenia becomes herself a priestess of human sacrifice and nearly kills her brother Orestes, until a recognition occurs, followed by an escape.

6 See J. Mossman, *Wild Justice: A Study in Euripides' Hecuba*, Oxford: Oxford University Press, 1995.

See also in this book

Aeschylus, Aristophanes, Ovid, Seneca the Younger, Sophocles

Texts, translations and commentaries

The plays are available in two OCT volumes. There are also Teubner versions of individual plays.

The Loeb editions are currently being revised, in a projected set of six volumes, four of which (by D. Kovacs) have appeared to date.

There are Penguin editions of all the plays, and some in World's Classics (seven plays, plus the *Rhesus* which is probably not by Euripides).

Editions with commentary in the Cambridge Greek and Latin Classics Series are in preparation for *Alcestis, Ion* and *Medea*.

Further reading

Burnett, A.P., *Catastrophe Survived: Euripides' Plays of Mixed Reversal*, Oxford: Oxford University Press, 1971.

Foley, H.P., *Ritual Irony: Poetry and Sacrifice in Euripides*, Ithaca, NY, and London: Cornell University Press, 1985.

Powell, A. (ed.), *Euripides, Women and Sexuality*, London: Routledge, 1990.

Rabinowitz, N.S., *Anxiety Veiled: Euripides and the Traffic in Women*, Ithaca, NY, and London: Cornell University Press, 1993.

Segal, C.P., *Dionysiac Poetics and Euripides' Bacchae*, Princeton, NJ: Princeton University Press, 1982.

Segal, C.P., *Euripides and the Poetics of Sorrow: Art, Gender and Commemoration in Alcestis, Hippolytus and Hecuba*, Durham, NC, and London: Duke University Press, 1993.

Vellacott, P., *Ironic Drama: A Study of Euripides' Method and Meaning*, Cambridge: Cambridge University Press, 1975.

Zeitlin, F., *Playing the Other: Gender and Society in Classical Greek Literature*, Chicago, IL: University of Chicago Press, 1995.

THUCYDIDES

When Thucydides in 431 BC started gathering material and writing about the war which had just broken out between the great sea-power Athens on the one side and the powerful land-based combination of Sparta and her allies on the other side, he was either very lucky or else (as he implies at 1.1.1 of *History of the Peloponnesian War*) had superb instincts. For it was this war which would eventually break the back of Athenian imperial power when it ended in 404 BC, and which would provide the material for Thucydides' extraordinarily influential (but incomplete) narrative.

However, all that was in the future in 431 BC. Thucydides himself was an Athenian, born perhaps around 460 BC, the son of a man called Olorus, whose father may have had links with a prosperous family from Thrace. This was one of the reasons why Thucydides, who owned property and had the right to work the goldmines there (4.105), shows a general interest in the area in his account of the war. Yet there was also a more unhappy personal association with Thrace. In 424/423 BC, Thucydides, having been elected as one of the ten generals for the year, was duly sent off to Thrace with a small fleet to help Amphipolis. This was an important city, founded by Athens in 437 BC, which provided her with a rich source of timber, so crucial for a naval power. Nevertheless, when the Spartan general Brasidas attacked the city, Thucydides wasn't able to save it and was exiled as a result, although he doesn't mention this until later in the narrative (5.26). His banishment from Athens lasted for twenty years and he died not long after the end of the Peloponnesian War in 404 BC.

In these circumstances, his account of the fall of Amphipolis is remarkably restrained (4.102–8). He is even able to understand why her citizens responded so favourably to Brasidas' offer of moderate terms and why the other cities in the area went over to Sparta, driven by

> the pleasurable excitement of the moment, and the fact that it looked for the first time as though they were going to find the Spartans acting with real energy.
>
> (*Peloponnesian War* 4.108)[1]

One might have expected to find some personal animosity being vented against Brasidas, the Spartan general whose actions led to Thucydides' exile, but, if anything, he is presented as a talented general, whose qualities as a leader pull against the stereotypical Spartan traits. We are shown his ingenuity in beginning his attempt on the city on a stormy winter's night, his exploitation of local tensions between Amphipolis and Argilus, and his speedy crossing of the bridge which allowed him to dominate the area immediately around the city's walls (4.103). Of course, the more cunning and impressive Brasidas appears in the narrative, the less culpable is Thucydides' response, and this hasn't been lost on modern commentators.

Rather than being cast down by his sentence of exile, Thucydides subsequently presents it as a unique opportunity to examine the war from both sides:

> It happened too that I was banished from my country for twenty years after my command at Amphipolis; I saw what was being done on both sides, particularly on the Peloponnesian side, because of my exile, and this leisure gave me rather exceptional facilities for looking into things.

> (*Peloponnesian War* 5.26)

It is hard to believe that he was really so sanguine about his personal fate, but here we need to separate his emotional life from his identity as an author. What he is attempting to do here is to enhance his authority as a historian and to address concerns about bias which may have existed among contemporary readers who knew something about his life. He achieves this both by choosing not to raise these issues until well after his account of events at Amphipolis and by the implication that the emotional blow of the initial banishment (which in any case he doesn't dwell on) was superseded by the intellectual advantages of being able to examine the war from both sides: when we are officially told about the exile, it is already twenty years (or more) in the past.

Thucydides' creation of a dispassionate, objective and rational authorial persona was a deliberate strategy, which had a lasting impact on the positive reception of his authoritative historical narrative. The way in which he presents his own exile is a particularly good example of his skill at winning the trust of his audience. So too is his understated reaction to having suffered from the plague, whose horrific symptoms he describes in impressive detail (2.49–50).[2] As he says, 'I myself caught the disease and myself saw others suffering from it' (2.48), which adds credibility to his account. Hornblower says that this is 'a rare autobiographical statement, followed by an emphatic (note the repeated "myself") claim to autopsy'.[3] This personal assertion is therefore an exception which proves a rule. Something which generally contributes to his detached persona is his tendency (especially in comparison with Herodotus) to avoid the first-person singular as a narrative mode, which creates the impression of a certain emotional aloofness.

It might be helpful at this point to summarise the narrative, which documents in eight books events from the start of the war until the autumn of 411 BC. Book one presents the background of the war, including disputes over Epidamnus (435–433 BC), Corcyra (433 BC) and Potidaea (432 BC), which led to the disintegration of the Thirty Years' Truce between the Athenians and the Peloponnesians.

Particularly distinctive is the opening section known as the *Arkhaiologia* (1.1–23),[4] where Thucydides outlines his attitude to important areas of historiography, such as speeches, whose precise words, he reasonably claims, are difficult to remember. Therefore he explains that

> my method has been, while keeping as close as possible to the general sense of the words that were actually used, to make the speakers say what, in my opinion, was called for by each situation.

> (*Peloponnesian War* 1.22)

For a modern historian, this policy is problematic in that it is precisely when speakers failed to say what was appropriate in a particular situation that a historical narrative potentially becomes most interesting. There is also the thorny issue of whether Thucydides is tampering with the truth. Still, Thucydides is at least grappling with a question which doesn't seem to have worried his predecessor Herodotus, and we must also acknowledge that there are crucial differences between ancient and modern historiography. None of Thucydides' audience would really have expected him to supply versions of speeches which accurately reflected what was said on a particular occasion.

Book 1 also contains a fairly long digression (1.89–118), known as the *Pentecontaetia*, which examines events between 479 and 435 BC (a period of almost fifty years – hence the name) in order to establish why Athens was so strong at the start of the war. This section serves as a bridge between the Persian and the Peloponnesian wars, or, to put it another way, between the works of Herodotus and Thucydides. At the same time, it is unusual because Thucydides generally prefers to avoid digressions of the sort which characterise Herodotus' narrative. Digressions can often be charming, but they are also messy and don't really cohere with the sort of rational narrative persona which Thucydides was trying to create.

Book 2 moves from the outbreak of war in 431 to 428 BC and contains some of Thucydides' best-known passages, most notably Pericles' funeral speech and the description of the plague in Athens. Book 3 also covers a three-year period from 428 to 425 BC and incorporates the revolt of Mytilene from Athens, the fall of Plataea to the Spartans, civil war in Corcyra and the first Athenian expedition to Sicily. Book 4 narrates the Athenian capture of Pylos in the south (425 BC) and Spartan successes in the north, particularly at Amphipolis (424/423 BC). At the start of Book 5, we hear about the deaths of the Athenian general Cleon and the Spartan general Brasidas, followed by the conclusion of the (ineffectual) Peace of Nicias in 422–421 BC, which marks the end of the first ten-year phase of the war (known as the Archidamian War).

After a second introduction (5.26), the rest of Book 5 (which shows distinct signs of being work-in-progress rather than a completed section) narrates events as far as 415 BC, including the Athenian capture of Melos in 416 BC and the famous Melian dialogue. In Books 6 and 7, Thucydides shifts the focus of his account to the disastrous Athenian expedition to Sicily between 415 and 413 BC, while in Book 8 (again showing signs of incompleteness), he returns to the Aegean and presents an account of the oligarchic coup in Athens, which led to the creation of the government of the Five Thousand in 411 BC.

The narrative unfortunately breaks off in mid-sentence before Thucydides has reached the end of the war. He probably died before he had a chance to carry out his final revisions, leaving some sections, notably 5.26–116 and Book 8, without speeches, and other sections with 'doublets', one of which he might have eventually removed (for example, 1.20 and 6.54–9). Certainly, Cratippus of Athens, Xenophon and Theopompus of Chios all decided to begin their own histories from 411 BC, just where Thucydides' account stopped; in this case, the continuation is more than simply a gesture of respect towards a brilliant predecessor in the genre, as it often is elsewhere in Greek and Roman historiography. Thucydides' *History of the Peloponnesian War* really was incomplete and (in that sense) needed someone to continue it.

So how is it that Thucydides gained such a reputation as one of the most distinguished historians of the ancient world when his work isn't even finished? Despite his rational approach to the war, some scholars see his achievement in terms of the emotional, calling him a 'prose tragedian'. One of the most disturbing aspects of his account is that the Athenian defeat seems to have been triggered by internal faults rather than by external successes. Thucydides makes Pericles signal this danger in a speech:

> I could give you many other reasons why you should feel confident in ultimate victory, if only you will make up your minds not to add to the empire while the war is in progress, and not to go out of your way to involve yourselves in new perils. What I fear is not the enemy's strategy, but our own mistakes.
>
> (*Peloponnesian War* 1.144.1)[5]

Pericles doesn't live long enough to enforce his views, but his words of warning are eventually vindicated by the failure of the Sicilian expedition. To make matters worse, Thucydides makes the decent but weak politician Nicias deliver a speech advising the Athenians not to embark on such a reckless venture: 'Our country is now on the verge of the greatest danger she has ever known' (6.13). Of course, he would subsequently play his own part in the unfolding disaster, but here his speech heightens the impending tragic downfall of the belligerent Athenians, who refuse to listen to sensible advice.

Our sense of tragic historical patterning is further enhanced by Thucydides' conviction that the very same features of the system which made Athens so strong at the start of the war may ultimately have caused her downfall. In the first place, Athens was a naval power, which gave her a distinct advantage over the land-based Peloponnesians. Yet by sending her navy to Sicily with the war on the mainland still unresolved, Athens left herself vulnerable. So long as Athens was conducting the war defensively rather than offensively, as Pericles had recommended, then all was well. However, overconfidence and bad luck led to disaster. Thucydides says that the scale of the defeat in Sicily in 413 BC was terrible:

> their sufferings were on an enormous scale; their losses were, as they say, total; army, navy, everything was destroyed, and out of many, only a few returned.
>
> (*Peloponnesian War* 7.87)

In fact, as Thucydides himself remarked (2.65), the Athenians held out for another eight years. If he had lived to complete his history, he might have modified his presentation, but in the overarching tragic structure of the narrative as it stands, the destruction of the fleet in the harbour at Syracuse signals the beginning of the end. As Rood suggests,

> the Athenian defeat in Sicily foreshadows the defeat of Athens as a whole – rather as, in the *Iliad*, the death of Hektor is proleptic of the fall of Troy.[6]

In the second place, although the democratic system could produce good politicians such as Pericles, it could also create leaders such as Alcibiades, whom Thucydides sees as being prepared to put desire for personal gain above the needs of the state. If the dynamic Alcibiades hadn't intervened, then the Sicilian expedition might never have happened and the war might have had a very different outcome. Even so, in an analysis from earlier on in the narrative which may have been written at a relatively late stage, Thucydides suggests that the expedition needn't have been so self-destructive. He argues that the initial decision to sail to Sicily, misguided though it was, was compounded by the subsequent lack of support from Athens:

> Because they [the demagogues] were so busy with their own personal intrigues for securing the leadership of the people, they allowed the expedition to lose its impetus, and by quarrelling among themselves began to bring confusion into the policy of the state.
>
> (*Peloponnesian War* 2.65)

In Athens' twilight years, Thucydides implies that Pericles' policies were sensible and that the politicians who came to prominence in the city afterwards were second-rate.

There are other reasons why Thucydides' account has achieved such a positive critical reception. Some episodes continue to strike a chord today because the issues which they address transcend the immediate historical circumstances which produced them. A case in point is the Melian dialogue of Book 5 (5.84–116). Although the Aegean island of Melos hadn't succumbed to Athens when Nicias invaded in 426 BC (3.91), she faced another attack in 416 BC when the

Athenians, keen to force her to join their empire, sent thirty ships to apply pressure. Melos, originally a Spartan colony, wanted to remain neutral, but this was not to be.

Thucydides presents the discussion between the Athenian representatives and the Melian council in the form of a dramatic dialogue. The discussion raises some very basic concerns about the impact that warfare has on collective morality and presents a provocative clash between might and right. The Athenians argue that it is expedient for the Melians to submit and that all arguments against that outcome are pointless. At a very early stage of the discussion, they make the unattractive point that 'the strong do what they have the power to do and the weak accept what they have to accept' (5.89). The Melians, faced with this relentless imperialist juggernaut, try to redirect the debate to questions of justice, but the Athenians, insisting that they abandon their forlorn hope, warn them not to turn to 'prophecies and oracles and such things which by encouraging hope lead men to ruin' (5.103). Even when the Melians articulate their confidence that Sparta will rescue them, the Athenians accuse them of folly.

In the event, the aggressive Athenians are proved right. For when the Melians insist on maintaining their liberty, the Athenians initiate a blockade, which the Spartans do nothing to prevent; when the Melians are eventually forced to surrender unconditionally, the Athenians put to death all the men of military age and sell all of the women and children into slavery (5.116). In the Melian dialogue, we are presented with the brutal reality of an imperial power deciding what they want and imposing this decision on a weaker group. The Athenians don't even bother to justify their actions, but present submission as the only option for the Melians, who will only have themselves to blame for the consequences if they insist on holding out. The issues which are raised in the Melian dialogue continue to be relevant today, so the episode strikes a powerful chord among modern readers. On a broader scale too, Thucydides' *History of the Peloponnesian War* has had an impact on modern politicians. In 1947 the US secretary of state George Marshall, drawing an analogy between the Peloponnesian War and the Cold War, commented:

> I doubt seriously whether a man can think with full wisdom and with deep convictions regarding certain of the basic issues today who has not at least reviewed in his mind the period of the Peloponnesian War and the fall of Athens.[7]

Even though scholars have certainly questioned the absolute authority of Thucydides' voice as narrator of the war, they still appreciate the basic rigour of his historical techniques, particularly in comparison with his successors in the genre. Cawkwell has commented on how zealously Thucydides carried out research for his narrative, calling him a 'monster in his enquiries' and noting how commendable it is that he managed to dig so much information up about the secretive Sparta.[8] Moreover, the basic framework of his account, with its helpful self-contained system of dating events on a year-by-year basis from the beginning of the war, allows readers to negotiate their way around the war with relative ease. It can be contrasted with the subsequent practice of, for example, Xenophon, who in the *Hellenica* starts off well in his provision of chronology, but then runs out of steam and abandons all pretence of a dating system.

In addition, Thucydides is reluctant to place too much weight on the gods or on fate as an explanatory device, but looks instead for more pragmatic reasons in interpreting events. The religious sphere certainly features in the narrative, but more often than not Thucydides is interested in the impact of religious belief on human behaviour. There are two important examples to be considered.

First, when the Athenians discover that one night the Herms (sculptures of the god Hermes endowed with phalluses and considered to have protective powers) have been mutilated by a person or persons unknown, they offer large rewards to find the culprits, since the incident was regarded as a bad omen for the Sicilian expedition (6.27). Thucydides is careful to focalise this point of view through the Athenians rather than to claim it as his own, and he seems to be interested in the incident, not so much as a bad omen in itself (although it adds to the atmosphere of foreboding), but as something which reveals the self-destructive forces at work within Athens: we are shown how the enemies of Alcibiades exaggerate the whole affair in order to make personal attacks on him (6.28), which will eventually culminate in his disastrous removal from the Sicilian expedition to face charges in Athens (6.52). The mutilation of the Herms may have been an act of impiety, but Thucydides pursues the causal chain on a human level, making it clear that unscrupulous individuals have exploited it for their own short-term advantage to remove Alcibiades.[9]

Second, there is the disastrous impact of superstition on Nicias' leadership during the campaign in Sicily, just when the Athenian forces urgently need to withdraw from Syracuse. After an eclipse of the moon, the general refuses to move his troops for twenty-seven days, a strategy recommended by the soothsayers. Thucydides openly criticises Nicias for being 'rather overinclined to divination and such things' (7.50). Through this delay, the Athenians find themselves in a vulnerable position and are defeated in a sea-battle (7.52), which leaves them utterly disheartened (7.55). We have to face the possibility that if Nicias hadn't been so superstitious and refused to move his troops, then the Athenians might not have faced defeat at Syracuse. The delay wasn't the only reason for the disaster and Thucydides still feels able to say positive things about Nicias in his obituary (7.86), but it certainly didn't help.

Again, Thucydides documents the religious sphere, but is most fascinated by the impact that belief has on human behaviour. We can contrast this with Xenophon, who conspicuously resorts to the divine and religious spheres to explain historical events when he suggests that the Spartans were punished for seizing the citadel of Thebes in 382 BC by their defeat at the Battle of Leuctra in 371 BC (*Hellenica* 5.4.1). As Cawkwell has observed, 'The hand of god is an explanation that dulls the quest for truth'.[10] Thucydides, who is one of the great rationalists of the ancient world, doesn't fall into this trap. He tends to apply logic to the world around him, as when expressing his belief that a series of damaging tidal waves are caused by earthquakes (3.89): the gods are conspicuous by their absence at such moments.

It wouldn't be right to leave Thucydides without emphasising the distinctive and sometimes difficult Greek in which he wrote. Thucydides' mode of expression was very different from the style of his predecessor Herodotus and arguably had a more lasting impact. Dionysius of Halicarnassus, a historian and literary critic who lived in the first century BC, wrote a short piece about Thucydides and commented on his style, particularly his 'poetical vocabulary, great variety of figures, harshness of word-order, and swiftness in saying what he has to say' (*Thucydides* 24). Thucydides' distinctive style had a pervasive impact on the Latin historian Sallust, who favoured deliberate imbalance, archaisms and 'truncated epigrams, words coming before you expect them, obscure brevity' (Seneca *Moral Epistle* 114.17). Style isn't just a matter of taste, but allows writers to suggest an intellectual affinity with a particular historical approach. So the orator Quintilian suggests a connection between the style of Herodotus and Livy on the one hand, and between Thucydides and Sallust on the other (*Training in Oratory* 10.1.101). There is no doubt that Thucydides' Greek is difficult, but it is one of the reasons why he is such a fascinating author. As Rusten has observed, 'Thucydides alone created a personal style to match his subject'.[11]

Notes

1 Translations are by R. Warner, *Thucydides: The Peloponnesian War*, Harmondsworth: Penguin, 1972.
2 See S. Hornblower, *A Commentary on Thucydides Volume I: Books I–III*, Oxford: Oxford University Press, 1991, pp. 316–27, on the plague.
3 Hornblower, *op. cit.*, p. 321.
4 See J.R. Ellis, 'The structure and function of Thucydides' *Archaeology*', *Classical Antiquity*, 10, 1991, pp. 344–75.
5 Cf. Augustus' advice to his successor Tiberius not to extend the empire any further (Tacitus *Annals* 1.11.4).
6 T. Rood, *Thucydides: Narrative and Explanation*, Oxford: Oxford University Press, 1998, p. 197.
7 A. Kemos, 'The Influence of Thucydides in the Modern World', online at http://www.hri.org/por/thucydides.html.
8 G. Cawkwell, *Thucydides and the Peloponnesian War*, London: Routledge, 1997, p. 8.
9 On Thucydides and Alcibiades, see D. Gribble, *Alcibiades and Athens*, Oxford: Oxford University Press, 1999, pp. 159–213.
10 See Cawkwell, *Xenophon: A History of My Times*, Harmondsworth: Penguin, 1979, p. 45.
11 J. Rusten, *Thucydides: The Peloponnesian War Book II*, Greek and Latin Classics Series, Cambridge: Cambridge University Press, 1989, p. 21.

See also in this book

Herodotus, Lucian, Polybius, Sallust, Tacitus, Xenophon

Texts, translations and commentaries

The Greek text is available in OCT, Teubner and Loeb.
As well as the Loeb, there is a Penguin translation by R. Warner (1972).
There are commentaries on *Peloponnesian War* 2 by J. Rusten in the Cambridge Greek and Latin Classics Series; on *Peloponnesian War* 2, 3 and 4.1–5.24 by P.J. Rhodes and on 4.2–41 by J. Wilson in the Aris and Phillips Series; and on the whole *Peloponnesian War* by S. Hornblower for Oxford University Press (with volume 3 forthcoming).

Further reading

Badian, E., *From Plataea to Potidaea: Studies in the History and Historiography of the Pentecontaetia*, Baltimore, MD, and London: Johns Hopkins University Press, 1993.
Cawkwell, G., *Thucydides and the Peloponnesian War*, London: Routledge, 1997.

De Ste Croix, G.E.M., *The Origins of the Peloponnesian War*, London: Duckworth, 1972.

Dover, K.J., *Thucydides*, Greece and Rome New Surveys in the Classics 7, Oxford: Oxford University Press, 1973.

Hornblower, S., *Thucydides*, London: Duckworth, 1987.

MacLeod, C., *Collected Essays*, Oxford: Oxford University Press, 1983.

Rawlings, H.R., III, *The Structure of Thucydides' History*, Princeton, NJ: Princeton University Press, 1981.

Rood, T., *Thucydides: Narrative and Explanation*, Oxford: Oxford University Press, 1998.

Stadter, P.A. (ed.), *The Speeches in Thucydides*, Chapel Hill, NC: University of North Carolina Press, 1973.

ARISTOPHANES

No holds were barred in Aristophanes' magnificently outrageous and outspoken flights of fantasy, and once he had got his teeth into a victim or an idea, he wasn't going to let it go, but would make it pop up again repeatedly like a jack-in-the-box, thus getting a laugh out of the laugh itself, and then out of doing it again. One of Aristophanes' favourite victims was his fellow demesman, the populist politician Cleon, whom he described as having 'a voice like a scalded sow' (*Wasps* 36) and a 'camel's rump and monstrous unwashed balls' (*Wasps* 1035, *Peace* 758). And that's just for starters.

Aristophanes was born some time around 450 BC, into a wealthy Athenian family, who may also have lived or had property in Aegina (*Acharnians* 652, but the evidence is slight). He began writing plays for the Athenian dramatic festivals at a very early age. He was perhaps as young as 17 when he wrote *The Banqueters*, which, like his other early plays and some of the later ones, was produced by a man called Callistratus. He lived through turbulent times, surviving not only the years of especially intense war with Sparta (the Peloponnesian War) and the plague exacerbated by overcrowding in the besieged city, but also the internal political turmoil of the later years of the fifth century, and went on producing plays well into the fourth, with his last extant play (*Wealth*) being produced in 388. Between *Wealth* and Aristophanes' death, at least two more (lost) plays were written and were produced, in conjunction with his son Araros. Aristophanes wrote probably about forty plays, of which eleven are extant.[1] He died in around 385.[2]

Aristophanes tells us in no uncertain terms that he was the best of the writers of Old Comedy. But before we go on to talk about Old Comedy and Aristophanes as if they were the same thing, we might note that the genre didn't in fact spring fully formed from the genius-mind of Aristophanes, but developed through interaction (both comically figured as rivalry and really so) between many exponents, among whom the names of Cratinus and Eupolis are to be mentioned. Moreover, it was (like all literature) parasitic on other literary and cultural forms of expression, such as dithyramb (song in honour of the god Dionysus), invective, epic, but most of all comedy's respectable big sister: tragedy.

Like tragedy, comedy was performed at the major Athenian festivals of Dionysus: at the Great (or City) Dionysia from at least 486 BC and at the Lenaea from before 440. In structure, there seems to have been a fairly strict framework on which a comedy was hung, although, like most things comic, it is there as much for the breaking as for the making. This framework is built around the movements of the chorus. Three important moments mark out the play: the parodos, when the chorus enter; the parabasis, when they walk forward to speak directly to the audience; and the exodos, when they leave (usually in triumph and celebration, this being comedy). The other crucial beam of the play's framework is the agon, or contest. The agon is generally both the 'big plot' of the play and also actually an antagonistic confrontation, often between the chorus and one of the protagonists.[3] As such, it is a good reflection of the agonistic nature of Athenian society.

Also like tragedy, albeit differently, Aristophanic comedy was thoroughly grounded in the Athenian state and intimately involved in its characters (like Cleon – politics; Socrates – philosophy; and Euripides – tragedy), its characteristics and its civic concerns. Comedy can often be seen as the equal and opposite of tragedy: tragedy turned upside down and inside out. But in comedy you *can* turn the world upside down, for comedy is about getting away with hubris. We can see this especially in the form of the typical Aristophanic hero (again, the deviations are many): it is easy to think of him as characteristically a little man with a big idea (often a selfish one), who transgresses the bounds of normal behaviour and *gets away with it*. Normally he is suggestively associated with the solid backbone of Athenian society, conservative, neither rich nor poor, and not very tolerant of anyone different from himself. But one of the laws of this kind of comedy is that everyone and everything gets sent up – even the play itself.

Comedy is a remarkably difficult genre to talk about critically, and the more 'broad-brush' the comedy, the more tricksy the work of the critic, because this literature is posing as being vernacular. Moreover, comedy tends to encourage generalisations – so here are a few. It seems to me that Aristophanic comedy encompasses elements of two very common strands in the history of comedy: irreverent subversion and comforting reinforcement of the status quo. The example of the political satirist is a useful illustration of this duality: the political satirist (like other humorists) is duty bound to attack those in power, but this very fact has the tendency to consolidate their power. The essence of comedy is the carnival, in which traditional power structures are overturned for a licensed time, and yet this very comic licence to insult and debunk is itself inclined towards the reinforcement of the structures it pricks. This isn't to say that resistance is useless, that comedy cannot ever be 'really political' or 'really critical', but rather to suggest, for example, that the fact that we can say 'hey, it's a joke' makes it all potentially comfortable. It will be helpful to keep this contradictory nexus of forces in mind if we are to make any sense of Aristophanic humour – or his politics, or anything else.

But even before that, we need to be careful about trying too hard to 'make sense'. An eternal feature of broad-brush humour in the Aristophanic mode is its magnificent disregard for the ordinary rules of logic or even plausibility. Comic plots/plays/characters are likely to have a good laugh at us critics trying to 'make sense' of them. That said, here is a bit of a schema of Aristophanic humour.

Like many comedians after him, a great deal of Aristophanes' humour is reductive; that is, it attacks people, institutions and ideas, with jokes and jibes that are racist, sexist, ageist and classist in several directions. This is in part a matter of creating an in-group sense of solidarity, by contrast with Others, but the psychological dynamics of humour are even more complex than that. After all, in Aristophanes the worm often turns.

A crucial special case of reductive humour is topical reference, and here Aristophanes is a master and we are sadly disabled. For really powerful topical humour, the Attic norm of single performance at a particular moment in time and place is the ideal medium, palely imitated by modern television.[4] But since Athenian drama is itself a civic institution of democratic Athens, it is hardly surprising that in political satire Aristophanes is in his element, however hard it may be to work out exactly what he means by it. Arguments rage among the critics: Cartledge sees Aristophanes as an arch-conservative pandering to democratic tastes only in order to win, but really offering (or at least hinting at) an oligarchic, pro-Spartan message; Heath reads the whole thing as a big joke which isn't political at all; Goldhill destabilises the opposition between 'serious politics' and 'apolitical fun', and argues that what is to be taken from

Aristophanes (how serious? how political? how dangerous or harmless?) was (and still is) a question which was replayed and debated by every audience member's engagement with the play.[5]

Easier for us (or at least easier to think it is easier) is the intertextual parody (also a 'topical reference') that pervades so much of Aristophanes' drama, which is littered with quotations, misquotations and deformations of contemporary and earlier literature, especially tragedy. Two plays are entirely structured around intertextual parody: in *Thesmophoriazusae* ('Women at the Thesmophoria'; called *The Poet and the Women* in the Penguin translation), the women of Athens are using the cover of their all-female festival to plot revenge on Euripides for his misogynistic (but, it seems, not 'untrue') representations of them. Euripides gets an old relative of his to dress up as a woman in order to infiltrate the festival and speak in his favour, but the virile old guy is discovered and is eventually rescued by Euripides himself (also dressed up as a woman), after a series of attempts which mimic different Euripidean 'escape' plays. In *Frogs*, Dionysus, god of drama, sits as judge of a contest between the dead Euripides and Aeschylus as to which of them should be brought back to life in order to 'save the city'. Both plays are thick with tragic parody and generic games, for Aristophanes was one of the sharpest literary critics of antiquity – and managed to make it funny.

Then there is the extraordinary verbal humour: the puns, wordplay, neologisms (made-up words). One play, *Birds*, is entirely constructed on the basis of puns, from the moment when two Athenians attempt to 'go to the crows' (Greek equivalent of 'go to hell' or 'get lost') but cannot find the way (27–9). They are actually joining the birds and, when they find them, they create a city (*polis*) in the sky (*polos*) with their feathered friends ἐκ τοῦ πόλου τούτου, κεκλήσεται πόλις, *Birds* 184; nicely translated by D. Barrett in the Penguin volume as 'turn this vast immensity into a vast, immense city'). Along with this verbal humour comes something which is almost entirely opaque to us, but which would have been crucial in original performance – visual humour. The old men somehow dressed up as or suggesting wasps (in *Wasps*); Trygaeus up on the tragic crane (and not very comfortable about it) in *Peace*; later in the same play, everyone (the audience symbolically included) helping to pull out the statue of Peace from the cave in which she had been hidden; and much more that we can only imagine.

Translating these things into modern performance is fraught with difficulty, but I once saw a production of *Lysistrata* that seemed to me suitably Aristophanic in its visual humour. This is the play in which the women of Greece go on a sex-strike in order to persuade their men to stop the Peloponnesian War. In one scene (904ff.), a young wife is following her instructions to the letter, seducing her husband, raising his hopes, but constantly dashing them again by 'going to fetch a pillow', then a mattress, a blanket, perfume, and so on. In ancient performance, at least some of the characters wore costumes depicting erect padded phalluses. In the London production I saw, the phallus was raised and lowered in time with the inflation and deflation of the character's hopes. I don't imagine that exactly this could or would have been done on the Athenian stage, but as visual humour it was a pretty good historical translation. And Aristophanic humour is very, very obscene. This has something to do with the involvement of comedy in the positive aspects of Dionysus – fertility and peace as an active celebration of life; something to do with the carnivalesque atmosphere of sticking two fingers up at authority; and a whole lot to do with making people laugh. The interrelations of fertility, obscenity and abusive invective all come together under the patronage of Dionysus, and are channelled into comedy from its forerunner in naming and shaming with a laugh: iambic poetry (see ARCHILOCHUS).

That schema only scratches the surface of Aristophanic humour. What I want to do for the rest of this essay is to look briefly at four ways in which comedy is the equal and opposite of tragedy – fantasy/ realism, hubris, gender-bending and politics.

First, fantasy. Because Aristophanic comedy dances on the edge of the dramatic illusion and the illusion of normality, it would be possible to see it as both more and less realistic than tragedy. While tragedy takes its subject matter overwhelmingly from the world of heroic myth and so is formally distant from the concerns of contemporary Athens, Aristophanes' plays are set right here, just outside (or even inside) the theatre in which we are watching them, now as we watch. Moreover, tragedies only very rarely and never unambiguously acknowledge the existence of the audience and the actualities of dramatic production (although they are often implicitly metatheatrical, especially Euripides), while comedies constantly do so. Finally, there is an awful lot of food in Aristophanes, good ordinary scrummy food. In tragedy, eating is always deviant, except when Euripides is being deviant with tragedy (*Electra*). On the other hand, as I have mentioned before, Aristophanic Athens isn't bound by the laws of nature. His plays are fantasies: the hero flies to heaven on a giant dung beetle to demand peace from the gods (*Peace*); the hero creates a city of birds (*Birds*); the hero makes a personal peace treaty with Sparta, embodied in a flagon of finest wine, which miraculously causes his own farm to be immune to the ravages of war and famine (*Acharnians*); the hero goes down to the Underworld to bring back a dead poet (*Frogs*); the sex-strike of wives forces the men to capitulate, rather than take the obvious rationalist option of alternative sexual gratification (*Lysistrata*); and, most outrageous of all, the government of Athens is handed over to the care of women (*Ecclesiazusae*, or 'Women in Assembly'). And everything always comes right in the end.

Many of these fantasies are fantasies specifically of hubris. Hubris could be seen as a failure, whether intentional or simply through external situation, to keep to the bounds appropriate to one's station. In the civic sense, it has to do with the right treatment of other members of the *polis*; in the larger frame, it has to do especially with the relation of man to the gods (and, on the other hand, the beasts). The tragic hero is characterised by hubris which makes him both great and fallen; the comic hero grabs hold of hubris and milks it for all it is worth. In the civic sense, we can see this in the behaviour of the old man of *Wasps*. Philocleon ('Cleon-lover') has supposedly been cured of his excessive love of jury-service and persuaded to join upper-class polite society. But he misbehaves at a party, steals a music girl, insults people, beats them up and refuses a summons to court (1299–1363). His hubristic, antisocial behaviour constitutes, paradoxically, a robust statement of the vitality of Athenian society, based on the virility of the men 'with stings' (the wasps are undoubtedly phallic), in a way that even old age cannot ultimately threaten (1071–5, 1121). Another thing about comedy is its power of rejuvenation.

On the larger scale, hubris can be seen in almost every play: the private peace in *Acharnians* that the hero (Dicaeopolis = Justice for the City) refuses to share; the flight to Heaven in *Peace*, doubly transgressive in that both flight and challenging the gods are about as hubristic as you can get; the siege of Heaven in *Birds*, where Peisthetaerus and his bird-friends cut off the lines of communication between men and gods, by blocking the passage of sacrificial smoke, and force the gods to terms. These are all things that hit at the heart of ancient Greek and particularly Athenian social codes – and the comic hero gets away with it.

He also gets away with gender-bending. In tragedy, inversions and instabilities of gender are inherent in the tragedy: the unmanning of Agamemnon in the bath and the manly Clytemnestra (Aeschylus' *Oresteia*), Pentheus unable to grow up into a proper man (Euripides' *Bacchae*), Medea and Hecabe taking into their own female hands the male ethic of 'helping friends and harming enemies' (Euripides' plays of those names), and so on. In comedy, by contrast, just about every possible inversion and perversion of gender takes place – and serves to affirm the confident masculinity of the Athenian.

Or does it? It would be possible to say, with Cartledge, that the original audience would probably have seen the eponymous hero (if we can call her that) of *Lysistrata* as an enormous joke on women, while it is just modern sensibilities that make us see it as subversive of Athenian patriarchal society. Perhaps so for many members of the audience, but comedy's hyperconventional streak has cracks in it as well, and all these powerful women, men in drag and effeminate tragedians might also offer the Athenians hints of different ways of looking at things, just as tragedy offered them the space to explore the potential horrors of those perversions.

And so to politics. When in 405 BC the city is in desperate trouble from the prolonged war and the financial and political difficulties which arise from it, Aristophanes sent Dionysus down to the Underworld to fetch Euripides because a poet was needed 'to save the city' (*Frogs* 1419). He came back, however, with Aeschylus, because comedy tends towards the comfortably conservative and Aeschylus embodies a past age of glory. Aristophanes won a civic crown for this play, which remains his most well known, partly for the croaking chorus of Frogs (*brekekekex koax koax*), partly for the outrageously funny interactions between Dionysus, his slave Xanthias and the god-hero Heracles, partly for the extraordinary competition between the two dead tragedians and partly for the moving but indefinable political 'message' that everyone senses in the play. If we read this play, there really should be no debate about whether Athenian tragedy is political, because Aristophanes tells us it is. Exactly *how* tragedy and comedy might be held to be integral to the city's welfare may not have been any more obvious to the original audience than it is to us – it may even be an outrageous joke! – but the play doesn't even let you consider any other possibility than that it *is*.

That doesn't mean, however, that the play, or any Aristophanic play, has a clear political message. In the parabasis of *Frogs*, when the second chorus (initiates of the Eleusinian mystery religion) address the audience directly on the subject of the re-enfranchisement of those citizens who had suffered penalties after the oligarchic coup of 411 BC, and those slaves who had extraordinarily been granted freedom and citizenship after their part in the Battle of Arginusae (406 BC), it poses as being a clear message. The famous money metaphor (the good old citizens are solid Athenian coin, none of your tacky modern rubbish; 718ff.) looks like it is telling us something straight. But this is a play all about bringing back the dead, reviving the good old times, reliving the golden age, returning to the values of Aeschylus – and satirising them all! The money metaphor is almost as daft as the 'wool-carding' metaphor which Lysistrata uses to describe how women will run the city, and everyone laughs at that. 'But money is a serious matter.' In comedy? Nothing escapes from satire and the message will not be tied down.

A similar radical instability of political message, which is nonetheless political, can be seen in the two most prominent 'Cleon' plays: *Knights* and *Wasps*. Both plays attack the politician mercilessly, but in each case the terms of the attack are ambivalent. In *Knights*, the Paphlagonian slave (Cleon) who has got Demos (embodiment of the Athenian people) under his control is ousted from his position by the Sausage-seller, who is an even bigger rogue than the Paphlagonian. In *Wasps*, the Cleon-lover's addiction to his favourite politician is cured only by removing him from the democratic process altogether – and ends up with him at a party with the villain himself. Do these plays then constitute an attack on the Athenian people, on the institutions of democracy? For some readers, perhaps so, but I think more readers would have seen them as explorations of the pleasures and dangers of people-power.[6] After all, you can always hide behind the highly personalised conventions of Athenian political rhetoric and insult, and the comedian's licence to insult the audience – as long as you keep them on your side.

Notes

1　*Acharnians, Knights, Clouds, Wasps, Peace, Birds, Lysistrata, Women at the Thesmophoria, Frogs, Women in Assembly, Wealth.*

2　445/4 to 385 BC are the dates given by P.A. Cartledge, *Aristophanes and His Theatre of the Absurd*, Bristol: Bristol Classical Press, 1990, pp. xiv–xv. Dover (in the *Oxford Classical Dictionary*) is more conservative, offering some time between 460 and 450 for the birth, and 'in or shortly before 386' for the death.

3　Strictly speaking, only the first actor is the prot-agonist (protos = first), but the word has come to be used for all the actors, and indeed for anyone centrally involved in a work of literature or a situation perceived as dramatic.

4   The British political satire television programme *Not the Nine O'Clock News* has a go. But I once saw 'Ten Years of the Best of *Not the Nine O'Clock News*', with programmes stretching back over the previous decade, and although I knew the earlier ones *were* funny, I couldn't actually *see how* they were.

5   See Cartledge, *op. cit.*: for example, where he calls Aristophanes 'politically reactionary' (p. 53); M. Heath, *Political Comedy in Aristophanes*, Göttingen: Vandenhoeck and Ruprecht, 1987, esp. pp. 41–3; S.D. Goldhill, *The Poet's Voice*, Cambridge: Cambridge University Press, 1991, p. 201. See further the discussion of this question in J. Hesk, 'Intratext and irony in Aristophanes', in A.R. Sharrock and H.L. Morales (eds), *Intratextuality: Greek and Roman Textual Relations*, Oxford: Oxford University Press, 2000, pp. 227–62. He takes the example of the reactionary comic figure Alf Garnett: 'Alf seemed to be funny whether you agreed with him or not'.

6   See especially J. Hesk, *Deception and Democracy in Classical Athens*, Cambridge: Cambridge University Press, 2000, p. 257.

See also in this book

Euripides, Menander, Plautus

Texts, translations and commentaries

The plays are all available in OCT, Penguin and Loeb editions. There is so far only one volume of World's Classics translations, by S. Halliwell, comprising *Birds, Lysistrata, Assembly-Women* ('Women in Assembly') and *Wealth*.

There are useful commentaries on all the plays by A. Sommerstein in the Aris and Phillips Series. The following plays have good recent commentaries published by Oxford University Press: *Frogs, Peace, Birds, Clouds, Lysistrata* and *Wasps*.

Further reading

Bowie, A.M., *Aristophanes: Myth, Ritual and Comedy*, Cambridge: Cambridge University Press, 1993.

Cartledge, P.A., *Aristophanes and His Theatre of the Absurd*, Bristol: Bristol Classical Press, 1990.

Dover, K.J., *Aristophanic Comedy*, London: Batsford, 1972.

Heath, M., *Political Comedy in Aristophanes*, Göttingen: Vandenhoeck and Ruprecht, 1987.

MacDowell, D.M., *Aristophanes and Athens: An Introduction to the Plays*, Oxford: Oxford University Press, 1995.

Sandbach, F., *The Comic Theatre of Greece and Rome*, London: Chatto and Windus, 1977.

Silk, M.S., *Aristophanes and the Definition of Comedy*, Oxford: Oxford University Press, 2000.

Taaffe, L.K., *Aristophanes and Women*, London: Routledge, 1993.

Whitman, C.H., *Aristophanes and the Comic Hero*, Cambridge, MA: Harvard University Press, 1964.

FOURTH CENTURY

LYSIAS

In the law courts today, we do occasionally see defendants who represent themselves, such as the pair who took on the might of the McDonald's corporation. Yet such figures are unusual in a system which is operated by highly paid professionals whose job it is to undertake prosecution or defence on behalf of others. In Athens, things were rather different. The president of the court was appointed by lot and the jurors were ordinary citizens, who needed both to be over thirty years old and one of the 6,000 Athenians who had sworn the dikastic oath at the start of the year. Perhaps the biggest contrast with the system today is that litigants were supposed to represent themselves in court rather than to turn to somebody else to do this for them.

As with any system, however, there were ways of making it work to one's advantage without breaking the rules. This is where the logographer comes in – that is, the professional rhetorician who would, for a fee, produce a polished speech which the client would then deliver in court on his own behalf. This was a potentially tricky business for all concerned. The logographer would, realistically, have to work with his client's talent (or lack of it). It was no good writing a brilliant speech if the litigant then became tongue-tied, or if the speech bore no resemblance to what the litigant might have been able to concoct for himself. Quintilian, looking back over the historical development of oratory, was particularly aware of these pitfalls and praises Lysias as 'having done excellently in those speeches which he wrote for unskilled people because he preserved the credibility of a true portrait' (*Training in Oratory* 3.8.51).

Indeed, the logographer needed to be a real chameleon and to keep a low profile, particularly before the case was heard. Plato makes his Phaedrus say that an unnamed politician had recently attacked Lysias and that throughout the tirade he had disparagingly called him a 'speech-writer' (*Phaedrus* 257c). Litigants themselves may have been sensitive to the problems of hiring a logographer. Quintilian claims that Socrates, who was quite capable of defending himself, thought it dishonourable to use a speech which Lysias had composed for his defence (*Training in Oratory* 2.15.30). The speech in question may actually have been epideictic and written after Socrates' death, but the story still illustrates the pitfalls associated with hiring a logographer. So too, if the jurors realised that the litigant had hired a professional to compose his speech, then they were quite likely to react to his case in a hostile way.

Athenians certainly admired clever speakers, sometimes excessively so, but at the same time they were suspicious of those who
acquired eloquence by (what were perceived as) unfair means. As the
fifth century progressed, Sophists came in for increasing criticism on
the grounds that they enabled their clients to trick gullible audiences
into taking flawed decisions. Some people might argue that this
divorce between rhetoric and morality was inevitable once it became
clear that clever speaking could get results, but it was the Sophists
who were blamed for triggering the process. One of the first Sophists
was Protagoras of Abdera (c. 490–420 BC), whose claim that he
could make the weaker argument the stronger caused concern in
some circles, although Plato makes Socrates defend Protagoras and
tackle directly the notion that he corrupted young men by his
teaching methods (*Meno* 91c6–92a6). Even so, Aristophanes in the
Clouds notoriously tars Socrates with exactly the same brush. It isn't
surprising that logographers, who were in some sense an offshoot of
the Sophistic movement, had an increasingly shady reputation,
particularly as the Athenian empire began to get into difficulties in
the final stages of the Peloponnesian War.

Against this backdrop, the outline of Lysias' life can be
reconstructed, although scholars have disagreed about some details.
Lysias' father was Cephalus, a wealthy man from the Sicilian town of
Syracuse, who moved to Athens, possibly as a political exile. His house
serves as the setting for Plato's *Republic*. Lysias himself was born in
Athens, perhaps in 459/458 BC (although Dover would prefer a later
date of 445/444 BC). Dionysius of Halicarnassus tells us that when
Lysias was about 15, he went with his two brothers, Polemarchus and
Euthydemus, to join a colony at Thurii in southern Italy, which may
have given Lysias the chance to meet some important people. The
Sophist Protagoras is supposed to have been asked by Pericles to draw
up a constitution for the new colony, which could conceivably have
brought Lysias into contact with him. In addition, southern Italy (and
especially Sicily) had its own tradition of honing talent in rhetoric,
and the main practitioners of the art in the region were said to be
Corax and Tisias. According to pseudo-Plutarch (*Moralia* 835d),
Lysias was taught by Tisias, although this could be a convenient
assumption based on little more than the geographical proximity of
two men who plied the same trade. Plato's Socrates is made to link
Tisias with the Sophist Gorgias (another Sicilian):

> they saw that probabilities were to be given precedence over
> truths and they make small things appear large and large

things small by the power of speech, and put new things in an old way and things of the opposite sort in a new way, and discovered conciseness of speech and infinite length on every subject.

(Plato *Phaedrus* 267a5–b1)

At any rate, Lysias was eventually forced to return to Athens in 412/411 BC after the defeat of the ill-fated Sicilian expedition. This move back to Athens seems to have been financially successful for a while, in that Lysias and his brothers set up a shield-making business, a lucrative choice during a war. Since Lysias was free from money worries, he could devote time to writing speeches and essays, such as the discourse on love which appears in Plato's *Phaedrus*, although whether this is a real piece by Lysias or merely something written in his style has been much debated.

However, Lysias' fortunes changed in 404 BC as the Peloponnesian War drew to a close and a new oligarchic regime, the Thirty, took power in Athens at Sparta's prompting. This was a grim and complex time, both financially and emotionally: the Athenian fleet had been defeated at Aegospotami in 405 BC, the Spartan general Lysander had been blockading the Piraeus and the Spartan kings Agis and Pausanias had invaded Attica. Athens, forced to concede victory to Sparta, began the depressing process of demolishing her defensive walls. After the end of the war, the Thirty drew up a citizenship list of 3,000 Athenians. Anyone not on this list faced real difficulties: considerable numbers were executed, while others had their property confiscated or left the city.

As the political climate deteriorated, the Thirty turned their attention to metics (long-term non-citizens), including Lysias. He and his family suffered greatly: his brother Polemarchus was executed and Lysias himself had to flee to Megara with the remnants of the democrats. In 403 BC, the Athenian general and statesman Thrasybulus seized the Piraeus and defeated the Thirty and their Spartan allies. Although this didn't instantly resolve the internal conflicts in Athens, it did at least mean that by the autumn of that year, the exiles (including Lysias) could return. Soon afterwards, Lysias began the prosecution of Eratosthenes, one of the Thirty, for killing his brother (*Against Eratosthenes*, speech 12). Whether or not this speech was successful (or even delivered), we don't know, but thereafter Lysias became a professional logographer. The date of his death, like that of his birth, has been disputed, but occurred at some point around 380 BC.

We have today thirty-four speeches by Lysias,[1] although whether they are all genuine is unclear. Porter has recently proposed that even Lysias' most famous speech, *On the Killing of Eratosthenes* (speech 1), was a fictional exercise, designed to advertise the logographer's skills, although Pelling stresses that it is nevertheless important that 'the texts *purport* to be delivered and deliverable'.[2] Lysias' style is usually characterised as clear and simple, the perfect example of Attic purity as opposed to the later Asiatic floridity of oratory in the Hellenistic period.[3] In addition, his speeches are portrayed as clear in their structure, which usually follows the simple pattern of proem, narrative, proofs and conclusion. Yet there is still scope for subtle manipulation of his listeners within this format. Dionysius of Halicarnassus praises Lysias' talents for 'smuggling persuasion past the hearer' (*Lysias* 18).

For example, in *On the Killing of Eratosthenes* (speech 1), which is a defence delivered by a man called Euphiletus against a charge of killing his wife's lover Eratosthenes, Lysias incorporates a dramatic pause (1.22) just after narrating the crucial encounter between the cuckolded Euphiletus and the maid, who has been acting as a go-between in the affair. Euphiletus recalls his words to the maid and his little speech ends:

> I require that you show me their guilt in the very act. I do not want words, but manifestation of the deed, if it is really so.
>
> (Speech 1.21)

This is a tremendous moment. The use of direct speech vividly characterises Euphiletus, who still cannot quite bring himself to believe that his wife's flagrant affair is real. Moreover, the formulation of his demand, with its antithesis between word and deed, prompts the audience to expect a grand showdown where the lovers are caught in the act, rather like a latterday Aphrodite and Ares trapped by the bumbling Hephaestus (Homer *Odyssey* 8). However, Lysias doesn't satisfy this curiosity just yet: noting that four or five days passed, he then makes Euphiletus say 'First, I want to explain what took place on the last day' (1.22). We are left in suspense as Lysias has Euphiletus narrate a chance meeting with his friend Sostratus, who came to dinner that night and who will later become a useful witness for the defence (1.39–40). Lysias' narratives often appear to be simple on the surface, but they can adeptly draw listeners into the case, prompting us to think that it *must* have happened like that.

Lysias is also good at grabbing his listeners' attention at the very start of the speech, when there was a real opportunity for the speaker to make a favourable impression on the jurors. A nice example is the speech *On the Property of Eraton* (speech 17), which opens with a fine *captatio benevolentiae* (winning of good will):

> Perhaps some of you, gentlemen of the jury, suppose that, since I desire to be a person of some account, I must be able to excel others in speaking; but, so far from my being competent to speak on matters that do not concern myself, I fear that, even on matters of which I am obliged to speak, I may be unable to say what is necessary.

> (Speech 17.1)

This delicately judged opening casts the speaker as a demure, self-effacing litigant whose chances of success are hampered by his lack of rhetorical talent. One could argue that his hiring of a logographer to put words into his mouth only reinforces this impression, but of course the jurors would (presumably) have been unaware that Lysias had provided this help for the speaker.

Another adept opening comes in speech 3, *Against Simon*. In this case an unnamed speaker has to defend himself against a charge of wounding a man called Simon with the intent to kill him during an incident which took place four years beforehand. The speaker, a mature man, and Simon, who was evidently younger, had both been in love with the same boy, Theodotos, and had competed with one another for his affections, but it was the speaker who was successful. Simon was allegedly unhappy about this outcome and eventually organised an ambush against the pair, which culminated in a violent fight at a fuller's shop where Theodotos had sought refuge.

Lysias creates a beautifully crafted proem, where the personalities of the speaker and of Simon are strongly polarised. From the very start, the speaker hints that Simon is a rotten character (albeit for unspecified reasons), presenting guilt and innocence in black-and-white terms:

> Although I was aware of much that was disreputable about Simon, gentlemen of the Council, I did not believe that he would ever come to such a pitch of daring as to lodge a

complaint as the injured party about things for which he
should have paid the penalty ...

(Speech 3.1)

The speaker then butters up his listeners by pointing out that
although he would normally be terrified about defending himself in
a legal system which is prone to intrigues and accidents, in this
instance he feels confident about obtaining justice since the case is
being tried before the court of the Areopagus (or *you* as he calls
them, placed emphatically at the start of the sentence – 3.2). The
flattery isn't subtle, but it may have been effective, although here (as
elsewhere) we are left guessing because we hear neither the
opponent's arguments nor the result of the case.

In addition, Lysias makes the speaker turn on the charm and
invite his listeners to empathise with him:

What especially vexes me, gentlemen, is that I shall be forced
to speak to you about such matters. Since I felt shame about
this business in case many men might get to know about me,
I held back even though I had been wronged.

(Speech 3.3)

The speaker presents himself as an unwilling defendant, who feels
acutely embarrassed that his personal life should be put under the
microscope in this very public manner, all because the malicious and
litigious Simon has driven him into court. He finishes the
introduction by asking for indulgence: they might think that, given
his age, he has been rather silly about Theodotus, but they should
remember that everybody can be overcome by sexual desire (3.4).
The speaker therefore anticipates the audience in concluding that he
is evidently older than is proper for an *erastes* (lover), and short-
circuits their disapproval.

These opening touches are all subsequently developed at greater
leisure in the narrative, which also contains humour, such as when
Simon throws a stone at the speaker but accidentally hits his friend
Aristocritus instead (3.8). One might compare this to the shambolic
Calydonian boar-hunt in Ovid *Metamorphoses* 8. Deft humour,
often a good way to short-circuit people's analytical skills during
court cases, is well used in this speech. In the description of the
'battle' which ultimately led to the court case, Lysias suggests that
there was an inevitable escalation, so that everybody in the vicinity

became involved: Simon's drunken gang even beat up Molon the fuller as he was trying to defend Theodotus (3.16). The fact that he and other passers-by were prepared to intervene on the boy's behalf doesn't reflect well on Simon. Carey notes that Lysias deliberately describes the climax of the battle in a 'remarkably clumsy sentence' (3.18), despite his usual clear style.[4] One of Simon's claims (apparently) was that the speaker split his head open, but Lysias' avoidance of clear syntax neatly implies that sorting out who inflicted Simon's injury is likely to be very difficult, if not impossible.

Not all of the cases for which Lysias wrote speeches had such scope for humour, and indeed the particular combination of cases in which he chose to become involved at different points in his career is sometimes disturbing. So, although Lysias wrote *Against Eratosthenes* (speech 12) on his brother's death at the hands of the Thirty, he also chose to defend a client accused of having supported the Thirty (*Defence against a Charge of Subverting the Democracy*, speech 25).[5] It is clearly problematic that Lysias, who himself suffered under the Thirty, could nevertheless offer legal help to one of their supporters.[6] What is going on here? Was Lysias inconsistent, hypocritical or just plain ruthless, the sort of man who was prepared to put his ethics on hold while taking money from a client who supported the regime which destroyed his family? Some have argued that Lysias' client was in fact a moderate, so it shouldn't worry us unduly that the logographer defends him. Yet in order to defend the man, Lysias had to make out that he was moderate, so that line of argument doesn't really get us very far.[7] Certainly there is no easy solution to this dilemma. Without a clearer knowledge of the circumstances in which such speeches were composed and delivered (if they were indeed delivered), perhaps we should defer any final judgement on Lysias' morals.

Notes

1 S.C. Todd, *Lysias*, Austin, TX: University of Texas Press, 2000, p. 318, explains that

> whereas speeches 1–31 derive from mediaeval manuscripts of Lysias' speeches, what we call Lysias 32–34 are the opening sections of three speeches that are quoted by the rhetorical theorist Dionysius of Halicarnassus in his essay *Lysias* as examples of Lysias' style in three genres of oratory.

2 J.R. Porter, 'Adultery by the book: Lysias 1 (*On the Murder of Eratosthenes*) and comic diegesis', *Échos du monde classique*, 41, 1997,

pp. 421–53; C.B.R. Pelling, *Literary Texts and the Greek Historian*, London: Routledge, 2000, p. 301 n. 89.
3 See G. Kennedy, *A New History of Classical Rhetoric*, Princeton, NJ: Princeton University Press, 1994, pp. 162–6, on Atticism.
4 C. Carey, *Lysias Selected Speeches*, Greek and Latin Classics Series, Cambridge: Cambridge University Press, 1989, pp. 100–1.
5 K. Dover, *Lysias and the Corpus Lysiacum*, Berkeley and Los Angeles, CA: University of California Press, 1968, pp. 188–9, suggests that this (incomplete) speech was written as a pamphlet rather than as part of a real case.
6 Todd, *op. cit.*, p. 6.
7 Cf. Pelling, *op. cit.*, p. 27, on the Profumo affair of 1963 and Mandy Rice-Davies, who when 'reminded in court that some distinguished personage had denied her embarrassing story … reasonably replied that he would, wouldn't he?'

See also in this book

Cicero, Demosthenes, Plato, Quintilian

Texts, translations and commentaries

The Greek text is available in OCT, Teubner and Loeb.

As well as the Loeb, there is a University of Texas translation by S.C. Todd in the Oratory in Classical Greece Series edited by M. Gagarin.

There is a commentary on *Lysias' Selected Speeches* by C. Carey in the Cambridge Greek and Latin Classics Series, on *Greek Orators I: Antiphon and Lysias* by M.J. Edwards and S. Usher in the Aris and Phillips Series, and on *Lysias: Five Speeches* (namely, *Speeches* 1, 12, 19, 22 and 30) by M.J. Edwards in the Bristol Series.

Further reading

Dover, K., *Lysias and the Corpus Lysiacum*, Berkeley and Los Angeles, CA: University of California Press, 1968.
Kennedy, G., *The Art of Persuasion in Greece*, Princeton, NJ: Princeton University Press, 1963.
Kennedy, G., *A New History of Classical Rhetoric*, Princeton, NJ: Princeton University Press, 1994.
Pelling, C.B.R., *Literary Texts and the Greek Historian*, London: Routledge, 2000.
Porter, J.R., 'Adultery by the book: Lysias 1 (*On the Murder of Eratosthenes*) and comic diegesis', *Échos du monde classique,* 41, 1997, pp. 421–53.
Todd, S.C., *The Shape of Athenian Law*, Oxford: Oxford University Press, 1993.

XENOPHON

Is Xenophon anything other than a second-rate Thucydides? The answer is certainly yes. Although perhaps best known as a historian, he also wrote technical treatises, dialogues, Socratic texts, a biography, economic and political works, and even a historical novel. In an era when authors tended to specialise in particular genres, Xenophon proved himself to be remarkably versatile. His two historical works are the *Hellenica* and the *Anabasis*, although the latter has a distinctly autobiographical tone and looks at intrinsic weaknesses in the Persian system from the viewpoint of someone who has observed them from close at hand. Xenophon also wrote a series of dialogues (the *Apology*, the *Symposium*, the *Memorabilia*, the *Oeconomicus* and the *Hiero*), technical treatises (the *Cavalry Commander*, *On Horsemanship* and *On Hunting*), a biography (the *Agesilaos*), and two works on economics and politics (the *Ways and Means* and the *Constitution of the Spartans*). Finally, there is the *Cyropaedia*, a fanciful and enjoyable account of the education of Cyrus the Great, the founder of the Persian empire.

The variety which characterises his literary output is mirrored in the various twists and turns of his life. Xenophon, born in *c.* 430 BC in the Athenian deme of Erchia (ten miles north-east of the city), grew up as the Peloponnesian War was raging between Athens and Sparta (431–404 BC). He soon gained practical experience of the conflict by serving in the Athenian cavalry, which may have helped to shape his political views. Xenophon had seen the Athenian democracy in action and came to the conclusion that there were deep-rooted flaws in the system. We can sense his despair by reading his account of the trial of the Athenian generals after their victory in the sea-battle of Arginusae in 406 BC: they didn't pick up survivors from the sea because of a storm and as a result faced prosecution upon their return. Xenophon regards the refusal to try the generals separately (rather than *en masse*) as outrageous and gives a version of a passionate speech by Euryptolemus in their defence (*Hellenica* 1.7.16–33). The fact that the Athenians subsequently aired regrets about their decision (*Hellenica* 1.7.35) must only have increased Xenophon's disquiet about the democracy. At any rate, while other Athenians (such as Lysias), who supported a democratic form of government, fled from Athens during the regime of the Thirty in 404–403 BC, Xenophon stayed behind. This didn't necessarily mean that he approved of the way in which the Thirty held power, as is clear from his moving description in *Hellenica* 2 of the execution of the moderate politician Theramenes. However, it must have caused

103

problems for him after the war when the democrats returned, even though there was an amnesty. Xenophon therefore decided to leave Athens either late in 402 BC or early in 401 BC.

What Xenophon decided to do next changed the course of his life. Stifled by the atmosphere in Athens, he decided to put his experience in the cavalry to good use by becoming a mercenary. Having received an invitation from a Boeotian friend called Proxenus (*Anabasis* 3.1.4–8), Xenophon offered his services to the Persian prince Cyrus, who was secretly planning to take power from his brother, Artaxerxes. Xenophon subsequently wrote about his experiences in the *Anabasis*, an account of Cyrus' unsuccessful rebellion which narrates in particular the experiences of the 10,000 Greek mercenaries. These men marched all the way from Babylon to the Black Sea after the defeat and death of Cyrus at the Battle of Cunaxa in 401 BC. Although they themselves fought well in the battle, the overall defeat led to the arrest and murder of their captains, and to the election of new ones, including Xenophon, who eventually became sole commander. He and his men served as mercenaries first in Thrace and then in Asia Minor, where they joined the Spartan army fighting against Persian satraps.

It was in this context that Xenophon in 396 BC met the Spartan king Agesilaos, who would go on to influence him hugely. When Agesilaos returned home in 394 BC to deal with Sparta's rebellious allies, Xenophon accompanied him and fought at the battle of Coronea, where he had to fight against the Athenians, among others. Since his departure, relations with his home city had deteriorated: he may already have been officially exiled, but he certainly was after the battle. It was fortunate under the circumstances that Agesilaos rewarded Xenophon with an estate at Scillus, just south of Olympia, where he lived quite happily for many years until Sparta was defeated by the Thebans at the Battle of Leuctra in 371 BC. In the chaos which followed, Xenophon had to leave his pleasant estate and decided to move to Corinth. There was a distinct improvement in his relations with his home city when Athens and Sparta joined forces against the increasingly powerful Thebes, and his son Gryllus even fought and died for Athens at the Battle of Mantinea in 362 BC. Xenophon praises the Athenians for helping the citizens of Mantinea in this battle, even though they were far outnumbered by the Theban forces, observing in a moving but restrained way: 'Good men among them were killed' (*Hellenica* 7.7.17). Xenophon himself died at some point in the late 350s BC.

As a historian, Xenophon has often been compared unfavourably with his predecessor Thucydides, partly because the starting point of the *Hellenica* falls pointedly in the autumn of 411 BC, just where Thucydides' narrative ends. This is deliberate, as Marincola observes: 'Xenophon's *Hellenica* is the first instance of "continuing" a predecessor, and this tradition has a long history in writers both Greek and Roman'.[1] It is conspicuous that there is no preface to the *Hellenica* (an account of Greek affairs from 411 to 62 BC) so a reader is left in the dark about why this particular period seemed worthy of treatment. Even Xenophon's identity as a narrator isn't highlighted, in marked contrast with Herodotus and Thucydides, who both open their historical accounts boldly with their names and provenance: we *know* that Thucydides is an Athenian and that Herodotus comes from Halicarnassus, but who is Xenophon? Critics have noted that Xenophon's narrative manifests a distinctly Spartan perspective, particularly in the last five books, which leads him to make some peculiar omissions. So, there is no account of the formation of the Second Athenian Confederacy: we do hear about it, but only incidentally when Athens is suffering from financial problems (*Hellenica* 6.2.1).

Critics have also suggested that Xenophon likes to see history rather crudely in terms of momentous single events, such as the Spartan seizure of the Theban citadel in 382 BC. This he saw as being punished subsequently by the gods when the Spartans were defeated at Leuctra in 371 BC (*Hellenica* 5.4.1). In general, the problematic features of his account are brought even more sharply into focus through reading Diodorus Siculus' universal history, the *Bibliotheke*: Books 13–15 rely heavily on the lost narrative of the historian Ephorus, which allows us to see Xenophon's account from another angle. Ephorus himself used as a source the so-called 'Oxyrhyncus historian', a reliable writer and another continuator of Thucydides. Two sets of papyrus fragments from his narrative were discovered in 1906 and 1942, and Xenophon's reputation suffered as a result. As George Cawkwell has observed of Xenophon:

> Like the grin on the Cheshire Cat, his literary charm remains, but his high esteem as a reliable historian is a thing of the past.[2]

We should never forget that even now discoveries can still be made which force us to rethink our assessment of a particular author.

Is there anything positive to be said about the quality of the *Hellenica* as a historical narrative? We can (and should) make some points in its defence. Particularly since most other continuous historical narratives of the fourth century BC have not survived intact, it is fortunate that this one too has not perished. In fact, Xenophon may even have had his own doubts about finishing the narrative: this work conspicuously falls into two halves, the first of which (*Hellenica* 1.1.1–2.3.10) was completed many decades before the second (*Hellenica* 2.3.11–7.5.27).

That said, Xenophon is at least a contemporary witness for many events and somebody who knew personally many of the major protagonists, including Agesilaos, Theramenes and Critias. His version of the incidents which led up to the overthrow of the Thirty, for example, is particularly vivid and valuable (*Hellenica* 2.4.2–43) since many others had fled from Athens. Even if we feel entitled to complain of a pro-Spartan stance in subsequent parts of the *Hellenica*, this does at least turn the tables on most other historical narratives, which (if anything) relate events from an Athenian perspective. His account of the Spartan campaigns in Asia Minor between 399 and 394 BC probably draws extensively on his own personal experiences. This sometimes leads Xenophon to include events not so much for their historical value, but because he felt well placed to preserve them for posterity. One such instance is the engaging episode where Agesilaos cunningly manipulates the Paphlagonian king Otys and the Persian Spithridates so that the former marries the latter's daughter (*Hellenica* 4.1.4–15). The betrothal itself wasn't particularly important historically, but the incident is certainly revealing about Agesilaos' personal qualities.

Moreover, the first half of the fourth century BC was a period of history on which it was very difficult to impose any overarching analysis as successive Greek city-states rose to prominence, only to be brought down again. Even the end-point of the narrative, the Battle of Mantinea, didn't change anything. As Dillery has observed: 'That Xenophon did not find Mantinea epochal is perhaps the most important feature to notice about the *Hellenica*'.[3] If Xenophon had lived long enough to see how the dynamic Philip of Macedon was able to exploit internal problems among the Greek city-states, then he might have created a more explicitly teleological narrative. However, even as things stand, the prognosis for Greece isn't good. Xenophon's focus on the essential disorder and continuing power struggles within Greece allows us to see how ripe the time was for Philip (or for somebody like him) to strike. Before explicitly passing on the baton to an unnamed future historian, Xenophon finishes his narrative: 'In fact, there was even more uncertainty and confusion in Greece after the battle than there had been previously' (*Hellenica* 7.5.27). As a formal closure to a historical account, this is remarkably weak, but the ending is still eloquent in other ways: the vulnerability of the Greek city-states is encapsulated forcefully by this disturbing final sentence.

Xenophon has received a warmer critical reception for some of his other works. His *Anabasis*, written after the Battle of Leuctra in 371 BC, has something in common with Julius Caesar's commentaries, since the work narrates in the third person events in which the author himself participated.[4] Xenophon's Greek, like Caesar's Latin, is usually clear and accessible, but the *Anabasis*, rather than offering (or purporting to offer) raw material for a professional historian, is a polished and exciting narrative in its own right. The text offers polarised images of Greek and Persian national characters: where the Persians are presented as servile, wealthy and militarily flawed, the Greeks are shown to have a powerful sense of liberty and to remain untainted by a life of luxury. At one point Xenophon says to his troops:

> But I am afraid that if we once learn to live in laziness and to pass our time in luxury, and to associate with the beautiful, tall women and girls of the Medes and Persians, we might forget our way home like the Lotus Eaters.
>
> (*Anabasis* 3.2.25)

Persia, it seems, is a dangerous place, above all because of its potentially enervating impact on the wholesome Greek mercenaries.

Xenophon's allusion to Homer's Lotus Eaters makes us recall that Odysseus had to force his men to abandon their painless but lethargic existence in this new land: the Homeric heroes cry on rejoining the expedition, but they do regain their identity (*Odyssey* 9.82–104). Through this allusion Xenophon suggests that however tempting it was to live like a Persian, it is far better to be Greek, an interesting perspective from a man who turned his back on Athens. It may also suit Xenophon's purposes for his audience to see him momentarily through the filter of Odysseus. This is, after all, the point in the text where Xenophon takes on a more active leadership role when the Ten Thousand have to respond to the treacherous murder of the Greek generals after the Battle of Cunaxa. We have already seen him marked out as someone special when he dreams that his family home was set ablaze by a thunderbolt (*Hellenica* 3.1.11).[5] Although Xenophon doubts whether this is a significant dream, it does galvanise him to act and therefore becomes important in the light of subsequent events.

The *Anabasis* has also been appreciated for its powerful descriptions of the Greek soldiers enduring terrible hardships. It is often the smaller points which are most telling. So, Xenophon graphically captures the perils of the cold as the soldiers make their way to Armenia:

> in all cases where men slept with their shoes on, the straps sunk into their flesh and the shoes froze on their feet; for what they were wearing, since their old shoes had given out, was footwear made from freshly flayed ox-hides.

> (*Anabasis* 4.5.14)

One might have thought that given the cold it was logical to sleep wearing shoes, but the opposite proves to be true.

There are also more light-hearted moments of survival, such as the incident in a Colchian village involving some potent local honey. As the soldiers rest, they notice that there are many bees around and so some of them decide to try the honey. The results are alarming: those who eat only a little seem very drunk, but those who consume a lot resemble mad or even dying men (*Anabasis* 4.8.20–21). However, on the following day, the men begin to recover at exactly the same time as they originally ate the honey. Xenophon is playing with our expectations that Colchis, home of the mythical sorceress Medea, could present hidden dangers to these Greeks, such strangers in a strange land.

As well as successive military encounters, the *Anabasis* also contains its fair share of ethnographic descriptions.[6] When the Greeks meet the Mossynoecians, they consider them to be the most uncivilised people whose country they have crossed during the expedition. The Mossynoecian customs are presented as being diametrically opposed to those of the Greeks, in an exaggerated manner that is fairly typical of such ethnographic portraits:

> For they habitually did in public the things that other people would do only in private, and when they were alone they would behave just as if they were in the company of others, talking to themselves, laughing at themselves, and dancing

in whatever spot they chanced to be, as though they were giving an exhibition to others.

(Anabasis 5.4.34)

In addition, Xenophon deploys the familiar ethnographic strategy of describing peculiar foreign customs through the filter of more familiar Greek habits: so the Mossynoecians are said to use dolphin blubber just as the Greeks use olive oil (*Anabasis* 5.4.28). Perhaps they aren't so different after all.

There are many overarching themes which one could highlight from Xenophon's diverse body of work, such as his interest in the best forms of military leadership, his fascination with dynamic individuals (whatever their nationality), his belief in divine retribution, his didacticism and his pan-Hellenism. Even if he had written nothing, the details of his life would have served as an eloquent marker of the upheaval and uncertainty which gripped Greece during the late fifth and early fourth centuries BC. As it is, however, Xenophon has left us a remarkable range of different works. I have focused for the most part on his historical writings, but we shouldn't forget the *Apology*, *Symposium* and *Memorabilia*, in which he presents us with a warm portrait of Socrates, which can be set alongside Plato's accounts. Moreover, there is also the creative *Cyropaedia*, which has been called the first historical novel. Although Xenophon's reputation went into decline after the discovery of the fragments from the Oxyrhyncus historian, there has recently been a revival of interest in his works: scholars are now increasingly willing to analyse Xenophon's writings for their own sake, rather than criticising them for what they don't offer us.

Notes

1   J. Marincola, *Authority and Tradition in Ancient Historiography*, Cambridge: Cambridge University Press, 1997, p. 237.
2   G. Cawkwell, *Xenophon: A History of My Times*, Harmondsworth: Penguin, 1979, p. 16.
3   J. Dillery, *Xenophon and the History of His Times*, London and New York: Routledge, 1995, pp. 22–3.
4   See J.K. Anderson, *Xenophon*, London: Duckworth, 1974, pp. 61–72, on the *Anabasis*.
5   See Marincola, *op. cit.*, p. 208 n. 142, for the Homeric overtones of this dream.
6   See Anderson, *op. cit.*, pp. 134–45, on the presentation of barbarians in the *Anabasis*.

See also in this book

Herodotus, Julius Caesar, Plato, Polybius, Thucydides

Texts, translations and commentaries

The Greek text is available in OCT (5 volumes), Teubner (3 volumes) and Loeb (7 volumes).

As well as the Loeb, there are Penguin translations of *History of My Times* and *The Persian Expedition* by R. Warner (with notes by G. Cawkwell), *Conversations of Socrates* by H. Tredennick and *Hiero the Tyrant and Other Treatises* by R. Waterfield, as well as an Everyman translation of *Education of Cyrus* by R. Stoneman.

There are commentaries on *Hellenika I–II.3.10* and *Hellenika II.3.11–IV.2.8* by P. Krentz, *Symposium* by A. Bowen, and *On Hunting* by A.A. Phillips and M.M. Willcock in the Aris and Phillips Series (with *Apology and Memorabilia I* by M.D. MacLeod 2001); and on the *Oeconomicus* by S. Pomeroy published by Oxford University Press.

Further reading

Anderson, J.K., *Xenophon*, London: Duckworth, 1974.

Cartledge, P.A., *Agesilaos and the Crisis of Sparta*, London: Duckworth, 1987.

Dillery, J., *Xenophon and the History of His Times*, London and New York: Routledge, 1995.

Gera, D., *Xenophon's Cyropaedia: Style, Genre and Literary Technique*, Oxford: Oxford University Press, 1994.

Gray, V., *The Character of Xenophon's Hellenica*, London: Duckworth, 1989.

Marincola, J., *Authority and Tradition in Ancient Historiography*, Cambridge: Cambridge University Press, 1997.

Strauss, L., *Xenophon's Socrates*, Ithaca, NY, and London: Cornell University Press, 1972.

Tatum, J., *Xenophon's Imperial Fiction: On the Education of Cyrus*, Princeton, NJ: Princeton University Press, 1989.

PLATO

Plato's thinking has been extraordinarily influential, and yet he himself does not once appear in the dialogues. Instead, his ideas are articulated through other characters, above all Socrates. Partly because of Plato's low profile in the works themselves, ancient biographers used their creative powers to fill in the gaps for successive audiences hungry for details about his life. We only have biographies written from the second century AD onwards, but these drew material from earlier versions, including the picturesque detail that bees came and placed honey on Plato's lips as a baby, foreshadowing the wise and beautiful words which he would speak as an adult.[1]

This anecdote acknowledges that Plato wasn't only a philosopher, but a literary artist as well. Similar stories were also told about other Greek writers, particularly poets, but its application to Plato suggests a desire to fill out the picture of the man who existed behind the mask of Socrates. To untangle the historical Socrates from the Platonic version is a task fraught with difficulties, although that has certainly not deterred critics from trying. Since Socrates himself left no direct written record of his ideas, it is perhaps more constructive to read Plato's dialogues without attempting to sort out arguments neatly into Socratic and Platonic piles. In any case, it is probable that even in the early dialogues, Plato presents us with a synthesised set of ideas in new contexts, which may build on original debates with Socrates, but don't necessarily allow us access to those debates.[2]

Plato was an Athenian, who was born in *c.* 428 BC during the troubled period of the Peloponnesian War. At some point he became a follower of Socrates (469–399 BC), who in his time had been a soldier and a politician, as well as a philosopher. Socrates increasingly came into conflict with the democracy at crucial moments, such as when he voted against the motion to execute the generals after the sea-battle at Arginusae in 406 BC. Nor did Socrates fare much better when the Thirty Tyrants came to power: Plato tells us about one occasion when Socrates refused to cooperate with the oligarchy by arresting an innocent man (*Apology* 32c–d).

This cannot have been an easy time for Plato, since two of his uncles, Critias and Charmides, were among the Thirty Tyrants. Family ties were pulling him in one direction, while his intellectual affinities were pulling him in another. Once the democracy was restored, Plato had to witness the arrest and trial of his friend Socrates, who was charged with introducing new gods and with corrupting the young. One can get a sense of the popular image of Socrates from Aristophanes' *Clouds*, originally produced in 423 BC, in which he is cast as an unscrupulous Sophist who profits from teaching young men how to make the weaker argument the stronger. Despite an amnesty which had been established to prevent individuals seeking revenge after the fall of the Thirty Tyrants, the real motives of Socrates' prosecutors may still have had a political edge.

At any rate, after Socrates' conviction and death through drinking hemlock in 399 BC (*Phaedo* 116d–118), Plato turned away from a public career, although his life as a philosopher didn't mean that he ignored politics. His depiction of the ideal state in the

Republic is partly a response to his own experiences, and his abortive attempt to serve as tutor to the Syracusan ruler Dionysius II in Sicily during the 360s BC suggests that he didn't want his philosophical precepts to exist in a vacuum. As his Socrates says,

> The philosophers must become kings in our cities, or those who are now called kings and potentates must learn to seek wisdom like true and genuine philosophers, and so political power and intellectual wisdom will be joined in one.
>
> (*Republic* 473c–d)

Nevertheless, we should be wary of imposing heavy-handed connections between Plato's life and his works, especially since the ancient literary community often liked to use (or even to create) biographical details to explain aspects of someone's writings: thus Juvenal's 'exile' is used to 'explain' his bitter satirical voice. In Plato's case there are the thirteen *Epistles*, most of which have been considered spurious (with the possible exception of *Epistle* 7). The failure of Plato's intervention in Sicilian politics has been used as a convenient bridge to connect the optimistic depiction of the ideal state in the *Republic* with the more pessimistic ideas of his final unfinished work, the *Laws*, but that may be to overschematise his thinking (and to read the *Republic* in particular much too straightforwardly). Just as Virgil's *Georgics* isn't by any stretch of the imagination a practical handbook for farmers, so Plato's *Republic* isn't simply a template to allow the setting up of an ideal city. At the end of *Republic* 9 (592b), Socrates certainly expresses his doubts about whether this place will ever really exist.[3] In any case, the main focus of the *Republic* is an investigation into the nature of justice.

One of Plato's projects which has been seen to reflect his desire for practical interaction with the political sphere is his foundation of the Academy. This school was established in Athens in the early 380s BC and survived for several centuries until it ceased to operate in the first century BC. Here those who originally attended (in due course including Aristotle) were encouraged to develop interests in philosophy, mathematics, astronomy, law and rhetoric, and the school remained a central focus for Plato until his death in 347 BC, despite various trips abroad, particularly to Sicily. Certainly, many of those who spent time with Plato at the Academy went on to become active in politics, but this doesn't mean that this was the *raison d'être* of the place. It may be that only those with time and money on their hands could afford to spend time in this sort of intellectual environment.[4] Likewise, many politicians today may have gone to university, but that doesn't mean to say that the purpose of these institutions is to churn out politicians.

The most distinctive feature of Plato's works is that, apart from in the *Apology*, the dialogue format dominates throughout, even if in the later pieces (such as the *Timaeus* and the *Critias*) the conversation tends to serve as a launchpad for long speeches delivered by one particular protagonist. Plato is particularly adept at producing vivid dramatisations of those actively engaged in trying to solve philosophical problems. The illusion is thereby created that we, as readers, are witnessing real discussions which took place on particular historical occasions.

So, for example, in the *Ion* Socrates meets the rhapsode Ion on his way back from Epidaurus where he had won first prize at the festival of Asclepius, or in the *Phaedrus* Socrates meets Phaedrus on the way back from hearing Lysias reciting a speech about love. In other dialogues there can often be an abrupt beginning, which creates the impression that the discussion has already started before the narrative begins, as when Meno asks: 'Can you tell me, Socrates, whether excellence can be taught?' (*Meno* 70a). Where necessary, we have to fill in details about context from the dialogue itself, as in this case, where it later emerges that Socrates and Meno had already met for a discussion on the previous day (*Meno* 76e).

Moreover, particularly with a central figure such as Socrates, who participates in so many of the dialogues, there is progressive development in his characterisation. In a piece such as the *Parmenides*, we see Socrates as a young man whose initial enthusiasm is rather dampened by Parmenides' criticisms of his theory of Forms, whereas in the *Meno* Socrates is more dominant, gently guiding the discussion and teasing Meno for trying to steer it in the wrong direction (*Meno* 76a–c). In the end, Socrates disappears from view, playing only a small role in the *Timaeus* and the *Critias*, and not featuring in the *Laws* at all.

Personality often meshes in provocative and creative ways with the arguments being put forward in a dialogue. So, in the *Gorgias*, where an enquiry into the nature of rhetoric serves as a springboard for a discussion about excellence and about what one must do to become truly happy, Socrates faces a series of increasingly difficult challenges from three rhetoricians, Gorgias, Polus and finally Callicles. The boastful and flamboyant Gorgias is first eliminated from the discussion by Socrates when his desire to impress his audience traps him into adopting a self-contradictory position (*Gorgias* 457b, 460a).[5]

Next Socrates deals successfully with the young and impatient Polus by proving that inflicting wrong is much worse for an individual than suffering wrong (one of the so-called 'Socratic paradoxes').[6]

His most difficult opponent, however, is the ruthless and amoral Callicles, who criticises Gorgias and Polus for exposing themselves to attack through their misguided sense of shame (*Gorgias* 482c).[7] Callicles cares very little about what people might think of him, which makes it particularly difficult for Socrates to undermine him: unlike Gorgias and Polus, Callicles isn't going to put himself into an untenable position just in case people disapprove of him. In the event, Callicles suggests that nature herself desires that the strong should dominate the weak, who only use the concept of justice as a way to disparage the strong (*Gorgias* 482c–486d).[8] More specifically, he suggests that the 'excellence' which the competent orator should pursue is the unlimited capacity to satisfy his desires according to the laws of nature (*Gorgias* 491e). Socrates retaliates by arguing at length that pleasure cannot be equated with what is good, which forces Callicles to back down. Szlezák has emphasised that although Plato could have debated the issue on a dispassionate, theoretical basis, he raises the stakes and draws us in by filtering an abstract issue through the personality of Callicles, whose 'direct expression of his pathological ambition and his boundless egocentrism' prove particularly shocking.[9]

What were Plato's most important philosophical ideas? It is impossible in this context to offer a comprehensive overview, but we can at least pick out some highlights. Plato's most significant doctrine is the theory of Forms, which plays a crucial role in his epistemology (that is, theory of knowledge) and which features in a number of different dialogues (although not necessarily in a static or fully developed manner). Plato suggests that beyond the physical world which we can perceive, there is another realm. Here, there exists a range of perfect Forms, eternally uniform and unchanging, such as Beauty, Justice and Good. In the physical world, there are imperfect imitations of these Forms, which will decay or which will only possess (for example) beauty in relative terms. So, in the *Symposium*, Diotima draws an important contrast:

> while all beautiful things elsewhere partake of this Beauty in such a manner, that when they are born and perish, it becomes neither less nor more and nothing at all happens to it.

(*Symposium* 211b)

As human beings, we need to progress from seeing these beautiful physical objects with our eyes to contemplating the abstract Form of Beauty with our minds.

Even within the realm of perfect Forms, however, there is a hierarchy, which is dominated by the Form of the Good. In the *Republic*, Plato makes Socrates argue that just as the sun enables us to see physical objects in the world around us, so the Form of the Good allows the philosopher to understand abstract ideas. To illustrate the point, Plato introduces the famous allegory of the cave. He asks us to picture humans as chained up in a cave, with their backs to the opening, so that all they can see are shadows projected from objects being carried along outside the cave. The images are cast by means of a fire in front of which those carrying the objects pass. If the humans were released and forced to enter the outside world, they would initially be dazzled and mystified, since the realm of shadows was (for them) the only real world. Yet as they became accustomed to the light, they would come to realise that the shadows in the cave, which they believed were real, were only images of reality. Socrates concludes:

> The world of our sight is like the habitation in prison, the firelight there to the sunlight here, the ascent and the view of the upper world is the rising of the soul to the world of the mind ... . At least what appears to me is that in the world of the known, last of all, is the Form of the Good, and with what toil to be seen!
>
> (*Republic* 517c)

Not everyone is capable of making this journey, but it is the duty of the philosopher to try to help his fellow prisoners to reach this other world.[10]

Another central Platonic doctrine is the concept of the tripartite soul, a temporary inhabitant of the body which will survive after death. In the *Phaedo*, Plato argues that the soul is a single rational entity, hindered from the pursuit of wisdom by the sensual and hedonistic body, but he modifies this theory in the *Republic*, *Phaedrus* and *Timaeus* to posit a tripartite soul, which is made up of reason, appetite and spirit. In the *Phaedrus*, Plato makes Socrates clarify the nature of the soul by comparing it with a chariot consisting of a charioteer and two winged horses, the first one being noble and good, while the second one is troublesome. These horses are in constant conflict with one another, which makes the vehicle difficult to drive. The charioteer represents the rational part of the soul, while the good horse represents the spirited part of the soul and the natural ally of the rational element. However, the bad horse, symbolising the desire for sensual gratification, is potentially disruptive. In the worst-case scenario, this horse can cause the chariot to be dragged downwards so that the soul is locked back into a cycle of rebirth, moving from one corrupt body to the next until it can eventually escape altogether from this tedious corporeal existence (*Phaedrus* 246a–b).

One particular Platonic doctrine depends on this theory about the immortal soul, namely the notion that knowledge involves recollecting things which the soul has already learned in a previous life. This crops up in a number of dialogues, but particularly in the *Meno*, where Socrates and Meno discuss the question of whether excellence is teachable. With characteristic insistence on tackling matters in the right order, Socrates demands that they establish first of all what excellence is and, for a section of the debate, they play around with the idea that excellence is knowledge. This is when the theory of knowledge as recollection becomes relevant. To demonstrate this theory, Socrates uses one of Meno's slaves, who has no knowledge of geometry, but who still manages to solve a geometrical problem despite his professed ignorance (*Meno* 81a–86c). Socrates argues that he must be drawing on knowledge which his soul had acquired in a previous existence.

Plato's philosophy was constantly evolving throughout his life, and there are certainly instances where Plato himself expresses dissatisfaction with some of his ideas, even quite central ones, such as his critique of the theory of Forms in the *Parmenides*. Subsequent philosophers such as Aristotle, who had been taught by Plato, continued to engage with his thinking, even if Aristotle was prepared to criticise some of his teacher's theories (such as his doubts at *Ethics* 1.6 that Goodness is a single, universal Form). Despite a period where the Academy itself reacted sceptically to some of Plato's ideas, there were significant revivals of Plato's philosophy, beginning in the first century BC with philosophers such as Antiochus and Posidonius (who heralded the arrival of the intellectual movement known as Middle Platonism), and above all in the third century AD with Plotinus (who was the catalyst for the intellectual movement known as Neoplatonism).

Plato's work has continued to have an impact on readers in more recent times. There is one engaging story about how the poet Shelley, after an afternoon spent reading Plato with a friend, was walking through Oxford when they met a woman holding a baby. Grabbing hold of the child, Shelley twice asked the startled mother what the baby could reveal to them about 'pre-existence'. When the mother pointed out that the baby couldn't talk and added, 'glancing at our Academical garb', that it wasn't for her to dispute with them, the friends went on their way, whereupon Shelley remarked that, despite the baby's attempt to trick them, it was still clear 'that all knowledge is reminiscence'.[11] We can only assume that Shelley and his friend Hogg had previously been reading either the *Phaedo* (72e–76a) or the *Meno* (81a–86c), where Plato outlines his theory that learning involves the recollection of truths known before birth. No doubt the poet Shelley's excitement was triggered both by Plato's philosophical ideas and by his talents as a writer.

Notes

1 A.S. Riginos, *Platonica: The Anecdotes Concerning the Life and Writings of Plato*, Leiden: Brill, 1976, no. 3.
2 See R.B. Rutherford, *The Art of Plato*, London: Duckworth, 1995, pp. 21–3, for a summary of the 'Socratic question'.
3 See C.J. Rowe, *Plato*, Brighton: Harvester Press, 1984, pp. 137–42.
4 See P.A. Brunt, 'Plato's Academy and politics', in *Studies in Greek History and Thought*, Oxford: Oxford University Press, 1993, pp 282–342.
5 See Rutherford, *op. cit.*, pp. 143–9, on Gorgias.
6 See Rutherford, *op. cit.*, pp. 149–57, on Polus.
7 See Rutherford, *op. cit.*, pp. 157–71, on Callicles.
8 Cf. the arguments of the Melian dialogue at Thucydides *History of the Peloponnesian War* 5.84–113.
9 See T.A. Szlezák, *Reading Plato*, London and New York: Routledge, 1999, p. 6.
10 For further discussion of the Forms, see C.H. Kahn, *Plato and the Socratic Dialogue: The Philosophical Use of a Literary Form*, Cambridge: Cambridge University Press, 1996, pp. 329–70.
11 J. Sutherland, *The Oxford Book of Literary Anecdotes*, Oxford: Oxford University Press, 1987, pp. 190–1.

See also in this book

Aristophanes, Aristotle, Lysias, Xenophon

Texts, translations and commentaries

The Greek text is available in OCT (5 volumes, but a new edition is in progress), Teubner (5 volumes) and Loeb (12 volumes).

As well as the Loeb, there are Penguin translations of the *Symposium* by

W. Hamilton and by C.J. Gill, *Republic* and *Timaeus and Critias* by D. Lee, *Protagoras and Meno* by W.K.C. Guthrie, *Gorgias* and *Phaedrus and Letters VII and VIII* by W. Hamilton, *Laws* and *Early Socratic Dialogues* by F. Burney, *Philebus* and *Theatetus* by R. Waterfield, *Last Days of Socrates* by H. Tredennick, and *Classical Literary Criticism* by T.S. Dortsch (revised by P. Murray). There are Oxford World's Classics translations of the *Gorgias*, *Republic* and *Symposium* by R. Waterfield, *Phaedo* by D. Gallop, and *Protagoras* by C.C.W. Taylor. There is also a Clarendon translation of Plato's complete works by B. Jowett, originally published in 1892, which is currently being revised, and a Princeton University translation *Plato: The Collected Dialogues*, edited by E. Hamilton and H. Cairns.

There are commentaries on the *Apology* by M.C. Stokes, *Meno* by R.W. Sharples, *Phaedrus* by C.J. Rowe, *Republic V* and *Republic X* by S. Halliwell, *Statesman* and *Symposium* by C.J. Rowe, all in the Aris and Phillips Series, and on *Phaedo* by C.J. Rowe, *Symposium* by K. Dover, *On Poetry* (*Ion*, *Republic* 376e–398b9, 595–608b10) by P. Murray, in the Cambridge Greek and Latin Classics Series (with *Alcibiades* by N. Denyer 2001).

Further reading

Benson, H. (ed.), *Essays on the Philosophy of Socrates*, Oxford and New York: Oxford University Press, 1992.

Brunt, P.A., 'Plato's Academy and politics', in *Studies in Greek History and Thought*, Oxford: Oxford University Press, 1993, pp. 282–342.

Burnyeat, M. (ed.), *Socratic Studies*, Cambridge: Cambridge University Press, 1994.

Kahn, C.H., *Plato and the Socratic Dialogue: The Philosophical Use of a Literary Form*, Cambridge: Cambridge University Press, 1996.

Kraut, R. (ed.), *The Cambridge Companion to Plato*, Cambridge: Cambridge University Press, 1993.

Rowe, C.J., *Plato*, Brighton: Harvester Press, 1984.

Rutherford, R.B., *The Art of Plato*, London: Duckworth, 1995.

Szlezák, T.A., *Reading Plato*, London and New York: Routledge, 1999.

Vlastos, G., *Platonic Studies*, Princeton, NJ: Princeton University Press, 1981.

Vlastos, G., *Socrates. Ironist and Moral Philosopher*, Ithaca, NY: Cornell University Press, 1991.

DEMOSTHENES

If you read Plutarch's *Demosthenes*, you might well think that the life of Athens' greatest orator would make a good film. You could make so much of pivotal moments from his childhood and early youth. Since Demosthenes was a lean and sickly boy, his spiteful schoolmates called him Batalus (the name either of an effeminate flute-player or of a bawdy poet, or slang for the anus – Plutarch *Demosthenes* 4; cf. Demosthenes 18.180). His initial attempts to address the Athenian people simply made them laugh, but thanks to a kindly actor called Satyrus, and despite a speech impediment, Demosthenes persevered (Quintilian *Training in Oratory* 1.11.5) and built an underground practice room where he would often stay for two or three months in a row, shaving one side of his head to prevent himself leaving for fear that people would laugh at this bizarre haircut (Plutarch *Demosthenes* 7). His practice techniques included declaiming speeches while keeping pebbles in his mouth and exercising his voice by running up steps while reciting (Plutarch *Demosthenes* 11).

Whether such engaging stories are really true is debatable, although Demosthenes' determination to succeed is suggested by Pytheas, who complained that the orator's arguments 'smelt of lamp-wicks' (that is, were meticulously prepared late at night – Plutarch *Demosthenes* 8).[1] Nevertheless, Demosthenes, despite rather unpromising beginnings, successfully turned himself into a formidable political and rhetorical force, whose speeches offer us valuable insights about contemporary events. This is particularly lucky because the continuous historical narratives of Theopompus, Callisthenes and Ephorus have unfortunately not survived intact, although of course reading speeches for historical evidence is a tricky process. The Demosthenic *corpus*, like Julius Caesar's commentaries, can be read both from a literary and a historical angle.

Demosthenes, born in *c.* 384 BC, faced more serious problems than being teased at school. His father died when he was seven years old (*Speech* 27.4) and his guardians, especially Aphobus, subsequently tried to cream off as much money as possible from the estate. One of Demosthenes' first experiences of the law courts as a young man was to prosecute these money-grabbing guardians (*Speeches* 27–29), although he may have exaggerated the scale of his father's estate. In undertaking this prosecution, Demosthenes capitalised on his training by the talented logographer Isaeus (420–340s BC), who specialised in inheritance cases and eventually retrieved what was left of Demosthenes' property. Thereafter he began his career as a logographer in the mould of Lysias and Isaeus. One of his earliest speeches written for a client was *Against Spoudias* (*Speech* 41), about a disputed dowry, as well as *Against Callicles* (*Speech* 55), a claim for damages after a source of water had been diverted to the detriment of the plaintiff.

As time went by, Demosthenes emerged from the shadowy world of the logographers and became increasingly prominent in politics in his own right. In 354 BC Demosthenes himself delivered a speech, *Against the Law of Leptines* (*Speech* 20) in which he challenged

Leptines' law abolishing hereditary privileges awarded to public benefactors. A recurrent theme here, and in many of Demosthenes' speeches, is the problem of Athenian citizens no longer being prepared to contribute time or money for the greater good of the city. Whether Athenian citizens of past eras were ever really as selfless as Demosthenes would like to suggest is another question. His rhetoric was partly designed to stir up a sense of nostalgia in his audience, which would work to his advantage in the current court case.

In 354/353 BC Demosthenes delivered another political speech, this time a deliberative one. In *On the Symmories* (*Speech* 14) he addressed Athenian fears that the Persians might take advantage of them now that the power of the Second Athenian Confederacy was in decline. Demosthenes argued that the weakened Athenians should avoid war in the short term, but nevertheless build up their defences (particularly their fleet) in case the Persian threat became more pressing in the future.

His argument in this speech is finely balanced. If Athens behaved too aggressively, then the Persian king could exploit the suspicions of the other Greeks (always wary that Athenian imperialism might re-emerge) and isolate her; but if she prepared herself quietly, then the other Greeks would perhaps lay aside their differences with Athens and offer a united front against the Persian king. This scenario has something in common with Sallust's later theory that *metus hostilis* (fear of a common enemy) could unite the Romans in a beneficial way. Demosthenes concludes the speech:

> I recommend that you equip your forces against your existing enemies, but I add that you must employ those same forces in self-defence against the king [of Persia] and against all who venture to do you wrong, although you must not set the example of wrong, either in word or in deed.

(*Speech* 14.41)

This advice seems sensible in the circumstances. Although the collective memory of the Persian Wars had always exerted a tremendous emotional pull on the Greeks, the reality during the fourth century was that Persian money rather than Persian soldiers had caused trouble in Greece. There was no point in antagonising Persia, particularly when Athens' navy was in poor shape and the trierarchs were no longer so keen to equip and maintain triremes as they had done previously.

In the event, trouble came not from Persia, but from Macedonia, through the dynamic king Philip, who came to power in 359 BC. Theopompus said of him: 'Europe had never produced a man like Philip son of Amyntas' (Fragment 27). During the 350s BC, Philip, through military innovations, diplomacy and sheer guts, had transformed a country which had previously been ripped apart by civil war. Exploiting Athens' involvement in the Social War (357–355 BC, when her allies revolted), Philip began to expand his territories, taking Amphipolis and Pydna in 357 BC and Potidaea in 356 BC. The rise of the Macedonians didn't stop there. Philip soon gained Thessaly and exploited her resources, including the income from the harbour at Pagasai (*Speech* 1.9). Philip had also been active in Thrace, besieging Heraion Teichos on the Propontis in 352 BC, intending to gain power over Cersobleptes, one of the three kings of Thrace (*Speech* 3.4). Over this period Philip moved closer and closer to the vital Hellespontine corn route. Athens, in a panic, decided to mobilise forty triremes and to levy a war tax of sixty talents (*Speech* 3.4), but in the event the ships never sailed, since Philip was reported to be ill or dead.

In the spring of 351 BC Demosthenes delivered the *First Philippic* (*Speech* 4), the first of a series of speeches which attempts to mobilise the Athenians against Philip and the Macedonians.[2] To do this, he adopts a rather different strategy from that which he used in *On the Symmories* (*Speech* 14). Demosthenes boldly tries to shake up his listeners by triggering collective shame at their apathy towards Philip, whom he characterises as a menace:

> For observe, Athenians, the height to which the fellow's insolence has soared. He leaves you no choice of action or inaction. He blusters and talks big according to all accounts. He cannot rest content with what he has conquered. He is always taking in more, everywhere casting his net around us, while we sit idle and do nothing.
>
> (*Speech* 4.9)

Demosthenes sets up a constructive contrast between one blustering individual and the inexcusably lethargic Athenians (including Demosthenes himself: he uses the pronoun 'we'). Yet he also suggests practical measures: they should equip 50 war-galleys

(*Speech* 4.16), organise a force of 2,000 including 500 Athenians to fight Philip (*Speech* 4.19), enrol 200 cavalry (*Speech* 4.19) and resort to guerrilla tactics (*Speech* 4.23).

Demosthenes uses some typically vivid imagery in this speech: he compares the Athenians with men who model clay puppets, in that they choose their commanders for the market-place, not for the battlefield (*Speech* 4.26), and most famously he compares the Athenian reaction to Philip with a barbarian boxer, who only responds to his opponent's blows rather than attacking (*Speech* 4.40). Powerful stuff, but there were some problems with the proposals. The financial situation in Athens was dire, and even to maintain the small force suggested by Demosthenes would have presented grave problems. Also it is doubtful whether such a small army would be able to confront Philip's well-trained and experienced forces. As Cawkwell has observed, 'the great *First Philippic* was greatly wrong-headed'.[3] The Athenians (like barbarian boxers!) ignored Demosthenes' proposals for the time being, although the problems posed by Philip wouldn't disappear.

Demosthenes didn't give up, but in 349 BC delivered three speeches, the *Olynthiacs* (*Speeches* 1–3), urging the Athenians to fight Philip in the north if they wanted to avoid confronting him in Greece. The people of Olynthus hadn't always got on well with the Athenians, but Philip's successes in northern Greece had begun to worry the Olynthians, even though they were notionally his allies. Despite this, the Olynthians made peace with Athens, so Philip declared war on them. Demosthenes' *Olynthiacs* were delivered as the Athenians were considering how they should respond to the Olynthians' request for a formal alliance.

Demosthenes' practical advice was that the Athenians should send one group of soldiers to protect Olynthus and another to attack Philip's own territory (*Speech* 1.16–17). This was reinforced by some colourful denunciation of Philip and his supporters:

> All the rest about his court, he [the informant] said, are robbers and toadies, men capable of getting drunk and performing such dances as I now hesitate to name before you.

> (*Speech* 2.19; cf. Theopompus Fragment 225)

After his first two speeches, Demosthenes was partly successful since the Athenians sent a mercenary force to help the Olynthians, although it didn't include any citizens as the orator had requested.

This detachment gained a minor success against Philip, but Demosthenes was still not happy about the threat posed to Olynthus and so he delivered a third speech urging the Athenians to follow up their initial victory. It was all to no avail. In 348 BC Philip attacked Olynthus, which fell through treachery (*Speech* 19.266–67).[4] It must have been hugely shocking when Philip sold most of the inhabitants of this Greek city as slaves. To hammer the message home, Philip destroyed the city, a potent message for those thinking of defying the Macedonians.

Despite Demosthenes' consistent opposition to Philip, he was subsequently sent on an embassy to the king in 346 BC to discuss a peace settlement.[5] One result of the negotiations was the Peace of Philocrates between Athens and Macedonia; another was a bitter quarrel between Demosthenes and his fellow ambassador Aeschines, which would fester for the next sixteen years. In 343 BC Demosthenes delivered *On the False Embassy* (*Speech* 19), unsuccessfully prosecuting Aeschines for allegedly taking bribes from Philip during the negotiations. We also have Aeschines' speech in his own defence (Aeschines *Speech* 2), which criticises Demosthenes, not because he was corrupt, but because he lost his nerve in front of Philip. It is very difficult to decide which of the two speeches we should believe (or mistrust) the most, but back-to-back they make fascinating reading.

The rather shaky Peace of Philocrates just about lasted for six years, although as soon as terms were agreed it was almost inevitable that war would erupt again at some point. During this period Demosthenes attacked Philip again in the *Second Philippic* (*Speech* 6), delivered in 344 BC, and in the *Third Philippic* (*Speech* 9), delivered in 341 BC after the Macedonians had invaded Thrace. In this rousing speech Demosthenes even advised that Athens should approach Persia for money (*Speech* 9.71). Finally, in 340 BC Philip attacked the city of Perinthus (Diodorus Siculus 16.74), whose citizens were aided by the King of Persia and by the people of Byzantium. In itself, this offensive didn't concern the Athenians unduly, but when Philip concentrated on Byzantium as well, they became anxious, because the corn-ships had to pass this city on their journey from the Bosporus (Diodorus Siculus 16.77). Demosthenes, who had been waiting for just such an opportunity, arranged an alliance with the beleaguered Byzantium. Philip's response was predictable: *Speech* 12 in the Demosthenic *corpus* is actually a version of his declaration of war.

Demosthenes' hopes for a united Greek effort against Philip were boosted in 339 BC through an alliance with Athens' old enemy,

Thebes, which got jumpy when the city of Amphissa asked Philip to intervene in central Greece during the Fourth Sacred War. For a brief spell, the balance tipped in favour of the Greeks: at the Dionysiac festival of 338 BC, Demosthenes was even awarded a golden crown for his efforts. Unfortunately, it all went sour later that same year, when Philip beat the Greeks decisively at Chaeronea and imposed a political settlement on them.[6] Demosthenes, who participated in the battle himself, had to deliver the funeral oration for the dead soldiers (*Speech* 18.285).[7] It must have been devastating, but perhaps he got some comfort in 336 BC when, in a sensational *peripeteia*, Philip was assassinated at his daughter's wedding. This could have happened at any point, but it was too late for Greece. Philip's place was quickly filled by his son, Alexander the Great, and although Demosthenes briefly tried to exploit Alexander's inexperience, the boy proved even more capable than his father.

For many critics, the high-point of Demosthenes' career came in 330 BC when he delivered *On the Crown* (*Speech* 18), a defence against charges brought against him by his old rival Aeschines and a continuation of the original quarrel of 346 BC. The case centres on Ctesiphon's proposal in 336 BC that Demosthenes should receive a golden crown, which was not only a mark of respect for the orator, but also reassured those Athenians who harboured anti-Macedonian feelings. Six years later, Aeschines, seeing that Alexander had now beaten the Persian king Darius and that the Spartan revolt against Macedonia had failed, thought it was timely to prosecute Ctesiphon on the grounds that his proposal to give Demosthenes a crown had been illegal. Although Aeschines was ostensibly prosecuting Ctesiphon, his real target was Demosthenes.[8]

The trial was conducted over a single day in 330 BC, and pretty miraculously, we have both Aeschines' prosecution speech (Aeschines *Speech* 3) and Demosthenes' defence (Demosthenes *Speech* 18). These two speeches (together with Demosthenes' *On the False Embassy*, *Speech* 19, and Aeschines *Speech* 2, discussed above) are the only precisely matching pairs of prosecution and defence speeches in (what survives of) the Greek orators. If we look at all four speeches, it emerges that the version of the original events at the embassy in 346 BC presented by each orator at the *Crown* trial in 330 BC is incompatible not only with each other (which is hardly surprising), but also with their own earlier versions at the previous *Embassy* trial of 343 BC!

Demosthenes, cleverly burying his weaker arguments in the body of the speech, proudly reviews his own political career and makes a spirited personal attack on Aeschines. Despite initially claiming to find such degrading exchanges distasteful, he (and more importantly his audience) must have enjoyed the onslaught. Personal invective had a firm place in Greek (and in Roman) rhetoric, and Demosthenes deploys various modes of attack. He denounces Aeschines' father Tromes as a slave who wore thick fetters and a wooden collar (*Speech* 18.129), and who changed his name to Atrometus in a futile attempt to disguise his origins (*Speech* 18.130). Aeschines himself is characterised as a market-place hack (*Speech* 18.127), as a collaborator (*Speech* 18.139) and ultimately as the root of all evil within the city:

> I am surprised that you did not turn away from him at first sight, except that it seems a thick darkness masks you from the truth.

> (*Speech* 18.159)

We might today regard such personal attacks as inappropriate, but Demosthenes was successful. Aeschines lost the case and retired to Rhodes to teach rhetoric.

We might have expected Demosthenes to retire peacefully after his active life in politics, but this was not to be. In 324 BC, Alexander the Great's disgraced treasurer, Harpalus, arrived in Athens seeking refuge and Demosthenes advised that he should be arrested. Despite this, an allegation was soon made that Demosthenes had accepted a bribe from Harpalus, so the orator was sent into exile once it emerged that he couldn't pay his fine. After Alexander the Great died unexpectedly in 323 BC, Demosthenes was briefly recalled to Athens, but fled after the Macedonian general Antipater defeated the Athenian army at Crannon in Thessaly in 322 BC. Demosthenes escaped to the island of Calauria, but was tracked down by Antipater's soldiers, led by Archias, who was rumoured to have been a tragic actor (Plutarch *Demosthenes* 28). Demosthenes' death proved as dramatic as his early years: while pretending to write a message to his family, Demosthenes bites into a pen, which he has thoughtfully infused with poison in advance, and dies, beating his Macedonian rivals one last time (Plutarch *Demosthenes* 29).

After his death, Demosthenes was generally regarded as the most talented of the Attic orators. Several decades later, the Athenians put up a bronze statue of him, after a proposal from Demosthenes' nephew. While talking about this statue, Pausanias notes proudly that Demosthenes 'was the only Greek exile whom Archias failed to bring back to Antipater and the Macedonians' (*Description of Greece* 1.8.2–3). Physical memorials were one thing, but it was the librarians at Alexandria whose efforts to assemble Demosthenes' speeches ensured their preservation for posterity. Today we have about sixty speeches and several letters by Demosthenes, but whether these letters are genuine has been questioned.[9]

Demosthenes' influence continued to grow during the Roman period. When Cicero attacked Antony in a series of speeches, he jokingly referred to them as the *Philippics* (*Letters to Brutus* 2.3.4) and the name stuck. When Tacitus' Messalla considers the relative merits of various Attic orators, he proposes:

> Just as amongst the Attic orators the first place is awarded to Demosthenes, while Aeschines, Hyperides, Lysias and Lycurgus win the next places, so at Rome, Cicero far outstripped the other speakers of his own day.

(Tacitus Dialogus 16.3)

Indeed, Demosthenes and Cicero are often mentioned together as an idealised pair, the most talented orators of Greece and Rome respectively (for example, Juvenal *Satires* 10.114). This association was no doubt reinforced when Plutarch chose to treat Demosthenes and Cicero in the fifth book of his *Parallel Lives*. Demosthenes' works continued to be read. Pliny the Younger, sending one of his own speeches to a friend, claims to have tried to imitate Demosthenes, although he engagingly admits that he may not have succeeded (*Letters* 1.2). In his *Training in Oratory*, the rhetorician Quintilian gives many examples of Demosthenic technique for the budding orator to imitate, drawing material most frequently from *On the Crown* (*Speech* 18).

These days, we tend to be rather suspicious of clever speakers and Demosthenes is perhaps read less frequently than he deserves to be. The passion of his deliberative speeches was certainly generated by a genuine desire to counter the threat posed to Athens by Philip of Macedon (even if his proposed methods of defence have sometimes been seen as unrealistic). Tacitus' Messalla, citing Demosthenes as an example, observes that, to create decent orators, there must be decent enemies to stir their talents (*Dialogus* 38.6). Perhaps if Philip of Macedon had been assassinated much earlier, the monumental Demosthenes would have remained a competent but shadowy logographer. As it was, Demosthenes' desire to make the Athenians wake up to the threat posed by Philip resulted in a fascinating series of speeches.

Notes

1 C.B.R. Pelling, *Literary Texts and the Greek Historian*, London: Routledge, 2000, p. 14, draws attention to Demosthenes' counter-argument, that his labour was a sign of his democratic nature, since 'it showed his respect for a popular audience who needed to be persuaded, not dragooned'.
2 See H. Yunis, *Taming Democracy: Models of Political Rhetoric in Classical Athens*, Ithaca, NY, and London: Cornell University Press, 1996, pp. 257–68, on Demosthenes' speeches against Philip.
3 G. Cawkwell, *Philip of Macedon*, London: Faber and Faber, 1978, p. 82.
4 See R. Sealey, *Demosthenes and His Time: A Study in Defeat*, Oxford and New York: Oxford University Press, 1993, pp. 137–43, on the Olynthian war.
5 See Sealey, *op. cit.*, pp. 143–50, on the peace with Philip.
6 See Sealey, *op. cit.*, pp. 196–8, on Chaeronea.
7 We have what purports to be the funeral speech (*Speech* 60), but most scholars think that it is too dull to be genuine.
8 See E.M. Harris, *Aeschines and Athenian Politics*, Oxford and New York: Oxford University Press, 1995, pp. 142–8, on the Ctesiphon trial.
9 See J.A. Goldstein, *The Letters of Demosthenes*, New York and London: Columbia University Press, 1968.

See also in this book

Aristotle, Cicero, Lysias, Quintilian

Texts, translations and commentaries

The Greek text is available in OCT (3 volumes), Teubner (3 volumes) and Loeb (7 volumes).

There is the Loeb translation by J.H. Vince, but there are currently no Penguin or Oxford World's Classics translations.

There are commentaries on *Selected Private Speeches* by C. Carey and R.A. Reid in the Cambridge Greek and Latin Classics Series (with *On the Crown* by H. Yunis 2001), on *On the Crown* by S. Usher in the Aris and Phillips Series, and on *Against Meidias* and *On the False Embassy* by D. MacDowell, these last two both published by Oxford University Press.

Further reading

Cawkwell, G., *Philip of Macedon*, London: Faber and Faber, 1978.
Goldstein, J.A., *The Letters of Demosthenes*, New York and London: Columbia University Press, 1968.

Harris, E.M., *Aeschines and Athenian Politics*, Oxford and New York: Oxford University Press, 1995.

Pearson, L., *The Art of Demosthenes*, Meisenheim am Glan: Hain, 1976.

Sealey, R., *Demosthenes and His Time: A Study in Defeat*, Oxford and New York: Oxford University Press, 1993.

Todd, S.C., *The Shape of Athenian Law*, Oxford: Oxford University Press, 1993.

ARISTOTLE

In a discussion about the damaging effects on human health of drinking snow-water, the Roman polymath Aulus Gellius called Aristotle 'most skilled in all human knowledge' (*Attic Nights* 19.5.3). The sheer range of subjects tackled by Aristotle is indeed extraordinary: ethics, philosophy, politics, formal logic, psychology, rhetoric, literary theory, zoology and botany are all there.[1] Yet despite Aristotle's towering reputation today, the process by which his works reached us is unconventional, and needs clarification if we are to understand the nature of his *corpus*. His style isn't polished and elegant in the manner of Plato, but there is a reason for this.

Aristotle, as we will see, was the focus for a number of extraordinary and often romantic stories. One such tale even surrounds the publication of his writing. According to Plutarch (*Sulla* 26) and Strabo (*Geography* 13.54), the works weren't published by Aristotle himself during his lifetime, but were left at his death to his colleague Theophrastus, who in turn entrusted them to Neleus of Scepsis in Asia Minor.[2] This man's descendants kept the works hidden away in a cellar until they were eventually sold in the first century BC to a collector, who brought them to Athens. When Sulla captured the city in 86 BC, he acquired Aristotle's writings and sent them to Rome, where a grammarian, Tyrannion, bought them. The books were neglected until Andronicus of Rhodes, who was the last head of the Lyceum, the school originally founded by Aristotle, acquired them and edited them for publication in *c.* 60 BC. Andronicus tried to put the collection into some sort of order, writing notes about which works he considered genuine or spurious.

This story contains a number of startling elements. It is of course ironic that a pivotal figure in the survival of a great thinker's writings was Sulla, who spent most of his life fighting and conquering. Moreover, critics have questioned whether the members of the Lyceum would really have permitted the writings of their founder to be taken from the site in this way, whatever Theophrastus' wishes had been.

However, even if the story has been embellished, it does account for some of the distinctive characteristics of Aristotle's writings as they survive today. The various treatises haven't been polished for publication and are often compared with working drafts or lecture notes, which evolved over time but were never intended to communicate the author's views to posterity. 'Reading Aristotle, as the poet Thomas Gray put it, is like eating dried hay.'[3]

Moreover, the order of individual books within a particular work may not derive from Aristotle himself, and sometimes material is duplicated between different works (for example, *Nicomachean Ethics* 5–7 are the same as *Eudemian Ethics* 4–6). Aristotle is still eminently readable, but we should not, in these circumstances, expect him to write like Plato. In this context, we should remember Plato's critique of writing in the *Phaedrus*, where he argued that true understanding can only be generated from face-to-face discussion, not from reading a static written text. Aristotle's works as we have them were originally used as teaching tools, in conjunction with active discussion of the issues. Aulus Gellius records that Aristotle divided his work into the 'exoteric' type, which was suitable for a wide circle, and the 'acroatic' type, which was only to be heard (NB: heard) by his pupils (*Attic Nights* 20.51–6). All of the works which we have are in this second category, which 'explains why there are relatively few illustrations and almost no jokes'.[4]

Aristotle's background was rather different from that of Plato. He was born in 384 BC in the small town of Stagira in northern Greece. His father Nicomachus had moved in high circles as a doctor working for Amyntas III, the king of Macedonia, whose son, Philip II (born in 382 BC), was almost exactly the same age as Aristotle. When Aristotle was seventeen, he travelled to Athens where he joined Plato's Academy, staying there until Plato himself died in 347 BC. For someone of Macedonian origin, this was an uncomfortable time to have been living in Athens. By this stage, Philip II had started to extend his influence in such a way as to unsettle Athens (and particularly Demosthenes), so Aristotle decided to gather a group of congenial friends and to leave the city. He had accepted an invitation from Hermias, ruler of Assus in Asia Minor, to set up a school on the model of Plato's Academy. While he was doing this, he married Hermias' niece, Pythias, who bore him a daughter. Aristotle stayed at Assus for three years, after which he moved to Mytilene on the island of Lesbos, where he became particularly engaged in research on biological topics.

The tranquillity of his research was interrupted in *c.* 342 BC when he was asked by Philip II of Macedon to come to Pella and be tutor to his young son, Alexander the Great, which was an offer that Aristotle could hardly refuse. Aulus Gellius quotes a letter allegedly written by Philip to Aristotle on this topic, in which the king thanks the gods that his son was born at a time when he could profit from his teaching (*Attic Nights* 9.3).

Alexander was only thirteen at this point, but, whatever the reality of the relationship between Aristotle the philosopher and his pupil the future conqueror, it has captured the imagination of writers and painters ever since. In the twelfth century AD, for instance, the epic poet Walter of Châtillon depicts a scene in which Aristotle gives advice to his young charge. The philosopher is introduced as follows: 'It happened that his teacher, lean, pale and with uncombed hair – for his appearance did not belie his studying – had come out through the open door of his chamber, where, having recently perfected the whole *corpus* of logic, he was sharpening the weapons of proof' (*Alexandreis* 1.59ff.). One of the sources for Aristotle's subsequent speech was the *Secret of Secrets*, a book of advice on politics allegedly written for Alexander by his teacher, but really written in Syriac in the eighth century AD and translated into Latin in the twelfth century AD. There are also many illuminated manuscripts and paintings which show Alexander's education in progress, such as the illustration of Aristotle teaching Alexander from the *Treasury* of Brunetto Latini (*c.* 1210–95). This work, completed in 1265, was a compendium of history, philosophy and legend, and readers were perhaps meant to be inspired by the idea that they were following in the young Alexander's educational footsteps, led by their very own 'Aristotle'.

In reality, the teaching arrangement lasted for about three years until *c.* 339 BC, when Aristotle returned to Stagira. In 336 BC, Philip was assassinated and Alexander was proclaimed king of Macedonia in complicated domestic circumstances, which were hardly the ideal basis for his campaigns of conquest. Aristotle returned to Athens where, just outside the city, he established his own school, the Lyceum, which must in some sense have been a rival to Plato's Academy. Here, Aristotle gave lectures on a wide variety of topics, until the death of his old pupil Alexander the Great in 323 BC once again triggered a wave of hostile feelings against Macedonia in Athens. Aristotle felt that it was safer to leave, even though five years earlier in 328 BC, his own nephew, Callisthenes, had been charged with treason by Alexander and put to death. Aristotle retreated to the relative safety of Chalcis in Euboea, where he died in 322 BC. His pupil, Theophrastus, became head of the Lyceum after his death.

What were Aristotle's main intellectual achievements? His work in the area of logic has had a particularly significant impact.[5] Aristotle wrote broadly within this field (*Categories, On Interpretation, Prior Analytics, Posterior Analytics, Topics* and *Sophistical Refutations*), but his *Prior Analytics* has perhaps been most influential. In this work, he investigates a process of deductive argument known as the syllogism, which is a technical system of reasoning based on two premises and a conclusion, and which can be perfect or imperfect, depending on whether the premises are valid.[6] Aristotle explains:

> A Syllogism is a form of words in which certain things are assumed and there is something other than what was assumed which necessarily follows from things being so. By 'from' I mean 'because of' ...

> (*Prior Analytics* 24b)

Barnes gives an example: 'Every animal that breathes possesses lungs; every viviparous animal breathes; therefore every viviparous animal possesses lungs'.[7]

It is particularly impressive that Aristotle's system became the basis for formal logic as a distinct discipline until the nineteenth century. It also enabled Aristotle to question certain propositions put forward by Plato, such as his suggestion in the *Meno* that knowledge is recollection (*Prior Analytics* 67a). Aristotle thought that the study of logic was necessary to acquire knowledge in other areas, whether science or philosophy. Later commentators on Aristotle's treatises on logic coined the name *Organon* ('tool') for them, which reflects their utilitarian nature.

Aristotle addresses broader questions about existence, being and knowledge in his *Metaphysics*.[8] This work includes a valuable summary of the ideas of some pre-Socratic philosophers about the constituent elements from which things are made and about the agent who made them. Aristotle sets up his own ideas against the backdrop of a philosophical tradition, which he is prepared to criticise. His main concern is to investigate the 'theory of being as being and of what "to be" means' (*Metaphysics* 1003a), but not in an isolated or piecemeal way as others had done before him. This desire to see the whole picture also manifests itself in his works on natural history, where his concern is to look at phenomena (such as movement) which transcend different species of animals. The *Metaphysics* also contains a useful glossary of terminology such as 'being', 'beginning' and 'necessary'.

A significant proportion of Aristotle's writings deals with natural science, although his work in this area was gradually superseded from the sixteenth century onwards. In the *Physics*, he examines fundamental concepts such as motion in relation to space, position and time, which culminates in his theory of the 'Unmoved Mover' as the ultimate cause of motion. This idea became particularly important in the thirteenth century in the thinking of Thomas Aquinas, who tried to explore the connections between faith and reason and to link the existence of God with Aristotle's notion of the 'Unmoved Mover'.

As well as this general discussion of movement, Aristotle turned his attention to specific aspects of the natural world in *On the Heavens, On Generation and Corruption, Meteorology, History of Animals, Generation of Animals* and *Parts of Animals*. He argues that there is no animal from which we cannot learn something: 'We must avoid a childish distaste for examining the less valued animals, for in all natural things there is something wonderful' (*Parts of Animals* 645a). His interests are broad, ranging from why front teeth are formed first and the grinders later (*Generation of Animals* 788b) to whether the foetus has a soul (*Generation of Animals* 736a).

Nor does Aristotle examine the physical nature of animals in isolation from psychology.[9] Other treatises include *On the Soul, On Memory, On Sleep* and his fascinating discussion *On Dreams*. Here, he argues that dreams are a product of overactive sensory perceptions, which continue to perceive impressions when the real object has gone: if someone looks at the sun or another bright object and then closes their eyes, then the image will persist, turning from crimson, to purple, to black, until it eventually disappears (*On Dreams* 459b). This pattern mirrors what happens when a person dreams. Dreams are therefore presented as a phenomenon which can be explained scientifically, rather than as being sent by the gods. Aristotle is an independent thinker, as we can see from another work: 'That, therefore, the soul or certain parts of it, if it is divisible, cannot be separated from the body is quite clear' (*On the Soul* 413a). We see here that he is prepared to diverge from one of the central doctrines of his teacher Plato.

His most popular works today address ethics and politics, namely the *Nicomachean Ethics*, the *Eudemian Ethics* and the *Politics*. The *Nicomachean Ethics*[10] examines some fundamental issues, such as the object of life, moral goodness, responsibility, justice, the nature of pleasure and the grounds for friendship. Aristotle hopes that by enhancing our knowledge of what is good, we will have a clearer target at which to aim in conducting our lives. He presents himself as a benign guide, who is prepared to embrace diversity and to deal with practical issues, rather than as a distant and authoritative figure who has all the answers. His narrative persona is that of a realist, as when he observes: 'Conscious of their own ignorance, most people are impressed by anyone who pontificates and says something that is over their heads' (*Nicomachean Ethics* 1095a). He often backs up his points with references to familiar examples from the poets and tragedians, particularly Hesiod, Homer, Sophocles and Euripides. Thus, his discussion of abstract moral questions is often rooted in the audience's familiarity with particular works of literature. In the end, Aristotle proposes that the rational activity of contemplation is the best way to secure happiness in human life.

In the *Politics*, Aristotle takes up some of the same questions, but looks at them in a broader context of communal life.[11] He considers that man is an animal meant to live in a *polis* and examines how mankind interacts with different kinds of states and societies. Issues of slavery, property, education and citizenship are discussed, as well as the reasons for the disintegration of order within a state. This task is undertaken systematically in order to determine how each type of state can avoid being crippled by revolution. In this work, Aristotle began a description of his own ideal state, which is incomplete and stops in the middle of a discussion of music.

Finally, Aristotle also wrote about literature and oratory in the *Poetics* and the *Art of Rhetoric*.[12] Plato in the *Gorgias* had examined the question of whether rhetoric was an art or a *techne*, and proved himself ultimately to be ambivalent about the role of rhetoric within a state, at least as it was practised by men like Gorgias, Polus and Callicles. Aristotle sees rhetoric more positively as the technique of discovering the persuasive aspects of any given subject, and sets out to explore the mechanisms by which it achieved its effects. In particular, Aristotle is interested in the character of the speaker, in the susceptibility of the audience to emotion and in the arguments used in the speech itself. There are certainly points of contact between the *Art of Rhetoric* and the *Poetics*, particularly through the focus of both works on pity (*Art of Rhetoric* 1385b–1386b, *Poetics* 1453b). There was originally a second book of the *Poetics*, now lost, which contained Aristotle's views on comedy,[13] and which became a focus for Umberto Eco in his novel *The Name of the Rose*.

Aristotle's influence on later thinkers was considerable and extended over many centuries. Alexander of Aphrodisias, who taught Aristotelian philosophy at the end of the second century AD, was perhaps the most important commentator on Aristotle in antiquity.[14] There was an explosion of interest in Aristotle's thinking during the twelfth-century Renaissance, after his works were translated into Latin via the Greek and the Arabic versions. One of the leading figures in making the works of Aristotle accessible for a wider audience was the Moorish author, Averroes (Ibn Rushd, who died in 1198), who produced commentaries on Aristotle's works.[15] Once the 'Latin Aristotle' had become established in the scholarly community, it led to the emergence during the twelfth century of Scholasticism, the intellectual system which employed Aristotelian logic to investigate the relationship between revelation and reason, and which was soon used to challenge accepted theological systems.

As a result, Aristotle's works had potentially become a dangerous area for scholars. In 1210, for instance, a committee of Parisian clergy decided to ban the *Notebooks* of one Aristotelian, David of Dinant, decreeing at the same time that there were to be no lectures on Aristotle's natural philosophy held in Paris publicly or privately. The ban may have caused temporary problems, but interest in Aristotle continued unabated all over Europe in the following centuries. Leading figures included Leonardo Bruni, George of Trezibond, Pietro Pomponazzi, Jacopo Zabarella and John Case. Aristotle's ideas were not always used judiciously, however, as when the *Politics* was taken up by defenders of Spanish colonial policy in the sixteenth century to argue that slavery was a natural state for Indians. It was fortunate that a priest, Francesco de Vitoria, felt obliged to step in and to use his knowledge of Aristotle's philosophy to attack this stance. The reception of Aristotle's writings is a fascinating topic in its own right.

Notes

1   There is a huge amount of modern bibliography on Aristotle. See J. Barnes (ed.), *The Cambridge Companion to Aristotle*, Cambridge: Cambridge University Press, 1995, pp. 298–384, for invaluable guidance.
2   On Neleus of Scepsis, see L. Canfora, *The Vanished Library*, Berkeley and Los Angeles, CA: University of California Press, 1990, pp. 26–9.
3   Barnes, *op. cit.*, p. 12.
4   *Ibid.*
5   On Aristotle and logic, see R. Smith in Barnes, *op. cit.*, pp. 27–65.

6 See further G. Patzig, *Aristotle's Theory of the Syllogism*, Dordrecht: Reidel, 1968.
7 Barnes, *op. cit.*, p. 30.
8 On the *Metaphysics*, see J. Barnes in Barnes, *op. cit.*, pp. 66–108.
9 On Aristotle and psychology, see S. Everson in Barnes, *op. cit.*, pp. 168–94.
10 See further D.S. Hutchinson in Barnes, *op. cit.*, pp. 195–232.
11 See further C.C.W. Taylor in Barnes, *op. cit.*, pp. 233–58.
12 See further J. Barnes in Barnes, *op. cit.*, pp. 259–85.
13 See R. Janko, *Aristotle on Comedy*, London: Duckworth, 1984.
14 See further R. Sorabji (ed.), *Aristotle Transformed: The Ancient Commentators and Their Influence*, London: Duckworth, 1990.
15 See further M. Fakhry, *Averroes, Aquinas and the Rediscovery of Aristotle in Western Europe*, Washington, D.C.: Georgetown University Press, 1996.

See also in this book

Cicero, Lucretius, Plato

Texts, translations and commentaries

The Greek text is available in OCT and Teubner, although neither publishes all of Aristotle's works. It is also available in Loeb (23 volumes).

As well as the Loeb, there are Oxford World's Classics translations of *Nicomachean Ethics* by D. Ross (revised by J.R. Ackrill and J.O. Urmson), *Physics* by R. Waterfield and *Politics* by E. Barker (revised by R.F. Stalley), and Penguin translations of *De Anima*, *Art of Rhetoric* and *Metaphysics* by H. Lawson-Tancred, *Athenian Constitution* by P.J. Rhodes, *Politics* by T.A. Sinclair, *Classical Literary Criticism* (includes the *Poetics*) by T.S. Dortsch (revised by P. Murray), *Ethics* and *Nicomachean Ethics* by J.A.K. Thomson and *Poetics* by M. Heath, and a Hackett translation of the *Nicomachean Ethics* by T. Irwin. There is also *The Complete Works of Aristotle: The Revised Oxford Translation*, Princeton, NJ: Princeton University Press, 1984, edited by J. Barnes and very useful, and the 'Clarendon Aristotle' translated by W.D. Ross.

There are commentaries to *On the Heavens I and II* by S. Leggatt and *On Sleep and Dreams* by D. Gallop, both in the Aris and Phillips Series, and on the *Athenian Constitution* by P.J. Rhodes, published by Oxford University Press.

Further reading

Ackrill, J.L., *Aristotle the Philosopher*, Oxford: Oxford University Press, 1981.
Barnes, J., *Aristotle*, Oxford: Oxford University Press, 1982.
Barnes, J. (ed.), *The Cambridge Companion to Aristotle*, Cambridge: Cambridge University Press, 1995.
Edel, A., *Aristotle and His Philosophy*, Chapel Hill, NC: University of North Carolina Press, 1982.

Lloyd, G.E.R., *Aristotelian Explorations,* Cambridge: Cambridge University Press, 1996.

Lynch, J.P., *Aristotle's School: A Study of a Greek Educational Institution,* Berkeley, Los Angeles and London: University of California Press, 1972.

Rihll, T.E., *Greek Science,* Greece and Rome New Surveys in the Classics 29, Oxford: Oxford University Press, 1999.

HELLENISTIC

MENANDER

The comic playwright Menander gives Classicists hope: hope that new discoveries of ancient texts might be just round the corner and hope that we might be the descendants of the intrepid Edwardian explorers who, like scholarly versions of Harrison Ford, boldly went into the dark places of Egypt and of museum mummy-collections to bring out these great lost treasures of the past. Menander is certainly one of the most romantic of ancient authors: fêted to excess in antiquity (the great literary scholar of the third century BC, Aristophanes of Byzantium, rated him second only to Homer;[1] a view echoed by, among others, Quintilian – *Training in Oratory* 10.1.69–72), his works were almost entirely lost in the eighth and ninth centuries, and were known only through a few scattered quotations until the late nineteenth century. They were also 'known', or guessed at, through the Roman adaptations of them by Plautus and Terence, which seemed to scholars to offer a dark glass in which glimpses of dramatic perfection might be caught. Then in 1898 came the publication of 80 lines of *Georgos* ('The Farmer'), followed in 1907 by substantial fragments of several more plays, discovered during the excavation of a sixth-century AD house in Egypt. The story goes quiet for half a century after this, until between 1959 and 1969 (living memory, just about, to Classicists active as I write this) large finds from papyri in the library of the Swiss collector Bodmer, and from papyri extracted from mummy wrappings, produced the complete *Dyskolos* ('Old Cantankerous') and several other substantial fragments, some new, some overlapping and elucidating what was already known.[2]

It is odd that this heroic story of discovery should come up with something so bourgeois, so nice, so understated as Menander's upmarket soap opera. The plays are stories of human relationships, romantic love, parents, children, siblings, friends and neighbours: their lives, fortunes, births and (occasionally) deaths, all in a small way, all set in contemporary Athens or possibly other Greek cities, nothing terribly dire or dramatic, but pleasant tales where the good win out and hardly anyone lacks at least a spark of goodness. The plays' virtues are neat plotting, clever characterisation, elegant diction and a kind of realist escapism.

Menander was an Athenian, born in 342 or 341 BC. He died sometime between 293 and 289 BC, by drowning while swimming in the Piraeus (the harbour of Athens) according to tradition. During his lifetime, he composed something like 105 plays, many but not all of which would have been produced for the major Athenian dramatic festivals (City Dionysia and Lenaea), others in lesser rural Dionysia and at festivals in other cities. There are only eight recorded victories. Athenian public life at this time was active, but troubled, with power changing hands several times between different factions, often with violent consequences for the ousted group. Menander is said to have been a friend of the oligarchic governor of Athens, Demetrius of Phaleron. Tradition has it that when Demetrius was expelled by Demetrius Poliorketes in 307 BC, Menander was only saved by the intervention of the liberator's cousin Telesphoros. The fact that Menander's comedy is domesticated, then, in contrast with the political activism of Old Comedy, is not because public life was no longer interesting.

The history of Western drama has an odd Menander-shaped hole in it. A giant in ancient literary history, yet lost for most of the post-antique period (it is worth remembering that Oscar Wilde wrote *The Importance of Being Earnest* three years before the publication of even the *Georgos* fragment), he nonetheless represents an important link in the chain from fifth-century Athens to the present day. In brief, Menander develops both the comedy and the tragedy of the late fifth and early fourth centuries, via the almost entirely lost Middle Comedy of the fourth century, into his social drama; Plautus and Terence then in some (complex) sense 'translate' the comedy of the late fourth and third centuries (Menander and others) into a Roman context. It is this Roman comedy which has an enormous influence over early modern playwrights such as Shakespeare, Marlowe, Molière, Sheridan and even, differently, on other genres such as the comic novel. Despite the loss of so much dramatic literature between the death of Aristophanes and the first plays of Plautus, however, it is possible to see something of what was happening, and to see the importance of Menander in the developments.

For example, as far as we can tell Menander adhered to the five-act structure, with song and dance, irrelevant to the play, performed by a chorus between the acts. Only on their first appearance are they even noted by the protagonists, who say something like 'let's get out of the way; I can see a band of young drunks arriving and this is no time to mix with them'. This chorus is the direct descendant of the integral chorus of fifth-century tragedy, and of such famous and outrageous Aristophanic choruses as the Frogs, the Birds and the women who go on sex-strike in *Lysistrata*. Afterwards, the Romans performed their plays continuously, mostly without choruses, even though traces of the five-act structure can be seen. Yet this structure was picked up, without a chorus at all, by the early modern playwrights.

Menander's new comedy is, formally, the direct descendant of Aristophanes' obscene, virile, politically outspoken Old Comedy (although even Aristophanes was softening towards the end); moreover, Menander's comedy is just as much derived from the tragedies of Euripides as it is from the comedies of Aristophanes. All ancient comedy has an important intertextual relationship with tragedy, but for Menander it isn't just a matter of reaction, or parody, or inversion, but of a more direct interaction. One place where we can seen this clearly, partly because he is explicit about it, is in *Epitrepontes* ('The Arbitrants').

The play is about a man who has left his wife because she produced a baby five months after marriage, the result of a previous rape when she was attending an evening festival. It will turn out that the rapist was none other than the husband himself. Unlike in Terence's *Hecyra*, which has a similar plot, the young man is allowed to realise his cruelty in rejecting his wife *before* it becomes known (to him) that the baby is his own. The arbitration from which the play takes its name is a vignette of the private/public life of Athens, home of justice, in which two lower-class people[3] ask a passing gentleman to settle their argument. Daos, a shepherd, had found an exposed baby, together with some jewellery and other items. Syros, a charcoal-burner, begged to be allowed to bring up the baby. This was granted, but the trinkets kept. The charcoal-burner now demands the return of the tokens to the baby. The old gentleman decides in favour of the baby, who unknown to him (but known to the audience) is his own grandson, the product of the pre-marital rape. During the scene, the charcoal-burner draws explicit attention to the importance of such tokens for dramatic recognition, giving examples from tragic myth. Just in case we missed the point, at the resolution of the play, as the slave Onesimos is explaining the plot to the old gentleman Smikrines, he starts quoting a speech from Euripides' *Auge* (now lost) and offers to give him the whole thing if he still doesn't understand what has happened. That play must have had a similar plot to *Epitrepontes*, but it is only one of many.

Recognition of children exposed or stolen by pirates or otherwise lost, recognition that a beloved girl is a citizen and so marriageable, that an apparent rival is the beloved's brother, or (as here in *Epitrepontes*) that the rapist is now the husband, or that for some other reason the Problem of the play isn't a problem – these are the stuff of comedy. But recognition, as Aristotle showed, is also the stuff of tragedy. The greatest tragic plots, according to Aristotle (*Poetics* 1452b10), are those where the recognition (anagnorisis) and the change of fortune (*peripeteia*) are intimately bound up in each other, as in classic examples like Sophocles' *Oedipus the King*. Indeed, so they are in many plays of Menander. Moreover, plays like *Epitrepontes* share, in their different way, with great tragedies like *Oedipus the King*, the themes of personal and civic identity, of legitimacy, and of the preciousness and precariousness of family relationships.

Most of the plays are gentle love stories in one way or another. But just a minute! To say that is to buy into the plays' treatment of women, which involves young girls being casually raped, blamed for it, made to expose their babies and then expected to slip happily into marriage with the man whom society says is Mr Right. Gentle? Well, yes, in their own terms. Perhaps it is possible, without undermining the seriousness of ancient misogyny, to see these rapes as failed attempts at the marriage which is the ultimate aim of comedy – deriving as it does from the big celebration of sex, consensus, unity, fertility, stability and feasting that ends an Aristophanic play. It is hardly surprising that the plays fail to see things from the woman's point of view. This is a society in which, in the normal way of things, a girl with whom a young man can respectably meet and form a relationship is not a girl whom he can respectably marry. Therefore, if he knows her to be a citizen, the interaction must be rape, while if it is a consensual relation he must believe her to be for some reason not marriageable, most likely because she is thought to be not a citizen.

Okay, let's call them gentle love stories. But they are also about many other things, and this fact, in the eyes of many critics, is what raises them to the level of high art. *Samia* ('The Woman from Samos') is about adoption and relationships between father and son, as well as between (male) neighbours; *Aspis* ('The Shield') is about the effects of war and of Athenian inheritance law on family life, offering a clever variation on the moral that money is the root of all evil. It is an interesting play for social historians, because the plot is based around the Athenian practice of the epiklerate, according to which if a man dies leaving only a daughter, then the nearest male relative, often (as here) an uncle, can marry her and inherit the estate, in trust, so to speak, for the expected child who will be the descendant of the girl's father.[4] If he doesn't wish to marry her, he should arrange an appropriate alternative. The marriage of niece and uncle wasn't considered incestuous, nor indeed was that between half-siblings, as long as the father was the common parent.

The best known Menandrian play, although unfortunately not the best, is *Dyskolos* – best known not only because it is the only complete play in existence, but also because the 'angry old man' has so important a progeny in European comedy (but see below). Again, the love story is a hook for a study of antisocial behaviour. The old man rejects society – because *it* is bad, not because *he* is – and tries to live in total independence. He will not even enter into that crucial aspect of societal interaction, arranging a marriage for his daughter. This kind of behaviour is anathema to the communitarian ethos of ancient Athens and so Knemon must learn to join in. The play is resolved by Knemon falling down a well and acknowledging that he needs help (and therefore also marrying off his daughter to the right person); this resolution is given an unusually comic turn in the final scene, when the old man is ragged and teased by a cook and slave into joining in the party. This is almost the only farcical scene in extant Menander.

The 'angry old man' becomes a very important stock character in Roman comedy, although whether one could simply call it a stock character in Menander is, I think, open to debate. Likewise, the soldiers of *Misoumenos* ('The Hated Man') and *Perikeiromene* ('The Girl whose Hair is Cut'), if rather impulsive and inclined to violence, display no more than a hint of the arrogance and absurdity of the Roman boastful warrior. New Comedy, whether Greek or Roman, is easily associated by critics with stock plots and stock characters; indeed, it is a crucial feature of this kind of drama that the audience should be able to recognise the type of character easily, have certain expectations of it, and enjoy both the fulfilment and the neatly judged breaking of those expectations. Sometimes even the names of characters will point us into particular ways of reading them, although we should be careful about being taken in. Smikrines in *Epitrepontes* isn't really a villain, although his namesake in *Aspis* is, and critics often judge the *Epitrepontes* Smikrines harshly partly as a result. The same point about recognition also goes for plot: the eternal comfort of comedy is that everything will turn out right in the end.

This brings me to a final and crucial point about Menander – his realism. Famously, Aristophanes of Byzantium apostrophised Menander like this: 'Menander, life, which of you imitated the other?' He thus sets Menander firmly within the aesthetic of illusionist realism, which dominates large areas of ancient artistic theory. Given the hegemony of realist theatre in the last two centuries, Menander's development of the realist drive in Euripides and to a lesser extent Aristophanes is particularly important for his reception, as well as for the history of drama. We can see this realism in technical ways: although the plays are in verse, they are mostly in iambic trimeter and trochaic tetrameter, metres that reflect the rhythms of everyday speech; the actors wear masks, but ordinary Athenian clothes (no padding, no over-sized phalluses); the settings are local and contemporary; the plots are credible, give or take the odd extraordinary coincidence. But there is more to it than that. Perhaps something which Menander understood better than some of his critics have done is that 'character' in life and in literature is a complex amalgam of the conventional and the individual. Much has been made of the tradition that Menander was a friend and pupil of the philosopher Theophrastus, himself a pupil of Aristotle, and the author of a treatise on *Characters*, while (conversely) Menander's many admirers wax lyrical about the delicacy and realistic power of his characterisation of individuals. We need not see a contradiction here, if we remember that 'all the world's a stage'.

Notes

1 The statement is frequently quoted, for example as *testimonium* 61 in the Teubner edition of Menander.

2 Details of this story, told more soberly, can be found in the introduction to A.W. Gomme and F.H. Sandbach, *Menander: A Commentary*, Oxford: Oxford University Press, 1973, pp. 3–4.

3 Their names, Daos and Syros, suggest that they could be slaves; their comparative independence might suggest otherwise, although that might be a joke. They are considered slaves by Gomme and Sandbach, *op. cit.*, p. 290.

4 In this play, the epiklerate possibility is raised twice. The first is the case of a brother who dies, apparently leaving his sister in the situation in which she would have been, had the brother predeceased the father and the father now died. This play offers the only recorded case of a sister as apparently epikleros, which makes it particularly interesting for sociolegal historians, as does the fact that Smikrines assumes priority because he is older. Primogeniture is not normally significant in Athenian inheritance law.

See also in this book

Aristophanes, Euripides, Plautus, Terence

Texts, translations and commentaries

The OCT is by F.H. Sandbach, revised with appendix (1990). There is also a Teubner, edited by A. Koerte and A. Thierfelder (1953). The Loeb edition has been revised recently (2000).

The 1987 Penguin translation by N. Miller is fine, and a World's Classics edition was published in 2001.

A major scholarly commentary is A.W. Gomme and F.H. Sandbach, *Menander: A Commentary*, Oxford: Oxford University Press, 1973. There are Aris and Phillips editions of *The Bad-Tempered Man* (*Dyskolos*, sometimes called 'Old Cantankerous') and *Samia*.

Further reading

Goldberg, S.M., *The Making of Menander's Comedy*, London: Athlone, 1980.

Hunter, R.L., *The New Comedy of Greece and Rome*, Cambridge: Cambridge University Press, 1985.

Segal, E. (ed.), *Oxford Readings in Menander, Plautus and Terence*, Oxford: Oxford University Press, forthcoming.

Webster, T.B.L., *An Introduction to Menander*, Manchester: Manchester University Press, 1974.

Wiles, D., *The Masks of Menander: Sign and Meaning in Greek and Roman Performance*, Cambridge: Cambridge University Press, 1991.

CALLIMACHUS

'A big book is a big evil' (fragment 465). This judgement on literature and size by the Hellenistic scholar-poet Callimachus is ideal for quoting in a range of circumstances, but what exactly this author of 'many thousands of lines' (fr. 1.4) may have meant by his indictment of 'bigness' has become a matter for scholarly debate and polemic which would no doubt have amused him. For later Roman poets and for modern critics, Callimachus embodies a particular kind of poetry: short (in a sense), highly wrought, self-conscious, polished, sophisticated, erudite, abstruse, playful, delicate, ironic – in sum: 'literary'. The Roman poets, almost to a man, were devoted to him, and would frequently claim, directly or indirectly, to be 'Callimachean', although the exact nature of this 'Callimacheanism' is as shifting and unstable as an artful literary aesthetic may be.

Callimachus, born in around 320 BC (or possibly as late as 305), was a native of Cyrene, where he is likely to have belonged to the local aristocracy. He claims (whether really or as a literary game) descent from the legendary king Battus. He spent much of his life writing and studying at the courts of the Ptolemaic kings of Alexandria, in what was no doubt a privileged position within that highly cultured environment. Ptolemy I Soter and his successors aimed to make the great library at Alexandria into the ancient equivalent of a copyright library, in which the librarians sought to collect copies of every Greek manuscript in existence. Recent evidence shows that Callimachus was never chief librarian (we should be wary of imagining that such terms translate directly from our own experience) but it is clear from his encyclopedic works that the library was part of his life. Indeed, he is believed to have drawn up a catalogue of the library's holdings.[1] Like most literary men in Greek antiquity, he travelled widely. Callimachus probably lived until some time in the 240s or 230s BC.[2]

On the evidence of the *Suda*, Callimachus' output was vast, some 800 books, but the only works to have survived by manuscript tradition are the six *Hymns*, plus a selection of epigrams (very short poems in elegiac couplets). Other works survive in fragmentary form, through quotations in later ancient writers, through the *diegeseis* (singular: *diegesis*) which are summaries and first lines of Callimachean stories, and through papyrus finds, which have been relatively kind to Callimachean scholars. The main fragmentary works are the *Aetia* (an elegiac poem on origins), the *Hecale* (a mini-epic poem about Theseus and an old woman who entertained him) and the *Iambs* (miscellaneous poems in iambic metres). Callimachus also wrote other epic and elegiac poems (of which there are a few fragments), and many learned works in prose and verse, including studies of *The Names of Months according to Peoples and Cities, On the Rivers of Europe* and *On Changes in the Names of Fishes*, to mention but a few from the selection recorded in the *Suda*. There were also cataloguing works, such as one of 'those who distinguished themselves in all branches of learning, and their writings, in 120 books' (so claims the *Suda*) and a 'catalogue and record of playwrights, arranged chronologically from the beginning'. This isn't to mention the tragedies, comedies, satyr plays and songs that the *Suda* throws in almost incidentally. Even if the *Suda* is exaggerating, and giving Callimachus at least one of everything, there should be no doubt that his work was formidable. A big book is a big evil?

It isn't surprising that this most literary of geniuses should be also a highly intertextual poet. Not only was Callimachus extraordinarily well read, but also he tended to couch his thoughts on the nature of poetry in terms of comparisons with other poets (more on this below). Despite the 'newness' which many people have seen in Hellenistic poetry, all of Callimachus' works beg to be read against the background of great predecessors. Homeric vocabulary, phrases, stories, structures and scenes are used and neatly twisted, while archaic lyric and iambic, drama, and more recent literature in various forms, all contribute to Callimachean texts. Moreover, in common with many ancient poets, Callimachus saw poetry as a dynamic creative process rather than a finished product. Although the Latin poets seem to have inherited this interest from Callimachus, it is prevalent also in the archaic Pindar, among others. The metaphors for poetry of weaving, sculpting, building and painting reflect this emphasis, as (differently) do those of flying and driving, and (differently again) drinking. This approach is perhaps foreign to many modern readers' expectations of poetry, but is fundamental to ancient ways of reading.

Callimachus' six hymns were probably written for performance, but not actually as part of the ritual itself, as would have been the case for the hymns of archaic poets such as Pindar or the *Hymns* attributed to Homer.[3] The game the Callimachean hymns play with their audience and with the archaic hymns is to create an atmosphere of greater naïve religiosity and mimetic (imitative) realism than do the genuinely cultic hymns.[4] At the opening of *Hymn* II (to Apollo), for example, the speaker heralds an actual epiphany of the god, calling attention to the shaking of the sacred emblems which indicates that the divinity is approaching. No-one is meant straightforwardly to believe this, but rather to see it as a literary, cultural and intertextual pose which is hymnic, poetic and antiquarian.

In the first *Hymn* (to Zeus) celebration of the god is interspersed with learned enquiry (for example, into Zeus' birthplace); playful, enigmatic jokes like the famous proverb 'Cretans are always liars' (8); mythic narrative; learned (but also pious) correction of common misconceptions about the god; and a delicate hint at courtly praise, when the justice of Zeus is presented as communicating itself into the greatness of 'our king' (probably Ptolemy II Philadelphus). In all the hymns the extraordinary (even bizarre), the delicate and the divine are exquisitely balanced. We see the unborn Apollo giving his mother advice from the womb (*Hymn* IV, to Delos, 162–95); the three-year-old Artemis tearing out the hair from a Cyclops' chest (*Hymn* III, to Artemis); the nymph Chariclo's grief and sense of betrayal when her son Tiresias is blinded for seeing Athene bathing (*Hymn* V, On the Bath of Pallas, 85–92: Chariclo was a companion of the goddess). The Greek gods are still powerful and terrible, still beautiful and superhuman, even when tempered with Hellenistic realism and interest in the emotional.

The *Hecale* has been taken by critics ancient and modern as Callimachus' answer to epic. It is a continuous narrative of a heroic subject, written in hexameters – yet it cannot have run to more than 1,000 or perhaps 1,500 lines.[5] The heroic story of Theseus' battle with the bull of Marathon is the minor key in a contrapuntal relationship with the hospitality offered by the poor old woman, Hecale, to the hero on his outward journey, and the institution of rites in her honour after he returns to find her dead. But the hospitality in Hecale's hut is itself bound up in the Homeric scene in the hut of Eumaeus, when Odysseus returns to Ithaca, disguised as a beggar (*Odyssey* 14). This is how Callimachean intertextuality works: it must belie any attempt to make simplistic judgements about rigid generic difference. Despite its fragmentary state, the poem exhibits many traits we would associate with Callimachus and Hellenistic poetry: an interest in obscure myths about famous heroes, compressed heroic narrative, emphasis on realism and the emotions, heroism cut down to size but still heroic, intertextuality and generic playfulness. Even this relatively short poem has a complex, highly wrought structure, with embedded narratives such as the story of the birth of Ericthonius (a foundation story for Athens), which may well have been narrated by the crow who is also part of the story. Embedded narratives are as old as Homer, but this subtle interweaving of levels is something in which Callimachus excelled and which later poets, such as Ovid, learned in part from him.

One place where the use of alternative speakers was expected was in the epigram. This literary form derives from the inscriptions carved on dedications and tombstones, in which it is common for the item itself or the dead person to be represented as the speaker: from these beginnings develops a genre of short elegiac poems on a range of topics. Callimachus' own contributions now exist only in a few fragments; there are many other Hellenistic and later epigrams collected in the *Greek Anthology* (available in a Loeb edition).

Callimachus used the conceit of the variant speaker also in other poems, where gods/statues or other items speak. In *Aetia* fr. 97, it is apparently a wall which speaks. Boundaries were of course very significant in myths of origins. In *Iamb* 7 it is clear from the *diegesis* and the one extant fragment that a statue of Hermes Perpheraios speaks, explaining his name by relating the story of how his divinity had been proven to some fishermen who tried unsuccessfully to destroy him (the statue/god). A rite was established which involved them passing the statue from one to another (hence the name – 'carried around').

The most delightful example of the talking god is fr. 114 of the *Aetia*, in which the statue of Apollo at Delos gets into conversation with the poet, describes his spectacular attributes in response to questioning, and finally explains why it is that he carries a bow in his left hand, but in his right hand the Graces (he is more inclined to give blessings than punishment). What would it be like to question the art-treasures in the British Museum or the cathedral at Turin about themselves? Yet alongside this fantasy comes the image of the reporter interviewing a famous and rather conceited star. The statue even, quite naturally, swears 'by me' (that is, by Apollo) in affirmation of the question about his height (eighteen cubits – about 27 feet).

The talking Apollo should be seen in the same light as the dialogue between the poet and the Muses through which the first two books of the *Aetia* are structured. Not only is this a clever way of creating a framework for a range of stories, a way of writing catalogue poetry without it getting monotonous, but also it is a playful development of the traditional relationship between the poet and the Muse, going back at least to Hesiod's meeting with the Muses on Helicon (reflected in fr. 2 of the *Aetia*), and made into a hint at a metaphor for studious research. The *Aetia* is both a 'sweet' poem (the term is Callimachean) and a learned catalogue of how things came to be as they are. Just how much 'unity' the collection (or the poem) has, or whether the poem (or collection) is really a set of disparate tales loosely linked (quite possibly later than their original composition) by a weak framework and a common interest in beginnings, remains a matter for scholarly debate, hampered by the fragmentary state of the text.

An aetion is a story of how things came to be as they are. Some of the narratives that arise out of aetia are only a few lines long, or even just a hint, but others are developed into longer stories. Probably the most famous, and one of the longest that can be pieced together, is the story of Acontius and Cydippe (frr. 67–75). It is a beautiful story of a young man's success in love – and his grotesque manipulation of the power of speech. Acontius is in love with Cydippe, both as lovely as each other. In the temple of Artemis, Acontius throws down an apple inscribed with the words 'I swear by Artemis to marry Acontius'. Cydippe duly reads this aloud and thereby binds herself unwittingly. Several attempts to marry her to other men are forestalled by sudden illness, until her father consults the oracle at Delphi, which tells him that he must marry his daughter to Acontius. All ends, of course, happily. The poet tells us (fr. 75) that his source was Xenomedes, who wrote a mythology history of Ceos (from where Acontius came). As we might expect, he doesn't lose the opportunity for glances at a few more myths briefly told, as if in conversation with his hero Acontius, whom he addresses as something between epic hero and beloved boy.

Another well-known aetion is again spoken by the subject being explained. The queen Berenice, wife of Ptolemy III Euergetes, swore to dedicate a lock of her own hair if her husband returned victorious. She fulfilled her vow in the temple of Arsinoe Aphrodite,[6] probably in September 245 BC, but the lock disappeared. Conon, the court astronomer, declared that the lock had undergone catasterisation – it had become a constellation of stars and thus divine. Callimachus' poem will have contributed to the elegant compliment to the queen (frr. 110 and 112). The tone of the aetion is light and humorous, but there is no reason to think it subversive of its compliment. The poem, or its shadow, we might say, is known to us through the creative translation which is Catullus 66.

All poets talk about their poetry, but Callimachus was particularly adept at capturing a vocabulary and a style for poetics that was to last. As mentioned above, he had a tendency to couch his poetic programme in terms of an argument with opposing critics. Certain passages have, from antiquity to modern times, been interpreted as reflections of real and acrimonious conflict with other men of letters, including the epic poet Apollonius of Rhodes. Most people nowadays reject the idea of a bitter feud between Apollonius and Callimachus, not least because the rigid generic divisions (epic and not-epic) which were thought to be the bone of contention have been shown to be more fluid and unstable.

Iamb 13, the last in the collection of iambic poems, presents its poetic programme through both a quarrelling answer to Callimachus' (supposed) critics and a description of the quarrels between poets that keep happening. The complaint (real or, more likely, imagined) against Callimachus is that he writes in too many genres. Although the poem is fragmentary, we can tell that Callimachus extended his defence to include not only range of genres but also range of dialect, in which he was proficient and diverse, and metrical variety (metre was an important defining characteristic of genre in antiquity). Whether or not there were arguments between pluralists and purists in the Senior Common Room of the Alexandrian

Museum (my description is a playful fantasy), Callimachus chooses to use the form of the quarrel in order to make statements about the type of poetry he writes and values.

So, finally, to the great debate about length and epic. It is the prologue to the *Aetia* which most emphatically (if not clearly) lays out the lines of the debate. There is a quarrel again, with some 'Telchines' (mythical craftsmen and evil magic-workers, standing, it is hinted, for other poets) who complain about Callimachus' poetry

> because I did not accomplish one continuous poem of many thousands of lines on ... kings or ... heroes, but like a child I roll forth a short tale, though the decades of my years are not few.
>
> (Loeb translation)

Somehow, various poems are compared, perhaps longer and shorter ones. Critics and readers are invited (17–18) to judge poetry 'by [the canons of] art, not by the Persian chain' (that is, not by length). Callimachus will not thunder his poetry, because thunder belongs to Zeus. Then the poet recalls a visit from Apollo, god of poetry, when he first started to write. The god told him to 'feed the victim fat, but keep the Muse slender' (23–4) and to drive along 'unworn paths, though your course be more narrow' (27–8).[7] This looks like a choice for short poems over long, for originality over traditional forms, for the delicate style over the bombastic.

It has long been assumed that Callimachus, and the other Hellenistic poets who followed his aesthetic, rejected epic: not Homer himself, who was great but inimitable, but the later imitations of Homer, including the poems of the 'epic cycle' (the term usually refers to early Greek epics other than the *Iliad* and *Odyssey*, covering myth from the creation through the heroic age – only fragments survive). Good poetry, the argument goes, should be in lighter genres, shorter, more delicate, more original than the repetition of hackneyed epic themes. Cameron (1995) has argued that Callimachus doesn't reject epic at all. He claims that the target of Callimachus' abuse is the poetry of the older contemporary elegiac poet Antimachus, and in particular his *Lyde* (a collection/poem not unlike the *Aetia*). Whether or not Cameron is right, Callimachus clearly rejects epic bombast and a high-flown style (as Cameron agrees), and comes near enough to 'rejecting epic' for it to be very easy for later poets to use his poetic programme in that way, for their own purposes.

Callimachus gives (at first sight) an explicit statement of the anti-epic view when he opens *Epigram* 30 (a six-line poem) with 'I hate the cyclic poem, nor do I take pleasure in the road which carries many to and fro'. That seems pretty clear, but it should be noted that this is an erotic poem, the main point of which is the desire for exclusivity in relationships (with a young boy, as are all Callimachus' erotic poems). The boy is lovely, but the poem ends with 'someone' saying 'Another has him'. The desire is for exclusivity in both poetics and erotics. When Callimachus says 'I drink not from every well' (3–4), we should see the reference both to love and to poetry. It is also fairly certain that any statement Callimachus makes about 'length' and 'littleness' is at least in part also a statement about poetic style, not simply the number of verses employed.

The metaphor of littleness has a vast progeny in Roman poetry. Callimachus' own most delicate example of it ends the *Hymn* II (to Apollo). Personified Envy has been whispering against Callimachus (again, this is a device to introduce a programmatic statement), but Apollo rejects the complaint. Envy complains about the 'poet who sings not things in number like the sea' (106), but Apollo enigmatically reminds him that the River Euphrates, great though it is, carries 'much filth of earth and much refuse' with it. The loveliest water is 'the trickling stream that springs from a holy fountain, pure and undefiled' (111–12). Williams' convincing interpretation of this passage is to take the sea as referring to Homeric epic, the Euphrates as cyclic epic and the spray from the fountain as Callimachean poetry.[8] While Apollo and Callimachus spurn Envy (yet need it also as a guarantor of fame), they do not despise the greatness of sublime poetry like that of Homer and Pindar. Callimachus himself aspires to be both the 'little winged one' (a cicada, symbolising delicate poetry – *Aetia* fr. 1.29) and a great poet. The paradox is as playful as the *Aetia* is long.

Notes

1   See L. Canfora, *The Vanished Library*, Berkeley and Los Angeles, CA: University of California Press, 1990, pp. 42–3.
2   For an extended discussion of Callimachus' life, see A. Cameron, *Callimachus and His Critics*, Princeton, NJ: Princeton University Press, 1995, ch. 1. It is worthwhile to note that this extremely important book has as its overt agenda the debunking of commonly held views about Callimachus.

3 We now call these the *Homeric Hymns*, although we don't treat them as having been written by the author of the *Iliad*. They may be found in the Loeb edition of Hesiod.

4 See M. Depew, 'Mimesis and aetiology in Callimachus' *Hymns*', in M.A. Harder, R.F. Regtuit and G.C. Walker (eds), *Callimachus, Hellenistica Groningana I*, Groningen: Egbert Forsten, 1993, pp. 57–77.

5 See A.S. Hollis, *Callimachus: Hecale*, Oxford: Oxford University Press, 1990, pp. 337–40.

6 Arsinoe, in life, was the wife of Ptolemy II Philadelphus. Callimachus wrote a lyric poem on her deification, of which a brief *diegesis* and a mutilated but substantial (seventy-five-line) fragment survive. See the discussion in Cameron, *op. cit.*, p. 107.

7 All the main Augustan poets wrote a scene in imitation of this epiphany of Apollo, in a range of variations.

8 See F. Williams, *Callimachus' Hymn to Apollo: A Commentary*, Oxford: Oxford University Press, 1978, p. 89.

See also in this book

Apollonius Rhodius, Catullus, Hesiod, Horace, Martial, Ovid, Pindar, Propertius, Theocritus, Virgil

Texts, translations and commentaries

The scholarly edition of the works of Callimachus is by R. Pfeiffer (Oxford: Oxford University Press, 1985): two volumes, with introduction and commentary, cover the *Fragments* (1st edn, 1949) and then the *Hymns and Epigrams* (1st edn, 1953).

There are two Loeb volumes, *Hymns and Epigrams* (with Lycophron and Aratus) and *Aetia, Iambi, Hecale and Other Fragments* (with Musaeus).

There is a new translation by Frank Nisetich, with introduction, translation and commentary (*The Poems of Callimachus*, Oxford: Oxford University Press, 2001).

Editions of individual works with commentary include:

Hollis, A.S., *Callimachus: Hecale*, Oxford: Oxford University Press, 1990.

Hopkinson, N., *Callimachus: Hymn to Demeter*, Cambridge: Cambridge University Press, 1984.

Kerkhecker, A., *Callimachus: Book of Iambi*, Oxford: Oxford University Press, 1999.

Williams, F., *Callimachus' Hymn to Apollo: A Commentary*, Oxford: Oxford University Press, 1978.

Further reading

Bing, P., *The Well-Read Muse: Present and Past in Callimachus and the Hellenistic Poets*, Göttingen: Vandenhoeck and Ruprecht, 1988.

Cameron, A., *Callimachus and His Critics*, Princeton, NJ: Princeton University Press, 1995.

Hutchinson, G.O., *Hellenistic Poetry*, Oxford: Oxford University Press, 1988.

Zanker, P., *Realism in Alexandrian Poetry: A Literature and Its Audience*, London: Croom Helm, 1987.

APOLLONIUS RHODIUS

The Greco-Roman tradition of epic poetry is dominated by the two giants, Homer and Virgil. Almost midway in time between these two comes a poet who deserves to be better read – Apollonius Rhodius. The subject matter of his epic has been immortalised in modern popular culture: it is the tale told in the Hollywood blockbuster *Jason and the Argonauts*. Apollonius' modernisation of primitive epic and his development of the genre to include intense interest in intense emotion both bloom in Virgil's *Aeneid*. Although the *Argonautica* has not always found favour, someone liked it well enough to set it on a path towards transmission – it is one of very few Hellenistic works to survive by manuscript tradition through the Middle Ages.

Apollonius was really more Alexandrian than Rhodian, for he was tutor to Ptolemy III Euergetes and was chief librarian of the Royal Library at Alexandria, probably for many years.[1] It is possible that the surname 'Rhodius' comes from his having spent a considerable time in Rhodes, or it may be that he or his family originated there. The common story is that he left Alexandria after the first draft of the *Argonautica* was badly received, and retired to Rhodes to work on and improve it. This may be fantasy. Still more likely to be fantasy is the tradition that he was involved in an acrimonious dispute with Callimachus over the right way to write poetry. Like Callimachus, Apollonius was a scholar as well as a poet. He wrote scholarly poetic works (now lost) on local history, cults and origins, as well as epigrams. He also wrote prose works, including literary criticism of early poets. Despite this learning, in his great epic the Argonauts' journey follows a wildly inaccurate geographical path, whether through the ignorance of Apollonius or because the geography is mythic rather than real.

The *Argonautica* is an epic poem in four long books, telling how Jason and a band of heroes travelled in the divinely made (and occasionally talking!) ship *Argo*, out of the Greek world to Colchis, on the shores of the Black Sea. His purpose was to retrieve the Golden Fleece, which had belonged to the ram on which the Greek hero Phrixus had escaped sacrilegious attempts to sacrifice him.

Jason gains the support of Medea, the daughter of the Colchian king Aeetes. She uses her magic powers to help Jason perform the supernatural tasks which Aeetes requires before he can take the Fleece (intending that it would be impossible for Jason). They flee from Aeetes' wrath and eventually get back to Greece, Jason and Medea having married on the way. Many people will know how Euripides developed the story: years later, Jason decides to take a new wife and Medea kills their children in revenge; she escapes on the chariot of Helios, the sun god who is her grandfather.

Jason's story conforms to the common folk-tale pattern of the Quest, in which the hero undertakes some dangerous task through which he wins the prizes of adulthood, often throne, wealth and marriage to the king's daughter. The Quest is often, as here, for some magic talisman: the Golden Fleece plays a role similar to that of the Holy Grail in Arthurian legend. The hero's enemy is monstrous. In this case, the king Aeetes is a terrifying barbarian. Although many of the Argonauts are sons or grandsons of the gods, Aeetes seems a stage closer to *his* father, Helios, who is a primitive chthonic deity rather than an Olympian god. Hera, wife of Zeus, directs all the action, so that the Greek king Pelias will get his punishment for scorning her. It is not told in the poem, but it is several times foreshadowed, that Medea will trick Pelias' daughters into killing him, thinking it is a magical rite of rejuvenation. That, as far as Hera is concerned, is the goal or telos of the epic. She plays a role which will be developed into that of Juno in Virgil's *Aeneid*.

With a highly self-conscious, scholarly and artistic poet like Apollonius, it is hardly surprising that his poem is a complex web of intertextual relations. The main intertextual lines work in three ways, which we might simplify as genre, content and style. As regards genre, the *Argonautica* is written as a Hellenistic answer to Homer, and is shot through with Homeric echoes and reworkings of Homeric scenes. Its content centres on the famous myths of Jason and Medea: of still-extant texts those most crucial to Apollonius are Pindar *Pythian* 4 and Euripides *Medea*, but given the popularity of the myth in literature and art it seems likely that there are other important intertexts that we are missing. Finally, style: Apollonius writes, however problematically, however idiosyncratically, in the style of Callimachus. He is a thoroughly Hellenistic poet, so much so that it seems hard to imagine how the old critical myth, that he was opposed to the fashionable canons of Hellenistic literary taste, ever arose. There are passages in the *Argonautica* which treat the same material as does Callimachus (see, for example, Callimachus *Aetia* frr. 7.19–21 on the return of the Argonauts) and also Theocritus (for example, the famous Hylas episode in *Argonautica* Book 1 and Theocritus *Idyll* 13). But perhaps more important are the artistic self-consciousness and the abstruse learning, aetiological, geographical, historical and mythic, which pervade the epic almost as much as the *Aetia*.

What kind of an epic poem is this? Apollonius plays with the way in which it is, in a sense, both before and after Homer. Near the beginning of the journey, for example, the centaur Chiron and his wife wave to the passing Argonauts and show Peleus his infant son Achilles, whom they are rearing after the breakdown of Peleus' and Thetis' marriage. The Argonauts don't stop, for it is not yet time for the *Iliad*, and yet there is a clear echo of the opening line of the first epic, when the centaur lifts up 'son of Peleus Achilles' for his father to see (*Iliad* 1.558). Likewise elsewhere, where there are adventures which are clear replays of Odyssean escapades, there is always a sense of 'not yet', of something even older than the Homeric poems – but referring to them, backwards in poetry, forwards in chronology.

The Argonauts themselves are almost overwhelmingly heroic, but not unproblematically so. Their leader Jason is at times the loveliest of all heroes: a clever strategist, a persuasive speaker and a heroic fighter. In the climactic trial of strength and endurance through which Aeetes puts him, Jason is fully heroic (3.1278–1339). At times, however, Jason seems weak and indecisive, such as when the heroes realise they have accidentally left Heracles behind, and deceitful (for example, 4.338ff. and in the matter of Apsyrtus, discussed below). It usually falls to Peleus, or occasionally to Orpheus, to encourage the companions and set them in the right direction.[2]

Heracles himself is an old-style hero who does not belong comfortably with this expedition. He aggressively refuses the leadership early on, insisting that only Jason can lead. He wards off various dangers, and even rows the whole ship on his own (1.1161–71) – until he breaks his oar! He then does the only thing a superhero can do, which is to pull up a young pine tree to make another one (1.1187–1205). While he is off hunting for his pine, however, his beloved boy Hylas is stolen by the nymphs of a pool. Heracles and Polyphemus are so busy looking for the boy that the Argonauts leave them behind. But Glaucus is right: Heracles shouldn't really be coming to Colchis, because he is too big a hero (1.1315–20). The Argonauts only find a trace of him much later

(4.1432–84), in the deserts of Libya on their way home, and one of them just gets a glimpse of him from afar.

Narrative is crucial to the question of genre. Although the poem has a properly epic powerful sense of forward movement – encapsulated in the journey itself, which is a metaphor for the poem – the narrative has often been seen as disunified and disjointed. Before we look at Apollonius' narrative, it is important to remember that Homeric narrative (teleological and relatively straightforward though it is) contains many digressions, and one major and famous narrative disruption in the form of Odysseus' story-telling in the palace of Alcinous (*Odyssey* 9–12).

We can get a sense of the odd, disjointed, tricksy narrative of the *Argonautica* if we follow its path for a little way. The poem opens with an appropriately epic invocation of the god of poetry and prophecy, Apollo. Then the trouble starts. It is written for those who know, as if the poet is recalling rather than creating. We hear about the ultimate *telos* from the beginning, when brief mention is made of Pelias' fear of a prophecy about the man with one sandal (1.5–7) who will eventually cause his death. Pelias sets his own fate in motion by trying to avoid it, when he decides to send Jason away (to get the Fleece to try and get rid of him, but in fact Jason brings back Medea, who kills Pelias). Then (1.18) the poet jumps to the building of the *Argo*, but refuses to tell of it, on the grounds that earlier poets have done so (but he will nearly tell it again at 1.111–14), and immediately we are thrown into the long roll-call of heroes who joined the expedition (in imitation of the catalogue of ships in *Iliad* 2 – but we are only at 1.20). Nothing so simple as 'so Jason called on heroes to join him in a quest' – rather, the roll-call seems almost unmotivated. It is only at 1.123 that we hear how the heroes came to be summoned; at 1.209 that we learn – incidentally to something else – that Jason, in between Pelias' decision and the gathering of heroes, went to Pytho to consult the oracle about his journey; at 1.301 that we hear the oracular response was favourable; and finally at 1.410 we have a re-recital of Jason's prayer at Pytho. The disjunction, the allusiveness and the compression of this narrative are features we are inclined to see as typically Hellenistic.

Despite the odd disruptions, changes of tone and authorial intrusions, the poem is full of structuring elements. The simplest of these is the journey itself, for this is a tale of 'there and back again' which nearly divides the poem into two groups of two books each. To emphasise this, the first two books end with dawn, while the third ends with dusk and the last with an oddly clipped closure, as if the poet refused to give it a proper ending. And yet the poem does have a perfectly proper ending, for the last word, 'disembarked', is really all there is to say, and also echoes the opening word, 'beginning'. At a micro-level, also, there are plenty of instances of structural architecture, even when they tease and deny our expectations. After the Argonauts' departure from Lemnos, we hear about some monsters with six hands (1.942–6) – but the expected conflict doesn't materialise (yet). Instead we have the aetiological story of the Argonauts swapping their small anchor-stone for a larger one, the discarded one becoming an object of reverence to the local inhabitants (1.953–60). Then there is a civilised meeting with the local king of the Doliones. Then there is a battle with the monsters (1.989–1011), mostly fought by Heracles. It looks as though this section is over, until the Argonauts' attempt to leave is stalled by some confused night-time sailing and they are driven back, without them realising, to the Doliones, who think they are enemies attacking. In the confused battle which ensues, the king is killed and the Argonauts are victorious – to their dismay when they realise what has happened. So, the structure has gone something like this: wild monsters, civilised guest-friendship, battle between the monsters and the monster-slaying (but preternaturally monster-like) Heracles, 'civilised' war in which we see a mini Iliadic battle, followed by suitably Homeric funeral games for the dead king. The individual elements are all broadly Homeric, but the totality is totally Apollonian. Apollonian also is the embarrassing stasis when storms stop the heroes getting away from the site of their accidental battle.

One feature that marks out Apollonius' epic as 'Hellenistic' as opposed to Homeric is the sensitive way in which it dwells on Medea and her love for Jason. Medea is a startling character and startlingly realistic, unless one requires a 'realistic' character to be entirely predictable. For large sections of Book 3, and some of Book 4, the narrative focalises with her. It would be easy (and true) to say that Medea represents the common ancient fear of the female, and in particular female control of life and sexuality, but there is more to Medea than that. Her character is tied up with crucial issues of the poem, for example the relationship between stratagem, persuasion and deceit. We can see this innocent maiden with a tricksy mind early on in her ordeal, when Medea spends a sleepless night thinking of going to see her sister, in order to manipulate *her* into persuading Medea herself to help the Argonauts – and then shame overwhelms her and she doesn't go (3.640ff.). But eventually she meets her sister, and at first 'cannot speak' (for shame – 3.681–2) but then 'speaks with guile' (3.687). The young girl in love and the powerful witch are both part of Medea. This is a maiden who routinely uses magic to open her bedroom door (4.41–2). That is frightening and fascinating, rather than good or bad.

The horrific side of Medea, and her tragedy, are treated delicately in the poem. She and Jason lure her brother Apsyrtus to his death through a trick, but Medea doesn't chop him up and scatter his body over the sea as in Euripides' and other versions. Rather, his death is bound up in the web of trickery, persuasion, stratagem and guile which pervade the story and problematise its moral values.[3] Medea's famous tragedy – her killing of her children – is foreshadowed in the description of Apsyrtus coming to his death, like an innocent child to be slaughtered. In addition, another passage even more powerfully and shockingly 'foreshadows' (backwards) the Medea of Euripides' *Medea*. Apollonius describes the last part of the night (that dark, cold hour which is often the deadest part of living time) as the time when sleep comes to 'a mother whose children are dead' (3.747–8). This, precisely, is what Medea will be like. The fact that she will be responsible for their death only makes the tragedy greater, and the image more poignant.

In true Hellenistic style, there is considerable interest in mothers and children in the poem. One passage with strong epic predecessors and descendants is when the goddesses Hera and Athene visit Aphrodite (3.36ff.) to ask her to get Eros to make Medea fall in love (the parallel with Virgil's Dido is close). Aphrodite is a troubled goddess, and her worst problem is her wayward son. She finds him playing dice with Ganymede (and cheating him – 3.114ff.) and berates him like any loving but distracted and not totally capable mother. She promises him a Playstation if he will do what she asks. (Actually, the toy is a cosmic globe of the type used by Alexandrian scholars.) Like Medea, Eros is a mixture of playful child and terrifyingly powerful force.

Notes

1 POxy 1241 – second-century AD list of librarians at Alexandria.
2 See J.J. Clauss, *The Best of the Argonauts: The Redefinition of the Epic Hero in Book 1 of Apollonius' Argonautica*, Berkeley and Los Angeles, CA: University of California Press, 1993.
3 See R.L. Hunter, *The Argonautica of Apollonius: Literary Studies*, Cambridge: Cambridge University Press, 1993, pp. 58–62.

See also in this book

Callimachus, Homer, Ovid, Statius, Virgil

Texts, translations and commentaries

The OCT is by H. Fraenkel. There is a good World's Classics by R.L. Hunter (using the title *Jason and the Golden Fleece (The Argonautica)*, 1993); also a Penguin translation by E.V. Rieu (1971). The Loeb, by R.C. Seaton, dates from 1912.

There is an excellent commentary on Book 3 by Hunter, in the Cambridge Greek and Latin Classics Series (1989).

Further reading

Beye, C.R., *Epic and Romance in the Argonautica of Apollonius*, Carbondale, IL: Southern Illinois University Press, 1982.
Campbell, M., *Echoes and Imitations of Early Epic in Apollonius Rhodius*, Leiden: Brill, 1981.
DeForest, M.M., *Apollonius' Argonautica: A Callimachean Epic*, Leiden: Brill, 1994.
Hunter, R.L., *The Argonautica of Apollonius: Literary Studies*, Cambridge: Cambridge University Press, 1993.
Hutchinson, G.O., *Hellenistic Poetry*, Oxford: Oxford University Press, 1988.

THEOCRITUS

The *Idylls*, the title generally applied to Theocritus' poems since antiquity, can create a misleading impression of their variegated nature. In English, 'idyllic' (in its widest sense) implies something which is charming or picturesque. Yet the lives of Theocritus' shepherds and goatherds are often torn apart by love which is destructive and unrelenting, however beautiful the landscape which they inhabit. This gulf between the idyllic topography of the countryside and the harsh power of love generates disturbing undercurrents. In addition, the title seems to exclude significant elements in the *corpus* of his poetry: as well as his bucolic pieces, which would prove so inspirational to Virgil in his *Eclogues*, there were the so-called 'urban mimes' (2, 14, 15), political poems (16, 17) and compositions based on myth (11, 13, 18, 22, 24, 26).[1] Yet it is in the creation of a new genre, pastoral poetry (or perhaps in the definitive pulling together of pre-existing strands), that critics see Theocritus' main achievement.

Theocritus wrote in Greek in a variety of dialects, mainly Doric (albeit of an artificial, literary type), although occasionally he used Aeolic and Ionic, and the predominant metre of his poems is the dactylic hexameter. He came from Syracuse on the east coast of Sicily. This was part of a wider area known as *Magna Graecia*, which had been colonised by Greeks from the eighth century BC onwards and included the coastal area of southern Italy. Sicily was therefore an island with a vibrant Greek culture, although it had been plagued by turbulent wars, initially against Athens and then against Carthage (and ultimately Rome).

At the period when Theocritus flourished (the first half of the third century BC), Hieron II, a general who had gained power through a military coup, had managed to create relative stability on this strategically located island, which he controlled between 270 and 216 BC. The historian Polybius greatly admires Hieron's qualities as a leader:

> During a reign of fifty-four years he kept his country at peace and his authority undisturbed by conspiracies, and he even contrived to escape envy, which all too often pursues a man of superior abilities; indeed on more than one occasion when he tried to lay down his power, he was prevented from doing so by the united action of the citizens.

> (*Histories* 7.8)[2]

Without Hieron, perhaps the environment which initially allowed Theocritus' creative talents to flourish would not have existed. The shadow of danger from which Hieron shields the islanders is vividly captured through Theocritus' hopes that war will be kept at bay: 'may spiders weave their slender webs over the weapons, and may the name of the war-cry no longer exist' (*Idyll* 16.96–7). Hieron himself is cast as a Homeric hero: 'Among them, Hieron, like one of the heroes of old, girds himself, and horse-hair plumes shade his helmet' (*Idyll* 16.80–1). No wonder that a certain anxiety and tension infiltrates parts of Theocritus' poetry, even when the action takes place in an apparently safe and picturesque world. Poetry was often about escape, but that presupposes that there was something from which there was a need to escape.

Later on, Theocritus went to Egypt, where he spent time in Alexandria and joined the circle of poets and writers granted royal patronage by King Ptolemy II Philadelphus. His gratitude to this ruler is expressed in poem 17, a panegyric for Ptolemy. Under the Ptolemies, the great library at Alexandria was created, which attracted many intellectuals to the city. While Theocritus was in Alexandria, he would certainly have come to know Callimachus, whose life was intimately bound up with the library.[3] Callimachus too paid homage to the ruling dynasty, writing one poem celebrating Ptolemy's marriage to his sister Arsinoe Philadelphus ('brother-loving') (fr. 392, Pfeiffer) and another (fr. 228, Pfeiffer) on the queen's subsequent *apotheosis* (transformation into a goddess) after her death in 270 BC.

If we put on one side for a moment fifteen poems (2, 11–18, 22, 24, 26, 28–30) which are either non-pastoral or different in some way,[4] and the eight pieces commonly thought to have been written by imitators (8, 9, 19–21, 23, 25, 27), there are actually only eight works (out of thirty in the *corpus*) from which Theocritus' reputation as the creator of the pastoral genre derives (1, 3–7, 10, 12). Although we should certainly remember Hutchinson's warning that 'a view of the poet which concentrates on one-third of his output is bound to be distorted',[5] nevertheless there are certain generalisations that one can make about the bucolic poems. Often (though not always) the action centres on a singing competition between two male rustics, conducted either in a pugnacious or a friendly spirit (4: Battus/ Corydon, 5: Comatas/Lacon, 6: Damoetas/Daphnis, 7: Simichidas/ Lycidas, 10: Milon/Bucaeus). In most cases, the first song is completed before the second begins (6, 7, 10), but sometimes there is only one song (1, 3, 4) or the singers engage in an alternating exchange of verses (5). The narrative framework may either be in a dialogue format centring on direct speech (1, 4, 5, 10) or else it may be set up as a third-person (6) or a first-person narrative (3, 7) with direct speech incorporated.

We also tend to get topographical description, either in the frame or within the inset songs – although in the dialogue poems such details have to be included obliquely, as the rustics describe the landscape through their direct speech. So the shepherd Lacon urges the goatherd Comatas to sing in a particular place:

> You'll sing better sitting under the wild olive and this coppice. There's cool water falling there, and here is grass and a green bed, and the locusts are chattering.

> (*Idyll* 5.31–4)

In this instance, the countryside gets absorbed into the agonistic milieu of the competing rustics, as Comatas asserts:

> I will never come over there. Here I have oaks and the cypress, and bees humming beautifully at the hives. Here are

two springs of cool water, and birds chattering on the tree,
and for shade, your patch is not the same. What is more, the
pine overhead is dropping her nuts.

(*Idyll* 5.45–9)

This confident piece of one-upmanship by Comatas foreshadows his
eventual victory in the singing match, which he dominates from the
start.

It was clearly much easier for Theocritus to include extended
topographical description in the non-dialogue version of the bucolic
poem, as in the famous *Idyll* 7, where the urban poet Simichidas
(sometimes thought to be a cipher for Theocritus himself)[6] recalls a
singing contest which took place on Cos as he and two friends made
their way to a harvest festival. Once they reach their destination,
Theocritus offers an elaborate and sensual description of a *locus
amoenus* (7.135–46). The passage opens with aspens and elms
rustling above their heads, while sacred water wells up from a cave of
the nymphs; crickets, the nightingale, larks, finches and bees inhabit
the spot, which is thick with the scent of the grain harvest and the
fruit crop. Various poetic devices provide technical enhancement of
the pure aesthetic pleasure. This is a particularly fine example of a
set-piece description of a beautiful place, the earliest example of
which is perhaps the depiction of Alcinous' garden by Homer
(*Odyssey* 7.112–31).

In this passage, according to Hunter, Theocritus

> establishes the dialectic of art and nature which was to
> dominate all subsequent 'pastoral' literature, which claims to
> describe 'the natural', but does so in overtly artificial ways.[7]

We can perhaps compare in this context the programmatic ekphrasis
of the elaborately wrought wooden cup, which serves as a prize in
the opening poem. It might initially appear to be an everyday object,
but the craftsman's hand has turned it into a work of art, much in the
manner that Theocritus has turned simple shepherds' songs into
intricate poetry. Longus uses a similar device at the start of *Daphnis
and Chloe* to complicate his apparently simple depiction of an
idealised landscape.

Some of the impact of these bucolic poems is generated from
conflicts and contrasts that are set up between the two main

characters, who serve as mouthpieces for the inset songs. So the goatherd Battus constantly teases and undermines the pretensions of Corydon, who temporarily takes care of some cows for Aegon, absent because he is participating in a boxing match at Olympia. Corydon pompously proclaims: 'Men say that he [Aegon] rivals Heracles in strength' (4.8). Battus is scornful: 'And my mother says that I'm another Polydeuces' (4.9). This sarcastic reference to the divine Polydeuces, the champion boxer, has an added resonance in the light of Theocritus' subsequent description of the violent boxing match between Polydeuces and Amycus (22.83–134).

Likewise in *Idyll* 7 the Cretan goatherd Lycidas teases Simichidas as he makes his journey from the town through the midday sun:

Are you going off to a meal though you haven't been invited?
Or are you rushing off to the wine jar of one of your fellow
townsmen? For as your feet travel along, every stone sings as
it stumbles from your shoes.

(*Idyll* 7.24–6)

Some critics have suggested that Lycidas may be intended to represent Apollo.[8] This would add engaging ironies to the poem, as, for example, when Simichidas calls Lycidas 'dear to the Muses' (7.95). If Lycidas is indeed meant to represent Apollo, the god who is (among other things) responsible for poetry, then this piece of flattery is truer than Simichidas can possibly know.

One theme which transcends the individual poems within the collection is love, whether unreciprocated or misfiring in some way. Some of the rustics are themselves love-sick, such as the unnamed goatherd (3) who sings to his darling Amaryllis outside her cave, Battus (4) who promises never to forget the dead Amaryllis, and Bucaeus (10), the reaper who is so distracted by love that his work suffers. More often, however, the rustics approach love at one remove through the filter of the inset songs, which present erotic vignettes. So Thyrsis sings of Daphnis (1.64–142) who pined away through love until foxes and wolves howled at his death. In another poem, Daphnis (now a singer) tells the cyclops Polyphemus that the lovestruck nymph Galatea is trying to attract his attention (6.6–19); next Damoetas plays the role of Polyphemus to explain that by ignoring the nymph he hopes to stir up her passion (6.21–40). Finally, Simichidas sings about his friend Aratus' passion for the boy Philinus (7.96–127).

In the non-bucolic poems, love is also a dominant theme. *Idyll* 2 is particularly dramatic, as a Coan girl called Simaetha puts a spell on her evasive lover Delphis. She wants the young athlete to burn with passion like the bay leaves she is putting in the fire, and to melt with desire like the wax figure she throws into the flames. In *Idyll* 11, we see a less happy version of the relationship between Polyphemus and the nymph Galatea, as he tries to soothe the wounds caused by love through song. This lovelorn cyclops is very different from his harsh and violent counterpart in *Odyssey* 9. Ovid was later inspired to recast Theocritus' version of Polyphemus' song in a rather more frivolous way (*Metamorphoses* 13.789–869). Finally, there is *Idyll* 14, an urban mime, in which a man called Aeschinas meets his friend Thyonichus on the road and tells him how he has recently lost his girlfriend Cynisca to the predatory (and aptly named) Lycus ('Wolf'). We can tell that Theocritus is in a different mode here, because instead of offering a consolatory song, Thyonichus suggests that his friend should forget his troubles by going to Egypt and joining the army of King Ptolemy.

As we have already seen from *Idyll* 2, not all of Theocritus' pieces are delivered by men. A particularly engaging dialogue appears in *Idyll* 15, another urban mime, where two women, Gorgo and Praxinoa, make their way to the festival of Adonis at the palace of Ptolemy II in Alexandria. Here, we are closer to the real world: Gorgo has a baby and both women have difficult husbands, Dinon ('Terrible') and Diocleidas ('Key-holder'). The streets on the way to the palace are packed with crowds and, once they are inside, the women meet a rude man, who mocks their accents, particularly their broad vowels (15.87–8). This criticism, coming just after Praxinoa has been admiring the delicate depiction of Adonis, is a particularly unwelcome intrusion of the male voice into their female world.

Burton has recently offered an intriguing analysis of the poem in terms of gender and power, as the two women (who are both from Syracuse) try to negotiate their way from the private to the public sphere.[9] As in the bucolic pieces, the prevailing tone of the poem is agonistic, but the competitive element is recontextualised and set in the real world. There is also a link with the bucolic mode as the woman who sings of the ephemeral but beautiful union between Aphrodite and Adonis (15.100–44) provides escapism for Gorgo and Praxinoa. This is only temporary, however. We are thrown back into reality by the poem's ending, which shows Gorgo expressing her anxiety about being away from home:

I must be getting back. It's Diocleidas' dinner-time and that man has a real temper; I wouldn't advise anyone to come near him when he's kept waiting for his food.

(*Idyll* 15.147–8)

Even Gorgo's enjoyment of female company (Praxinoa) is curtailed by her duties as a wife.

Subsequent writers have been rather selective in choosing what to imitate and admire from Theocritus' *corpus*. The fundamental nature of bucolic poetry continued to evolve after Theocritus' death, and authors often side-stepped certain elements of his writing if these did not cohere with their own agenda. The Syracusan poet Moschus in the mid-second century BC and Bion of Smyrna in the late second century BC were among the first to take up the torch, but it was perhaps Virgil through his *Eclogues* who did most to reinvent the genre for a new audience.

As Gutzwiller has observed,

The polarity of rustic and urban, largely implicit in Theocritus, is not only made explicit in Vergil but revised as a series of related and interwoven polarities – peace and war, security and fear, private and public.[10]

Particularly through the creation of an Arcadian landscape, Virgil's conception of bucolic poetry exerted its influence on post-Classical pastoral writing, although even this was progressively reshaped in later years.[11] Even when Theocritus himself was writing, the notion of simple shepherds and goatherds competing with one another in a beautiful landscape was a bit of an anachronism in the increasingly urbanised Hellenistic world. Nevertheless, Theocritus had triggered a creative process which flourished until the eighteenth century.

Notes

1   R. Hunter (ed.), *Theocritus: A Selection*, Greek and Latin Classics Series, Cambridge: Cambridge University Press, 1999, p. 3 n. 12, observes that

the origin of the term *eidullia*, which the scholia apply to all of Theocritus' poems (not just 'the bucolics'), is unclear; Pliny uses it of his own hendecasyllables without any bucolic reference (*Epistles* 4.14.99, cf. *Corpus Inscriptionum Latinorum*

VIII 5530), but in Greek, the term seems exclusively attached to Theocritus. 'Little types' is a plausible book title, particularly given the variety of Theocritus' poetry, but no date can firmly be attached to it ...

2 Rulers who try to abdicate, but paradoxically strengthen their position by appearing to reject autocratic power, are common in ancient literature: Gelon of Syracuse (Diodorus Siculus 11.26.5–6), Aristagoras, governor of Miletus (Herodotus 5.37.2), and even the Roman emperor Augustus' 'restoration of the republic' (Augustus *Res Gestae* 34.1) can be thought of in this light.

3 L. Canfora, *The Vanished Library*, Berkeley and Los Angeles, CA: University of California Press, 1990, pp. 39, 42–3.

4 *Idyll* 11, about the love-sick cyclops Polyphemus, is difficult to categorise. Hunter, *op. cit.*, pp. 218–19, observes that 'the framing addresses to Nikias provide a quite different structure from the "bucolic" mimes of *Idylls* 1, 3, 4, 5 and 7', but raises the intriguing possibility that the linguistic and metrical roughness of *Idyll* 11 is deliberately parodic, with 'the Cyclops ... given a style appropriate to his lack of sophistication'.

5 G. Hutchinson, *Hellenistic Poetry*, Oxford: Oxford University Press, 1988, p. 143.

6 See further Hutchinson, *op. cit.*, pp. 203–5.

7 Hunter, *op. cit.*, p. 193.

8 F. Williams, 'A theophany in Theocritus', *Classical Quarterly,* 21, 1971, pp. 137–45. One of Apollo's titles was Lykios.

9 J.B. Burton, *Theocritus' Urban Mimes: Mobility, Gender and Patronage*, Berkeley, CA, and London: University of California Press, 1995, pp. 52–62.

10 K.J. Gutzwiller, *Theocritus' Pastoral Analogies: The Formation of a Genre*, Madison, WI, and London: University of Wisconsin Press, 1991, p. 181.

11 R. Jenkyns, 'Virgil and Arcadia', *Journal of Roman Studies*, 79, 1989, pp. 26–39

See also in this book

Callimachus, Longus, Ovid, Virgil

Texts, translations and commentaries

The Greek text is available in OCT (in the *Bucolici Graeci* volume) and Loeb (in the *Greek Bucolic Poets* volume).

As well as the Loeb, there is the Penguin translation by R. Wells.

There are commentaries on *Theocritus: A Selection* by R. Hunter (in the Cambridge Greek and Latin Classics Series) and on *Select Poems* by K. Dover (published by Macmillan and Bristol Classical Press), and a commentary (with translation) by A.S. Gow, published by Cambridge University Press.

Further reading

Burton, J.B., *Theocritus' Urban Mimes: Mobility, Gender and Patronage*, Berkeley, CA, and London: University of California Press, 1995.

Goldhill, S., *The Poet's Voice*, Cambridge: Cambridge University Press, 1991.

Gow, A.S., *The Greek Bucolic Poets*, Cambridge: Cambridge University Press, 1953.

Gutzwiller, K.J., *Theocritus' Pastoral Analogies: The Formation of a Genre*, Madison, WI, and London: University of Wisconsin Press, 1991.

Hunter, R., *Theocritus and the Archaeology of Greek Poetry*, Cambridge: Cambridge University Press, 1996.

Hutchinson, G., *Hellenistic Poetry*, Oxford: Oxford University Press, 1988.

Jenkyns, R., 'Virgil and Arcadia', *Journal of Roman Studies*, 79, 1989, pp. 26–39.

Williams, F., 'A theophany in Theocritus', *Classical Quarterly*, 21, 1971, pp. 137–45.

EARLY ROMAN

ENNIUS

Ennius ingenio maximus, arte rudis ('Ennius greatest in genius, crude in art' – *Tristia* 2.424): so Ovid encapsulated the laudatory if slightly ambivalent attitude of the Augustan poets to this great predecessor. Ennius was a 'strong father' for later Roman poets, a model for emulation, an icon of the patriotic glories of a past and simpler age (so it was perceived), an alternative model, however problematically so, to the Callimachean ideal – and at times a figure of fun. Little over a thousand lines of Ennius' work now survive out of a huge oeuvre, mostly in fragments of not more than one or two lines. The longest fragment is only twenty lines long, the shortest are single words. The result of this loss is that the poems themselves are barely readable now, except by the determined or as a scholarly enterprise, but the influence and importance of Ennius for later poets is such as to justify his inclusion as a 'Key Author'. He was known and read throughout antiquity.

Ennius lived at a crucial time in the cultural development of Rome. He was born in Rudiae (in Calabria in southern Italy) in 239 BC, two years after the end of the First Punic War. The cultural mix of the area and of Ennius' own upbringing is expressed in the poet's statement (reported by Aulus Gellius at *Attic Nights* 17.17.1) that he had 'three hearts' – Greek, Latin and Oscan (the language of those areas of southern Italy which were not Greek-speaking). According to a tradition that isn't particularly reliable, Ennius joined the Roman army, which brought him to the notice of M. Porcius Cato, the later Censor (184).[1] Since Cato is supposed to have developed a rhetorical, cultural and political strategy of opposition to all things Greek, the connection between the two men has a particular interest and some tension. Ennius was not Greek, but no small part of his achievement as a poet is in the interaction of the Latin language and Roman patriotism with Greek poetic forms and literary traditions. It is partly this that later critics are referring to when they call him 'half Greek' (Suetonius *On the Grammarians* 1), as well as to his culturally Greek education, probably in the city of Tarentum (in the heel of Italy).

In 204, Cato brought Ennius to Rome, where he worked as a poet, teacher and playwright, and lived until his death in 169. Ennius was also friendly with other Roman nobles, who weren't always friendly to Cato: at least some members of the Scipio family, which presented itself as cultured and philhellene (Ennius wrote a *Scipio* celebrating Scipio Africanus' victory over Hannibal), and Marcus Fulvius

Nobilior, whom Ennius accompanied on campaign to Greece in 189–187 and whose military exploits he celebrated in *Ambracia*, which was probably a tragedy *praetexta* (tragedy on a Roman historical theme). Pliny the Elder (*Natural History* 7.101) says that Ennius wrote *Annals* 16 in honour of two Caecilii brothers, adding Books 16–18 to the original fifteen books at a later date.

The fragments of Ennius survive not through scraps of manuscript but in quotations by later authors. This makes the work of reconstruction enormously complex, since the later authors are not very reliable or precise in giving what we would call complete references. Moreover, the manner of survival is liable to distort our image of the poetry, particularly in the case of those fragments that exist precisely because some later writer wanted to give an example of an odd usage or an archaic peculiarity. Others are quoted in commentaries on later poets, especially Virgil's *Aeneid*, as parallels or allusions or alternatives; others are used as 'proof texts' from this authoritative ancient source. The longest fragment (80–100 Loeb; Liber I, xlvii Sk),[2] which relates the taking of auguries to decide whether the new city will have Romulus or Remus for its foundation-leader, is quoted by Cicero in *On Divination* 1.107–8 in order to show the seriousness with which augury was taken by the heroes of the past, and to refute the charge that auguries are fabrications.

Ennius can seem like the grandfather of Roman poetry, but even grandfathers have relatives. If anyone could claim the 'beginning' of Latin literature it would be Livius Andronicus, the Greek former slave who was brought to Rome in the mid-third century BC. Andronicus composed tragedies and comedies, including, in 240, what was traditionally held to be the first play for the Roman stage, and among other works translated the *Odyssey* into Latin using the Italic 'saturnian' metre. The poet Naevius, dramatist and writer of historical narrative poetry, was also active before Ennius, and the comedians Plautus and Caecilius were near contemporaries. The important point is that Ennius made developments which changed the face of Latin poetry without which the great literary monuments of the Augustan age and later could not have come about.

Ennius was often quoted or otherwise mentioned by later poets in antiquity. During his own lifetime, Plautus parodied him, as did Terence soon afterwards. The Republican satirist Lucilius (mid-second century BC) and the didactic poet Lucretius both used him extensively. Cicero, who loved tradition, Cato the Elder and the second century BC, had a particularly great admiration for Ennius, in whom he saw the marriage of Greek culture and Roman patriotic values, made into a 'truly Roman' artistic whole, which he himself sought to achieve. On Virgil Ennius' influence is huge, while the other Augustans praise him, albeit with a sense that the shaggy hero of virile Republican epic lacked the polish of Callimachean art (or so it suited them to pretend). After the Augustan period nothing is quite the same, no doubt because poets and readers now had Virgil onto whom poetic *mos maiorum* ('ways of our ancestors') could be projected and because, after Ovidian polish had codified Latin verse, the archaism of Ennius seemed just too crude. Yet Ennius continued to be read and admired right into late antiquity. It must be among the worst accidents of textual tradition that no manuscript survived into the Middle Ages.

Ennius' output was huge. The *Satires*, a collection of poems in a variety of metres, were in some sense the beginning of the satiric genre, although the Roman grammarian Quintilian saw Lucilius as the founder of the genre which Quintilian famously claimed as 'entirely our own' (that is, 'Roman' – *Training in Oratory* 10.1.93). The fragments, such as they are (thirty-odd lines in eighteen separate fragments), suggest that the vituperative diatribe or even the gentler satiric abuse which we associate with Juvenal and Horace respectively played only a relatively small role in Ennian satire. There were also comedies; a didactic poem on food (*Hedyphagetica*), of which the surviving fragment, a mutilated eleven lines quoted by Apuleius, details the characteristic and the best fish from various places; a minor and quite probably virulently obscene work called *Sota*; philosophical works (*Euhemerus*, *Epicharmus*, and *Protrepticus*) which probably aimed to popularise the theories of various Greek thinkers; the *Scipio* poem in honour of Africanus mentioned earlier; and epigrams, including some honouring Scipio (and some honouring Ennius himself).

Ennius' greatest work was the epic poem on Roman history, the *Annales Populi Romani* (*Annals of the Roman People*). The poem relates, in eighteen books, the history of Rome from its foundation to the poet's own day. After the programmatic proem, the first fragment of the story itself begins with the destruction of Troy and Aeneas' escape: 'when ancient Priam succumbed beneath Pelasgian warfare' (15 Loeb; Liber I, xii Sk). Books 1–3 take the story through the foundation and the reign of the kings up to the expulsion of the Tarquins; Books 4–6 describe the early republic up to the outbreak of the Second Punic War; Books 7–9 relate that war, up to the peace of 201. It is almost shocking for the reader used to Augustan and later epic to note that the story has now reached well into Ennius' own lifetime, and three years after his arrival in Rome. The remaining books treat the first war against Macedonia, that against Antiochus III, the Aetolian War, the Istrian War, the Third Macedonian War (172–168/7 BC). The exploits of many great men are recounted: Cato at home and on campaign, the Scipiones, Fulvius Nobilior, lesser men such as the tribune Aelius, and the Caecilii, for whom Ennius says the last three books are a 'monument' more lasting than the statues and noble tombs of kings. (This claim is echoed in Horace's famous *Ode* 3.30, and in Ovid's imitation of it and of Ennius at the end of the *Metamorphoses*.) It is difficult to structure and write a poem up to the *end* of your own lifetime, since the *terminus ante quem* (the final cut-off point before which it must have been written) is unpredictable. Ennius almost certainly included events within two years of his own death.

Ennius' achievement in the *Annals* consists above all in the Romanisation of Greek poetic sophistication. It was Ennius who first adopted the Greek hexameter, the metre of Homeric epic, for Roman poetry, which previously had used native Italian metrical forms. To the reader trained through Virgil and Ovid, Ennius' hexameters can seem rough and awkward, but the later poets were in no doubt of their debt to the poet of the *Annals* and sometimes consciously imitated his style for the sake of its rough grandeur, which seemed to them to express and embody the values of the glorious (nostalgic) past.[3] But he is 'first founder' also in the expression of Roman patriotic values and was the Roman national poet until Virgil took his place. As Virgil would do after him, so Ennius appropriated the Homeric poems as intertexts for a story of Roman themes and values. What in Ennius is a narrative of the linear evolution of the Roman people towards world conquest becomes in Virgil a teleological aetiology for the imperial system.

Allusions to the *Annals* are pervasive through the *Aeneid*. Some are close verbal parallels, which are undoubtedly intended to evoke the Ennian poem for the reader. For example, Virgil's *est locus, Hesperiam Grai cognomine dicunt* ('there is a place, the Greeks call it Hesperia by name' – *Aeneid* 1.530 (repeated at 3.163)) is an allusion to Ennius' *est locus, Hesperiam quam mortales perhibebant* ('there is a place, which mortals called Hesperia' – 24 Loeb; Liber I, xvii Sk). In that case, Virgil is imitating the 'Aenean' part of the *Annals* and so is evoking the subject matter as well as the diction of the earlier text. He also makes allusions to later parts of the historical poem, however, which are well beyond his chronological scope. For example, Ennius' *tollitur in caelum clamor exortus utrimque* ('a shout, going up from all sides, rises to heaven' – 433 Loeb; Liber XVII, i Sk), which the Virgilian scholar Macrobius says is from Book 17, is imitated by Virgil at 11.745 *tollitur in caelum clamor, cunctique Latini* ... ('a shout rises to heaven, and all the Latins ...') and again at 12.462. Exactly how Virgil is using the subject matter of the Ennian passage is hard to tell, since the context is uncertain. We can be sure, however, that we have lost some of the richness of Virgil's text in the loss of Ennius'.

An interesting example of Ennius' role in the multiple intertextuality which creates the *Aeneid* comes from a fragment about the tribune Aelius (or possibly Caelius), who fought heroically during the Istrian War (178–177 BC), recounted in Book 15 or 16.[4] Macrobius says that there are some passages which Virgil is believed to have transferred from Homer, but Macrobius wants to show that they are taken from earlier Latin poets who themselves took them from Homer. The description in *Aeneid* 9.803–11 of Turnus, hemmed in and valiantly defending himself on all sides, evokes the Republican tribune from Ennius, as well as that embodiment of heroic defence, Ajax (Homer *Iliad* 16.102–11). So, by means of this multiple intertextuality, Turnus 'is' both Homeric hero and, perhaps more troublingly, native Italian, (pre-)Roman, (proto-)Republican hero.

Another Ennian legacy to later poets is the explicit self-consciousness about the poetic persona and the poet's voice and role. Ennius opens his great work, appropriately, with an invocation to the Muses: *Musae, quae pedibus magnum pulsatis Olympum* ('Muses, who beat great Olympus with your [dancing and metrical] feet'). The allusion is to Homer, both of whose poems open with such an invocation; to Hesiod, whose Muses now, however, dance no longer on Helicon but on the Homeric Olympus (*Il.* 1.530); to Naevius, who invoked the native Italian 'Camenae' as the inspirers of his song of the Punic War and is 'corrected' by Ennius' self-conscious Greek and epic superiority; and to Livius Andronicus, who translated the Odyssean opening Muse with Camena. The invocation is followed by an account of a dream in which Ennius met Homer, who told him that he, Ennius, was a reincarnation of himself, Homer. He had also been a peacock in between! The dream itself is an allusion to such poetic dreams in Callimachus and Hesiod, who met the Muses.

A distinctive feature of early Latin style is alliteration. Because Plautus uses it to such good comic effect, it is easy for modern readers to find highly alliterative lines funny, but it is probably the case that early Latin sought also to express heightened emotion through heavy alliteration and simply to use it to structure a poetic phrase. The most famous example from Ennius is the line *o Tite, tute, Tati, tibi tanta, tyranne, tulisti* ('o Titus Tatius, tyrant, what great things [evils, death] you have brought for yourself' – 108 Loeb; Liber I, lx Sk). The line is an exclamation, possibly by Romulus (so Skutsch), or perhaps by the poet himself or one of the murderers, reacting to the death of Titus Tatius, who had ruled with Romulus but had been murdered in revenge for various deeds considered tyrannical. There are several examples almost as alliterative as that one, like *machina multa minax minitatur maxima muris* (24 Loeb, fragments of uncertain work;[5] sedis incertae fragmenta [fragments of uncertain place], clvii Sk), and others which come closer to the kind of soundplay that a later poet would allow, such as *premitur pede pes atque armis arma teruntur* (sed. inc., cxxii Sk),[6] imitated by Virgil at *Aeneid* 10.361 (*haeret pede pes densusque uiro uir*, 'foot clings to foot and man, dense-packed, to man').

The Republican stage, known to us mostly from the extant plays of Plautus and Terence, was highly prolific. Ennius himself was a successful writer of tragedies throughout his life, his *Thyestes* being produced in the year of his death, and his nephew Pacuvius followed him in the genre. One of the longer tragic fragments (nine lines), which probably comes from the opening of Ennius' *Medea*, shows quite a close relationship with Euripides' well-known play of that name. The titles of most of Ennius' tragedies suggest that they used Greek mythological themes and were based, in some way, on Greek plays. There were also Latin tragedies using Roman themes and setting: Ennius' *Ambracia*, his work celebrating Fulvius Nobilior, and his *Sabinae*, on the rape of the Sabine women, were probably 'tragedies in Roman dress'. Certainly Ennius was better known in later antiquity as a writer of epic than of tragedy, but Cicero, for one, clearly knows his plays well and expects the same from his audiences.

Notes

1 Silius Italicus, in his epic poem on the Punic wars, has Ennius fighting as a centurion in the front rank of the Roman side in Sardinia (12. 393–414).

2 Throughout this essay I give references both to Skutsch's edition and to the Loeb.

3 For a full discussion of Ennius' hexameter, in all its experimental exuberance, see Skutsch's introduction to his commentary.

4 Skutsch places the passage in 15. Warmington, in the Loeb translation, places it in 16.

5 In fact, Warmington thought that the fragment is spurious, having been invented by the ancient grammarian who transmits it for his own purposes. I see no reason to reject it on the grounds of style, but the very fact that such alliterative sound-patterning would be ascribed to Ennius is telling.

6 Skutsch's reconstruction of this line is much more convincing than that printed by Warmington: *[hic] pede pes premitur, armisque teruntur/ arma* ..., 507–8).

See also in this book

Homer, Lucan, Ovid, Plautus, Virgil

Texts, translations and commentaries

The fragments of Ennius are collected and translated in Volume 1 of *Remains of Old Latin*, in the Loeb Classical Library, trans. E.H. Warmington (1935). The edition of the *Annals* by O. Skutsch (Oxford, 1985) is a work for the scholar, as is H. Jocelyn's edition of the *Tragedies* (Cambridge, 1967). Both volumes contain introductions and full notes, as well as the text.

Further reading

Dominik, W.J., 'From Greece to Rome: Ennius' *Annales*', in A.J. Boyle (ed.), *Roman Epic*, London: Routledge, 1993, pp. 37–58.

Goldberg, S.M., *Epic in Republican Rome*, Oxford: Oxford University Press, 1995.

Jocelyn, H., 'The poems of Quintus Ennius', *Aufstieg und Niedergang der römischen Welt*, I.2, 1972, pp. 987–1026.

The entry by A. Gratwick in the *Cambridge History of Classical Literature* is particularly worthwhile.

PLAUTUS

A Funny Thing Happened on the Way to the Forum. If you want to see what Plautus' plays looked like to their original audience (with a fairly big leap of historical translation), then see the musical produced in 1966 by Melvin Frank. It is a marvellous mishmash of Plautine plots, in which (like the mid-Republican Romans) you can play 'spot the allusion' or you can just enjoy the songs and jokes. Or watch the old television comedy series *Up Pompeii*, in which Frankie Howerd plays the clever slave who directs the action. The authors of that series expressed the metatheatrical power of the controlling slave by having Howerd sometimes spend an entire episode intermittently trying to deliver the prologue, but keeping on getting distracted and interrupted. Plautus himself never used exactly this technique, but the point is well made – the slave builds up a relationship with the audience, in which he stands outside the play and inside it at the same time. It looks as if the plot is constantly about to fly out of control, out of his hands, but we know that however much he slips, however much he seems to be making it up as he goes along, he'll present it to us on a plate at the end.

What can we say about the 'life' of a comic playwright whose name has come down to us meaning something like 'Prick, son of Flatfoot, the mime actor',[1] Titus Maccius Plautus? Either it is too good to be true or more likely it is a nickname. Likewise, the stories which the ancient biographical tradition tells of his life are a tissue of guesses and fabrications, invented on the basis of his plays and from a sense of what *ought* to have happened. It would be worth stressing that the life of Plautus offers an extreme case of something which is often true for ancient authors: much of what we say about their lives is invented from their works. Plautus is supposed to have been a native of Umbria, who began a career in drama. He then lost all his money, was imprisoned for debt and was forced to work in a mill (the slave-punishment so often threatened in his plays), during which time he, improbably, is supposed to have written three plays which made his name and set him on a path to the theatrical top. An appropriately dramatic life – which probably has no basis in fact. We do know, however, that Plautus wrote plays of the genre *fabula palliata* ('comedy wearing a little Greek cloak' – that is, comedy set in Greece and in some sense translated from Greek New Comedy) between about 205 and 184 BC. Although he was undoubtedly a popular entertainer, there was enough interest in his works as 'literature' for there to be a lively debate in antiquity about the authenticity of plays attributed to him. The first-century BC scholar Varro is reported by Aulus Gellius (*Attic Nights* 3.3.3) in the second century AD as having listed twenty-one plays that were generally thought to be genuine, a list which probably corresponds with the group that has survived into the modern world.[2] The snobbish attitude of the critics to 'broad-brush' comedy has harmed Plautus more in modern scholarship than in antiquity (although he was never as well accepted by the po-faced lettered mainstream as was Terence): Cicero, when he wants an example of sophisticated and urbane humour (*On Duties* 1.104), mentions Old Comedy, Socrates and Plautus.

Plautus isn't the easiest Classical author to get to know. For people who have learned Latin largely through the texts of the Late

Republic and Augustan ages, there are some linguistic oddities that take a bit of getting used to. It is worth the effort, however, because Plautine language is spectacular. For those who are reading the plays in translation – and there is a strong tradition since the Renaissance of both reading and performance of these plays in translation – it is worth shopping around for one that captures something of the exuberance and magnificent disregard for realism that the best Plautine characters exude.[3] One particular feature of Plautine style is alliteration – which can be spectacularly funny, although we should also remember that this is a feature of archaic style generally and isn't only used to raise a laugh (see ENNIUS). Here is just one example among many. A character celebrates the opportunity to bring good news to a rich man – and earn himself a fine meal (*Captivi* 768–74).

> *Iuppiter supreme, seruas me measque auges opes,*
> *maxumas opimitates opiparasque offers mihi,*
> *laudem, lucrum, ludum, iocum, festiuitatem, ferias,*
> *pompam, penum, potationes, saturitatem, gaudium,*
> *nec quoiquam homini supplicare nunc certum est mihi;*
> *nam uel prodesse amico possum uel inimicum perdere,*
> *ita hic me amoenitate amoena amoenus onerauit dies.*

> Jupiter, serve me and minister unto my plumpness!
> Boundless abundance, abundance unbounded, you bring me.
> Joy, praise, profit; festivity, jollity, pleasure;
> banqueting, pompous with edibles, roaring with goodies.
> Never again shall I toady to mere human beings.
> Now I can praise friends, damn all my enemies freely,
> daylight's delighted me so with delights so delightful![4]

Successful comedies depend, among other things, on the skilful interweaving of the expected and the unexpected. The audience want both to feel comfortably superior and to be pleasantly shocked. Plautus achieved the first part by what we perhaps unhelpfully call 'stock plots' and 'stock characters'. By a range of semantic signs, including appearance (probably, although not certainly, with masks), actors presented themselves to the audience in immediately identifiable roles. The audience is offered the comfort of recognising characters for what they are/represent: for example, the *senex* ('old man') will have his authority undermined, either by being made into a fool in love or by being bamboozled by his son and slave into paying for the son's affair, unless he has the fortune to be an 'affable' old man, in which case he will assist the young man's affair anyway; a slave will either be clever and 'bad' (although not, of course, evil) or stupid and 'good'; a young man will be *amans et egens* ('in love and in need') – in need of the help of the clever slave to get him out of this mess. And so on. Likewise, the audience will have a pretty shrewd idea of how the plot will turn out, both because the prologue tells them (although, in comic fashion, he often spends ages telling them not very much of substance), and because this is 'how it always works' in comedies.

At the same time, these stereotypes are there for the breaking and the audience will expect all forms of the unexpected: the well-timed quip, the sudden inversion of normality, the momentary puncturing of the dramatic illusion – all the better to draw the audience into the world of the play. A simple example of typical Plautine playfulness with stock characters would be the 'running slave' routine. In its 'pure' form, this involves a slave coming charging onto the stage with important information (such as the unexpected arrival of the father) and then engaging in a virtuoso performance of verbal and visual jokes without actually *telling us what has happened*. To do it properly, the slave should have bundled his cloak up on his shoulder. One way Plautus plays with this routine occurs in a play in which the distinctions of status between slave and free are complex and ambiguous. In *Captivi* ('The Captives'), the parasite Ergasilus (a parasite is a free man who lives by his wits, dependent on dinner invitations for his next meal) metatheatrically decides to do a running slave routine when he has the opportunity to come in with the news that the old man's *son* (there is another inversion) has arrived at the harbour (*Captivi* 778ff.). That is in a play in which one son, Tyndarus, was kidnapped as a child, brought up as a slave in another country, captured in war with his master and sold into slavery with him – to his own father. The father is trying to find someone to ransom for his other son, who has been captured and enslaved by the other side. Anyway, Tyndarus and his master change places, so that the master can get away back home. So Tyndarus is a free man who is a slave who is pretending to be a free man who is a slave. When you add to this the fact that the actor may have been either a slave or free, you get a complicated situation. And it is in that situation that Plautus plays around with the conventional slave scene.

Many of the themes of Roman comedy are self-referential to the act of playing itself. For example, deceptions and disguises drive many plots: as in *Captivi* just described, in *Mostellaria* the clever slave convinces his master that the house is haunted, in *Casina* the women dress up a male slave as the slave-girl 'bride' loved by the old man (you can guess the result), in *Miles Gloriosus* the clever slave has the young man dress up as a sailor to get the girl back, while his rival the soldier is deceived by a prostitute pretending to be a matron adulterously in love with him, or in almost any other play. These deceptions are metatheatrical images of what is happening in the theatre itself – people dress up as other people and deceive a third group.

Likewise, many plays depend on some kind of twinning or duplicitous (doubly deceiving) repetition. This, as several theorists of comedy have argued, is because repetition is inherently comic. For Bergson, repetition of words, lines, characters, plots and so on is part of a comic scheme of things which would also include twinning and miming, and which he attributes to a kind of mechanical inelasticity in the mimicry of life, which constitutes comedy.[5] Plautus has plenty of examples: the two sisters both called Bacchis, who have two friends as their lovers (only the lovers don't realise there are *two* Bacchises and so think they are each other's rival);[6] the doubled-up captives mentioned previously; the very many pairs of rivals (for example, *Asinaria*, *Casina*, *Mercator*); and the imagistic twins, like the pregnant girl and the pot of gold that symbolises her (*Aulularia*), or the recurrent ring with two roles (*Curculio*).

But the finest examples are two plays (two!) which centre on the complexities of twinning: *Menaechmi* and *Amphitruo*. These two are specially important for the history of comedy, because of the influence they had on Shakespeare in the construction of *The Comedy of Errors*, itself a self-referential sign of what is going on in dramatic comedy. Both are stories not only of twins, tricks and doubles, but also of the confusion of identity which is crucial to drama. In *Menaechmi*, a young man is searching for his identical twin brother, lost in childhood, and whose double and replacement he has become by being given his name when the first boy was lost, presumed dead. So they are both called Menaechmus. Already big questions of identity are thrown up. The 'lost' brother has done well for himself in his adopted town, and is now rich, married and stealing from his wife to buy the favours of his mistress, a prostitute. The searching brother, of course, gets mistaken for the lost one by both wife and mistress, while the lost brother is mistaken for the searcher by his slave. And so on. The resolution comes about when they meet face to face, recognise each other and what has happened, and tidy up the messy world of comedy in fraternal harmony. (Not very nice for either wife or mistress, but that's comedy ... .)

Amphitruo is even more complex, although less confusing, and is remarkable for being the only extant play of Roman comedy to have a mythological plot. Here there are two pairs of 'twins': on the one hand, the hero Amphitruo and his slave Sosias, on the other, the god Jupiter and his son Mercury. The latter disguise themselves as the first pair so that Jupiter can sleep with Amphitruo's wife Alcmene and engender the great Hercules. (He whose conception required two nights stuck together. And he was a twin.) Here, then, we have scope for multiple interactions between the two sets of twins, whose confusion of identity is further enhanced by the issues of mortality and status. The play jokingly reminds us that 'Jupiter' is a slave – a slave actor, that is – thus adding an extra level to the disguise.

The greatest Plautine deceivers are slaves. The 'clever slave' is a 'stock character', of course, but this is something of an understatement. Not only does the clever slave arrange the trick which will be needed in order to achieve the desired end of the play; not only does he win love for his young master, humiliation for his old one, praise and possibly even freedom for himself (and certainly no punishment), but more importantly he controls the play – not just the plot – and holds the audience in his hand. He is the playwright. The most highly developed example is Pseudolus, 'hero' of his eponymous play (and appropriately the name of the clever slave in *A Funny Thing* ...). Palaestrio in *Miles Gloriosus* is pretty good too, directing his play within the play as well as the play itself. But Pseudolus takes comic control to a high art. So confident is he of his skill that he even warns his master early on to beware of him and tells him straight that he is going to cheat him that very day. And he does. The issue is a music girl who needs to be bought for the young man, her lover, before she is sold elsewhere by the pimp who owns her. Pseudolus manages not only to get the girl, but actually to get the sum of money required twice over.

What is at stake in using a slave character in this way? I don't think there is any one answer to this question, but there are a number of things which are almost certainly going on. One is the topsy-turvy carnivalesque nature of the comic world, in which, for a licensed period, people do outrageous things, often involving exact inversions of status. Such inversions may, as with Aristophanes, in fact have the effect of enhancing the status quo. Another important point has to do with the relationship between the playwright and the audience: it is an odd kind of power-relation, a mixture of suppliancy and control, since the playwright directs what is going on in the theatre, but relies on the audience for it to work. Using a slave for his mouthpiece is a trick of self-deprecating *captatio beneuolentiae* ('capturing of good will'), allowing the playwright to control his audience without causing offence and always just slightly undermining the authority of his own position. There might even be a little bit of social comment – not an abolitionist manifesto, certainly, but a way of raising questions about identity, status and worth, questions which the audience can take or leave at their pleasure, this being comedy.

This 'take it or leave it' attitude to social comment, serious message, intellectual sophistication, and so on, is part of the rhetoric of Plautine comedy and its relationship with its audience. Plautus always wears his learning lightly and jokes with us about the possibility that he might ever be serious. Take, for example, references to tragedy: the opening of *Rudens* is almost certainly a sustained intertextual game with the tragedies of Ennius, particularly the *Alcmena*. Is this a programmatic sign of the tragicomic nature of this play? Well, it could be, for *Rudens*, like Shakespeare's *The Tempest* which has many affinities with it, skirts along the edges of the distinction between comedy and tragedy. It is also deeply imbued with Euripides. This is what happens: Plesidippus is in love with Palaestra, who is in the control of a pimp, Labrax. Labrax had promised to meet Plesidippus at a shrine of Venus, on the coast near Cyrene, but reneged on his promise. He set sail with Palaestra and other girls, intending to sell them lucratively in Sicily, but they were shipwrecked and washed ashore in the vicinity of said shrine. Living nearby is a man called Daemones, who had a daughter stolen by pirates years ago. Palaestra and her friend take refuge with the priestess of the shrine, and later with Daemones himself, and are almost abducted by the pimp. Plesidippus involves a group of supporters to help him remonstrate with Labrax, to whom he had already made part-payment for Palaestra. Palaestra is particularly concerned about the loss of trinkets which will enable her to recognise her parents. When the pimp's chest is fished out of the sea by one of Daemones' slaves, she gets back not only the trinkets but also the parents – Daemones and his wife. Palaestra marries Plesidippus; her friend and fellow-sufferer Ampelisca marries Plesidippus' slave (now freed) Trachalio.

It is no accident that the play ends with probably the most extreme visual statement of comic harmony and integration – the pimp and the newly found father of the girl he was about to sell off go in to dinner together, along with her legitimate lover. Aristotle described a non-tragic ending, which he says is proper to comedy rather than tragedy, as Aegisthus and Orestes going off arm-in-arm and no-one killing anyone at all (*Poetics* 1453a35–9). That is more or less what we have here, and we have it precisely because the play has been generically ambiguous. On the other hand, however, that potentially programmatic statement in the prologue is all blown away by the response of the first character to enter after it. 'What a dreadful storm', he says, 'why, it's like the overblown nonsense of Euripides' (83–8 – I am paraphrasing slightly). In this way – and it is a highly Aristophanic way – tragic pretensions are cut down to size.

Notes

1 Or, as Gratwick beautifully puts it in his edition of *Menaechmi*: 'Dickie Clownson Tumbler' (p. 3).

2 *Amphitruo, Asinaria, Aulularia, Bacchides, Captivi, Casina, Cistellaria, Curculio, Epidicus, Menaechmi, Mercator, Miles Gloriosus, Mostellaria, Persa, Poenulus, Pseudolus, Rudens, Stichus, Trinummus, Truculentus* and the fragmentary *Vidularia*.

3 It is difficult to recommend any version unequivocally, as some plays are better in some versions, others in others. The best of the Slavitt–Bovie series are among the best overall, but unfortunately not all live up to that standard.

4 I have used here the translation of Richard Moore in the Slavitt–Bovie series (p. 232 – the line numbering doesn't follow that of the Latin). It is creative, but captures something of the exuberant spirit of Plautus.

5 See H.L. Bergson, *Laughter: An Essay on the Meaning of the Comic*, London: Macmillan, 1911.

6 This play, *Bacchides* ('The Bacchises'), is the only play where we have any really firm knowledge of the New Comic original. In this case, it is a play by Menander, called *Dis Exapaton* (the 'Double Deceiver'). In 1968 a fragment of about sixty lines was published by Eric Handley, allowing the direct comparison of a Plautine passage with its original. It is worthwhile to remember that this isn't much to go on. See E.W. Handley, *Menander and Plautus: A Study in Comparison*, London: H. K. Lewis & Co., 1968.

See also in this book

Aristophanes, Ennius, Menander, Terence

Texts, translations and commentaries

There is an OCT edition in two volumes. There are two volumes of Penguin translation, and one of World's Classics, neither giving complete coverage. *The Complete Roman Drama in Translation*, edited by D.R. Slavitt and P.

Bovie (*Plautus*, Baltimore, MD, and London: Johns Hopkins University Press, 4 vols, 1995), is a good alternative to the standard translations. There are three Greek and Latin Classics commentaries: A. Gratwick on *Menaechmi* (1993); M.M. Willcock on *Casina* (1976); and D.M. Christenson on *Amphitruo* (2000). There is also Willcock on *Pseudolus* (Bristol Classical Press, 1987).

Further reading

Beacham, R.C., *The Roman Theatre and Its Audience*, London: Routledge, 1991.

Gruen, E.S., *Culture and National Identity in Republican Rome*, London: Duckworth, 1993.

McCarthy, K., *Slaves, Masters and the Art of Authority in Plautine Comedy*, Princeton, NJ: Princeton University Press, 2000.

Moore, T.J., *The Theatre of Plautus: Playing to the Audience*, Austin, TX: University of Texas Press, 1998.

Segal, E., *Roman Laughter: The Comedy of Plautus*, 2nd edn, Oxford: Oxford University Press, 1987 (first published, 1968).

Segal, E. (ed.), *Oxford Readings in Menander, Plautus and Terence*, Oxford: Oxford University Press, forthcoming.

Slater, N., *Plautus in Performance*, Princeton, NJ: Princeton University Press, 1985.

Wiles, D., *The Masks of Menander: Sign and Meaning in Greek and Roman Performance*, Cambridge: Cambridge University Press, 1991.

POLYBIUS

The anonymous author of a work on men who lived exceptionally long lives says that the Greek historian Polybius died in 118 BC aged eighty-two, after falling off his horse (Pseudo-Lucian *Macrobioi* 23). Such was the end in impressively active circumstances of the writer whose *Histories*, Mommsen says, are

> like the sun shining on the field of Roman history; where they open, the mists ... are lifted and where they end a perhaps even more vexatious twilight descends.[1]

Polybius is indeed an invaluable source, although unfortunately not all of his account has survived intact.

Although Polybius wrote various works, including a piece on military tactics, a monograph on the Numantine War, a biography of Philopoemen and an investigation into the habitability of the equatorial regions, today we only have his fragmentary *Histories*, which originally consisted of forty books about events between 264 and 146 BC. Only the first five books survive (covering 264–216 BC), together with substantial fragments from some other books.[2] After the introductory Books 1 and 2, the material is arranged in Olympiads (periods of four years), with a geographical focus which moves from west to east. It would have been fascinating to have had Polybius' account of the events from his own lifetime, but in some ways the survival of the first five books is a fortunate accident, since they help to fill the gap left by the loss of Livy's *Ab Urbe Condita* 11–20 (292–219 BC), which included the Pyrrhic War (280–275 BC) between Rome and Pyrrhus of Epirus, as well as the First Punic War (264–241 BC) between Rome and Carthage. Livy was sensible in using Polybius as a source for his own narrative, although he often embellishes the Polybian framework for his own purposes.

Polybius, born in *c.* 200 BC, lived during a century which saw the balance of power shift from east to west, as the Hellenistic world (the legacy of Alexander the Great) disintegrated in the face of unprecedented Roman expansion.[3] He came from the fortified Greek city of Megalopolis in Arcadia, which had been created after the Thebans defeated the Spartans in the Battle of Leuctra in 371 BC. His father, Lycortas, was a politician who was actively involved in the federal Achaean League, which Megalopolis had joined in 235 BC. Polybius himself would also become involved in the Achaean League, which he describes using the analogy of a city:

> An area which embraces almost the whole Peloponnese only differs from the situation of a single city in the sense that the inhabitants are not encircled by a single wall; in other respects, whether the region is considered as a whole or city by city its institutions are virtually identical.
>
> (*Histories* 2.37)[4]

This idealised passage was probably written before the Achaean League became involved in a war with Rome in 146 BC, which ultimately led to its dissolution.

A formative experience for Polybius occurred in 182 BC when he was chosen to carry the funeral urn containing the ashes of Philopoemen (Plutarch *Philopoemen* 21).[5] This man had been a particularly dynamic leader of the Achaean League, who had consistently resisted the Romans when they wanted to intervene in the League's internal affairs. Polybius subsequently wrote an appreciative biography of Philopoemen (*Histories* 10.21.6), which has not survived, but we do have some relevant passages from the

Histories. In one debate about how the Achaean League should best handle relations with Rome, Philopoemen is presented as an honourable realist:

> I know very well that the time will come when the Greeks will be obliged to give complete obedience to Rome. But do we wish this to happen as soon or as late as possible? Surely the latter.

(*Histories* 24.13)

It wasn't long before Polybius himself had to consider questions about Roman power, after his election in 170/169 BC to cavalry leader in the Achaean League (*Histories* 28.6.9). The Romans were currently fighting Perseus of Macedon, whom they went on to defeat in 168 BC at Pydna. After that victory, the Romans were concerned that the Achaeans had not supported their cause with sufficient enthusiasm and so a pro-Roman politician of the Achaean League, Callicrates, drew up a list of 1,000 people, including Polybius, all of whom were brought to Italy against their will by the Romans. Their presence there was partly designed to control the actions of the Achaean League. Polybius spent the next seventeen years in Rome, which gave him the chance to observe the Roman national character at first-hand.

The quality of his life during this enforced absence from Megalopolis was distinctly improved after becoming friends with the young Publius Scipio and his brother Fabius, the sons of Aemilius Paullus, the general who had successfully defeated Perseus at Pydna. As Polybius tells us, Scipio, together with his brother, petitioned the praetor so that he might be allowed to remain in Rome (*Histories* 31.23) and they developed 'a mutual affection, which could truly be compared to that of father and son, or of kinsmen of the same blood' (*Histories* 31.25).[6] Polybius presents Scipio as a fair-minded man, who swam against the tide in rejecting the corrupt lifestyle so favoured by his contemporaries. As well as becoming a highly competent military man, Scipio was also a literary patron, who supported the playwright Terence, the satirist Lucilius and the Stoic philosopher Panaetius. Scipio had wide cultural and political interests, and Cicero in *On the Republic* depicts a discussion between Scipio and his friends about government.

In 151 BC, Scipio travelled to Spain on military service and persuaded his friend Polybius to accompany him. The pair also went to Africa and Polybius, always keen to interview eye-witnesses, seized the chance to talk to the elderly king of Numidia, Masinissa, about Hannibal (*Histories* 9.25). Polybius also decided to return to Italy over the Alps, following in Hannibal's footsteps, 'to obtain first-hand information and evidence' (*Histories* 3.48) and adding authority to his version of events as a result. He criticises previous historians who distorted the facts and made self-contradictory statements in order to impress readers with the wonders of these mountains (*Histories* 3.47). Portraits of Hannibal as a leader combining supreme courage with utter lack of foresight in crossing the Alps provoke his particular irritation.

Of course, Polybius also witnessed important events in his own right. After he and the surviving Achaean exiles were finally allowed to return home in 150 BC, Polybius joined Scipio again and saw for himself the destruction of Carthage (146 BC) after its capture by his friend, who allegedly cried at the sight (*Histories* 38.21–22). Whereas Sallust would later see Carthage's destruction as deadly for Rome (through the removal of a foreign enemy who had previously kept Rome on her toes), Polybius allows for the possibility that the annihilation of the city was a necessary evil, although he reports various reactions to the final defeat of the Carthaginians by the Romans (*Histories* 36.9).[7]

Since Achaea was now at war with Rome, Polybius decided not to return immediately and, after borrowing some ships from Scipio, he went on a voyage of exploration down the African coast and through the Straits of Gibraltar, as Pliny the Elder records (*Natural History* 5.9).[8] Not much is known about this voyage but, after returning to Achaea, Polybius became involved in rebuilding the government after the Achaean league was dissolved. He died in or soon after 118 BC.

It is clear that Polybius' own personal experiences shaped his historical perceptions and made him choose this particular period (264–146 BC) rather than any earlier one. He formulates his subject in powerful terms:

> There can surely be nobody so petty or so apathetic in his outlook that he has no desire to discover by what means and under what system of government the Romans succeeded in less than fifty-three years in bringing under their rule almost the whole of the inhabited world, an achievement that is without parallel in human history.
>
> (*Histories* 1.1)

All historians had to convince readers that their subject matter was significant, but Polybius isn't just paying lip-service to a hackneyed topos. His sense of urgency is conveyed through his utter disbelief that there could be anybody not interested in the process by which the Romans extended their power. Walbank has suggested that Polybius' intended audience is indeed a broad one, and was meant to include both Greeks and Romans, even if his primary target was actually his Greek readership.[9] Certainly, he carefully explains terms derived from Latin for his non-Roman audience: so there is clarification about the procedure at a *fustuarium* ('beating'), by which miscreant soldiers were punished (*Histories* 6.37).

The period of less than fifty-three years in question runs from 220 BC, shortly before the start of the Second Punic War, to 168 BC, when the Romans defeated Perseus of Macedon at Pydna. In fact, the narrative actually begins before 220 BC and ends later than 168 BC. Polybius' first two books explore the background from 264 BC onwards to allow his readers to orientate themselves, before reaching the real starting point of 220 BC. As for the end point of the narrative, it is clear that Polybius' original plan changed as he wrote: instead of thirty books, his history went on to fill forty books. So he explains in a passage added subsequently that he wants to extend his account down to the end of the Achaean War in 146 BC:

> In this way our contemporaries will be enabled to see clearly whether the rule of Rome is something to be welcomed or to be avoided at all costs, and future generations to judge whether they should praise and admire or condemn it.

> (*Histories* 3.4)[10]

This focus on praise and blame is common in ancient historiography (cf. Tacitus *Annals* 3.65). However, the remark has a particular resonance for Polybius' shifting conception of the purpose that his historical narrative should serve. In the beginning, Polybius saw his work in fairly practical terms, as a means to satisfy contemporary Greeks' desire for information about this emerging Roman imperial power. His plan is to provide 'a comprehensive view, and thus encompass both the practical benefits and the pleasures that the reading of history affords' (*Histories* 1.4). Once the Achaean League had collapsed, however, and it became clear that the Romans would be dominant for some time to come, Polybius explicitly embraced a moral as well as a practical dimension (although, arguably, sensitivity towards the moral dimension must have been there from the very beginning, even if this isn't spelled out). His already wide-ranging audience is extended to include posterity.

So what did Polybius want us to think about the Romans? There is no easy answer to this question, partly because Polybius' own views about the Romans were progressively redefined in the process of writing his *Histories*. The Romans are certainly presented as having admirable qualities at the start of the narrative, as when Polybius notes their collective response to defeat by the Carthaginians at the Battle of Cannae in 216 BC, despite initial panic:

> For although the Romans had beyond any doubt been defeated in battle and their military reputation annihilated, yet through the peculiar virtues of their constitution and their ability to keep their heads, they not only won back their supremacy in Italy and later defeated the Carthaginians, but within a few years had made themselves masters of the whole world.

> (*Histories* 3.118)

It is striking here that Roman national character only partially explains the success story: the other crucial elements are Rome's constitution, which Polybius will analyse extensively (*Histories* 6.11–18), and (as is made clear later) its army (*Histories* 6.19–42).[11] At the same time, Polybius is prepared to acknowledge the role of 'the unexpected' in the generation of Rome's empire (*Histories* 1.1), although in general he doesn't allow the concept of Fortune to serve as a substitute for sound analysis of cause and effect. Even when deploying the image of Fortune as a good umpire in his account of the First Punic War (*Histories* 1.58), he subsequently presents the Roman decision to use naval force against the Carthaginians as the crucial factor. Although Fortune features in the narrative, Polybius is above all a rational writer who sees himself as writing 'pragmatic history' and who discerns that the rise of the Romans can be explained logically.

However, if one considers Polybius' portrait of the young Scipio (so different from his contemporaries), it is clear that he sees a subsequent decline in Roman public morals during the war against Perseus and the Macedonians (*Histories* 31.25).[12] Not every Roman was like Scipio, which raises questions about the Roman imperial machine. One point should be added about Polybius' presentation of his material. He frequently gives multiple viewpoints about particular Roman actions, such as the final defeat of the Carthaginians, where he offers four different interpretations (*Histories* 36.9) without endorsing any single analysis, either positive or negative. Perhaps the destructive reality of imperial power made Polybius feel uneasy (cf. *Histories* 5.11 on Philip V's destruction of Thermum), but by presenting multiple viewpoints he leaves the ultimate judgement about Roman imperial conduct to posterity.

During extensive criticism of the historian Timaeus, Polybius conjures up the figure of Odysseus to exemplify the man of action (*Histories* 12.27) and argues that the ideal historian needs to be just this sort of figure.[13] By implication we are meant to see Polybius himself as the embodiment of this active and practical Odyssean researcher. History isn't an activity to be conducted amidst the dusty shelves of libraries, but needs a practitioner who will investigate matters in the real world. In this context we should remember Polybius' journey across the Alps and his voyage of exploration around the coast of Africa and beyond the Straits of Gibraltar. No doubt he would have been unsettled if he had discovered that his own work would later be used as a source by another 'armchair historian': Livy.

Notes

1 Quoted and translated by F.W. Walbank, *The Hellenistic World*, 3rd edn, London: Fontana, 1992, p. 19.

2 The fragments of Polybius are much more substantial than those of (for example) Ennius.

3 See Walbank, *A Historical Commentary on Polybius' Histories Volume I*, Oxford: Oxford University Press, 1957, pp. 1–8.

4 Translations are by I. Scott-Kilvert, *Polybius: The Rise of the Roman Empire*, Harmondsworth: Penguin, 1979.

5 See further R.M. Errington, *Philopoemen*, Oxford: Oxford University Press, 1969, pp. 193–4.

6 See A.E. Astin, *Scipio Aemilianus*, Oxford: Oxford University Press, 1967, pp. 16–20, on Scipio and Polybius.

7 See further Walbank, *A Historical Commentary on Polybius Volume III*, Oxford: Oxford University Press, 1979, pp. 663–8.

8 On the Straits of Gibraltar (or Pillars of Hercules), see J.S. Romm, *The Edges of the Earth in Ancient Thought*, Princeton, NJ: Princeton University Press, 1992, pp. 17–19, 147–9. Walbank, *A Historical Commentary on Polybius Volume I*, p. 5, dates the trip to 146 BC.

9 Walbank, *Polybius*, Berkeley, Los Angeles and London: University of California Press, 1972, pp. 3–6.

10 See further Walbank, *A Historical Commentary on Polybius Volume I*, p. 301.

11 See further Walbank, *A Historical Commentary on Polybius Volume I*, pp. 673–97 on *Histories* 6.11–18 and pp. 697–723 on *Histories* 6.19–42.
12 See A.M. Eckstein, *Moral Vision in The Histories of Polybius*, Berkeley, Los Angeles and London: University of California Press, 1995, pp. 225–36, on the deterioration of the Romans.
13 See Walbank, *A Historical Commentary on Polybius Volume II*, Oxford: Oxford University Press, 1967, pp. 142, 409.

See also in this book

Cassius Dio, Herodotus, Livy, Sallust, Tacitus, Thucydides, Xenophon

Texts, translations and commentaries

The Greek text is available in Teubner (5 volumes) and Loeb (6 volumes), but there is no OCT.

As well as the Loeb, there is a Penguin translation, *Polybius: The Rise of the Roman Empire*, by I. Scott-Kilvert.

There is an Oxford commentary by F.W. Walbank (3 volumes).

Further reading

Davidson, J., 'The gaze in Polybius' *Histories*', *Journal of Roman Studies*, 81, 1991, pp. 10–24.
Derow, P.S., 'Polybius', in T.J. Luce (ed.), *Ancient Writers. Greece and Rome*, New York: Scribner, 1982, pp. 525–39.
Eckstein, A.M., *Moral Vision in The Histories of Polybius*, Berkeley, Los Angeles and London: University of California Press, 1995.
Sacks, K., *Polybius on the Writing of History*, Berkeley, CA: University of California Press, 1981.
Walbank, F.W., *Polybius*, Berkeley, Los Angeles and London: University of California Press, 1972.
Walbank, F.W., 'Supernatural paraphernalia in Polybius' *Histories*', in I. Worthington (ed.), *Ventures into Greek History*, Oxford: Oxford University Press, 1994, pp. 28–42.

TERENCE

Terence, comic playwright of the 160s BC, is almost as different from Plautus as two exponents of the same genre can be, while at the same time being deeply involved in a complex relationship of influence, intertextuality and reaction with his Roman predecessor(s) and with his principal Greek model, Menander. It is worth remembering that Plautus and Terence represent only a fraction of the original strength of Roman comedy. According to the ancient scholar Vulcacius Sedigitus, whose treatise *de poetis* ('On Poets') is mentioned by Aulus Gellius (*Attic Nights* 15.24.1), Caecilius (between Plautus and Terence in date) is best, Plautus next best by a long way, Terence comes sixth, Ennius tenth. Terence's work has little of the exuberance, vitality and towering magnificence of Plautus' more farcical, broad-brush comedy; instead it is a comedy of manners and is an important ancestor of the modern domestic drama. Terence has been admired for his lucidity of style, his gentle humanity, and the apparent timelessness and universality of his work. Six plays were written, all extant: *Andria* ('The Girl from Andros'), *Heauton Timorumenos* ('The Self-Tormentor'), *Eunuchus* ('The Eunuch'), *Phormio*, *Hecyra* ('The Mother-in-Law') and *Adelphoe* ('The Brothers').

We have plenty of stories about the life of Terence, though we should be wary of believing any of them. From antiquity there survive numerous testimonials, the most important of which are Suetonius' *Life* (first century AD) and Donatus' commentary (some six centuries after the playwright lived). The story is wonderfully romantic: Publius Terentius Afer, freedman of Terentius Lucanus, born *c*. 185 BC in Carthage in north Africa, died *c*. 159 BC in Greece. A slave, perhaps even a black slave, brought to Rome from Africa, freed for no other reason than that he was a genius (although his looks may have contributed also, as some sources say with varying degrees of maliciousness), became an international playwright before he was twenty, was befriended and fêted by the great and good of the land, produced a play (the *Eunuch*) which was the biggest 'box-office hit' of any up to its time[1] and was about to embark on the next stage of his sparkling career when disaster struck: on a trip to Greece, which he undertook to further his education and 'study Greek manners more closely', also to look for more material in the form of Greek plays, Terence died, a young man in his middle twenties, in a shipwreck which also claimed the 108 new Greek plays he was bringing home (so claims Suetonius) and/or (our sources get vague here) new plays he had written. The story is thus doubly romantic, playing on the huge sense of wonder and loss we feel at the vulnerability of literary works, as well as the poignant story of doomed genius. There is, however, no good reason to think it is true. Note how motifs in poets' lives have a habit of recurring – Virgil also died on a trip to Greece, where he went to put the final touches to the *Aeneid*.

One point in Terence's life which certainly is important for the reading of his work is his historical moment. The second century BC was a time of rapidly increasing Hellenism, there having been a great influx of Greek culture during and after the Second Punic War (ended 201 BC), and after the conquest of Macedonia in 168. Terence appears to have been friendly with several philhellenic nobles (lovers of Greek culture), including the younger Scipio Africanus.[2] Terence and his powerful friends played a major role in the Roman appropriation of and interaction with Greek culture.

The tone of Terentian comedy is quite similar to that of Greek New Comedy, for he eschews the farcical and other elements which are seen as 'Roman' (sometimes as 'Roman dross') by the critics of Plautus. There is the odd reference which might be topical, but in general Terence seems to strive to produce a realistic representation of Greek bourgeois life. In what sense, then, are his plays 'Roman'? Take the *Brothers*, thought by many to be Terence's finest play, based on a play of the same name by Menander, with a bit of one by Diphilus thrown in for good measure. The production notice, showing the Roman occasion for this play, and its philhellenic Roman aristocratic sponsors are a succinct hint at the play's complexities. It was performed at the funeral games for Lucius Aemilius Paullus, held by his sons Quintus Fabius Maximus and Scipio himself (both had been adopted into other aristocratic families, as was common). The story revolves around two sets of brothers: Demea has two sons, one of whom has been adopted by Demea's brother Micio. Each young man, in the way of things in Terence, is involved in an awkward love affair: Micio's son Aeschinus with a poor but free girl, whom he has made pregnant and whom he will eventually marry, Demea's son Ctesipho with a prostitute, whom he will eventually possess. These kinds of details of Terentian plots are fairly predictable, and it is part of the pleasure in the comic world and genre that they should be so. But the play is about the difficulties of education and the right way of influencing people. Micio maintains a liberal regime, which he hopes is based on trust and friendship, while Demea's policy is authoritarian. It would have found favour with the great Censor of the second century BC, Cato. By contrast, Micio's liberal educational policy, whether or not it is really a Greek sort of approach, can be perceived by a second-century Roman as 'Greek', or at least as 'Hellenising'. So we have a kind of opposition set up in the play between Greek licence and Roman strictness. In the end, Micio, with whom we have identified throughout the play, is the butt of an almost farcical ragging (suitable to provide closure to a comedy). Can it be, then, that Demea and Roman strictness have won? I don't think so. After all, Demea has been mocked and humiliated for four-fifths of the play and *his* son looks silly. Rather, the answer to the play is that there is no simple answer to the problem of the right way to bring up children; and there is no straightforward route for the development of Roman culture. For better or worse, the play seems to say, Roman culture is now bound up with Greek. 'Rome' is still 'Roman', but being Roman is a complex matter. And comedy is always at the father's expense.[3]

While issues of national culture are certainly important, Terence also has a reputation for a kind of universal humanity. Amusingly, the most famous line of Terence, which gives easy support for Terentian humanity, has a hint of irony in its own context. In the *Self-Tormentor*, Chremes says, in response to his neighbour Menedemus' thanks for Chremes' advice about how to manage Menedemus' relationship with his son: 'I am human, so nothing to do with humans do I consider foreign to me' (*homo sum: humani nil a me alienum puto*, 77). Chremes means that he is driven by universal altruism, but as the play progresses it becomes clear that Chremes is a busybody and even something of a hypocrite. Not that he is a bad character, as few in Terence are, but his pretensions to wisdom and disinterested neighbourly concern don't bear close examination. This gentle irony and complex development of character in Terence invites comparison with Jane Austen.

Terence took up a genre which was full-to-bursting with character-types and expectations placed on them, as he himself makes plain in the prologue to the *Eunuch*. Terence has peopled his world with variants on the characters of New Comedy, many of them made much nicer in the process (such as the 'noble prostitutes' of *Eunuch* and *Hecyra*), but the real innovation in his characterisation is the manner in which our expectations are provoked and then undermined. Terence uses a 'clever slave', for instance, not to develop that magnificent character into a higher art-form, as did Plautus in the *Pseudolus*, but rather *not* to 'use a clever slave'. A nice example comes from the *Eunuch*, often said to be Terence's most Plautine play. The supposedly 'clever slave' character, Parmeno, thinks up the crucial ruse in the play (right on character) but then tries to back away and finally confesses all to the old master (right off character, refusing it).[4] The humour and artistry of this situation is enhanced by the existence of strong 'clever slaves' in the tradition, against which Parmeno's character can react.

Crucial to this intertextual cheating-of-expectation is Terence's policy of not telling us the story in advance. He thus seduces us into picking up the prejudices surrounding particular characters, which he will then show to be inappropriate. This is particularly (although not exclusively) true with regard to female characters. Instead of the expository prologue, Terence uses protactic characters – that is, characters whose purpose is to set the scene and give out some information which the audience needs. A lovely example comes in *Hecyra*: a discussion about men between two prostitutes is interrupted by the arrival of the slave (another Parmeno) of one of the central families, who then gives them some of the story as a piece of gossip. The representation here of the courtesan Bacchis is not borne out by the development of the play, being rather the stereotype against which her character reacts. Although we get some information we need in order to understand the confusions of the play, we are not told (because Parmeno doesn't know) some other crucial elements, and we are tempted into expecting something quite different from what we get. The scene has the effect of undermining the reliability of *any* of the speakers in the play, all of whom are influenced by their own wishes, desires and prejudices. Part of the point of the play, perhaps, is to expose those influences among the audience also.

It is hardly surprising that the play was not well received at first (it failed twice, according to Terence's own testimony, before finally gaining a successful hearing). Perhaps the most important cheating of expectation in this play is in the characterisation of the mother-in-law herself. Damned to eternity by comedy, the older woman, particularly if she is married and if she is a 'false mother' (mother-in-law or stepmother), 'cannot' be other than the view we get of her in the first scene after the introduction – or so the stereotype has it. Laches, the husband of the title figure (Sostrata), bursts out of the house shouting abuse of his wife as the worst, and the teacher, of 'the whole tribe of women' (198–204). We eventually learn that nothing could be further from the truth, when Sostrata turns out not only to be willing to do anything to further the happiness of the young people, but also to be particularly sensitive to the nature of relationships between the generations. But the point here isn't just that Terence has started with a stock character and undermined its function by completely changing its complexion. Rather, it is also that he has provoked and undermined his *audience*'s prejudices, and their whole way of reading comedy. He has encouraged us to make judgements in a particular way, and then he has overturned them.

Hecyra could be held to be unusually sympathetic to women, both in the undermining of the stereotypes of mother-in-law and courtesan, and also in the exposure of the ancient dual standard between the genders in sexual morality. The girl, Philumena, was raped. She was then married to a man (Pamphilus) who didn't really want her, being in love with the prostitute Bacchis, but married her to please his parents. He didn't sleep with her for the first few months. After a while, however, he came to love her, but was then sent away on business. During his absence, it became apparent that Philumena was pregnant as a result of the earlier rape. It would be possible to pass the baby off as Pamphilus' own (and a little early), except for the fact that he would know it couldn't be because of the delayed consummation. Philumena leaves the house of her parents-in-law in order to conceal her condition, and the story gets around that she has quarrelled with Sostrata.

The upshot of it all is that it turns out Pamphilus himself was the assailant, so the baby is indeed his own and all is well. Does this expose the double standard or reinforce it? Terence is more concerned to jolt us out of our easy responses to stock characters than to make radical changes in the way the audience thinks about young women. In the *Eunuch*, he has one girl raped by a pseudo-eunuch actually during the play itself (offstage, of course), a unique event in extant comedy, and has the noble prostitute shared, at the end, between her two lovers, one of whom (at least) is a fool. A contribution to explaining what is going on here may come from noting that the *Eunuch* was produced at the Games in honour of Cybele, the Great Mother of the gods, whose cultic worship involves castrated priests. It is possible also to note that the rape is a kind of 'failed marriage', which will be put right by a proper marriage at the end. Both these points would allow us to view the whole thing in ritual terms, but none of this should entirely smooth over the discomfort that many readers and audiences will feel at Terence's challenging comedy.

Towards the end of *Hecyra*, Pamphilus speaks a rare piece of self-referential metatheatre. He says that he doesn't want things to end up 'as they do in the comedies, with everyone knowing everything' (866–7). Unlike Plautus, Terence rarely breaks the dramatic illusion in any direct way, preferring to maintain throughout the plays the naturalism we have seen in the expository opening scenes. This is not to say, however, that he is at all coy about metatheatrical sophistication. Throughout his work, there is a playful though understated and indirectly expressed awareness of his own place among the conventions of drama and with the strong playwrights who preceded him. Some of this awareness is played out in the highly literary prologues which he has substituted for the more integrated exposition favoured by Plautus. Terence uses his prologue to argue with his critics, to present his own philosophy of drama, to celebrate his friends and to capture the goodwill of the audience. In all this, his prologue may have some conscious connection with the parabasis of Old Comedy (see ARISTOPHANES). Much (too much) has been made by the critics of Terence's running battle with the older comic playwright, Luscius Lanuvinus, who is said to be the 'malevolent old playwright' who accused Terence of 'spoiling' Greek plays by putting together scenes from different plays, of plagiarism, of presenting as his own work plays largely written by his powerful friends and generally of being a bad thing. It would be worth noting, however, that the only evidence for this is Terence's own programmatic prologues and that this is an appropriately *comic* way of carrying on a debate about dramatic issues: for it is in the nature of ancient comedy to be agonistic. The antagonism expressed in the prologues, whatever else it might be, is programmatic for the genre of comedy.

The mixing of scenes from different plays connects with a particularly important Terentian feature: the double plot. All Terence's plays are structured around duality, focused on two brothers (*Brothers* [two sets], *Eunuch*, *Phormio* [brothers and cousins]) or two friends (*Andria* [which has two sisters], *Self-Tormentor*). There are usually two intertwining affairs, various minor characters acting as go-betweens for the two plots. The exception is *Hecyra*: if there is a double plot here, it would be the two halves of Pamphilus' relationship with his wife. On the one hand is the known marriage, on the other the unknown rape. The affair with Bacchis provides the link between the two, and allows the resolution which fuses the two stories into one. Pamphilus is his own double. Everything turns out well when he realises that his 'rival' (Philumena's rapist) is himself. Recognition and the fusion of opposites brings happy closure, because this is comedy.

Notes

1 According to Suetonius, it received the highest fee ever paid for a comedy: 8,000 sesterces.
2 Publius Cornelius Scipio Aemilianus Africanus (Numantinus – an unofficial extra name), consul in 147 and 134 BC.
3 See the brilliant, if difficult, discussion of this play and of the issues it raises about philhellenism, Roman-ness and education, by J.G.W. Henderson (*Writing Down Rome*, Oxford: Oxford University Press, 1999, ch. 2).
4 Chaerea is to dress up as a eunuch-slave, so that he can be near to a

young slave girl (supposedly) with whom he has fallen instantly in love. So he rapes her ...

See also in this book

Menander, Plautus

Texts, translations and commentaries

The OCT dates from 1963, the Loeb from 1912. Betty Radice's Penguin translation, first published complete in 1976, is elegant. There is also a translation by Palmer Bovie in the *Complete Roman Drama in Translation* (Baltimore, MD, and London: Johns Hopkins University Press), edited by D.R. Slavitt and P. Bovie.

Eunuchus and *Adelphoe* have editions in the Cambridge Greek and Latin Classics. All the plays except *Andria* have editions in the Aris and Phillips Series, or will do very soon.

Further reading

Duckworth, G.E., *The Nature of Roman Comedy: A Study in Popular Entertainment*, Princeton, NJ: Princeton University Press, 1952 (republished with preface and bibliography by Richard Hunter, Bristol Classical Press, 1994).

Goldberg, S., *Understanding Terence*, Princeton, NJ: Princeton University Press, 1986.

Konstan, D., *Roman Comedy*, Ithaca, NY, and London: Cornell University Press, 1983.

Norwood, G., *The Art of Terence*, Oxford: Blackwell, 1923.

Segal, E. (ed.), *Oxford Readings in Menander, Plautus and Terence*, Oxford: Oxford University Press, forthcoming.

LATE REPUBLICAN

CICERO

Cicero is responsible for the most famous of all Latin phrases: *o tempora! o mores!* ('o times! o morals!'), so good he used it four times.[1] It is a phrase which has been much used to deprecate later times and morals, both seriously and jokingly, as Cicero did himself. The combination of a serious moral and an act of self-parody here brings together some significant features of Cicero's work. On the one hand, it shows him characteristically deploring the way in which society in his own day failed to live up to the great example of the past, the *mos maiorum* or 'ways of our ancestors' which played such an important role in regulating and forming expectations about Roman behaviour. On the other hand, a joking response is also highly Ciceronian. If one's image of Cicero is formed mainly by the traces of the Victorian schoolmaster, or from expectations of Roman *grauitas* (seriousness implying authority – important indeed for Cicero), one may not appreciate how great a humorist he was, or, as Cato dryly and rather disparagingly remarked, 'what a comic consul we have' (Plutarch *Cato the Younger* 21). Cicero can in fact be very funny, and is even able to laugh at himself, despite the vanity and pomposity of which he is justifiably accused.

Cicero's life and his work are intimately bound up in each other – and are both extensive. Much of the evidence for his life comes directly from himself, which means, of course, that it is partial, but still it is a rich historical resource. The vast correspondence, for example, allows us to follow certain episodes in late Republican history from one well-informed man's perspective, day-by-day, even hour-by-hour, while most of the speeches are themselves acts of late Republican politics. A brief account of Cicero's life will have to suffice here. Marcus Tullius Cicero was born on 3 January 106 BC, a native of Arpinum, a town which had achieved Roman citizenship in 188 BC. He embarked on the career of a Roman aristocrat, passing through all the traditional stages in appropriate though unhurried order. His successful defence of Roscius of Amerina in 80, against a charge of having killed his father, made Cicero's name in oratory. The trial, like so many, was politically motivated.

As quaestor (the first magistracy on the way up the senatorial ladder) in 75, Cicero served in Sicily, where he seems to have shown himself an able administrator. Five years later, he was asked to undertake the prosecution of the outgoing governor of the province, Verres, on a charge of exploitation. Verres had powerful friends, but was defeated. Cicero passed through the other magistracies and in 63 became consul, in partnership with M. Antonius Hybrida, the uncle of Mark Antony. During the year, Cicero exposed the conspiracy of Catiline. It is likely that the threat to the state was not quite so appalling as Cicero's later celebration of his actions would suggest, but nonetheless most people accept that there was a real danger and that Cicero was responsible for its removal. In the process, however, he put some of the conspirators to death without trial (with the agreement of the Senate), after Catiline had fled the city. As a result his worst enemy, Clodius, was able to force Cicero into exile a few years later.

Although Cicero was recalled in 57, his position was necessarily much weakened. A governorship, of the province of Cilicia in Turkey, followed in 51. The civil war between Caesar and Pompey (early 40s BC) and its aftermath generated a period in the political wilderness for Cicero, but the situation was transformed by the assassination of Caesar in 44 and the ascendancy of Antony. For a few months in late 44 and 43 he enjoyed a position of considerable prominence and influence in the Senate, during which time he made a series of blistering attacks on Antony.[2] But it all went wrong, partly because Cicero underestimated a young man who had been born in the year of his consulship, a man called C. Octavius, who became C. Julius Caesar Octavianus when he was adopted in the will of his great-uncle the dictator Julius Caesar, and who would eventually become Augustus and change the world. Octavian turned against Cicero and the Senate to join Antony. Cicero's name went on the list of the proscribed and he was killed by Antony's men on 7 December, 43.

For Cicero, like many elite men at the time, upholding the republic was of paramount importance: their overwhelming political goal was to avoid too much power accruing to any individual. Cicero sought to preserve the social order and the authority of the Senate, although he was also ready to present himself when convenient as a friend of the people. His political rhetoric was usually conciliatory, emphasising the 'harmony of the orders' (that is, the Senate, the equestrian order of respectable and wealthy citizens, and the lower orders right down to freedmen). This developed into a rhetoric of the 'consensus of all *boni*', all 'good' men, by which he means all men who seek to uphold the status quo. As a 'new man' (that is, someone from a family which had never entered the Senate before and didn't have a ready-made network of social relations), he had to struggle to achieve acceptance by the political elite. It is a sign not only of his own hard work but also of the porousness of the Roman aristocracy that he did achieve a certain greatness in Roman politics. If that greatness was less than he would have us believe, it was still an outstanding achievement. He was also an important literary figure and the writer of the most marvellous Latin prose.

In the late Republic, it is impossible to separate literature and politics, particularly in Cicero's primary genre: oratory. When the contemporary poet Catullus ironically, but nonetheless admiringly, calls Cicero *optimus omnium patronus* ('the best patron of all' – Catullus 49.7), he is paying tribute to Cicero's domination over the forum, in both political and forensic speeches. Oratory was a major form of literature and was also the crucial tool by which men swayed the Senate and the people,[3] drove policy, pursued glory and personal vendettas, and accused and defended enemies and friends in the courts. 'Serving the state' in this way was, alongside farming and fighting, the one truly respectable occupation for an upper-class Roman. Oratory was entirely amateur, at least in theory. It would have been regarded as disgraceful for an advocate at law to accept payment. That is not to say, however, that there were no material benefits to be had, as well as outright corruption. The courts were heavily political; relationships of obligation and friendship were the central structuring motives in Roman political life. We will under-stand the cruel humour, the invective, the slander rather better if we realise that it played an important role in defining an elite Roman male's free position, first by seeking to make the victim into an outsider and second by constructing the identity of the speaker as someone who has the right and the personal authority to say these things about another member of the elite. Forensic and political oratory, as practised by Cicero and his contemporaries, depended on the political culture in which men (a group of them, that is) had the freedom to speak and the possibility of *making a difference* by speaking.

Some fifty-eight speeches of Cicero are still extant (although not all are complete). A few of them were never delivered, such as the famous second *Philippic* which was circulated as a pamphlet and the whole second *actio* ('case' – five speeches) against Verres, which was rendered unnecessary when Verres fled after the first speech, but which was too good to waste. We have both more and less than Cicero actually said in public: more, because many of the speeches were written up for publication; less, because we have only the script of the performance and Cicero is quite explicit that oratory has much in common with acting. We also lack the interactions of political debate, the questioning of witnesses and the other speeches that make up a court case.

Cicero's style tended towards the exuberant, with great rolling periods, sonorous sentiments and an astonishing command of rhythm. This last aspect is something which the modern reader can find hard to appreciate: the Romans, even when listening to prose, were very sensitive to the sounds and rhythms of speech, which could be varied for different purposes and which were particularly marked at the ends of sentences, in the cadences which take on almost a poetic metrical form (adapted to prose). It would be only a slight exaggeration to say that Cicero sometimes won cases by the sheer music of his speech. Cicero was master also of changes of tone: his oratory moves from biting irony, sarcasm, thundering invective and humour to tragic pathos, old-fashioned moral seriousness and companionable, plain-speaking friendliness. He was well versed in the theories of the well-formed speech, which moves from exordium (introduction) through narrative, proofs and refutation of opponents to the final peroration. This formal structure is standard, but Cicero was no slave to it. His work is enlivened, and his cases supported, by his wide knowledge of law and of Roman history, for precedent and ancient example are crucially important in persuading a Roman audience.

One of the most effective and entertaining aspects of Cicero's speeches are the vignettes, character sketches and anecdotes which sometimes have scant direct relevance to the matter at hand, but a great deal of relevance to winning over an audience and scoring a point. Let's take an example from the second *Philippic*. Cicero wants to show that Antony is even more of a threat to 'liberty' than the dead Caesar. The tyrannicides (Brutus and Cassius, with others, who killed Caesar) are praised. Caesar himself is attacked as being too powerful and overbearing, but not vilified as an utter profligate like Antony. If Caesar had to be killed, how much more should Antony be regarded as a public enemy whom all good men should aim to see dead! Cicero tells the story (*Philippic* 2.85–7) of how Antony offered a diadem to Caesar, inviting him to take the kingship. Caesar rejected the offer: he probably even engineered the whole event so that he *could* publicly repudiate the suspicion of attempting the kingship. But Cicero's lively and evocative telling of the story serves to display both the threat of Caesar himself, enthroned in gold (*Philippic* 2.85), and the dangers of Antony, while avoiding attributing to Antony the kind of personal power and authority which was the basis for excessive influence. Traditionally, Romans won glory and influence by the exercise of military and political virtues. In the late Republic, certain individuals exploited such influence to acquire unprecedented power. Yet here comes Antony, without a virtue to his name, still revealing himself as hungry for power.

The anecdote ends with a catalogue of over-powerful men who had to be killed for the sake of freedom: 'was all this to be done so that Antony could set up a king at Rome?' The resounding *rex Romae constitueretur* ('a king at Rome should be established' – *Philippic* 2.87) ends the passage. The collocation of *rex* and *Romae* poses the ultimate, unspeakable horror to the Republic. And this man who sought to make Caesar king, now seeks tyranny for himself and the overthrow of the state – when he is sober enough to do anything about it! Antony is accused of all kinds of sexual irregularity (*Philippic* 2.84), but most of all passive homosexuality (which of all things most undermines his status as free Roman male); of drunkenness, which causes a tendency to vomit over the most sacred Roman political places and his own lap in an assembly (*Philippic* 2.63); of being in league with all the worst people (*Philippic* 2.67), including slaves; of greed, debt, deceit. The list seems endless; the telling so varied and subtle that one is served with an overwhelming weight of despicable behaviour, without getting bored of hearing of it.[4]

In a forensic case, the defending orator was by no means expected to stick to what we would regard as material pertinent to the defence of the client. He might seek to persuade the court to pity, to fellow-feeling, to indignation against the accusers. In this regard, it is fascinating to watch the complex relationships between Cicero as defending counsel (the position he preferred) and his client's accusers. Sometimes the accusers were political enemies of Cicero, but they were just as likely to be his friends. Each speaker in a trial (perhaps about six to eight people) would probably be involved in some relationship of obligation or opposition with other contestants. Such is the case in Cicero's defence of Marcus Caelius Rufus. In 56 BC, after Cicero's return from the exile into which his enemy Clodius had forced him, Caelius was accused on five charges, including plotting to poison a woman called Clodia, who was the sister of Clodius. Caelius had been attached to Cicero as a young man, for his induction into political life at Rome, but had become estranged from him and even become friendly with Catiline; Caelius had, only months before this trial, been prosecuting counsel against Cicero's (successful) defence, but now the tables are turned and Cicero is defending Caelius; on the other side, the accusers are men with whom Cicero has a good relationship, including L. Sempronius Atratinus, who is almost certainly the son of the man whom Caelius was attacking in the aforementioned case, and against whom he was about to bring another case. Cicero is able, therefore, to commend Atratinus' filial loyalty, admire his oratory and crush his case. But *behind* the accusation are the Clodii. It is on them that the full weight of Cicero's invective falls. The aim is to win the case, attack the enemies, but not offend the friends.

Catiline is a perennial enemy. Cicero needs to show both that Catiline was a public enemy (a constant refrain in his work) and that it wasn't too much to Caelius' discredit that he became attached to him. Cicero therefore represents Catiline as a strange mixture of virtues and vices. Catiline is shown to be attractive, and dangerously effective, but also repellent to those who have the maturity to see through him. His inconsistency is itself a vice: he is a *monstrum* (*Pro Caelio* 12), a sort of religious portent of a monster, in whom there were the outlines of excellent qualities at war with all the vices.

Clodia gets similar treatment. This woman, who is probably the inspiration for Catullus' Lesbia, is presented as the sort of dangerous emancipated woman who seduces young men and threatens the very fabric of the state: a 'courtesan'[5] with the wealth and influence of a Roman noble.[6] The various intrigues to do with Clodia are presented as a comedy. This is argument by entertainment: Clodia is effectively placed in the stock role of the grasping courtesan from comedy, and Caelius in the role of the young man, who may be foolish but is never expected to suffer in the end. It is also hinted that she murdered her husband, the 'excellent' Metellus (*Pro Caelio* 34, 60) and that she sleeps with her brother – Cicero pretends a slip of the tongue when he refers to Clodius as Clodia's husband: 'I meant to say brother. I always make that mistake' (*Pro Caelio* 32).

Cicero builds up to the attack on Clodia with a great show of moderation. How would she like him to deal with her? In the old-fashioned way or the modern way? He tries both, taking up the mask of two representative characters. The first character to be impersonated (*Pro Caelio* 3 – this is a device called *prosopopoeia*) is a hero of the Republic and ancestor of Clodia, Appius Claudius Caecus, censor in 312 (consul 307 and 296), builder of the Appian Way and the first Roman aqueduct. In suitably stern, archaic language, Claudius demands to know why his degenerate descendant has anything to do with Caelius at all. Did he build the aqueduct so that she could wash after her sexual debauchery? Build the Appian Way so that she could visit other women's husbands? At the end of his thundering speech, Cicero pretends that they should all be terrified by the voice of the great moral Roman past. The second mask is a complete contrast: it is the younger brother of Clodia, 'so nervous that he had to sleep with his sister' (*Pro Caelio* 36 – the implication is incest). This pathetic, wheedling weakling is made to protest that there are plenty of other lovers to be had, so she shouldn't pursue this Caelius who is no longer interested in her. The contrast with Appius Claudius could not be greater. The audience (I meant to say judges; I always make that mistake) are to enjoy the performance, condemn the Clodii, admire the Claudii (even while they may laugh a little nervously at Appius' old-fashioned severity), feel part of the group of good Romans who maintain *mos maiorum* but have a sense of humour – and acquit Caelius. They did.

Unlike collections of letters from later antiquity, Cicero's correspondence was not written for publication. That isn't to say, however, that some of it was not intended for public gaze, for some are official letters of a political nature which would certainly have been passed around a group. There are also letters which follow a set generic pattern (that isn't to question their sincerity), such as letters of consolation over a bereavement, encouragement in some political matter and personal recommendations, which are as formulaic as modern-day references. We have thirty-six books of letters to various friends and relatives, including many significant figures in late Republican history. Some letters from these people to Cicero are preserved with Cicero's own.[7]

The letters to Cicero's lifelong friend Atticus are collected together. These cover a vast range of subjects, including requests that Atticus should purchase some nice works of art on Cicero's behalf; expressions of affection for Atticus' little daughter Attica; accounts of civic events such as trials and debates in the Senate; desperate pleas, with recriminations, that Atticus should work for Cicero's return from exile; worried musings about which course of action Cicero should take on all sorts of matters. Two other collections are devoted to particular individuals: to Cicero's younger brother Quintus, including literary works on matters such as the right way to run a province; and to the tyrannicide Marcus Brutus, in which we see the Republic dying. Indeed, many of the letters of the last part of Cicero's life evoke in readers a sense of real-life tragedy: Cicero and his correspondents don't know, as we do, that the Republic for which they are fighting is doomed.

If in the speeches and the correspondence we cannot distinguish the literary from the political, in his theoretical writings also Cicero sees himself as a great writer in the service of the state. The most intensive periods of Cicero's production on theoretical works coincide with periods of relative political inactivity, for example after around 55 BC, when he wrote *On the Orator* while Clodius' gangs were most active, and during the dictatorship of Julius Caesar in the mid-40s, when he composed most of the philosophical works. We should note, however, that the famous *On Duties* (*De Officiis*) was composed at the same time as the *Philippics*.

Most of the theoretical works are in the form of dialogues, in conscious imitation of Plato's practice. Much of the material, also, is influenced by Greek writers. On the other hand, the characters involved in the dialogues are either heroes of the great days of the Republic or sound Republicans of Cicero's own day (including himself), and the issues raised are constantly considered with reference to the Roman political and social environment. In all this, we can see how Cicero combined a knowledge about and love of Greek culture with a strong sense of Roman-ness and the values of Roman *mos maiorum*. The theoretical works may be roughly divided into three groups: the rhetorical, the political and the philosophical.

Since oratory is so political a skill, however, the works of rhetorical theory could hardly be unpolitical. The dialogue *On the Orator* (*De Oratore*) is set in 91 BC, just before the outbreak of the Social War, with which began the long, slow death of the system which fostered political oratory. A dialogue of 46 BC, significantly called *Brutus* and dedicated to Marcus Brutus (himself an accomplished orator), tells the history of Greek and Roman oratory, while another work of the same year, the *Orator*, has detailed discussions of style, including rhythmic prose. The long-running contest between the flamboyant 'Asianic' style and the more restrained 'Attic' style is at issue in both works. Although Cicero became more restrained as his career developed, he was never in sympathy with the driest of Attic oratory.

It is only a small step to the political works. Again in imitation of Plato, Cicero wrote a dialogue *On the Republic* between 54 and 51. It is set in 129 BC, and features a hero of the second century whom Cicero particularly admires, Scipio Aemilianus, in dialogue with his friend Laelius about the best kind of constitution. Not surprisingly, the right answer looks rather like an idealised form of the Roman republican state. An interesting question is the role Cicero assigns to someone called the *princeps* ('first man'). It seems likely that this *princeps* was to be a brilliant leader who was in the forefront of aristocratic politics because of his fine qualities, but not at all like the monarchic emperor which the word came to signify under Augustus. The characters have a particular importance, for Cicero sometimes sought to position himself as a latter-day Laelius to Pompey's Scipio (see, for example, *Letters to His Friends* 5.7.3, to Pompey). In order to understand why 'monarchy' wins the debate as to which type of constitution is best, it may be relevant that the dialogue is set before the rise of the power-hungry characters from Sulla on, whose warring destroyed the Republic. In Cicero's own day, it was no longer possible to hold such an idealised view of rule by one man.[8] *On the Republic* was followed by *On Laws*, in which Cicero, his brother Quintus and Atticus played out the dialogue. This fictional discourse is presented with a realism that defies clear distinction from the 'active' works (that is, speeches and correspondence).

Cicero had studied philosophy from his youth, but only started to write overtly philosophical works in his last few years. There are three religious works surviving: *On the Nature of the Gods*, *On Divination* and *On Fate*. While he was convinced of the value of traditional religious practice within the political life of the state, Cicero was prepared to rehearse debates which questioned the existence and nature of the gods. His philosophy is eclectic, combining interest in a range of different philosophical schools,[9] but most committed to the academic tradition stemming from Plato. This academic tradition contributes to his attitude to religion: Cicero isn't the type of Sceptic who believed that nothing can be believed; however, he holds a theory of knowledge based around the most plausible opinion, rather than dogmatic truth. He is least sympathetic to the Epicurean tradition, of which Atticus was nominally an adherent. Epicureans were opposed to participation in public affairs, something which would be anathema to Cicero.[10] The hard-hitting morality of the Stoics attracted him, particularly after it was given a Roman edge by the very respectable Republican Cato, but Cicero was inclined to find it too rigid and, in its extreme forms, absurd. Among his philosophical works are the *Tusculan Disputations*, the dialogue *On the Ends of Good and Bad* and two short dialogues, *Greater Cato on Old Age* and *Laelius on Friendship*, addressed to the best of friends, Atticus.

In the treatise *De Officiis* (*On Duties*), Cicero uses philosophical theory to outline the ethical basis of his political ideals by describing the virtues of a statesman. 'Tully's Offices', as it became known, has been of all Cicero's theoretical works the most influential over European thought. The treatise doesn't use the dialogue form, but presents itself as an exhortation to Cicero's son, who was at the time studying philosophy in Athens. The main inspiration for *On Duties* is Stoic; the second-century Stoic philosopher Panaetius, connected with Scipio Aemilianus, is an important authority to whom Cicero often openly refers. Cicero's work is divided into three books. The first lays out the four virtues of wisdom, social virtue (justice and liberality), greatness of spirit and *decorum* ('seemliness' or 'appropriateness'). It might seem a little odd to us to include under the last heading thoughts on 'manners' such as conversation, appearance and even interior decor, but this is due to what we might perhaps call our more fragmented approach to life-issues. For a Roman, housing appropriate to one's station and avoiding luxury as it avoided poverty was a sign and part of a well-ordered whole. It was precisely this kind of harmony and integrity that Catiline lacked in Cicero's description discussed above. The second book considers various beneficial things, such as good reputation, health and wealth. The final book relates the first two: we learn that the truly beneficial is what is honourable and just, justice being an important theme of the work. The treatise ends with expressions of affection towards and hope for Marcus, somewhat undermined, for us, by the parting shot: 'be assured that you are very dear indeed to me, and will be far dearer if you take delight in such guidance and advice' (*On Duties* 3.121). Bullied sons are an inevitable element in Roman patriarchy, but it shouldn't be supposed that Cicero was even aware that anyone would consider his sentiments other than the most proper and appropriate for a father and a good citizen.

Notes

1 *Against Verres* 2.4.56, *Against Catiline* 1.2.1, *On His House* 137.3, *On Behalf of King Deiotarus* 31.1.
2 These speeches, fourteen of which are extant, were called *Philippics* – an allusion to the speeches of Demosthenes against Philip of Macedon. Quotations show that there were at least three more in antiquity.
3 The Senate was in theory an advisory group for the consuls (the top magistrates at Rome, who held office in pairs, for one year at a time) and was made up of former magistrates (quaestor, aedile, praetor and consul, in that ascending order of importance). In practice, the Senate's advice was taken as binding (usually). Orators also regularly addressed the Roman people, speaking from the rostrum to anyone who happened to be there or to various types of specially convened gathering.
4 An honest evaluation would have to say that Cicero can sometimes go on a bit too long for modern taste, which tends to prefer brief soundbites.
5 Clodia is called an *amica*. This feminine form of *amicus* doesn't have the positive political and social implications of the masculine form, but on

the contrary is used of a girlfriend or prostitute. At other points Cicero insists that the matron-behaving-like-a-courtesan he is talking about is *nothing to do with* Clodia (thereby of course talking about Clodia).

6 The siblings belong to the patrician family, the Claudii. Clodius uses the plebeian form of his name, and in fact got himself adopted into a plebeian family, so that he could stand as tribune of the plebs.

7 There are sixteen books of correspondence with Atticus, sixteen with various friends, three with Cicero's brother Quintus and one with Brutus.

8 See M. Fox 'Dialogue and irony in Cicero: Reading *de republica*', in A.R. Sharrock and H.L. Morales (eds), *Intratextuality: Greek and Roman Textual Relations*, Oxford: Oxford University Press, 2000, pp. 263–86.

9 A clear exposition of Cicero's philosophical position relative to the main schools of Greek philosophy may be found in M.T. Griffin and E.M. Atkins, *Cicero: On Duties*, Cambridge: Cambridge University Press, 1991.

10 This is perhaps not an adequate explanation, since there were politically active Epicureans around, such as Cassius, but the point isn't crucial.

See also in this book

Demosthenes, Julius Caesar, Lysias, Plato, Pliny the Younger

Texts, translations and commentaries

Cicero's extant works are so vast that the modern media of publication haven't quite kept up. Most of the works are available in OCT, but it gives a sense of the scale to realise that the speeches alone make up six volumes of OCT. The Teubner series is complete, although some editions are old. The Loeb series runs to twenty-nine volumes, mostly rather old, with only D.R. Shackleton-Bailey's four volumes of the *Letters to Atticus* being a modern edition (1998). Only three volumes of World's Classics are available (*On the Nature of the Gods, The Republic and The Laws, Defence Speeches*). Seven volumes of Penguin Classics together represent only a selection. Many individual works have editions with commentary, although there remains a lot to be done.

Further reading

Habicht, C., *Cicero the Politician*, Baltimore, MD: Johns Hopkins University Press, 1990.

Hutchinson, G.O., *Cicero's Correspondence: A Literary Study*, Oxford: Oxford University Press, 1998.

Mitchell, T.N., *Cicero: The Senior Statesman*, New Haven, CT, and London: Yale University Press, 1991.

Powell, J. (ed.), *Cicero the Philosopher*, Oxford: Oxford University Press, 1999.

Rawson, B., *The Politics of Friendship: Pompey and Cicero*, Sydney: Sydney University Press, 1978.

Rawson, E., *Cicero: A Portrait*, London: Allen Lane, 1975.
Stockton, D., *Cicero: A Political Biography*, London: Oxford University Press, 1971.
Wiedemann, T., *Cicero and the End of the Roman Republic*, Bristol: Bristol Classical Press, 1994.

JULIUS CAESAR

What would we think today if a general who was actively seeking political power wrote up his military campaigns for a wider audience? We would probably be rather suspicious, particularly if the author used the third person to describe events, thereby implying emotional detachment and impartiality. Today, the roles of politician and general are usually played by different people, but in the ancient world there was considerable overlap between the two spheres, particularly in the turbulent twilight years of the Republic.

Caesar not only wrote *Commentarii* about his operations in Gaul and about the civil wars, but also appears in works by other authors. Catullus treats Caesar scornfully in his poetry (though Caesar forgave him), Cicero refers to him constantly in his speeches and letters, Ovid narrates his apotheosis in the *Metamorphoses*, Valerius Maximus often depicts him positively in the *Memorable Deeds and Sayings*, Lucan casts him as a fiery character in his civil war epic (the *Pharsalia*) and both Plutarch and Suetonius wrote biographies about him. From brief snapshot to extended portrait, images of Caesar proliferate in ancient literature, so to distinguish between the man and the myth is never easy, given Caesar's own literary output and his role in terminating the Republican system of government.

It might be useful to begin by outlining the main events of his life.[1] Caesar, born in 100 BC into an ancient patrician family, became one of the most dominant politicians and generals of the century. After gaining military experience in Asia and winning a civic crown of oak leaves for saving a fellow soldier's life, he returned to Rome where he prosecuted two former supporters of the dead dictator Sulla (with whom he had fallen out). Although he was unsuccessful, he became popular as an orator through these early cases.

Caesar's career really took off in the 60s BC. He became quaestor in 69 BC, the same year as he delivered funeral orations for his wife Cornelia and his aunt Julia. In the second speech he even boasted that his aunt's father was descended from Venus (Suetonius *Divus Iulius* 6); indeed, he continued to court divine status right until his death. Meanwhile, his career progressed nicely with an aedileship in

65 BC, the post of *pontifex maximus* in 63 BC (usually held by an experienced magistrate)[2] and the praetorship in 62 BC. This was the year when he intervened in the case of the Catilinarian conspirators by proposing (unsuccessfully) that they should be treated leniently rather than executed (as Cato the Younger proposed): Sallust offers a version of his speech (*Catiline* 51.1–43), in which Caesar warns against taking decisions in anger which might injure the state.[3] In 60 BC Caesar joined a political alliance with Pompey and Crassus (the so-called 'first triumvirate'), after which Pompey married Caesar's daughter Julia, and in 59 BC Caesar became consul.

Through the *lex Vatinia*, Caesar was put in charge of Cisalpine Gaul and Illyricum. Between 58 and 51 BC, he engaged in successive campaigns which resulted in the subjugation of Gaul. Caesar also invaded Britain in 55–54 BC, lured, as Suetonius claims (*Divus Iulius* 47), by the country's supply of pearls. During this period, the relationship between the three triumvirs began to crumble: Julia died in 54 BC and Crassus was killed fighting a misguided campaign against the Parthians in 53 BC. Caesar wanted a second consulship in 49 BC but, blocked by his enemies in Rome, he invaded Italy, notionally to defend the tribunes of the people who had fled to him from Rome. Poets and historians alike see his crossing of the river Rubicon (near Ariminum in northern Italy) on this occasion as a symbolic moment.[4]

With legions experienced through campaigning in Gaul, Caesar was able to defeat Pompey at the Battle of Pharsalus in Thessaly in 48 BC. The historian Asinius Pollio suggests that after the battle Caesar revealed his true reasons for starting the civil war, namely a desire to avoid prosecution by acting first:

> They brought it on themselves. They would have condemned me regardless of all my victories – me, Gaius Caesar – had I not appealed to my army for help.

> (Suetonius *Divus Iulius* 30.4)

Although Pompey escaped to Egypt after Pharsalus, he was treacherously killed, which left Caesar free to deal with pockets of Pompeians in Africa (where he won a battle at Thapsus in 46 BC) and in Spain (where he won a battle at Munda in 45 BC). During this period, Caesar was consul in 48, 46, 45 and 44 BC, and was dictator in 49, 48, 46, 45 and 44 BC. He wanted to be deified and (ironically) succeeded shortly before the death which proved his mortality.

Caesar was assassinated by a group of conspirators led by Brutus and Cassius on 15 March 44 BC. The result was not freedom, but further civil wars which lasted until 31 BC.

Despite an active military and political life, Caesar still wrote prolifically. Suetonius lists various works which haven't survived, including a tragedy (the *Oedipus*), a piece called *In Praise of Hercules*, a volume of *Collected Sayings*, an essay *On Analogy*, two books *Against Cato* (written in response to Cicero's laudatory *Cato*) and finally a poem known as the *Journey* (Suetonius *Divus Iulius* 56), as well as various speeches, letters and military despatches. There are also his surviving works, the seven books *Gallic War* and the three books *Civil War*. This is an impressive output, but Caesar wasn't alone in combining an active military life with writing. Cicero's brother Quintus, for example, is supposed to have written four tragedies in sixteen days while campaigning with Caesar in Gaul in 54 BC (Cicero *Ad fratrem Quintum* 3.5.7). Warfare certainly involved a good deal of waiting around, which would have left time for writing for those who were so inclined.

Nor does quantity, of course, necessarily indicate quality. It may be significant that Caesar's adoptive son, Augustus, wrote to his coordinator of libraries, Pompeius Macer, forbidding the circulation of Caesar's minor works. Could this have been because not every book by the divine Caesar was a masterpiece? There are also various spurious works attributed to Caesar, including Hirtius' eighth book of the *Gallic War*, as well as the *Alexandrian War*, the *African War* and the *Spanish War*, narratives about the final stages of the civil war written perhaps by some of Caesar's officers.

The fact that Caesar's narratives were continued by unknown writers suggests the popularity of his original works. Cicero says that Caesar's memoirs are 'clean, direct and graceful, and divested of all rhetorical trappings' (*Brutus* 262), although the historian Asinius Pollio was more critical, claiming that the commentaries had been composed with disregard for the truth and that Caesar, whether deliberately or through absent-mindedness, had described his own actions incorrectly. Hirtius, the continuator of the *Gallic War*, suggests that Caesar had originally written the work to provide raw material for 'proper' historians to develop into a more polished narrative. No historian ever tackled this task.

The central question usually asked of the commentaries is how far Caesar distorted the truth. There is no simple answer, partly because the circumstances in which the commentaries were published remain unknown. For instance, were the seven books *Gallic War* written and published as a unit, or was each separate book published on an annual basis once it was completed?[5] It certainly would have been useful if, by annual publication, attention in Rome was regularly drawn both to Caesar's military successes in Gaul and to set-backs which made his continued presence there necessary. One could compare Ovid's strategy of regularly publishing separate books of the *Tristia* to remind readers of his absence from Rome. The annual appearance of a book from *Gallic War* could have been an invaluable defensive strategy. After all, Caesar's campaigns were expensive and needed justification, particularly once his enemy Domitius Ahenobarbus had tried to summon Caesar back to Rome in 56 BC to face prosecution.

There are similar questions about the publication of Caesar's other surviving work, *Civil War*, which has generally faced more serious charges of bias than *Gallic War*. Were the three books *Civil War* published by Caesar himself, despite the apparently unfinished state of the third book, or did somebody else take the decision to publish them after Caesar's death? Perhaps we will never know. We can, however, make some general observations about Caesar's self-portrait and his depiction of Pompey in this work. From the very beginning, Caesar emphasises that his enemies acted illegally and that most senators who voted for Scipio's motion that Caesar should disband his army before a certain date did so in fear after being threatened by Pompey's friends (*Civil War* 1.2). Pompey emerges as a dubious figure, who pretends to be a supporter of the Republic but resorts to all manner of dangerous and desperate techniques to get what he wants, such as arming slaves to fight on his behalf (*Civil War* 1.24; cf. 3.4.4, 3.21.4, 3.103.1). Caesar, by contrast, presents himself as having an extraordinarily good relationship with his own soldiers, although in order to create this impression he does gloss over some tense moments, such as the mutiny of his troops at Placentia (cf. Cassius Dio *Roman History* 41.27–35, Appian *Bella Civilia* 2.47.191–2.48.199).

This doesn't mean that Caesar idealises his men, partly because depicting their unruliness enables him to emphasise his own achievement in controlling such a potentially destructive force. So Caesar highlights the tension between his strategy of blockading the enemy general Afranius and the demands of his soldiers, who want a pitched battle (*Civil War* 1.82). Caesar prevails and Afranius surrenders. Here and elsewhere, Caesar presents himself as a buffer between order and chaos.

Other commanders in the narrative aren't so successful at controlling their soldiers, notably Pompey, who decides to fight a pitched battle at Pharsalus 'with the encouragement of his soldiers' (*Civil War* 3.86.1). Despite this, Caesar depicts Pompey deviously abandoning his men before the battle has been properly lost (*Civil War* 3.94). Pompey's hasty departure from the camp after the battle, together with his complaint that his soldiers are virtually traitors, is meant to seem particularly graceless and hypocritical (*Civil War* 3.96). In this chapter Caesar raises questions about the moral calibre of Pompey and his soldiers through his description of the camp, in which there are piles of silver, bowers, some tents floored with freshly cut turf and others wreathed with ivy. All these touches suggest that the Pompeians had been arrogantly preparing for their victory banquet before the battle had even started.

Caesar deploys various techniques to enhance the plausibility of his account, such as his use of internal focalisation to allow us to see what his opponents are thinking. So when the Pompeian general Bibulus finds thirty ships, which have just delivered Caesar's troops, he 'vented on them the anger and resentment produced by his own carelessness', burning the ships and putting the captains and crews to death (*Civil War* 3.8.3). Caesar adds that he did so 'in the hope of deterring the others by the magnitude of the punishment' (*Civil War* 3.8.4).[6] Such a reading of Bibulus' motives is certainly plausible, but Caesar may be exaggerating the intensity of Bibulus' emotions for his own purposes.

Another effective narrative technique was the creation of vivid speeches. As well as his own speeches, Caesar also includes set-piece speeches delivered by his enemies which he couldn't possibly have heard himself. So there is Vercingetorix's speech to his men, responding to the accusation that he preferred to hold power in Gaul through Caesar's gift rather than to acquire it through their favour (*Gallic War* 7.20). Even more striking, Critognatus delivers a speech to the Gauls blockaded inside Alesia advocating cannibalism rather than surrender, which Caesar doesn't want to omit because of its 'singular detestable cruelty' (*Gallic War* 7.77). Roman audiences were always ready to believe stories about Gallic cruelty and Caesar happily obliges.

Finally, there is Caesar's style of writing. While it is certainly possible to overestimate the clarity and simplicity of Caesar's Latin, there is certainly a directness about his style which discourages a reader from looking for hidden meanings or questioning the truth of what is being expressed. One commentator, Spilman, has observed that almost half of Caesar's subordinate clauses are ablative absolutes (not of the Tacitean variety!),[7] and Oakley has suggested that Caesar 'was content to string three, four or five instances of the same construction together'.[8] The avoidance of complex, hypotactic periods of Latin also enhances Caesar's identity as a military man. It was a topos of Latin historiography that soldiers tended to avoid intricate language in favour of straight-talking (cf. Subrius Flavus at Tacitus *Annals* 15.67.2), so Caesar's style reinforces his character. Nevertheless, there can still be artfulness in apparent simplicity. If one reads the *Spanish War*, written by an anonymous soldier or general, this will put things into perspective. Finally, even the famous third-person narrative voice, which we today tend to regard with some suspicion, may have been devised for practical reasons. Wiseman has recently suggested that if the commentaries were meant to be delivered by a speaker other than Caesar at a public meeting, then the third-person form was unavoidable.[9]

Not all readers have been prepared to take Caesar's accounts at face value. Lucan, in his epic about the civil war, the *Pharsalia*, deliberately includes events such as the mutiny at Placentia, which Caesar had carefully omitted from his own narrative.[10] In addition, Lucan recasts incidents with which his readers would have been familiar from their reading of Caesar's commentaries. So, as the Battle of Pharsalus is drawing to a close, Lucan's Pompey doesn't slip away from the fighting like a coward, leaving his soldiers to face the enemy without their leader. Instead, he goes around his troops and calls them back from an early death, saying that he wasn't worth so much (*Pharsalia* 7.666–9).

There are other examples of a critical response to Caesar's version of events. The historian Appian describes the capture of Gomphi in Thessaly and notes how Caesar's troops 'stuffed themselves endlessly with everything and became disgracefully drunk' (*Bella Civilia* 2.64.268). The climax of the attack is the moment when twenty distinguished elders of the town are discovered with goblets scattered around them, lying on the floor 'as if they had succumbed to drunkenness' (*Bella Civilia* 2.64.269), although in reality they have poisoned themselves. The genuine inebriation of Caesar's soldiers is poignantly juxtaposed with the apparent drunkenness of the desperate citizens. Caesar, naturally, doesn't include this scene in his account of events at Gomphi (*Civil War* 3.80) and Appian may have referred to the lost narrative of Asinius Pollio for his information.[11]

Caesar was ultimately perhaps more influential as the image of a model general and as a symbol of the end of the Republic than he was as a writer. Even so, his works provided a challenging intertext for subsequent authors, such as Lucan, and the artful simplicity of his style has meant, rightly or wrongly, that Caesar is often the first introduction to 'real' Latin experienced by modern students. This is a far cry from the purpose for which the commentaries were originally written, but perhaps Caesar, given his promotion of simple and austere Latin in his *On Analogy*, wouldn't have been unhappy.

Notes

1 See in general J.P.V.D. Balsdon, *Julius Caesar*, New York: Athenaeum Press, 1967; M. Gelzer, *Caesar: Politician and Statesman*, Oxford: Oxford University Press, 1968.
2 S. Weinstock, *Divus Iulius*, Oxford: Oxford University Press, 1971, p. 31, observes that Caesar was elected 'in preference to elder and more deserving competitors'.
3 D.S. Levene, 'Sallust's *Catiline* and Cato the Censor', *Classical Quarterly*, 50, 2000, p. 191, argues that

> Caesar argues for Catonian mercy at the expense of Catonian rigour, Cato [the Younger] for the reverse. In the Censor, these elements were combined: here they are fragmented and separated into contradictory opposites.

See further A. Drummond, *Law, Politics and Power: Sallust and the Execution of the Catilinarian Conspirators*, Stuttgart: Franz Steiner, 1995, pp. 25–50.
4 See Plutarch *Caesar* 32, Lucan *Pharsalia* 1.213–27, Suetonius *Divus Iulius* 31, Appian *Bella Civilia* 2.35.
5 See T.P. Wiseman, 'The publication of *De Bello Gallico*', in K. Welch and A. Powell (eds), *Julius Caesar as Artful Reporter*, London and Swansea: Duckworth and the Classical Press of Wales, 1998, pp. 1–9.
6 See further J.M. Carter, *Julius Caesar: The Civil War Book III*, Warminster: Aris and Phillips, 1993, p. 150.
7 M. Spilman, 'Cumulative sentence building in Latin historical narrative', *University of California Publications in Classical Philology*, 11, 1932, p. 238.
8 S.P. Oakley, *A Commentary on Livy Books VI–X Volume I*, Oxford: Oxford University Press, 1997, p. 131.
9 Wiseman, *op. cit.*, p. 8 n. 27.
10 See further E. Fantham, 'Caesar and the mutiny: Lucan's reshaping of the historical tradition in *De Bello Civili* 5.237–373', *Classical Philology*, 80, 1985, pp. 119–31.
11 See further R. Ash, *Ordering Anarchy: Armies and Leaders in Tacitus' Histories*, London: Duckworth, 1999, pp. 13–14.

See also in this book

Catullus, Cicero, Lucan, Plutarch, Sallust, Suetonius, Xenophon

Texts, translations and commentaries

The Latin text is available in OCT (2 volumes), Teubner (2 volumes) and Loeb (3 volumes).

As well as the Loeb, there are Oxford World's Classics translations of the *Gallic War* by C. Hammond and of the *Civil War* by J.M. Carter, and Penguin translations of the *Conquest of Gaul* by D. Browne (revised by J. Gardner) and of the *Civil War* by J.F. Mitchell.

There are commentaries on *Civil War I and II* and *Civil War III* by J.M. Carter in the Aris and Phillips Series. C.S. Kraus is working on a commentary on Book 7 of the *Gallic War* for the Cambridge Greek and Latin Classics Series.

Further reading

Balsdon, J.P.V.D., *Julius Caesar*, New York: Athenaeum Press, 1967.

Gelzer, M., *Caesar: Politician and Statesman*, Oxford: Oxford University Press, 1968.

Weinstock, S., *Divus Iulius*, Oxford: Oxford University Press, 1971.

Welch, K. and Powell, A. (eds), *Julius Caesar as Artful Reporter*, London and Swansea: Duckworth and the Classical Press of Wales, 1998.

Yavetz, Z., *Julius Caesar and His Public Image*, London: Thames and Hudson, 1983.

LUCRETIUS

Science in the modern world is generally thought to be 'objective', with science-writing a matter of simple fact, unadorned and uncomplicated by rhetoric. It isn't usually written as poetry. In antiquity, the wars of the disciplines were drawn up on different lines. Science and philosophy were the same thing: 'natural philosophy' was what physics was called until very recently. Moreover, there was a tradition of presenting factual or informative material in poetic form. It isn't so odd, then, that Lucretius chose to explain 'The Nature of Things' (the title is *De Rerum Natura*) through an epic-didactic poem. He was continuing a tradition which had begun with Hesiod, and derives also from the scientific poems of Parmenides and Empedocles. The didactic tradition of the Hellenistic scholar-poets such as Aratus (who wrote a poem on the constellations) is also a development from this origin. If Lucretius is reaching further back, behind the artificial learning of the Hellenistics into a tradition of poetic seekers after truth, that is part of the archaising tendency of his work that makes such important contributions to his elevated poetic style.

It would be wrong to deny that there was also a conflict between philosophy and poetry in antiquity, with exponents as famous as

Plato as well as Lucretius' master Epicurus, but nonetheless we must start with the understanding that poetry in antiquity was a medium far broader in scope than in the modern world. We might note, finally, that even among modern scientists, objective observers of fact as they supposedly are, there is a tendency to wax lyrical about the structure of a molecule or about the infinity of the universe. The American physicist Richard Feynman is an eloquent example.

Titus Lucretius Carus lived from around the mid-90s BC to around the mid-50s BC, in the time of Catullus and Cicero. He may have lived in Campania (the region around Naples), but that is only an inference from the fact that there were known Epicurean groups there. Few ancient writers have much to say about him. Cicero makes one mention, agreeing with his brother Quintus that Lucretius' poems have both genius and poetic art (*Letters to his Brother Quintus* 2.10(9).3), but has nothing at all to say about the claim which Jerome made over 400 years later, that he (Cicero) edited Lucretius' work for publication after the poet's death. The Augustan poets clearly know him, and Virgil is one of his most sensitive readers, but there is little reliable information about his life. The snippet of a 'life' we have from Jerome reports a story that he was driven mad by a love-potion, wrote *De Rerum Natura* in moments of lucidity between bouts of madness, and later killed himself. There is no reason to believe this story, every reason to suspect its ideological basis. The poem itself is an exposition of Epicurean philosophy in six books of archaic roughness and sublime poetic beauty. It is addressed to Memmius, a typical Roman aristocrat of the Late Republic, who was also a patron (political, rather than artistic) of Catullus. He was not converted.

In the third century BC, there grew up in Greece a plethora of philosophical schools. Although these schools of thought to a considerable extent defined their own beliefs by opposition to other schools, in practice there was a great deal that they had in common with each other.[1] One often-sought goal was the achievement and maintenance of *ataraxia*, or freedom from the fears and worries that make life miserable. There being so many rather more substantial things that can make life miserable, philosophers also needed to develop both a lifestyle to minimise them and an attitude of mind to cope with them. Epicurus' version puts the emphasis on pleasure as the goal of life. Both in antiquity and in the modern day, this has been (mis)interpreted as a form of hedonism. The modern understanding of the term 'Epicurean', epitomised by the brand of luxury foods called 'Epicure', is quite different from the rather austere lifestyle recommended by the master, with its emphasis on simple, natural pleasures and a diet which is 'good for you': the food label 'Epicure' has more in common with Horace's joking representation of himself as a fat and happy 'Epicurean pig' (*Epistles* 1.4.16).

According to Epicurean philosophy, the greatest pleasure is freedom from fear, especially fear of death and of the gods, and from physical pain, together with the realisation that the needs of life are few. Epicurean philosophy is essentially materialist: that is, it is based on the belief that the only things which have existence are material things. There is body and there is void (which is the absence of body). The 'soul' is in fact 'body' (in the sense of 'matter') and doesn't outlive the dissolution of the body. The gods live a life of perfect happiness and serenity, totally unconcerned with the affairs of mankind. All natural phenomena are just that – natural – not the effects of the gods' anger or design. In fact, there is no design in the universe, just chance. If you understand this, you will be able to look down unperturbed on the sufferings of human life. In general, therefore, it is not in the interests of your happiness to engage in public affairs: Lucretius' political quietism sets him apart from the mainstream of Latin literature (see, for example, *De Rerum Natura* 5.1129–35). True friendship, on the other hand, is a positive goal, and the truest form of friendly activity is engaging in Epicurean philosophical discussion.

But Epicurus was against poetry,[2] particularly the sort of mythic poetry which is so important in the elevated epic tradition, and this left Lucretius with a problem in writing an epic-didactic poem expounding Epicurean philosophy. Sensing the difficulties involved in Lucretius' position, the critics have for generations asked, in various forms, the question 'was the philosophy or the poetry more important in Lucretius?' Today we tend to be disinclined to make rigid distinctions between 'artist' and 'thinker', and to see the tension rather as the great challenge for Lucretius. We should also be aware that the persona who narrates the poem isn't straightforwardly to be identified with the author. We might also say that Lucretius' great achievement was to appropriate the poetic power of word and image, the mythic heritage, and even religious enthusiasm, all for Epicurean philosophy (and perhaps also the other way round).[3] Symbolic and programmatic of this creative difficulty is the invocation to Venus in the proem (the opening of Book 1). This atheistic poem begins, oddly, with a strikingly beautiful hymn to the goddess, mother of the Roman race (1.1), who is celebrated for the generative power which she embodies (as goddess of sex) and asked to bring peace to the Romans through her love affair with the war-god Mars. To attempt to resolve all the tensions and to deny all the conflicts would be to reduce the power of the poem and the challenge of its philosophy.

The subject of *De Rerum Natura* is nothing less than the nature of the universe, for only by understanding the universe can a man understand his own place in it and be happy (see 5.82–90, 6.58–66). The first two books are primarily concerned with laying out the groundwork of atomic theory: that everything that exists is matter or void; that all matter consists of tiny particles which are themselves neither created nor destroyed, but which are constantly moving and constantly forming new compounds as things are born and die; that matter is infinite, although the different *types* of atoms are not; that the activities of these atoms, which explain everything, happen without any design from an outside agency; that occasionally atoms swerve from their normal downward movement and this accounts for 'free will', which might otherwise look impossible in this highly mechanistic world-view. An atomic theory is older than Lucretius or even Epicurus.

Book 3 shows how, on the basis of the atomic theory, we can understand that the mind and the life-force of a person are material things, made up of very fine atoms with a loose texture and wide gaps between them (3.370–95), which dissipate when a person dies, like escaping water or smoke (3.425–44). There is no life after death, and so no reason to fear death. The materiality and mortality of the 'soul' thus crucially established, Book 4 considers the activities of the senses (for example, vision is caused by very faint images of things – a film of their particles – emanating from things and striking our eyes), of thoughts and the will, of dreams, and of how images stimulate responses. The book ends with Lucretius on sex, a famous tirade against the emotion of love (4.1058–1191), hinting at the kind of love displayed in the poetry of Catullus. Lucretius is writing in the style of the diatribe (as elsewhere in the poem) and is on good traditional Roman ground here: sex is fine, natural and useful, but love is quite another matter. It wastes your property (because of fine gifts foolishly given to the beloved) and destroys your autarky (control of the self). That can't be good ... .

The first two books lay out the theory; the second two consider how it explains the life of the individual; the final two do the same for the life of the universe and of mankind as a whole. Book 5 is primarily concerned with cosmology: how the world (one among an infinite number) was formed by a chance conglomeration of atoms and will be destroyed when eventually their bonds are dissolved; then with the development of human life, in which progress is seen to happen by chance or arising out of some need. This history of culture is consciously anti-religious and anti-Hesiodic, being concerned to show technological developments as human constructs, not gifts of the gods. The final book deals with natural phenomena, particularly those which traditional religion and myth would interpret as the activity of the gods: thunder, earthquakes, floods, and so on. The book and the poem end with a graphic description of the plague at Athens during the Peloponnesian War. If you can look untroubled on that, you have conquered fear and are fully fledged as an Epicurean.

Although he was writing at the time of the early neoteric movement (see CATULLUS), Lucretius staked his poetic position in the more archaic ground of earlier Latin poetry.[4] He expresses a particular admiration for Ennius (1.117–26), although, like Empedocles, the great man is said to have fallen into fundamental error (not being Epicurean) despite his genius. Lucretius has a preference for stylistic archaisms, like the genitive ending 'ai' (which makes two syllables) rather than the diphthong 'ae', often producing a resounding close to a hexameter line: the word *materiai* ('of matter': ma-te-ri-a-i) is particularly effective in this way. Students of Latin poetry will have grown up learning this form, and the passive infinitive ending '-ier', from Lucretius.

He also favours compound words, like *montiuagus* ('mountain-wandering', 2.1081), *altiuolans* ('high-flying', 5.433), *fluctifragus* ('wave-breaking', 1.305), not to excess, but much more frequently than is the Augustan norm, and periphrastic expressions like *uenti uis* ('force of wind' or just 'wind', 1.271) or *caeli lucida templa* ('the shining temples of the sky', 1.1014; this is a variant on an Ennian phrase, such as *caeli caerula templa*, *Annals* Liber I, xxix Sk). Like most early poets, he loves alliteration and assonance[5] and takes what later poets would consider liberties with his metre, such as dropping a final '-s' before another consonant in order to ensure that the syllable stays short, for example in *quominu' quo* (1.978). All this 'rough archaism' is part of the bardic persona: the elevated, prophetic pronouncements in which the priest of Epicurus expounds the master's revelation.

What he denies is often as poetically useful to Lucretius as what he affirms. For example, in illustration of the dangerous and impious potential of *religio* ('religion/superstition'), he tells the story of the sacrifice of Iphigenia (1.80–101) as emotively as any tragedian or epic poet. It is the graphic horror and pathos of the story, as much as the 'light of reason' (for example, 1.144), which is to turn us from the false belief that the gods can be placated by such means (or any means). Indeed, often Lucretius seems concerned to shock, entice or even amuse us into seeing the truth, even while he maintains that it is rational argument which will convince. That must be the force of the satiric picture of laughing and crying atoms in 1.919–20 (and again at 2.976–84, where the atoms even discourse on their own natures). The image is introduced in order to be denied (of course atoms don't hold their sides with laughter ...) but its effect works by being entertainingly absurd. The series of 'logical proofs' about the insensate nature of the atoms (2.865–972) is thus rounded off with a memorable rhetorical flourish.

It is perhaps above all Lucretius' imagery which brings his subject to life. This is a poem full of flowering fire (1.900, 4.450), grazing stars (5.523–5) and earth boiling over with worms (5.798–806).[6] Often the poetry is in the analogy, and indeed there is some slippage between simile, analogy and proof. One of the most famous and beautiful examples is the 'motes in the sunbeam' image (2.112–41), used to show that one should believe in the movement of atoms, even though one cannot see it. When a sunbeam 'sheds light into shadowy places' (2.115), you can see tiny particles dancing about in the bright beam of light. Lucretius uses the image of battle and offers this as an analogy for the movement of atoms constantly being tossed about in the void. But the analogy is 'proof' also, because we are meant to imagine that we are actually *seeing* atoms in the sunbeam, even though Lucretius has told us that the atoms are too small to see, for this is 'an actual indication of underlying movements of matter that are hidden from our sight' (2.127–8). It is as if the shaft of light has revealed to us the true structure of the atomic universe.[7] This light in darkness isn't just a pretty picture: it is the controlling image of the poem, that the 'divine mind' and 'golden words' (3.12–15) of Epicurus shed light into the dark places of human life. Without Epicureanism, we are like children terrified of the dark (2.55ff.), needing Dr Lucretius to apply the honey of his poetry to the bitter cup of philosophy that will make us better (1.936–50).

Notes

1 For a lucid introduction to the Hellenistic philosophical schools, and their influence at Rome, see M.T. Griffin and E.M. Atkins, *Cicero: On Duties*, Cambridge: Cambridge University Press, 1991. For more complex studies, see A.A. Long, *Hellenistic Philosophy: Stoics,*

Epicureans, Sceptics, London: Duckworth, 1974, and R. Sharples, *Stoics, Epicureans and Sceptics*, London: Routledge, 1996.

2 That statement is contentious. Texts in support of the view are Cicero, *On the Ends of Good and Bad* 1.72 and Diogenes Laertius 10.13. See D. Obbink, *Philodemus and Poetry: Poetic Theory in Philodemus, Lucretius and Horace*, Oxford: Oxford University Press, 1994.

3 Gale speaks of

> [Lucretius'] overall strategy of investing the truths of Epicurean philosophy with the beauty and attractive power [that is, power to attract the reader] of images derived from myth.

> (Gale 1994: 207)

4 He has some intertextual relationships with Hellenistic poetry, including a version of the Callimachean motif of 'being the first to' write in a particular manner (1.921ff.; 4.1ff.), and of course some connection with Aratus. But his path to Callimachus is not the same as that of the neoterics.

5 For a few examples, almost at random, try 1.979, 2.34 and 2.145–6.

6 See D. West, *The Imagery and Poetry of Lucretius*, Edinburgh: Edinburgh University Press, 1969 (esp. p. 16 for the worms).

7 See P.R. Hardie, *Virgil's Aeneid: Cosmos and Imperium*, Oxford: Oxford University Press, 1986, ch. 5.

See also in this book

Hesiod, Ovid, Plato, Virgil

Texts, translations and commentaries

The poem can be found in OCT, Loeb, Penguin and World's Classics translation (with introduction and notes by Don and Peta Fowler).

Books 3, 4 and 6 have Aris and Phillips editions, while Book 3 also has a Cambridge Greek and Latin Classics edition.

Further reading

Clay, D., *Lucretius and Epicurus*, Ithaca, NY, and London: Cornell University Press, 1983.

Gale, M., *Myth and Poetry in Lucretius*, Cambridge: Cambridge University Press, 1994.

Sedley, D.N., *Lucretius and the Transformation of Greek Wisdom*, Cambridge: Cambridge University Press, 1998.

Segal, C.P., *Lucretius on Death and Anxiety: Poetry and Philosophy in De Rerum Natura*, Princeton, NJ: Princeton University Press, 1990.

West, D., *The Imagery and Poetry of Lucretius*, Edinburgh: Edinburgh University Press, 1969.

CATULLUS

'We all like to learn facts about the lives of writers and artists, but this activity should not be confused with critical assessment of their works.'[1] So Godwin, a recent editor of Catullus, warns his readers when discussing the most constructive interpretative strategies to apply to the poetry. Investigating the relationship between ancient poetry and real life has always proved rather a minefield for critics, but this issue is naturally more central in some genres of poetry than in others. For instance, epic, with its conventional muted voice of the narrator and the predominance of mythically distant subject matter, offers little scope for those wishing to tease out a poet's biographical details from the text. However, other genres, particularly love poetry, satire and epigram, purport to look at the contemporary world from the poet's point of view and often use verbs in the first-person singular to do so. As a result, some critics have read the autobiographical element in the poetry rather literally.

Catullus himself problematises such critical approaches when attacking Furius and Aurelius for extrapolating too much about the author from his poetry: 'for you thought from the evidence of my little poems that because they are rather soft, I was not virtuous enough' (16.3–4). Fitzgerald suggests that in this poem Catullus 'is concerned with the power relations between poet and reader' and that his readers are 'in rather a different position from that assumed by Furius and Aurelius'.[2] We therefore need to read the poetry sensitively to distinguish between Catullus and 'Catullus'. The poet's apparently autobiographical world is a poetic construct, even if (as some concede) it has some connection with 'reality'.

We do know a little about Catullus from outside sources, but our information is fairly sketchy. Ovid says that Catullus was fairly young when he died (*Amores* 3.9.61). Jerome, writing in the fourth century AD, says that Catullus came from Verona and lived between 87 and 57 BC, but something is wrong with these dates, since Catullus refers at one point (11.9–12) to Caesar's invasion of Britain in 55 BC.[3] So Catullus' dates are more likely to be 84–54 BC, an era when Rome faced military crises posed by Sertorius and Spartacus, as well as the Catilinarian conspiracy and violence perpetrated in Rome by the armed gangs of Clodius and Milo. However, we get little sense of this turbulent political backdrop from the poetry itself, although there are poems on leading men such as Cicero (49), Mamurra (29, 41, 43, 57) and Caesar (54, 57, 93), with whom Catullus' father was supposed to have been friends (Suetonius *Divus Iulius* 73).

Catullus' *libellus* is eclectic by nature, consisting of short, polymetric pieces (1–60), the long poems (61–8) and the elegiac compositions (69–116). Certain groups of poems, such as those about his love affair with Lesbia (2, 3, 5, 7, 8, 11, 37, 43, 51, 58, 68b, 70, 72, 75, 76, 79, 83, 85–7, 92, 107), appear throughout the collection and bind it together. Other pieces feature people who appear only once, such as Arrius, whose comically aspirated Latin reveals his social pretensions (84). Some poems are linked not by recurrence of individuals, but by theme, such as those on the work of other poets (14, 22, 35, 36, 50, 95). The collection as a whole is dedicated to Cornelius Nepos (*c.* 110–24 BC), the biographer and historian whose production of a miniaturised universal history in three books seems to make him particularly receptive to Catullus' elegant little book of poetry.

Despite these elements of cohesion, Catullus' *corpus* is still strikingly diverse, both metrically and in its subject matter. Some have found it hard to understand that the same poet who wrote about the marriage of Peleus and Thetis, with its beautiful inset tableau of Ariadne on Naxos (64), could also produce pieces about oral sex (59), incest (90) and autofellation (88). One explanation for this inherently contradictory poetic voice lies in the dominant model of Hellenistic poetry. In particular, Catullus was strongly influenced by the Hellenistic poet Callimachus, who was equally at home writing polished, allusive pieces on mythical subjects and composing risqué epigrams. One of Catullus' long poems, the lock of Berenice (66), is a direct translation of an original in Callimachus' *Aetia* and in the last poem of the collection (116), Catullus recalls how he tried to write in the manner of Callimachus in order to soothe Gellius' anger. In both contexts, he refers to Callimachus as *Battiades*, 'son of Battus' (65.16, 116.2), which is a reference to the legendary founder of Cyrene, Callimachus' native city.

A particularly elegant set of references comes when Catullus, picking up on poem 5 in which he urges Lesbia to give him thousands of kisses, explains to her exactly how many will satisfy him:

> As great a number as the Libyan sands that lie on silphium-bearing ['lasarpiciferis'] Cyrene in between the oracle of sweltering Jove and the holy tomb of old Battus ...

> (7.3–6)

This is typically Catullan. It might initially seem like a passionate love poem, but Catullus twists a familiar poetic trope by adding

Alexandrian details. As Fitzgerald says, 'hidden learning is substituted for sexual secrets'.[4] This isn't just any old sand, but sand from Callimachus' home city, Cyrene, which is modified by an extraordinary new adjective (*lasarpiciferis*). The innovatory vocabulary and the ostentatious references to Jupiter's oracle and Battus' tomb suggest that Catullus' readers (and Lesbia) enjoy learning for its own sake in the Alexandrian manner.

The audience has already had fair warning of Catullus' literary heritage in the collection's opening poem, which signals a Callimachean aesthetic by referring to his *lepidum novum libellum/ arida modo pumice expolitum* ('elegant new little book, just polished off with dry pumice stone', 1.1–2). The reference here is not just to the finely produced physical artefact of the book, but also works on a metaphorical level, suggesting the highly refined nature of the poetry itself.[5] The diminutive, *libellus* ('little book'), triggers particular associations with Callimachus, who rejected the grandeur of epic in favour of delicate pieces on a small scale.

This Callimachean ethos didn't mean the exclusion of epic material altogether, but it did involve treating it in a rather specialised and circumscribed way. Instead of a grand all-encompassing narrative, Catullus in his poem about the wedding of Peleus and Thetis (64) creates a perfect segment of epic in miniature, which offers an alternative perspective on various Homeric characters. Peleus is no longer old, as in Homer, Thetis isn't yet a mother, and Achilles hasn't even been born (though there are extensive prophecies about his future). This tendency to depict familiar epic figures at unfamiliar periods of their lives is a favourite technique of Alexandrian poets and was also used by Theocritus (as in *Idyll* 18, the *Epithalmium* of Helen). Catullus' inset story of Ariadne, suffering after her abandonment by Theseus, accentuates the female perspective and qualifies the glory of the heroic age in important ways.[6] It is initially set up as a work of art, as we see Ariadne abandoned on the beach, frozen in time 'like a Bacchant in marble' (64.61), but the picture is expanded on an emotional level so that we come to know about Ariadne's feelings and how she came to be in this predicament.[7]

In addition, the poem as a whole is richly allusive and relies on the learning of Catullus' readers to supply the context and to unravel particular references. Thomas has argued that in the first section of the poem alone, Catullus alludes to at least five previous versions of the story of the *Argo*.[8] As a result of such techniques, Ovid (*Amores* 3.9.63) and Martial (1.61.1, 14.100) both call Catullus *doctus* ('learned'), but so too must have been his ideal readers, some of whom were probably poets themselves. Indeed, Catullus was part of a wider artistic community of poets who were called the 'neoterics' by Cicero (*Letters to Atticus* 7.2.1) and probably bounced ideas off one another in a creative atmosphere, enhancing the learning and inventiveness of the poetry. Or at least this is the impression created by Catullus in his account of a brainstorming session with fellow poet Licinius Calvus, who wrote a miniature epic, the *Io* (50), which is now lost. Godwin calls the poem 'a self-consciously ironic text, asserting the sort of passion usually associated with sexual love in a message to a fellow poet'.[9]

For many modern readers, Catullus' most enjoyable poems are those tracing his doomed love affair with a mistress known simply as Lesbia. At an early stage in the reception of the poems, Lesbia's mask was conveniently lifted to reveal a real woman called Clodia as Catullus' lover (Apuleius *Apologia* 10), quite possibly the same Clodia who is so memorably portrayed by Cicero in the *Pro Caelio* as an amoral and predatory adulteress.[10] In this speech, Cicero's naïve young client Caelius is presented as having had an affair with Clodia (who also has an incestuous relationship with her brother) before being ruthlessly dumped by her.

Whether or not Catullus' mistress can be conclusively identified with this particular Clodia is still open to question, but it has almost certainly enhanced the enjoyment of Catullus' poetry for some modern readers to equate Lesbia with this historical woman, whose character was so vividly attacked by Cicero. If the poetry is read seeing Lesbia through the filter of Clodia, the personalities of the two lovers become dramatically polarised from the very start, as sensitive young poet meets selfish older woman with tragic consequences.

This identification may say more about the taste of some readers for narratives of doomed romantic love than it does about the real identity of Lesbia. However, to be fair, it does also cohere with Catullus' depiction of the affair: he accentuates the vulnerability of his love, 'which because of her has fallen like a flower at the edge of the meadow, after it has been touched by the passing plough' (11.22-4). In choosing this image, Catullus poignantly alludes to Sappho's simile of a hyacinth trampled by herdsmen (fr. 105c), suggestively articulating his feelings through the voice of a female poet.[11]

According to traditional perceptions of gender in the ancient world, men were rational, while women were emotional, so Catullus' expression of his feelings in this way may contribute within the Lesbia cycle to a progressive feminisation of his persona (or 'gender dissonance', to use Skinner's terminology).[12] Yet at the same time we should remember that this is only one aspect of a multi-faceted poetic identity. Only a few poems later, Catullus is happily back in the world of aggressive male sexual posturing: 'I will bugger you and fuck your mouths, Aurelius the pansy and Furius the pervert' (16.1–2). The change of tone is all the more pronounced because the poem in which Catullus included the flower simile was addressed to the very same pair, Aurelius and Furius. Reading Catullus' poetry often involves tensions and disorientation, but we shouldn't try to iron these out.

Catullus' poetry, which (apart from poem 62) has only reached us thanks to a single manuscript, was especially attractive to later writers. In antiquity, Catullus' *libellus* was soon imitated by poets, who saw its potential for enriching their own works. Virgil alluded creatively to poem 64 in *Georgics* 4,[13] as did Ovid, both at *Amores* 3.11b.33–4 and elsewhere. Ovid indulges in a running joke about Ariadne's lament, partially because he knew that his audience would be so familiar with the Catullan original.[14] Ovid gives a tongue-in-cheek version of Ariadne's speech (*Fasti* 3.471–506; cf. *Heroides* 10), but then defies our expectations by not giving a rendition in the *Metamorphoses*, simply describing her as 'deserted and making many complaints' (8.176; cf. *Ars Amatoria* 1.536–7). Martial too alluded to Catullus for comic purposes in a wry reworking of poem 85: 'I don't like you, Sabidius, but I can't say why: I can only say that I don't like you' (*Epigram* 1.32). Even Statius wove clever references to poem 64 into his unfinished epic the *Achilleid*.

In more recent times, Sir Walter Ralegh, Richard Lovelace, Jonathan Swift, Lord Byron, William Wordsworth, Aubrey Beardsley and Arthur Symons all produced translations of at least some of Catullus' poems from the sixteenth century into the twentieth century. The world of Catullus' poetry may be a construct, but it certainly is one of the most successful to emerge from the Classical period.[15]

Notes

1 J. Godwin, *Catullus: The Shorter Poems*, Warminster: Aris and Phillips, 1999, p. 12.
2 W. Fitzgerald, *Catullan Provocations: Lyric Poetry and the Drama of Position*, Berkeley, Los Angeles and London: University of California Press, 1995, pp. 49–50.

3   See Godwin, *op. cit.*, p. 129.
4   Fitzgerald, *op. cit.*, p. 55.
5   W.W. Batstone, 'Dry pumice and the programmatic language of Catullus 1', *Classical Philology*, 93, 1998, pp. 125–35.
6   Some have seen in Ariadne reflections of Catullus, abandoned by Lesbia. See further Fitzgerald, *op. cit.*, p. 147.
7   There is also temporal dislocation, since Ariadne's story had technically not yet happened at the time of the wedding of Peleus and Thetis.
8   R.S. Thomas, 'Catullus and the polemics of poetic reference (64.1–18)', *American Journal of Philology*, 103, 1982, pp. 144–64.
9   Godwin, *op. cit.*, p. 169.
10 See further T.P. Wiseman, *Catullus and His World: A Reappraisal*, Cambridge: Cambridge University Press, 1985, pp. 15–53, on Clodia.
11 See further Fitzgerald, *op. cit.*, pp. 179–80.
12 M.B. Skinner, '*Ego Mulier*: The construction of male sexuality in Catullus', in J.P. Hallett and M.B. Skinner, *Roman Sexualities*, Princeton, NJ: Princeton University Press, 1997, p. 129.
13 A.M. Crabbe, 'Catullus 64 and the fourth *Georgic*', *Classical Quarterly*, 27, 1977, pp. 342–52.
14 See further G.B. Conte, *The Rhetoric of Imitation: Genre and Poetic Memory in Virgil and Other Latin Poets*, Ithaca, NY: Cornell University Press, 1986, pp. 57–69, and S. Hinds, *Allusion and Intertext: The Dynamics of Appropriation in Roman Poetry*, Cambridge: Cambridge University Press, 1998, pp. 3–4.
15 See further Wiseman, *op. cit.*, pp. 211–45, and Fitzgerald, *op. cit.*, pp. 212–35.

See also in this book

Callimachus, Julius Caesar, Martial, Ovid, Sappho, Theocritus, Virgil

Texts, translations and commentaries

The Latin text is available in OCT, Teubner and Loeb.

As well as the Loeb, there is an Oxford World's Classics translation by G. Lee and a Penguin translation by P. Whigham.

There are commentaries on *Catullus: The Shorter Poems* and *Catullus: Poems 61–8* by J. Godwin in the Aris and Phillips Series, *Catullus: A Commentary* by C.J. Fordyce (published by Oxford University Press), and *Catullus* by G.P. Goold (published by Duckworth).

Further reading

Ferguson, J., *Catullus*, Greece and Rome New Surveys in the Classics 20, Oxford: Oxford University Press, 1988.
Fitzgerald, W., *Catullan Provocations: Lyric Poetry and the Drama of Position*, Berkeley, Los Angeles and London: University of California Press, 1995.
Lyne, R.O.A.M., *The Latin Love Poets*, Oxford: Oxford University Press, 1980.

Newman, J.K., *Roman Catullus and His Modification of the Alexandrian Sensibility*, Hildesheim: Weidmann, 1991.
Wiseman, T.P., *Catullus and His World: A Reappraisal*, Cambridge: Cambridge University Press, 1985.

SALLUST

Fantham has recently suggested that the historian Sallust (*c*. 86–35 BC) would have made a brilliant journalist, thanks to his efficient assimilation of other thinkers' ideas, his skill at creating emotional effects and his memorable style of writing.[1] He could so easily have produced an exciting monograph about the Falklands War, perhaps, or documented the unfolding of the Watergate Affair. Sallust himself lived in turbulent times, which provided ample material for his distinctive historical narratives. The Republic was coming apart at the seams and, with no external threat to galvanise the Roman people into action, corrupt politicians and power-hungry generals were scrambling over one another to seize financial rewards to which they weren't entitled. Or at least this is the broad picture presented of the second and first centuries BC by Sallust, whose historical works are driven by his perceptions of ever-deepening moral decline wreaking havoc on the Roman national character.

Unlike Livy, Sallust himself played an active political role in Rome as well as being a writer, but (and this is significant) he didn't engage in these activities simultaneously.[2] After becoming tribune of the plebs in 52 BC, he opposed the politician Milo, who had been engaging in gang warfare with Clodius for several years but was now facing a murder charge from which even his defence counsel Cicero couldn't save him. Two years later, the censors expelled Sallust from the senate on a charge of immorality (Cassius Dio 40.63.4) for reasons which remain unclear, but which may have been connected with his involvement in the condemnation of Milo.

From politics, Sallust turned his attention to warfare and in 49 BC he appears as a commander of one of Caesar's legions. His leadership skills were severely tested in Campania in 47 BC when he tried and failed to control a mutiny among Caesar's troops, who were about to set off for Africa (Appian *Bella Civilia* 2.92.387, Cassius Dio *Roman History* 42.52.1). Even so, he did redeem himself during the following year when he participated in the African campaign, albeit in the low-key context of transporting supplies (*African War* 8.3, 34.1). His practical experience of the region prompted Caesar to put him in charge of a newly instituted province,

Africa Nova. This was created by Caesar after he defeated his enemies Scipio and Cato the Younger at the Battle of Thapsus in 46 BC. However, Sallust doesn't seem to have fulfilled his potential as a governor, since he was prosecuted for misconduct in the province soon after returning to Rome. It was Caesar himself who intervened on his behalf (Cassius Dio 43.9.2) but, after this brush with disgrace and danger, Sallust decided to remove himself from politics so that he could engage in the serious business of writing history.[3]

This basic outline of Sallust's life may raise more questions than it answers. Above all, there is the matter of hypocrisy. What right did Sallust have to adopt such an overtly moralising stance as a historian when his own public career appears to have been so tarnished by corruption? There are various possible critical responses to this dilemma. One constructive approach is to concede that Sallust speaks about political corruption from first-hand experience as someone who was himself caught with his hands in the till, but then to argue that we should give him some credit for having rejected this world in order to take up a more wholesome activity. To write perceptively about a debased political system, it was no good if an author was pure as the driven snow.

This is clearly the response which Sallust hoped to provoke in his audience by his pre-emptive admission of guilt in the preface to his first historical work:

> Although my spirit, being unaccustomed to evil ways, scorned temerity, bribery and greed, even so, as a helpless young man amidst such great vices, I was gripped by corrupt ambition; and although I tried to dissociate myself from the evil ways of the others, nevertheless desire for an honourable career exposed me to the same pernicious gossip as my rivals.
>
> (*Catiline* 3.4–5)

Sallust perhaps lays too much emphasis here on his youth and inexperience to absolve himself successfully from charges of corruption, which after all he perpetrated when he was more than forty years old. However, at least he acknowledges that the issue of his political career will generate problems for the particular type of history which he proposes to write and tackles the issue of hypocrisy directly.

Another response to this problem involves putting it into context. The world of the Late Republic was dominated by talented speakers and writers who used invective to attack leading figures (usually their personal enemies), and there were very few politicians who emerged from the period unscathed. A great number of hostile pamphlets were circulating at the time, which suggests that people had acquired a taste for such mudslinging, and it also became a popular exercise in the rhetorical schools to compose invective retrospectively, even when their targets were dead and buried. Such may be the provenance of two pieces which became attached to the Sallustian *corpus* at an early stage, namely the pseudo-Sallustian *Speech against Cicero*[4] and the pseudo-Ciceronian *Speech against Sallust*.

In these circumstances, it is hardly surprising that Sallust's public life became a target for exaggerated attack, even if the rhetoricians were building on a solid foundation of truth. Particularly after the publication of his moralising historical works, Sallust became vulnerable to criticism and the temptation to knock him off his pedestal must have been intense. A good example is the reference by Aulus Gellius to a lost work of Sallust's contemporary Varro, who allegedly claims that

> Sallust, the author of that serious and austere speech, whom we see in his history writing and acting like a censor, was caught in adultery by Annius Milo, was soundly beaten with whips and released only when he had handed over some money.

> (*Attic Nights* 17.18)

Perhaps in the original work Varro himself only reported the adultery, but for Aulus Gellius the gulf between Sallust's moralising authorial voice and degenerate life was a little too much to stomach.

What about Sallust's historical works themselves? His first attempt at writing history resulted in a monograph, the *Catiline*, published in 42–41 BC, in which he narrated the unsuccessful conspiracy led by Catiline in 63 BC.[5] Two points should immediately strike us about this project. First, the scale of this work is very much smaller than Livy's (subsequent) huge *Ab Urbe Condita*. Sallust chooses a monograph format, which had first been used by Coelius Antipater and enabled Sallust to circulate the finished product for public consumption far more rapidly than Livy could have done with his own grand narrative (even if he gave readings from individual books before the whole work was finished, as seems likely).

Second, Sallust chooses as his subject matter an event from relatively recent times, which meant that although Catiline, Cicero, Cato and Caesar were all dead by the time of publication, many contemporaries would have lived through the conspiracy and could have checked his account against their own memories of what happened. It was a notoriously difficult business to write recent history, and even Tacitus chose projects whose subject matter had progressively earlier starting points: so his first work, the *Histories*, covered the years between AD 68 and 96 while his second work, the *Annals*, is a 'prequel' dealing with the history of AD 14–68. Sallust therefore was choosing a difficult topic by focusing on the Catilinarian conspiracy.

Having chosen the monograph format, how does Sallust organise his material? The main events of the narrative do not actually begin until *Catiline* 14, which is striking, considering that there are only sixty-one chapters in the whole work. Before that, we are given a moralising prologue (*Catiline* 1–4), a memorable character-sketch of Catiline (*Catiline* 5) and a whistle-stop tour of early Roman history from Aeneas to Sulla (*Catiline* 6–13). Critics have noted a parallel with the opening book of Thucydides' *Peloponnesian War*, in which 1.1–23 (the so-called *Arkhaiologia*) sets the war against the backdrop of previous history, but we can also perhaps see here a Livian *Ab Urbe Condita* in miniature. Of course, Livy didn't begin his project until some point between 35 and 30 BC, after Sallust's death, but *Ab Urbe Condita*-type history was a well-established genre. That Sallust wants us to think of this monumental genre is suggested by the opening sentence of the historical survey: *Urbem Romanam, sicuti ego accepi, condidere atque habuere initio Troiani* ... ('The city of Rome, so I have heard, was founded and inhabited at first by Trojans ... '; *Catiline* 6.1. Cf. Tacitus *Annals* 1.1.1). This formulation celebrates the status of Sallust's compact monograph in comparison with works on a much larger scale.

If we find a miniaturisation taking place in the survey of Roman history, at the same time we can detect an amplification in other parts of the work. In the first place, Sallust emphasises the grandeur of his theme, which is 'a villainous enterprise, which I consider especially memorable because of the unprecedented nature of the dangerous crime' (*Catiline* 4.4). This sort of claim is conventional in ancient historiography, whose practitioners had to convince their readers that the subject matter of the narrative was suitably important, but there are real questions to be asked about whether the short-lived Catilinarian conspiracy was really as momentous as Sallust (and Cicero) made out.

We can also see magnification in the characterisation of Catiline himself. In the famous introductory character-sketch (which was later imitated by Tacitus at *Annals* 4.1 in describing Sejanus), Catiline is said to have 'an evil and twisted personality' (*Catiline* 5.1) and is endowed with the characteristics of an ideal general: 'a body capable of enduring hunger, cold and lack of sleep' (*Catiline* 5.3). These are qualities which would have been invaluable to the state, if only the right man had possessed them. Even though Catiline himself is absent from Rome for a large portion of the narrative, his larger-than-life personality still looms over the events and adds cohesion to the work.

Catiline is also given two speeches (*Catiline* 20, 58), which frame the action of the conspiracy itself and which help to impose his personality on the narrative, since the only other speeches in the monograph are delivered by Caesar and Cato the Younger (*Catiline* 51–2). In the second speech, Catiline addresses his soldiers before the final battle with Gaius Antonius. It is unsettling that what he says doesn't allow us to dismiss Catiline straightforwardly as a simple villain, and indeed at least one critical response to these final chapters has been to see Catiline as a tragic hero. That may be taking things too far, but the end of the monograph certainly belongs to Catiline. The rival general, Marcus Petreius, although perfectly competent, is not given a fully developed pre-battle speech of his own (*Catiline* 59.4–5) and Catiline finally dies bravely in battle: his body is found in the midst of the enemy forces and he 'keeps on his face the ruthlessness of spirit which he had possessed when alive' (*Catiline* 61.4). The Romans were perhaps fortunate that they managed to defuse the conspiracy, but the ending of the monograph still provokes disquiet. Levene has recently argued that Catiline certainly posed a threat to Rome (just as Carthage did before its destruction in 146 BC), but that removing him 'removes the moral order that made such a victory possible in the first place'.[6] The *Catiline* is therefore much more open-ended than the neat closural device of the final battle would suggest.

Sallust clearly felt comfortable with the monograph because he kept that format for his second work, the *Jugurtha*, composed perhaps in 41–40 BC.[7] Where the *Catiline* had looked inwards at a conspiracy hatched in Rome, the *Jugurtha* (notionally) looks outwards, at a war fought between 112 and 104 BC against the rogue king Jugurtha in Numidia, although Sallust still shows a strong interest in domestic affairs even in this narrative of a foreign war. As he makes clear in his programmatic statement, he chose the Jugurthine war as a subject 'both because it was great, bloody and of shifting fortunes, and because it represented the first challenge to the arrogance of the nobility' (*Jugurtha* 5.1).[8]

Sallust's interest in the internal problems at Rome is developed in his subsequent discussion of party strife (*Jugurtha* 41–2), where he formulates clearly one of his best-known views about the history of the Roman republic, namely that the destruction of her great enemy Carthage in 146 BC paved the way for the moral disintegration of Rome. Levene observes the intriguing paradox whereby Sallust deliberately adopts the distinctive Latin style of the moralising historian and politician, Cato the Elder, when it was this man who argued most vehemently for the destruction of Carthage and inadvertently paved the way for the moral deterioration of Rome.[9]

This monograph is almost twice as long as the *Catiline* and contains many more examples of historiographical set-pieces, such as the geographical excursus on Africa (*Jugurtha* 17–19)[10] and the assault by Marius' forces on the mountain stronghold of Jugurtha near the river Mulaccha (*Jugurtha* 92.5–94). One important difference between his first and second monographs is that the subject matter of the *Catiline* was relatively self-contained, since most of the events covered took place within a single year, but the *Jugurtha* is more complex, since the core of the narrative addresses affairs which happened over twelve years and alternates between internal and external matters in the manner of annalistic history. Sallust therefore needed to provide his readers with a reliable chronological framework, but modern critics haven't been overly impressed with his efforts. The *Jugurtha* is still a monograph, but one which foreshadows Sallust's decision to turn to the annalistic format in his final work, the *Histories*.

It is unfortunate that the *Histories* has not survived intact.[11] We do have some fairly substantial fragments, particularly four speeches and two letters, but many fragments are rather small and have survived only because they were quoted by grammarians, such as Nonius, or commentators, such as Servius. Thus we face familiar problems in trying to decide how faithfully many of these fragments reflect what Sallust actually wrote. It appears that Sallust started his narrative with the events of 78 BC, in the aftermath of the death of Sulla. Our last surviving fragment comes from 67 BC, but it isn't clear where the formal end of the narrative would have come. This was a turbulent period of history, which included Rome's war with the turncoat Roman commander Sertorius, the revolt of Lepidus, the outbreak of a slave rebellion under Spartacus and the third war against Rome's great foreign enemy of the first century BC: Mithridates, King of Pontus. There was plenty of scope here for Sallust to pursue his interest in decline and internal corruption.

One of Sallust's most abiding legacies was the extraordinarily distinctive style of his Latin.[12] He himself was a self-conscious archaiser, who used as his models Cato the Elder and Thucydides. Style wasn't just a matter of taste, but a way of aligning oneself with (or against) a particular ideology and historical tradition. Through his discordant, unbalanced syntax and through his perverse choice of archaic vocabulary, Sallust distances himself from the corrupt contemporary world in which words shift their meaning according to the immediate needs of the speaker. Instead of *uiuus* ('alive'), Sallust will write *uiuos*, or rather than *libido* ('lust'), we are given *lubido*.

Not everybody liked the way in which Sallust wrote. According to Suetonius, Augustus made fun of Antony for using words which Sallust had borrowed from Cato the Elder's *Origines* (*Augustus* 86.3), and according to Seneca the Elder, Livy criticised Sallust for the way in which he adapted an epigram from Thucydides (*Controversiae* 9.1.14). However, although Sallust went against the grain of contemporary tastes, his style subsequently inspired the historian Tacitus, who deliberately chose to write in a Sallustian manner (although with his own unique twists). Some critics have claimed that this stylistic (and hence ideological) alignment only serves to highlight the deficiencies of Sallust as a historian in comparison with his great successor, but that is hardly fair. Sallust's own annalistic history has not survived intact, so we cannot compare like with like. Syme notes the way in which Tacitus' early works, the *Agricola* and *Germania*, reveal an 'author in search of a style'.[13] Without Sallust, Tacitus' *Histories* and *Annals* could have been written in a completely different style.

Notes

1 E. Fantham, *Roman Literary Culture: From Cicero to Apuleius*, Baltimore, MD, and London: Johns Hopkins University Press, 1996, p. 96.
2 See R. Syme, *Sallust*, Berkeley, Los Angeles and London: University of California Press, 1964, pp. 29–42, on Sallust's career.
3 See J. Marincola, *Authority and Tradition in Ancient Historiography*,

Cambridge: Cambridge University Press, 1997, pp. 138–9, on the relationship between Sallust's historical writing and public life.

4   See Syme, *op. cit.*, pp. 314–18.

5   See Syme, *op. cit.*, pp. 60–82, and C.S. Kraus and A.J. Woodman, *Latin Historians*, Greece and Rome New Surveys in the Classics 27, Oxford: Oxford University Press, 1997, pp. 13–21.

6   D.S. Levene, 'Sallust's *Catiline* and Cato the Censor', *Classical Quarterly*, 50, 2000, p. 191.

7   See Syme, *op. cit.*, pp. 138–77, and Kraus and Woodman, *op. cit.*, pp. 21–30.

8   See Marincola, *op. cit.*, p. 40, on Sallust's amplification of his subject.

9   Levene, *op. cit.*, pp. 179–80.

10 See further T. Wiedemann, 'Sallust's *Jugurtha*: Concord, discord and the digressions', *Greece and Rome*, 40, 1993, pp. 48–57.

11 See Syme, *op. cit.*, pp. 178–213, and Kraus and Woodman, *op. cit.*, pp. 30–41.

12 See further Syme, *op. cit.*, pp. 240–73; Marincola, *op. cit.*, pp. 16–17; Kraus and Woodman, *op. cit.*, pp. 11–13.

13 Syme, *Tacitus*, Oxford: Oxford University Press, 1958, p. 340.

See also in this book

Cassius Dio, Herodotus, Livy, Polybius, Tacitus, Thucydides, Xenophon

Texts, translations and commentaries

The Latin text is available in OCT, Teubner and Loeb.

As well as the Loeb, there is a Penguin translation by S.A. Handford.

There are commentaries on the *Catiline* by K. Vretska (two volumes, published by C. Winter), by P. McGushin (published by Brill) and by J.T. Ramsey (published by Scholars Press); on the *Jugurtha* by G.M. Paul (published by F. Cairns); and on the *Histories* by P. McGushin (two volumes, including a translation) in the Clarendon Ancient History Series. There is a commentary on the *Jugurtha* by M.R. Comber forthcoming in the Aris and Phillips Series.

Further reading

Earl, D.C., *The Political Thought of Sallust*, Cambridge: Cambridge University Press, 1961.

Fantham, E., *Roman Literary Culture: From Cicero to Apuleius*, Baltimore, MD, and London: Johns Hopkins University Press, 1996.

Kraus, C.S. and Woodman, A.J., *Latin Historians*, Greece and Rome New Surveys in the Classics 27, Oxford: Oxford University Press, 1997.

Levene, D.S., 'Sallust's *Jugurtha*: An "historical fragment"?', *Journal of Roman Studies*, 82, 1992, pp. 53–70.

Levene, D.S., 'Sallust's *Catiline* and Cato the Censor', *Classical Quarterly*, 50, 2000, pp. 170–91.

Marincola, J., *Authority and Tradition in Ancient Historiography*, Cambridge: Cambridge University Press, 1997.

Scanlon, T.F., *The Influence of Thucydides on Sallust*, Heidelberg: Winter, 1980.

Syme, R., *Sallust*, Berkeley, Los Angeles and London: University of California Press, 1964.

AUGUSTAN

VIRGIL

'Virgil I only saw': so Ovid (*Tristia* 4.10.41) expressed the sense both of greatness and of otherness which Virgil inspired in him. Virgil was a legend in his own lifetime. His greatest work, the *Aeneid*, achieved the status of a classic before it was even finished – it was hailed by Propertius as 'something greater than the *Iliad*' (2.34.66) – and it immediately became a school text; it has never yet lost either of these elevated positions. After Virgil, things were never the same again in literary matters: as Conte put it, 'Virgil's *Nachleben* is western literature'.[1] If the 'Fifty Key Classical Authors' of this book were put in order of importance, Virgil would have to come first.[2]

There is surprisingly little to say about Virgil's life, except that it was almost entirely constituted by poetry. Virgil was born near Mantua in northern Italy in 70 BC (on 15 October, according to Donatus and other ancient biographers). His family were probably small landowners. There is a story that Virgil's family lost its farm during the confiscations of land for the settlement of veterans from the civil wars, but the farm was restored to them through the good offices of some great man, possibly the young Octavian himself.[3] The story may well be true: there is no doubt that Virgil's poetry is sensitive to the sufferings caused by the confiscations, and little doubt that Virgil himself never did anything other than study and write poetry. It is said that he studied in Milan, and in the school (called a 'garden') of the Epicurean Siro in Naples; he was clearly well acquainted with Epicureanism, as with other philosophical systems, and indeed with a vast range of knowledge.[4] Except for a note in Donatus that the poet once (and once only) acted in a law-court case, there is no evidence that Virgil had a conventional public career or was involved in any direct political activity, but he was a friend to several great men: Pollio, Varus and Gallus in his youth, then Maecenas and Augustus in his maturity. Moreover, his works are one of the central monuments of the Augustan age: that might legitimately be called 'political activity'. The sources (for example, Donatus) tell us that he was extremely shy and retiring, but clearly this didn't hamper his career.

Virgil's poetic life is as beautifully structured as one of his own poetry books. He wrote entirely in hexameters:[5] first a collection of ten short poems in the pastoral genre, called *Eclogues* (or *Bucolics*); then a more ambitious work of didactic poetry, in four books, on farming (the *Georgics*); then finally the epic climax, the *Aeneid*. Virgil died in 19 BC with the *Aeneid* unfinished (that is, 'unrevised', although most of the incomplete lines can be shown to work very well as they are). His order that it should be burned was disobeyed by his executors, on the encouragement of Augustus (Donatus 37–8). He died on return from a curtailed journey to Greece and Asia, whence he had gone 'to finish work on the *Aeneid*'. Donatus says (35) that he intended to devote the rest of his life to philosophy, after spending three further years on the *Aeneid* (in addition to the eleven already spent). Philosophy would be the study appropriate to old age, after the crowning glory of a poetic career. Virgil's poetic history thus becomes a paradigmatic case of the 'life of the poet'.[6]

What is the reason for this extraordinary success? To encapsulate Virgil's achievement is beyond me, but I offer the following as a starting point.[7] It consists above all in three areas, none of them exclusive to himself: intertextuality (the creation of a literary work out of a web of complex allusions and interactions with other literary works), tensions (the ability to keep multiple perspectives and levels of meaning in play at once, without allowing easy resolutions of the tensions involved, but without descending into chaos) and 'poetry' (that unfathomable notion which starts with formal aspects such as diction and metre, together with something readers often want to call 'sensibility').

Other poets are behind almost every Virgilian verse: Theocritus (and Callimachus and Gallus) in the *Eclogues*, Hesiod and Lucretius in the *Georgics*, Homer and Ennius in the *Aeneid*, and many others throughout his work; but Virgil's 'thefts' are creative. He himself is said to have remarked that 'it would be easier to steal his club from Hercules than a line from Homer' (so Donatus reports). Virgil's powerful intertext for the *Eclogues* is the *Idylls* of Theocritus, who together with Moschus and Bion created pastoral. But it was Virgil who gave the genre its classic form and mediated that form to later European literature and art. The designation 'pastoral idyll' probably conjures up for most people images of a fantasy world of nymphs and shepherds innocently cavorting in beautiful countryside, where it is always spring, there is no suffering and no-one ever does any work. It is most people's idea of heaven and regularly surfaces in mythology and literature as 'Eden' – the place of natural bliss. The world of Virgil's *Eclogues* gives glimpses of such beauty, and contains some gorgeous descriptions of nature; but there is 'trouble in Eden', for this is a beautiful world under threat, from the 'outside' in the form of the city, war and politics, but also from the 'inside'.

This 'inside' tension we can see not only from the fact that the shepherds are more often dying of love than enjoying it, but also more importantly because Virgil's pastoral world is *not* in fact an escapist fantasy. It is a world, and a genre, which confronts head-on the tension between art and nature. It would be a simplification even to say that the *Eclogues* offer an artificial and sophisticated view of a simple country world (although there is certainly an element of over-sophisticated longing for a simpler life). It is a highly artistic, even mannerist medium, but the pastoral world which is the content of the poetry and the object of its desire is itself not so simple and natural as it may seem. The *Eclogues* should be a central text for 'green theory'.[8]

A typical scene in an *Eclogue* is the singing contest between two herdsmen who may meet by chance and decide to sing, perhaps under the shade of the trees or in a natural cave overhung with wild vines (*Eclogue* 5.6–7). The contest is called 'amoebean' because the performers sing alternately: poems 3, 5, 7 and 8 take this form. *Eclogue* 9 also hints at it, but in that case it is a contest which never manages to happen, because the pastoral world is losing its voice under the threat of the land confiscations, during which real-life Italian peasants were forced off their land to make way for the settlement of war veterans. There may be a judge (for example, *Eclogue* 3) and sometimes prizes, which are suitably rustic: a pipe and a staff (*Eclogue* 5) or cups and a heifer (*Eclogue* 3). In some cases (for example, 5 and 8), the singers perform once each; in others (3, 7) they pass the song to and fro between them, the second singer answering and (he hopes) bettering the first. The songs are of country matters, with a preponderance of the erotic. Among the most beautiful of pastoral love songs, this time not in a singing contest but a lonely monologue, is the lament of Corydon for the boy Alexis (*Eclogue* 2).[9] Like much else in the *Eclogues*, the poem has a powerful intertext in Theocritus, particularly *Idyll* 11, in which the cyclops Polyphemus (translated from the Homeric world of the *Odyssey*) sings of his love for the nymph Galatea. Is Corydon a monstrous fool like Polyphemus – or not? One line from this poem seems to me to epitomise the intertextuality (it draws on Gallan elegy as well as Theocritean pastoral), the poetic sensitivity and the musicality of the *Eclogues*, perhaps with a touch of gently ironic humour as well: *a Corydon Corydon, quae te dementia cepit?* ('ah Corydon, Corydon, what madness has caught you?', 2.69).

In some poems, the pastoral setting interacts with other genres. *Eclogue* 6 begins with a set-piece in Augustan poetics, in the form of a meeting with Apollo, who advises the poet on the type and manner of his poetry, in imitation of the opening scene in Callimachus'

Aetia. Possibly for the first time, the Apollo-inspired refusal to write epic is given a political spin: thereafter, it always has political connotations. Instead of epic, Virgil sings of the meeting of two herdsmen who capture the countryside deity Silenus and force a song out of him. Silenus' song is a pastoral and neoteric version of the mythological epyllion (little epic) and didactic poem. *Eclogue* 10 brings Virgil into contact with love elegy, for the poem depicts the first (and lost) elegist Gallus dying of love in a pastoral context, singing his elegiac sentiments to the sympathetic countryside. The poem is closely modelled on *Idyll* 1 (the death of Daphnis), which has also been alluded to in *Eclogue* 5. In that poem, it is almost certainly the case that the dead and deified Daphnis stands allegorically for the dead and deified Julius Caesar.[10] Both poems (10 and 5) are good examples of how Virgil makes a completely new meaning out of a poem closely modelled on a predecessor.

Perhaps the most extraordinary element in the *Eclogues* has been alluded to already: some of the poems are highly politically charged. A number of contemporary figures appear in the poems, either as addressees (for example, Varus in 6, Pollio in 4) or participants (Gallus in 10 and 6), or as allegories (probably Julius Caesar in 5) or more nebulous hints and analogies (such as the 'young man' in 1, who may be Octavian). This variety of involvement is one of the ways in which the *Eclogues* break down the boundaries of fantasy and reality, calling into question distinctions between art and nature. It isn't possible to read off a single political message from the *Eclogues*. Poems 1 and 9 are caught up in the land confiscations and clearly 'oppose civil war', but since no-one does other than regret civil war not a great deal can be made of that. They are delicate poems, full of sensibility to the displaced and to the destruction of country values. But there is also celebration of the great men who protect their clients from such suffering, however much they may have been involved in its cause. The opening four-line speech of *Eclogue* 1 neatly balances these conflicting tensions. Throughout, song is a defining feature of the pastoral world.

I have left until last the poem which, above all, ensured Virgil's unbroken popularity through the Middle Ages. *Eclogue* 4 raises the pastoral voice 'a little higher' to sing a prophecy of a new Golden Age (there is an essential connection between Golden Age imagery and pastoral) and of a child about to be born who will rule the world 'made peaceful by the virtues of his father'. The year is 40 BC – Pollio's consulship in that year is stressed. The identity of the child has aroused colossal critical interest. In late antiquity and throughout the Middle Ages, because the poem was seen as a prophecy of the coming of Christ, Virgil was interpreted as a sort of proto-Christian prophet. Many modern scholars think that the child referred to is the hoped-for product of the political marriage between Antony and Octavian's sister Octavia, which took place that year in an attempt to forge a peace between the two most powerful men in the Roman world. No son in fact came of that short-lived and troubled union, but many would say that Virgil's language is sufficiently oracular and ambiguous to avoid any embarrassment from the failure of his prophecy. Others take the line that the child is no one single child but a 'spirit of the age'.[11] Whatever the 'right' answer may be, the poem epitomises the power of Virgil's pastoral voice to express political sensitivities in poetry of outstanding natural beauty and art.

The interactions of art and nature inform also Virgil's second major work, the *Georgics*, in which 'art', in the form of hard work, seems to have the upper hand. The poem constantly evokes the spirit (and often the details) of Hesiod, for whom hard work on the farm was the defining feature of morality and indeed of man's very existence. It plays also with the abstruse didactic poetry of the Hellenistic period, which made a virtue of turning unpromising material into poetry. Still more important is the relationship with Virgil's predecessor in Roman didactic: Lucretius. The ancient Lives tell us that Virgil assumed the toga of manhood on the day of Lucretius' death. This is precisely the sort of thing we expect from the ancient biographies of the poets – literary critical comments couched in biographical terms. Lucretian passion and vocabulary are powerful forces throughout the *Georgics*.

It can be very difficult for modern people to make sense of what ancient authors are trying to do in didactic poetry. It is more than 'poetry with a moral', but it isn't 'a handbook in verse'. While we may feel we are looking at the real Italian countryside in the *Georgics*, there is no attempt to make the picture match the Late Republican/Early Imperial reality of large, slave-run estates and absentee landlords (ironically, those things are more obvious in the 'fantasy' world of the *Eclogues*). Rather, the implied recipient of the poem's instruction is the small citizen-farmer. Such a position may no longer be the reality for most Romans, but the ideology of farming as a truly moral way of earning a living, as an aspect of citizenship and as intimately involved with political stability is still very active. How far Octavian really developed an agricultural economic policy at this time is less important than that he and others made political use of the rhetoric of 'back to the land'. That rhetoric worked, and Virgil's poem works not just as Augustan propaganda but as a Roman poem, precisely because the ideology of farming held a powerful position in the collective consciousness. By writing his poem about farming, Virgil seeks to tell us not 'how to run a farm' in the muddy details (though mud and details are there), but cosmically, socially and morally 'how to run a farm' – and thus how to be a good citizen.[12] The poem is addressed to Maecenas, patron of the arts, right-hand man to Octavian/Augustus and a lifelong friend of Virgil.

The first *Georgic* tells the farmer and the reader about ploughing, sowing, the cultivation of fields, seasons of the year and the weather. In the last section, description of weather-signs (which a modern audience can easily see as 'scientific') slips naturally into a description of portents (which a modern audience would more happily call 'superstition'). You can trust the natural world to tell you about itself, the argument goes (1.464ff.), because the natural world rightly foretold – by horrific disruptions of the natural order – the upheaval of the civil wars after the assassination of Julius Caesar. The portents, within the poem, constitute both a memory and a subliminal warning for the future. There is a striking image of a farmer, in the midst of his ploughing, digging up rotting armour and huge bones from the civil wars (1.493–7). This isn't just poetically effective but also symbolically and politically important: this whole book, after all, has been about farmers ploughing, and ploughing as a positive aspect of citizenship. The book ends with a prayer to the Roman gods to spare 'Caesar' (by which the poet now means Octavian) as the only hope against the wars raging throughout the world and the consequent neglect of the land. The tone is laudatory, but the hopefulness is tempered, for the closing image of the book is the war-god Mars raging like a charioteer who has lost control of the reins (1.511–14).

Georgic 2 is, above all, the book of the Italian farmer. He learns about the whole range of trees, including the crucial vines and olives, and their methods of cultivation and propagation. But he also learns that his Italy is the most beautiful and most farmable land in the world, and that his own occupation is the best. One much-quoted line expresses Virgil's praise for farmers (just tinged with anxiety): *o fortunatos nimium sua si bona norint/agricolas!* ('o how fortunate are farmers, if only they knew their own goods', 2.458–9). The exclamation opens a section detailing the delights of the farming life, the prosperous simplicity, the peace, the morality, the freedom from worry. The remainder of the book is devoted to this theme, interacting with a reflection on Virgil's own position as poet. He describes the Muses as his own highest joy (475), slipping easily between the didactic knowledge they impart to him and the love of the countryside which drives this poem.[13]

Then in comes Lucretius: *felix qui potuit rerum cognoscere causas* ('happy is he who was able to describe the causes of things', 2.490). The reference in 'causes of things' is specifically to *De Rerum Natura*. The vocabulary links the happy fruitfulness of the didactic poet to that of the farmers (2.458). But there is something of a challenge to the Lucretian world-view also, in that the 'one who knows the rustic gods' is also described as *fortunatus* (493), and the rest of the book continues the praise of the farming life. But that last *fortunatus* is clearly Virgil as well as his addressees (the farmers). He and the farmers live a life which now has more than a hint of the Golden Age, a hint which becomes explicit at the end of the book in a reference to nostalgic myths of early Rome: the Sabines, Romulus and Remus without the fraternal murder, and Golden Saturn ruling Italy (2.532–8). Virgil skilfully plays with a tension between the moral value of hard work (contrary to Golden Age imagery) and the Golden Age's natural fruitfulness. Octavian may be closely involved in this image, since his propaganda machine drew on Roman idealism about the past and hinted that Octavian/Augustus would bring a new Golden Age, but the touch is delicate and understated.

The third book is the oddest. It begins with an upbeat programmatic proem, including the most extravagant praise of Octavian yet, which involves the promise of a temple that Virgil will build with Caesar in the middle (3.3–16). It would be easy to say that 'the temple is the *Aeneid*', but it is probably not as simple as that. There is also an invocation to Maecenas to help in the execution of his *haud mollia iussa* ('not-soft orders', 41; there is, however, no reason to suppose that Maecenas in any sense literally ordered the *Georgics*). The subject of this book is the care and breeding of herds. It ends with a horrific plague.

First come noble animals – horses and cattle – described in heroic terms, exuding a sense of the powerful and wild force of these animals, potentially creative and fruitful, potentially destructive (for example, fire imagery at 3.97–100). Near the end of this section, this wild force becomes centred on the overwhelming sexuality of the animals (3.209ff.). The farmer is advised to keep the sexes separate if he wants to get the best out of them, for the sight of the females wastes the males. There follows a description of a battle between two bulls over a beautiful heifer. It is left to the reader to decide how anthropomorphically (or even allegorically) this is to be read, but at line 244 some wider implications are made explicit: all kinds of men and beasts are driven by the same madness, for *amor omnibus idem* ('the same love [exists] for all'). The very negative assessment of erotic love portrayed here finds resonances throughout Virgil's work, in Corydon (*Eclogue* 2), Dido (*Aeneid* 1, 4 and 6) and Turnus (*Aeneid* 7–12) above all. But it is most of all the mares who suffer from this madness. The section ends with the frenzied flight of the mares on heat, scaling the mountains to be made pregnant with the wind and dripping the poisonous love potion *hippomanes*.

The poet turns away, and considers goats and sheep, with a brief mention even of dogs. A digression on the sterile winter of Scythia, hostile to farming and civilisation, prepares the ground for the final section of this book: the plague. The set-piece description of a plague has a long history, from the opening of the *Iliad* through Sophocles, Thucydides and Lucretius, to mention only a few examples. Virgil's description subsumes all that history of suffering and expresses it in terms appropriate to his poem. One powerful moment is the vignette of the ploughman with two bulls (3.515–19), one of whom dies at the plough. The farmer, with calm desperation, unyokes the other (a 'young bull') and gives up on his task, leaving the ploughshare (symbol of the poem) stuck in the ground. The plague begins among the cattle, and only in the closing lines of the book does it affect mankind.

Then after the grief and suffering of the plague comes the sublime beauty of the opening of Book 4, with the description of bees and heavenly honey. The terrible plague which afflicted all kinds of creatures must have some link with the other horrific force which is the same for all – sexuality. The bees come as sublime relief from the horror, both of the plague and of sex, for the bees reproduce asexually. They represent a perfect society in miniature. After details regarding the care of bees, Virgil devotes almost exactly half of the book to a digression, telling the story of the mythological beekeeper Aristaeus and how he lost his bees. It was in punishment for causing the death of Eurydice, the wife of the singer Orpheus, whom Aristaeus tried to rape. The story of Orpheus' descent to the Underworld to retrieve his wife, and his fatal look which lost her a second time, is inset within the Aristaeus story (itself inset in the poem). When Aristaeus makes expiation for the death of Eurydice, he learns how to replace his bees, by the practice of bougonia, the sacrifice of four bulls from whose decaying flesh a new swarm appears (4.548–58).

The poet undoubtedly tempts us to make analogies between the bees and contemporary politics, as indeed with other parts of the

Georgics. It is typically Virgilian that a range of interpretations will find favour, but none of them is susceptible to exact one-to-one correspondence.[14] Just about everyone agrees, however, that the Aristaeus–Orpheus digression (it might be called an epyllion) contains some of the most sublime poetry from the ancient or indeed the modern world.

And so to a full-scale epic narrative: the *Aeneid*. The seed for the legend of Aeneas is a brief prophecy in Homer's *Iliad* (20.307–8; also in the *Homeric Hymn to Aphrodite*, 196–7) that the minor hero Aeneas, son of Trojan Anchises and Aphrodite, would save a remnant of dying Troy, and that his descendants would rule the Trojans. That Aeneas and his Trojans became the ancestors of contemporary Italians is a national myth developed over centuries of propagandistic accounts of the origins of Rome. A standard version is the one told by the second-century BC traditionalist statesman Cato ('the Censor') in the first book of his *Origines* ('Origins', the first work of history to have been written in Latin). Many Romans liked to trace their ancestries back to the Trojans: for Augustus, the purported lineage went back to Aeneas himself, through his son Iullus, who was said to have founded the family of the Iulii (of which Julius Caesar, Augustus' adopted father, was a member). Virgil takes up the mantle of this myth and makes it the basis of his national epic.[15]

The poem falls into two halves: the first six books describe the fall of Troy, the love and death of Dido, and the wanderings of Aeneas and his people in their attempts to find the object of their desire: 'receding Italy' (*Aeneid* 5.629); the last six describe the war in Italy between the Trojans and the native Italians, culminating in the death of the Italian hero Turnus. The sixth book, the pivot of the work, takes Aeneas down into the Underworld to meet his dead father and link his and Troy's past to his and Rome's future.

In writing an epic poem, Virgil was daring to take up the poetic challenge which neoteric and Augustan poetry had so far been refusing, but to which it had nonetheless been building up – rivalling Homer. 'Writing epic', in Augustan poetics, also at some level means 'celebrating Rome and the new regime'. It may be inappropriate to try to distinguish between these two aspects. Virgil succeeded in taking up both challenges without breaking faith with the poetic values of his day – rather, he became the apex of them. Let's begin with Homer.[16]

The *Aeneid* opens, famously, with 'arms' and 'the man': *arma uirumque (cano)*. In three words, both Homeric poems are evoked ('arms' = *Iliad*, 'the man' = *Odyssey*). The evocation is in reverse order: the two-fold structure of the poem also incorporates both Homeric poems, with the first half being broadly 'Odyssean' and the second half 'Iliadic'. The division is complex, however, because each half contains allusions to elements from the 'other' Homeric poem. For example, not only does Aeneas play an Odysseus-like role in the first half, when he is his own narrator in a flashback narrative diversion (as is Odysseus among the Phaeacians), when he is detained by a loving woman and when he narrowly misses hideous monsters like the Cyclops, Scylla and Charybdis (3.558–688), but also in the *Iliadic* second half he is a bit like the returning Odysseus who needs to fight to re-establish his position in his homeland. Virgil is following a version of the Aeneas legend in which the Trojan ancestor Dardanus is identified with a Dardanus who came to Troy ultimately from Italy, so that Aeneas is coming 'home' in coming to Latium. Conversely the *Odyssean* first half contains the description of funeral games for Aeneas' father Anchises which are modelled on the funeral games for Patroclus in *Iliad* 23; it also contains the fighting in Troy (Book 2) which most straightforwardly recalls the subject matter of the *Iliad*. Moreover, it is frequently the case that more than one Homeric scene is active in one Virgilian scene (and in more than one), as in the case of those games, which find resonance in the Phaeacian games in *Odyssey* 8 as well as the *Iliadic* scene. A good example is the way that Dido is drawn from all three of the women who delay Odysseus (Calypso, Circe, Nausicaa), as well as women from other literature and possibly Roman life. There is even a hint of Cleopatra in Dido (as there may be also in the cringing Helen in Book 2).

The *Aeneid* is the quintessential epic poem. As a work of sophisticated and self-conscious literary artistry, it is what is sometimes called 'secondary' epic, to distinguish it from the 'primary' epic – poems like the *Iliad* and *Beowulf* – coming from primitive societies. The epic form provides for the poet the mask or 'persona' of a 'bard': that is, a quasi-religious, prophetic channel of divine song, celebrating heroes greater than ordinary humanity. Even if this isn't straightforwardly real anymore for first-century Romans, the epic genre makes it 'real' in a symbolic sense.[17] But this elevated stance is risky – one of the risks of epic is that it may become ridiculous, for epic is ultimately susceptible to parody (as Ovid well exploited). Virgil manages to maintain his epic voice without bathos, partly by this intertextual bardic mask and partly by a certain moderation of tone: for all its epicness, the *Aeneid* is quite discreet. There are certainly all the ingredients – similes, complex images, high-sounding vocabulary, epithets and other repetitions which have a formulaic ring – but none of these is overdone. Likewise there is the obligatory divine machinery, but the cosmic order is carefully integrated into the fabric of the poem, and into the Roman sense of mission and identity which drives it.

Epic, then, is a matter of big themes, a big canvas, big heroes, big narrative, all bound together by the cosmic order. In this analysis, 'big' means serious, public and masculine. An epic narrative should add up to more than the sum of its parts. It should also be directed towards a goal or telos, which not only ends the poem but also gives it its overriding sense of purpose. It is no accident, therefore, that many epics, which are not only stories of war, are structured around a journey. But this need for a teleological and unified narrative doesn't mean either that the poem is all about the same thing, or that the narrative structure works 'and then, and then … '. The *Aeneid* is driven by a powerful sense of onward movement of the narrative towards a goal – Italy, the foundation of Rome and, beyond the end of the poem, into Eternal Rome by way of Augustus. It is this fusion of an epic necessity (teleologically directed narrative) and a political statement (celebration of Augustus or Rome or both) that makes the *Aeneid* into so great an Augustan and Roman monument and also a universally great poem. Virgil turned an old legend into a political statement partly by analogy between the old times and the present, which itself works because of the strong Roman reverence for *mos maiorum* ('the ways of our ancestors'), partly by prophecy from the ancient times of the greatness which is Rome and will be Rome in the future, and partly by the teleology of time.

But what is this goal towards which the poem is directed? The establishment of Rome, certainly, but that isn't how the poem ends. Rather, the climax of the poem is the death of Turnus, the native Italian leader, defending his home and his promised marriage from the foreign aggressor, Aeneas. In the very last line, Turnus' spirit goes down to the shades 'unworthy', not deserving it. Aeneas triumphs over his enemy because he is driven by madness (symbol throughout the poem of the forces opposing Aeneas) and the need for old-fashioned Homeric revenge. He has slipped from being a Trojan hero, a kind of Hector, into the role of Achilles. He kills Turnus in vengeance for the death of the boy Pallas, whose death at the hands of Turnus replays the death of Patroclus (Achilles' dear friend in the *Iliad*) at the hands of Hector, and so seals both Hector's and Turnus' fate. Aeneas fails at the last to follow his father's instruction for Romans: 'spare the defeated and war down the proud' (*parcere subiectis et debellare superbos*, 6.853). That is one reading of this ending, and implies one possible reading – the 'pessimistic' one – of the poem as a whole, in which the celebration of Aeneas, Augustus and Rome is undercut by the emphasis on the destruction they cause.

The death of Turnus is only the last in a series of poignant deaths of young people, especially men, before their time, not deserving it. His death replays that of his victim Pallas; of the young lovers Nisus and Euryalus (*Aeneid* 9), whose crazy night-time adventure to try and break through the Italian ranks is modelled on the much more successful night-time activities of Odysseus and Diomedes in *Iliad* 10, but ends in their death in mutual loyalty; of Lausus (*Aeneid* 10), the noble son of an unworthy tyrant father, whom Aeneas kills, and in killing loves, just as Achilles killed and loved the Amazon Penthesilea, not in the *Iliad* but in the epic cycle and frequently in art. That scene is interestingly intertextual, for the Penthesilea story is at work also in the exploits and death of the Italian warrior-maiden Camilla, who dies in *Aeneid* 11.

But, most of all, the death of Turnus provides a closure to the story of Dido, the Carthaginian queen whose love for Aeneas threatens to destroy his mission. Ovid claimed that Dido's story was the most popular part of the epic in his day, in the generation after Virgil (*Tristia* 2.533–6); and St Augustine in the fifth century AD described himself weeping over Dido's fate (*Confessions* 1.13). There are many memorable moments in Book 4: the 'wounded deer' simile (4.68–73), in which erotic and epic imagery are intimately and troublingly entwined, as they are in the language of fire; the cessation of activity in Dido's new city (4.86–9), as the world and the poem grind to a halt under the all-consuming influence of love; the cave scene, where Dido and Aeneas first make love, with Juno (goddess of marriage) as witness and nymphs on the mountains wailing (marriage song or death song? – it is deliberately ambiguous); the strange and terrible dreams (4.465ff.) in which Dido seems to be lost and to be searching for her people in an unknown land; the recriminations, culminating in Dido's curse (4.625–9) that an avenger should arise to pursue the Trojans, a curse which was fulfilled in the person of Hannibal; and finally the slow, painful death of Dido (4.663ff.), and the fire which Aeneas on his ship oddly, obtusely, fails to understand (5.1–7).

The loss of Dido is poignant and terrible, and so likewise is that of so many other victims of empire, including Aeneas himself. But there is another side to the story of the *Aeneid* and it is one which we can't ignore: the greatness of the Roman destiny. Virgil offers the reader these 'two sides' – empire and loss, the public and the personal (which are actually far more than 'two') – but doesn't allow the reader to resolve the tension or, in my opinion, finally to choose between them. These 'two sides' have found expression in a continuing debate among Virgilian critics between the 'pessimist' school of thought, which emphasises loss and is broadly anti-Augustan, and the 'optimist' school, which emphasises the glory of empire and is broadly pro-Augustan.[18] Even that simple division 'pro' or 'anti' Augustan has recently, and rightly, come under fire as too simplistic a response to a complex phenomenon.[19]

However much, with Augustine, we 'grieve for Dido', reading the *Aeneid* must also involve entering into the grand plan of the poem and of Roman destiny. That plan is structured around a series of set-pieces, the most important of which are the prophecy of Jupiter in Book 1, promising deification for Aeneas (and Augustus) and *imperium sine fine* ('empire without end', 1.279) for the Romans; the descent into the Underworld in Book 6, with its parade of unborn heroes who will people Roman history, culminating in the young Marcellus, on whom Augustus' dynastic hopes were pinned, and whose death finds resonance with that of the other young men in the poem; the visit to the future site of Rome in Book 8, which ends with the new armour for Aeneas, decorated with the future greatness of Rome; and finally the prophecy of Jupiter in Book 12, which seals the fate of Turnus and turns Juno into a friend of the new Trojan-Italian people who will become the Romans. This 'grand plan' might be called 'Fate'.

Notes

1 The quotation comes from G.B. Conte, *Latin Literature: A History*, Princeton, NJ: Princeton University Press, 1994, p. 284. See also R.F. Thomas, *Virgil and the Augustan Reception*, Cambridge: Cambridge University Press, 2001.

2 Some people might argue the case for Homer. But Virgil has had far greater influence on the literature of all periods after the end of antiquity.

3 The sources are vague on this point. The fullest Life is that by Donatus. He says, with marked lack of clarity, that Pollio, Varus and Gallus were responsible for saving the poet's land (19), as does the *Vita Probiana*; Servius attributes the restitution to Pollio and Maecenas (20).

4 For a convenient introduction to Virgil's philosophical interests, see S.M. Braund, 'Virgil and the cosmos: Religious and philosophical ideas', in C.A. Martindale (ed.), *The Cambridge Companion to Virgil*, Cambridge: Cambridge University Press, 1997, pp. 204–21.

5 There are various *iuuenalia* – works of the poet's youth – which are all or mostly spurious, although they are thought genuine by the ancient

commentators (Donatus 17–18, Servius 15). Not all of these are in hexameters. Statius refers to the *Culex* as Virgilian (*Silvae* 2.7.74).

6 The death of Terence follows a similar pattern: this may suggest that Virgil's life isn't the originator of the passage, although it is possible that the stories post-date either poet. On Virgil's end, see F. Cox, 'Envoi: The death of Virgil', in Martindale, *op. cit.*, pp. 327–36.

7 It is obvious, but perhaps worth repeating, that such success is self-perpetuating. Almost everyone who knows some Latin has read some Virgil, sometimes at quite an early stage, for it is quite 'easy' Latin for the beginner. I, like many classicists, had as a significant element in my undergraduate education to read the whole of Virgil in Latin.

8 So, for that matter, should the *Georgics*. See C.A. Martindale, 'Green politics: The *Eclogues*', in Martindale, *op. cit.*, pp. 107–24.

9 The sexuality of pastoral is often homoerotic, although it slips apparently easily between different sexualities. See E. Oliensis, 'Sons and lovers: Sexuality and gender in Virgil's poetry', in Martindale, *op. cit.*, pp. 294–311.

10 But note: Donatus tells us that Daphnis represents Virgil's brother Flaccus, whose death he laments in *Eclogue* 5. It would be entirely Virgilian for both allegories to be active.

11 See P. Alpers, *The Singer of the Eclogues: A Study of Virgilian Pastoral*, Berkeley and Los Angeles, CA: University of California Press, 1979, pp. 177ff.

12 On the metaphysical significance of farming in Hesiod and Virgil, see S.A. Nelson, *God and the Land*, Oxford: Oxford University Press, 1998.

13 See C.G. Perkell, *The Poet's Truth: A Study of the Poet in Virgil's Georgics*, Berkeley, CA, and London: University of California Press, 1989.

14 For a full discussion, see L. Morgan, *Patterns of Redemption in Virgil's Georgics*, Cambridge: Cambridge University Press, 1999.

15 See E.S. Gruen *Culture and National Identity in Republican Rome*, Ithaca, NY, and London: Cornell University Press, 1992, pp. 6–51.

16 J. Farrell's essay, 'The Virgilian intertext', in Martindale, *op. cit.*, pp. 222–38, is excellent on Virgil's relationship with Homer (and other poets). Other bibliography can be found in P.R. Hardie, *Virgil*, Greece and Rome New Surveys in the Classics 28, Oxford: Oxford University Press for the Classical Association, 1998.

17 See D.C. Feeney, *Literature and Religion at Rome: Cultures, Contexts and Beliefs*, Cambridge: Cambridge University Press, 1998, for a good discussion on the Roman attitude to myth and religion.

18 See R.J. Tarrant, 'Poetry and power: Virgil's poetry in contemporary context', in Martindale, *op. cit.*, pp. 169–87.

19 See Hardie, *op. cit.*, and especially D.F. Kennedy, ' "Augustan" and "anti-Augustan": Reflections on terms of reference', in A. Powell (ed.), *Poetry and Propaganda in the Age of Augustus*, London: Bristol Classical Press, 1992, pp. 26–58.

See also in this book

Apollonius Rhodius, Ennius, Hesiod, Homer, Horace, Lucan, Lucretius, Ovid, Statius, Theocritus

Texts, translations and commentaries

The authentic works of Virgil are collected in one OCT volume, while the Loeb runs to two books. There are very many translations, among which a good, readable, modern version is D. West, *Virgil – the Aeneid: A New Prose Translation*, Harmondsworth: Penguin, 1990. The World's Classics rival is by C. Day Lewis, with introduction by J. Griffin.

For the earlier poems, there is C. Day Lewis, *The Eclogues, The Georgics* in World's Classics, with introduction and notes by R.O.A.M. Lyne (1983). In Penguin, there is a translation of the *Georgics* and a dual-language (Latin and English) version of the *Eclogues*. There is also a *Virgil in English*, published by Penguin – a collection of snippets of different translations over the centuries.

The history of commentating on Virgil is vast: among modern commentaries useful for students are Cambridge Greek and Latin Classics editions of the *Eclogues, Georgics* (in two volumes), and Books 8, 9 and 11 of the *Aeneid*. Older, but still useful for those reading in the original, is the commentary by R.D. Williams, *The Aeneid of Virgil. Books 1–6* (London: Macmillan, 1972) and *Books 7–12* (London: Macmillan, 1973). The same author also produced *The Aeneid of Virgil: A Companion to the Translation of C. Day Lewis* (Bristol: Bristol Classical Press, 1985), which contains useful commentary for those reading in translation.

Further reading

The following highly selective list represents a tiny fraction of the secondary literature on Virgil.

Alpers, P., *The Singer of the Eclogues: A Study of Virgilian Pastoral*, Berkeley and Los Angeles, CA: University of California Press, 1979.

Camps, W.A., *An Introduction to Virgil's Aeneid*, Oxford: Oxford University Press, 1969.

Farrell, J., *Virgil's Georgics and the Traditions of Ancient Epic: The Art of Allusion in Literary History*, Oxford: Oxford University Press, 1991.

Feeney, D., *The Gods in Epic: Poets and Critics of the Classical Tradition*, Oxford: Oxford University Press, 1991.

Gransden, K.W., *Virgil: The Aeneid*, Landmarks of World Literature, Cambridge: Cambridge University Press, 1990.

Hardie, P.R., *Virgil's Aeneid: Cosmos and Imperium*, Oxford: Oxford University Press, 1986.

Hardie, P.R., *Virgil*, Greece and Rome New Surveys in the Classics 28, Oxford: Oxford University Press, 1998.

Hardie, P.R., *Virgil: Critical Assessments of Classical Authors*, London: Routledge, 1999.

Harrison, S.J. (ed.), *Oxford Readings in Virgil's Aeneid*, Oxford: Oxford University Press, 1990.

Hubbard, T.K., *The Pipes of Pan: Intertextuality and Literary Filiation in the Pastoral Tradition from Theocritus to Milton*, Ann Arbor, MI: University of Michigan Press, 1998.

Jenkyns, R., *Classical Epic: Homer and Virgil*, Bristol: Bristol Classical Press, 1992.

Lyne, R.O.A.M., *Further Voices in Vergil's Aeneid*, Oxford: Oxford University Press, 1987.

Martindale, C.A. (ed.), *The Cambridge Companion to Virgil*, Cambridge: Cambridge University Press, 1997.

Miles, G.B., *Virgil's Georgics: A New Interpretation*, Berkeley, CA: California University Press, 1980.

Otis, B., *Virgil: A Study in Civilised Poetry*, Oxford: Oxford University Press, 1963.

Putnam, M.C.J., *Virgil's Pastoral Art: Studies in the Eclogues*, Princeton, NJ: Princeton University Press, 1970.

Williams, R.D., *The Aeneid*, London: Allen and Unwin, 1987.

HORACE

Dulce et decorum est pro patria mori ('it is sweet and fitting to die for the fatherland', *Odes* 3.2.13), said Horace in celebration of traditional Roman upbringing. Or *is* it celebration? When Horace charts the civil wars and the 'glories' of the Augustan settlement, is he extolling Rome's greatness or exposing its horrors? His famous phrase was repeated bitterly from the trenches of World War I by Wilfred Owen, and it is in his quotation that most people know the lines. Whether the object of Owen's irony is Horace himself or, as I suspect, the Edwardian schoolmasters' teaching of Horace, there can be no doubt of the important role played by Horace in the English public and grammar school systems in the nineteenth and early twentieth centuries, directed towards fostering the spirit of British empire. In today's world, around the change of the millennium, when empire and education-through-Classics are both greatly changed, Horace is one of the most challenging of Latin poets: genial and comforting to some, troubling to others – or even both at once.

Horace lived in interesting times. He was a young man studying philosophy in Athens in 44 BC, when Brutus came there seeking support for the Republican cause after the elimination of Julius Caesar. Horace joined him and was given the rank of military tribune, a surprisingly high position for one both young and not from a great family. After Brutus' defeat, Horace accepted the triumvirs' 'clemency' and returned to Rome, where he took up (by purchase, as was usual) a post as a kind of administrative official (*scriba quaestorius*), which gave him a comfortable living. Horace had been born on 8 December 65 BC in Venusia in southern Italy. He says he was the son of a freedman (*Satire* 1.6.45–6) and of 'humble means' (1.6.71), but his means cannot have been all that humble, since his father, an auctioneer's agent (a more lucrative job than it sounds), gave him the best Roman education, sent him to study in Athens and set him up in a position from which he could enter the circles of the great. Even allowing for Horace's extraordinary talent, these beginnings suggest that the 'humility' of his position has a fair degree of pose in it.[1]

Horace soon came to the attention of Maecenas, the friend and adviser of Octavian (who became Augustus in 27 BC), and joined his circle, perhaps through the agency of Virgil. What exactly it means to say that Maecenas was the 'patron' of Horace is a question of some complexity: suffice it to say that he was a lifelong friend, that he gave Horace the gift of a farm and that, in his will, Maecenas asked Augustus to 'care for Horace as if for myself'. Horace died on 27 November 8 BC, only a few weeks after Maecenas, and was buried near him. After the death of Virgil in 19 BC, Horace had been in effect the poet laureate, and was commissioned in 17 BC to write the official hymn for the secular games which Augustus put on to celebrate the inauguration of a new 'age'. It was Horace and Virgil who produced the great poetic monuments of the Augustan culture. To call them 'court poets' would be both true and a simplification.

One of the principles of Horace's work is *uariatio* (variation): he wrote in several genres – *Epodes*, *Satires*, *Odes*, *Epistles* – and within each he produced collections of poems with great variety of tone and content. Another way of looking at Horace's construction of his persona is to see it, as Henderson does, as two poetic trajectories developing in parallel: a hexameter Horace (*Satires*, *Epistles*, *Ars Poetica*) and a lyric Horace (*Epodes*, *Odes*, *Carmen Saeculare*).[2] Yet at the same time, there are certain themes and principles which pervade his work: among the most important are *decorum* ('what is fitting'), moderation and friendship. None of these is wholly unpolitical, for if there is one overriding impression from Horace's work, it is the representation of what it might be to be a 'good citizen', a Roman (Ro-*man*, if you'll pardon the pun), in the world of Augustus. Much of this is indirect and, we might say, more insidious for that: Horace works by evoking an image of the sophisticated circle of Maecenas and other elite men, at work and at play, presented as a continuation of the aristocratic world of the Republic, but with subtle shifts of emphasis – and all very reasonable, of course.

Where elite men of the Republic were obsessed with their 'freedom' (that is, with stopping any one member getting too much influence), in Horace's world that 'freedom' is equally important, but emphasis is placed on autarky, on control of the self, on not being subject to excessive desires or fears of any nature. This includes fear of the tyrant: Horace helped Augustus to present himself not as a tyrant, but as rightly and reasonably powerful, powerful in a way that was a continuation of the moral authority of aristocratic heroes of the Republic. The discourse also enables Augustus/Horace to present (to invent) a role for Roman citizens to take pride in, now that the public 'rat race' of Late Republican politics was largely over. We can see *Epistles* 1.18 as an example of this shift from political to what we might call 'spiritual' autarky. The poem is a statement of independence, including independence from Maecenas himself, and involves a kind of political quietism, but it is also a political act, for it (a) shows the tolerance of Maecenas (and therefore Augustus) and (b) suggests one kind of lifestyle appropriate to an Augustan Roman.

But even this as I have just said is a simplification of Horatian complexity: that notion of 'spiritual autarky' is not an invention of the years after Actium (31 BC), but would have found resonance among such politically active Republicans as Cicero. Also, although I do believe my suggestion above – that Horace presents fear of the tyrant as *nothing to do with Augustus*, because Augustus' power (in Horatian propaganda) is just and reasonable, not tyrannical – is correct, I think we could also rightly say that when Horace represents that separation between the tyrant and the Augustan myth, it is performatively self-refuting. An aspect of Horatian *uariatio* is the ability to take up a whole range of subject-positions *vis-à-vis* the regime, including one that suggests (to put it simply) that maybe Augustus is a tyrant after all.

Horace is a poet of highly complex relationships, poetic as well as political. We cannot understand Horace, or indeed any Roman poet, without coming to terms with his intertextual agenda, that is his relationship with earlier poets, particularly Greek ones. Although the Romans were acutely aware of their culture as a variation on Greek culture, and it was Horace who spoke of how 'captured Greece took her fierce conqueror [Rome] captive' (*Epistles* 2.1.156), they saw their culture as rivalling as well as imitating its Greek model. Greek poetry is part of the Roman poet's material, a building block just as much as are the words of his language, the thoughts of his people, 'human nature', the countryside of his home, and so on. Horace is proud (*Epistles* 1.19.23) to be 'the first' to write Latin iambs[3] in the manner of Archilochus, in the *Epodes*, and the first to train Roman song in Greek lyric metres, in the *Odes* (*Odes* 3.30.13–14). If the *Satires* aren't so specifically 'Greek into Roman', nonetheless Horace is keen to emphasise their poetic ancestry in (and difference from) the poetry of the early Latin satirist Lucilius.

The *Epodes*, seventeen short poems, were written in the 30s BC. Their aggressive tone, obscenity and violence seem at first sight at odds with the 'genial Horace' of the *Odes* (and, differently, the *Satires*). Horace claims (*Epistles* 2.2.51–2) that he was driven by the bitterness of poverty to write in this way, but it is likely that the comment is meant in a literary-critical way, and that he was at least as much driven by the genre he chose. Archilochean iambics are poetry of excess, where violent abuse and rancorous invective are part of the 'rules' of the genre. Horace, we might say, writes with a *poetics* of excess.

Some *Epodes* are light pieces, like the delightfully playful invective against garlic (*Epode* 3) – if Maecenas ever serves it to him again, may he be cursed with bad breath that puts off his lover in bed. Some are straightforwardly political, like the diatribe against civil war (*Epode* 7). A number are grotesquely obscene, introducing the darkest side of Horatian representations of sexuality: *Epode* 8, for example, in which the speaker (let's call him Horace) violently abuses a woman with whom he claims to be impotent. Somehow his own virility remains intact, for how could a full-blooded Roman fail to be put off by this disgusting old woman? (I mean this ironically – just in case you were wondering.)[4] The poem is undeniably cruel and no amount of pleading about the generic appropriateness of invective will change that. Various equally disgusting witches occur elsewhere (*Epodes* 5, briefly 3, 17); in Horace, as in so many other places, the representation of the witch is tied up with a misogynistic fear of the power of woman, of sexuality and particularly women's control of sexuality.

Horace's *Satires* are not an ancient version of *Spitting Image*. While they do contain elements of parody, diatribe, invective and attack by distorted representation, these things are, in antiquity, as much characteristic of other genres as of satire. A partial clue to understanding the nature of Horace's satires is one of the ancient derivations of the word 'satire': from the *lanx satura*, the plate of mixed first-fruits offered to the gods. Satire is a mixed bag of different poems, with an earthy ethos for which food is a suitable metaphor – a variation on this derivation is the mixed sausage. (The other ancient derivation is that satire comes from the activities of satyrs.) In using the metre of epic poetry (the hexameter), satire does so with a slightly ironic tone, joking at its own presumption. Horace claims, indeed, that satire 'is not really poetry but more like conversation' (1.4.41–2). That is a rhetorical ploy, designed to make a statement about the stylistic level while also self-deprecatingly evoking a friendly, homely relationship between speaker and audience.

The two books of *Satires* contain poems that at first sight seem hardly satirical at all in the modern sense. One such (1.5) describes a journey made by himself, Maecenas and various other friends, including Virgil. The apparently simple subject hides a wealth of complexity. First, this is a poem modelled directly on one by Lucilius, which also relates a journey. But, second, this is indeed a real journey and one of rather more consequence than Horace implies.[5] The friends just happen to be wandering down to Brundisium – for a very sensitive political meeting between representatives of Antony and Octavian. What Horace presents is a picture of the friends of Maecenas, and therefore also Octavian, as a group of cultured, sophisticated, reasonable, amusing and thoroughly 'good chap' citizens, doing their utmost to preserve peace, while also preserving the aristocratic amateurishness of Republican political values. The story narrates their journey through war-ravaged Italy, the country that they are busy protecting.

Other poems are more obviously 'satires': the usual targets are luxury and excess of any form, and failures of autarky (control of the self) and proper Roman behaviour. These are themes which will be intensified by Horace's successors in the genre, Persius and Juvenal. An example is *Satire* 1.3, which begins with an attack on the excessive behaviour of an individual, before turning into a plea for tolerance (a big 'Augustan' virtue) in human relations. Other poems are entertaining anecdotes, like the story of Horace's famous encounter with the 'pest' (1.9) who tried to get Horace to arrange to have him introduced to Maecenas, or the preceding poem, which is told in the persona of a Priapus (a wooden statue of the ithyphallic god who was guardian of gardens). Priapus was troubled by the visit of some witches (them again) to the gardens of Maecenas on the Esquiline Hill, against whom his apotropaic (warding-off-evil) powers were useless until he emitted a fart which burst his buttocks and sent the witches off in terror. Horace, as he says, aims 'to instruct with a laugh' (1.1.23–5; cf. *Ars Poetica* 344).

This didactic stance is developed further in the *Epistles*. These poems aren't 'real letters' in the sense that Cicero's letters to friends are, but belong to a tradition of letter-writing as a literary and philosophic medium. Some, but not all, use the conventional formulae of letters. In the second book of *Epistles*, the focus is on a matter of pervading interest to Horace: poetry itself. The first letter, to Augustus, is a defence of the activity of the poet and of modern poetry at its best. Age, he says, shouldn't be an over-whelming criterion for value. It would be reasonable to think that the comment applies also to areas other than poetry. The second letter, to Florus, starts as an apology for not having produced some (supposedly) promised lyrics,[6] but develops into a highly elaborate disquisition on the nature of poetic activity and the relationship of poets and critics. The final 'letter', which is known as the *Ars Poetica* and is the culmination of Horace's hexameter persona, is nearly 500 lines of advice to budding poets, itself in poetic form. The main interest is in tragedy and epic, not only because these were the subjects on which Aristotle concentrated in his *Poetics*, but also because these are the acknowledged highest genres. Writing about writing epic and tragedy (and about decorum) is not an unpolitical gesture. The poem opens with images of what lack of decorum might produce in poetry: monsters. Immediately, the images problematise the poem's status, for 'poetic monsters' are precisely what Horace *does* offer us. This poem is not only a brilliant piece of literary criticism, but also is itself a performance of literature.

Horace's crowning achievement was the *Odes*. Three books were published in about 23 BC, a final book being added much later in 13 BC. These are works of superb poetic beauty, written in a variety of different lyric metres, in imitation of Greek lyric poets such as Alcaeus, Sappho and Pindar. The challenges and opportunities of these difficult metres should not be underestimated, nor should the importance of sound and rhythm in Roman poetics. But the genre is more than its metres. The lyric genre covers a range from the erotic and symposiastic to celebration of heroes and hymns to the gods. It also offers Horace a lyric stance, or rather a series of stances or personae, on which he can draw in order to speak at one remove. This is particularly important in the directly political odes, where the lyric persona allows Horace to get away with his celebration of Augustus precisely because he is speaking in a pose, 'in inverted commas'. This is not to suggest that Horace is insincere in his praise, but that the fact that 'this is how you write in this genre' means that he can be more extravagant without causing offence or embarrass-ment (or, at least, that is something of what this capturing of good will is posing as doing – though at another level it deliberately fails, and it *is* offensive and embarrassing). He can sing of having met Bacchus (god of wine, 2.19) in a cave, and we know that he is talking about poetry and talking poetically about culture.

Horace writes poems celebrating the Augustan regime. There is

nothing too un-Roman in effusive compliment, as the letters of
Cicero are witness, but at the same time it is true that in order to
write great poetry, and also to help to build up Augustan culture
(proclaiming moderation and the supposed continuation of Republican values), Horace had to find a way of moderating his encomium.
It was the lyric persona which gave him this. Because he is writing in
the voice of Alcaeus or Pindar, he can appeal to the appropriateness
of the genre to justify his poetry. In *Odes* 1.12, for example, he begins
in the hymnic style of Pindar (for example, the opening of *Olympian*
2): 'Is this poem, inspired by the muse, to be in praise of a man, a
hero, or a god?' All are suitable subjects for lyric encomium. The
stanzas work through a series of gods who might be celebrated in
lyric (and in effect they are being celebrated by this poem), slipping
naturally from the Olympian gods (with Jupiter first, as he should
be) through mythic heroes (like Hercules) into the mythic-historic
heroes of Roman history (Romulus), on into the great heroes of the
Republic (like Regulus, Camillus, Marcellus) and on from them into
the emperor's family, aided by the link between the Marcellus who
was consul five times in the third century BC and the Marcellus who
had recently married Augustus' daughter Julia (25 BC; he died two
years later). From there, by way of the Julian star (signifying the
deification of Julius Caesar), Horace slips Augustus neatly and
naturally into the list. By ring composition (returning to the
beginning of something at the poem's end), Jupiter returns in a
special relationship with Augustus. The result is an elevated lyric
hymn which celebrates the emperor – in a manner in keeping with
Horatian and Augustan ideals of propriety.[7]

This kind of suggestive connection between Augustus and great
figures of the past is one of the crucial ways in which his public
image was developed.[8] In *Odes* 3.5, a similar technique is at work.
The poem is one of the so-called 'Roman Odes' – the first six poems
of Book 3, all in Alcaics and all particularly involved in developing
the Augustan programme. One issue, throughout the *Odes* and
beyond, is whether or how to make Augustus a god during his
lifetime. There was a good deal of pressure that way, and the cult of
the living ruler was familiar in the East, but it was officially
discouraged. Horace has various subtle ways of just not quite
deifying Augustus. *Odes* 3.5 begins by saying that just as thunder in
heaven is a sign of Jupiter, so Augustus will be considered a *praesens
diuus* (a 'divinity in person') when he has conquered the Britons and
Parthians. The rest of the *Ode* tells the story of Regulus. This hero of
the Punic wars persuaded the Senate not to give in to Carthaginian

pressure and submit to a dishonourable (in Roman eyes) treaty and exchange of prisoners. Instead, Regulus went back to Carthage to his death – happy and unconcerned, as if he were going off to his country farm. He is thus the embodiment of autarky. What has this to do with Augustus? The poem elliptically commemorates the return in 20 BC of the Roman military standards lost thirty-three years previously in the disaster at Carrhae (53 BC). But there is more to it. Horace is suggesting something about how elite Roman men might find it appropriate to regard Augustus. People can think of him as a god, in the same way as they are terribly impressed by the weather as a sign of Jupiter. For the Roman aristocrat, the shared inheritance of Republican heroes provides a store of models and links which may allow them to regard Augustus as a present-day hero. That is what Roman rhetoric has been doing for years: what Horace is doing for Augustus is only a continuation and intensification of it. Thus the gulf between Republican aristocratic heroisation of the ways of the past and the imperial ruler-cult is subtly and subliminally breached.

The peak of Horace's career as Roman poet laureate is the *Carmen Saeculare*, the Secular Hymn (or rather 'Hymn of the New Age'), which he was commissioned by Augustus to produce for performance during the celebrations of the Secular Games in 17 BC. It was sung by a choir of citizen boys and girls, who embodied the hopes of the Augustan 'brave new world'. They pray to the gods, and especially to Apollo and Diana, that the Roman people may be granted peace, prosperity and social harmony – all the blessings of which the poem itself is a sign and an enactment.

Lyric has a private face also, one which in Horace encourages many scholars to identify with him as 'someone you could drink with'.[9] As I have mentioned previously, many of the symposiastic poems have a political angle to them also, showing the good Roman at leisure. Probably the most famous example is the delightful hymn to a wine jar (*Odes* 3.21). The wine jar in question has a special relationship with Horace, having been lain down in the year of his birth (marked by the consul, as is customary). The jar is invited to 'come down' like a god (3.21.7) because Corvinus, ruler of this drinking party, is calling for something stronger. Messalla Corvinus didn't just model himself on the great Republican hero Cato; he was also, we should note, the man who will propose the title *pater patriae* ('father of the country') for Augustus in 2 BC. The picture being built up is of sophisticated men at leisure, loosening up when the jobs of public life are done. Thus Horace organises the *Odes*, weaving personal, national, civic and poetic themes together into a mosaic to mime Augustan culture. Personally I find it exceptionally challenging to square my delight in the beauty of odes like the famous Soracte poem (1.9) or that of Pyhrra (1.5), or the oddly moving description of the kid that is unaware it will be sacrificed to the equally lovely spring of Bandusia (3.13), with the anxiety I feel in the face of Horace's powerfully insidious propaganda for the Augustan regime. Not everyone would agree.

Notes

1 It was conventional for poets to pose as being 'poor', throughout the Roman world and on into the Middle Ages. Sometimes it was also true, and for Horace it has been important in his reception. For discussion of Horace's conversion or treachery (him and everyone else), see J.G.W. Henderson, *Fighting for Rome*, Cambridge: Cambridge University Press, 1998, chaps 3 and 4.
2 Henderson, *op. cit.*, p. 108.
3 Metre makes a major contribution to defining genre in ancient literature. For an introduction to Horace's verse types in the *Epodes*, see D. Mankin, *Horace: Epodes*, Greek and Latin Classics, Cambridge: Cambridge University Press, 1995, pp. 18–22.
4 On this poem, see the very important though very difficult Chapter 4 of Henderson, *Writing Down Rome*, Oxford: Oxford University Press, 1999.
5 See E. Gowers, 'Horace, *Satires* 1.5: An inconsequential journey', *Proceedings of the Cambridge Philological Society*, 39, 1993, pp. 48–66.
6 Augustan and later poets get a lot of poetic mileage out of refusing to write or apologising for not writing poetry.
7 Yes, although it should be noted that the metre employed – Sapphics – may go some way towards undercutting the heroic pretensions of the grand style.
8 This was true also for other major figures of the time. It was a standard rhetorical ploy, which the Augustan machine was particularly adept at manipulating.
9 West comments, in the introduction to his World's Classics translation *The Complete Odes and Epodes* (p. vii), that

> Those who know Horace well find that of all dead writers there is none who is a closer friend, who speaks more usefully in easy and in difficult times, and none whom they would more happily sit down to drink with.

In a sense, he is right.

See also in this book

Archilochus, Callimachus, Juvenal, Martial, Virgil

Texts, translations and commentaries

The complete works are available in OCT (with the interesting oddity of starting with the *Odes*), Teubner, Loeb and Penguin. An excellent World's Classics edition of *The Complete Odes and Epodes* is by D. West (reissued in 2000).

The commentaries by R. Nisbet and M. Hubbard on *Odes 1* (Oxford University Press, 1970) and *Odes 2* (Oxford University Press, 1978) are among the classics of Classical commentary-writing. Valuable also are D. West, *Horace – Odes I: carpe diem* (Oxford University Press, 1995) and *Horace – Odes II: uatis amicis* (Oxford University Press, 1998), both offering text, translation and commentary; and K. Quinn, *Horace: The Odes* (Macmillan, 1980), which contains introduction, text and commentary.

There are Cambridge Greek and Latin Classics editions of the *Epodes* and the *Epistles*, and Aris and Phillips editions of the *Satires*.

C.O. Brink's editions with commentary of the *Ars Poetica* and the other poems in *Epistles* 2 (Cambridge University Press, 1963, 1971, 1982) constitute another monument of Classical scholarship.

Further reading

Commager, S., *The Odes of Horace. A Critical Study*, New Haven, CT, and London: Yale University Press, 1962.

Fraenkel, E., *Horace*, Oxford: Oxford University Press, 1957.

Freudenburg, K., *The Walking Muse: Horace on the Theory of Satire*, Princeton, NJ: Princeton University Press, 1993.

Harrison, S. (ed.), *Homage to Horace: A Bimillenary Celebration*, Oxford: Oxford University Press, 1995.

Lowrie, M., *Horace's Narrative Odes*, Oxford: Oxford University Press, 1997.

Oliensis, E., *Horace and the Rhetoric of Authority*, Cambridge: Cambridge University Press, 1998.

Rudd, N. (ed.), *Horace 2000: A Celebration. Essays for the Bimillennium*, London: Duckworth, 1993.

Santirocco, M.S., *Unity and Design in Horace's Odes*, Chapel Hill, NC: University of North Carolina Press, 1986.

West, D., *Reading Horace*, Edinburgh: Edinburgh University Press, 1967.

LIVY

Unlike some of his predecessors, Livy didn't come to write history during or after a long career of public service. It is therefore a bit of a paradox that he chose to compose the *Ab Urbe Condita*, a monumental work of Roman history in 142 books, dealing with military and political affairs from the capture of Troy at the beginning[1] until the events of 9 BC at the end.[2] Some critics might have seen Livy as an 'armchair historian'. It had after all been a traditional ingredient of Roman historiography that the *auctor* (author) should ideally also be an *actor* (protagonist), although not necessarily within the period of his narrative. So Cato the Elder (consul, 195 BC), the first Roman to narrate history in Latin in the third century BC, had served in the Hannibalic war, while Sempronius Asellio, who wrote a *Res Gestae* of his own time, was military tribune at Numantia in 134–133 BC.

Historians who couldn't add credibility to their writing through a public career risked criticism. For instance, the Roman historian Cassius Hemina, who wrote in the second century BC, refers in one fragment to a 'merely literary man' (fr. 28, Peter), which some have taken as a hostile comment about one of his sources, the Sicilian historian Timaeus, another 'armchair historian', who wrote in Greek. Livy's predecessor Sallust also anticipates an unfriendly response from his audience because he has withdrawn from public life to write history, even though he had been active in politics beforehand. In the preface to the *Jugurtha* Sallust argues that 'more benefit will come to the state from my leisure time than from the business activities of other men' (*Jugurtha* 4.4). The fact that he has to defend himself in this way suggests how unfavourably the Roman literary elite could view those who self-indulgently abandoned a public career to write history.[3]

Cicero even went as far as to argue that to be drawn away from active life by study was to disregard one's duty (*On Duties* 1.19). That was all very well, provided that contemporary politics offered the opportunity to serve the state honourably, but in his preface Livy presents an image of Rome torn apart by the troubles of the civil wars: in comparison with the current political scene, the world of the historian is wholesome and profitable, and can also present readers with useful examples to follow or to avoid (*Preface* 10). It is as if the usual hierarchy between the relative merits of literature and politics has been reversed. To create this impression was certainly advantageous for Livy, who was boldly swimming against the historiographical tide by devoting himself to writing history on a full-time basis. Although we might think today that Livy's detachment from contemporary politics was advantageous because it shielded him from charges of bias, ancient audiences had different expectations of their historians.

It is a reflection of Livy's isolation from a career in politics that we know very little about his life. He was born in about 59 BC in Padua, a town in northern Italy which also produced Asconius, the commentator on Cicero's speeches, and Thrasea Paetus, the Stoic philosopher who wrote a biography of Cato the Younger. As Kraus has observed, Livy refers tacitly to his roots at the start of the narrative when talking about Antenor's foundation of a city called Troy (later Padua) in the region of the Veneti, before turning to Aeneas' more famous adventures and the subsequent foundation of Rome.[4] Antenor's settlement in the north was superseded by Rome, but we are made aware (however obliquely) that history could have turned out differently to make Padua more important than Rome.

Various writers perceived the strength of Livy's connection with his home town. The historian Asinius Pollio teased Livy for his *Patauinitas* ('Paduan identity'; Quintilian *Training in Oratory* 1.5.56, 8.1.3), which some have seen perhaps as a general criticism of his provincial state of mind, while Martial notes more positively that the 'land of Aponus' (that is, Padua) was renowned because of Livy (*Epigram* 1.61.3). At any rate, Livy himself went to Rome, probably after the Battle of Actium in 31 BC, having already started to write his historical narrative, and there he met Augustus, who took an interest in his work even in its early stages.

Quite what Livy thought about the new emperor has been hotly debated among scholars. They have cast Livy as pro-Augustan, anti-Augustan, pro-Republican or even as someone who shifted from one end of the spectrum to the other through writing his history.[5] Tacitus makes Cremutius Cordus claim that Augustus teased Livy as a 'Pompeian' (*Annals* 4.34.3),[6] and there certainly seem to be pro-Pompeian elements in the late antique *Periochae*, the summaries of the lost books of Livy, but it doesn't look as if there was any serious quarrel between the two men. Livy refers to Augustus in positive terms as having closed the doors of the Temple of Janus after Actium to symbolise that Rome was no longer at war (1.19.3). There is a second positive reference to Augustus as a 'founder and restorer of temples' (4.20.7), as Livy discusses an inscription discovered by Augustus, although he ultimately questions the historical reliability of the information unearthed by the emperor.

Livy's association with the imperial family extended beyond Augustus. We hear that, along with a man called Sulpicius Flavus, he encouraged the young Claudius to write history (Suetonius *Claudius* 41.1). As it happened, Claudius didn't finish this work until he became emperor and, even then, he drew a diplomatic veil over events beyond the end of the civil wars.

As well as mixing with the imperial family, Livy spent time in the declamation schools and some scholars have seen a connection between this intellectual environment and Livy's digression on Alexander the Great in Book 9. Seneca the Elder remembers one debate where Livy criticised Sallust's translation of an epigram supposedly written by Thucydides (*Controversiae* 9.1.14). Historians often had confrontational relationships with other practitioners of the genre, but Livy may have developed a special rivalry with Sallust, whose terse and antithetical style was so different from the more expansive manner of writing in the *Ab Urbe Condita*.[7] We know that as well as his historical narrative, Livy also wrote dialogues 'halfway between history and philosophy' (Seneca *Moral Epistle* 100.9) and a letter to his son advising on appropriate reading for a potential orator (Quintilian 10.1.39). Livy eventually died in AD 17 in Padua.

Livy's *Ab Urbe Condita* is an extraordinary achievement, even if today only Books 1–10 and 21–45 survive. It would have been very easy for both writer and reader to lose their way through such a monumental narrative, but Livy uses various techniques to ensure clarity. The basic chronological unit of the text is the year, which is dated according to who the consuls were, while the basic structural unit is the book, which was created by Livy himself rather than by a later editor.

Within this framework, Livy could slow down or speed up his narrative according to the importance of particular historical events: for instance, we know from the *Periochae* that Livy narrated the events of the First Punic War, a period of twenty-four years (264–241 BC), in four books (Books 16–19), even though he took just one book (Book 20) to report what happened in the aftermath of the First Punic War, a period of twenty-three years (241–219 BC).[8] This highlights another helpful organisational device of Livy's work, namely the use of five- or ten-book units (pentads or decades) to present particular periods of history.[9] So, in the third decade (Books 21–30), Livy narrates the events of the Second Punic War (218–201 BC), and introduces the material with a new preface (21.1) which highlights the importance of the conflict that he is about to relate.

Another feature which helps to guide readers through the narrative is Livy's vivid depiction of the grand protagonists who dominate the action over the course of several books. They are often introduced or highlighted with separate character sketches, as happens with Hannibal (21.4) and Scipio Africanus (26.19). As well as describing these figures' qualities from an authorial viewpoint, Livy also uses internal focalisation to depict them from the point of view of another protagonist within the text. So, when Hannibal confronts the Roman general Fabius Maximus, who refuses to engage in battle with the Carthaginian army, Livy makes Hannibal declare scornfully that the Roman spirit has been broken and that the war has been won; yet at the same time Livy reveals the more subtle private thoughts of Hannibal, who is worried that, in Fabius, the Romans have finally found a general who will be a worthy adversary for himself (22.12).

Another method which Livy regularly used, both to illuminate the personalities of his protagonists and to expand his narrative, was the inclusion of speeches. Quintilian particularly admired this aspect of his work (*Training in Oratory* 10.1.101) and we know of one man, Mettius Pompusianus, who was executed by Domitian for carrying around with him speeches taken from Livy (Suetonius *Domitian* 10.3). Leaving aside the intriguing question of which excerpts provoked Domitian's anger, the fact that Pompusianus bothered to acquire copies of Livy's speeches suggests their power to captivate ancient readers.

Even relatively minor characters are given powerful speeches, such as the harangue of Marcus Minucius, who can no longer bear Fabius Maximus' policy of doing nothing while Hannibal goes on the rampage in Italy. Livy makes him conjure up the powerful image of smoke from burning houses and fields filling the Roman army's eyes and mouths as the legionaries hide from Hannibal. Livy also has Minucius sarcastically call Fabius Maximus a 'new Camillus' (22.14.9) and speculate that if Camillus had acted in 390 BC as passively as Fabius Maximus in 217 BC, then the Gaulish invaders would still be entrenched on the Capitol. Minucius will have to change his tune when he offers battle in an unfavourable position and has to be rescued by Fabius Maximus, but his speech is typical of the way in which Livy fills out personalities and heightens narrative tension.

Most speeches in Livy stand on their own, although there is one example of a pair of addresses by Scipio and Hannibal before their respective armies (21.40–4). Such speeches not only heighten the drama, but also usefully allow Livy to pursue his agenda of 'expansion of the past'. Particularly for the early books of his history, historical evidence was scarce and so there was a real need to flesh out the bare skeleton of facts with decorative touches such as speeches, colourful topographical descriptions (such as the site of the Caudine Forks ambush at 9.2) and dramatic battle narratives.[10]

As a result, scholars have debated the extent to which Livy's narrative is historically reliable. For some sections of the *Ab Urbe Condita*, we can measure Livy's narrative against other historical accounts, such as Dionysius of Halicarnassus' *Roman Antiquities*, which ran from the origins of Rome to 264 BC (although we now only have the narrative to 443 BC), or Polybius' *Histories*, which narrated the rise of Rome during the Punic wars (although only Books 1–5 now survive intact).[11] Such comparisons can shed valuable light on alternative historical traditions about particular events, but unfortunately we don't have access to parallel narratives for all of the surviving books of Livy. Still, Livy is at least prepared to admit when he is puzzled and often cites perplexing variations from his own sources, such as the confusion about which Roman, Lucius Cornelius or Papirius Cursor, won a triumph for exacting revenge on the Samnites after the Caudine Forks ambush (9.15.9–11).

Not everyone admired Livy, despite his achievements as a historian. Caligula is supposed to have come close to removing Livy's writings and busts from the libraries, criticising him as a long-winded and careless historian (Suetonius *Caligula* 34.2). Yet this story casts Caligula in a worse light than Livy. In addition, Martial jokes playfully in an elegant two-line epigram that his library cannot hold all of 'huge Livy' (*Epigram* 14.190), which might suggest impatience, but nevertheless the epigram was written to be inscribed on an edition of Livy being given as a gift. Perhaps Martial liked Livy after all, or knew of friends who did.

On a more positive note we might remember Pliny's story of a man who travelled all the way from Cadiz just to glimpse Livy (Pliny *Letters* 2.3.8). After his death, Livy influenced subsequent historians. Tacitus fairly frequently used Livian language, and there are also more extensive influences. For example, Dillius Vocula's appeal to his armies (Tacitus *Histories* 4.58) is modelled on a speech put into Scipio's mouth by Livy (*Ab Urbe Condita* 28.27–9).[12] There is also the *Epitome* of the second-century AD author Florus, who drew heavily on Livy's *Ab Urbe Condita* to produce a condensed version of Roman history for those who lacked the time to read monumental narratives. It wasn't just historical writers upon whom Livy had an impact. Livy also influenced the epic poet Silius Italicus, who wrote at the end of the first century AD about the Punic wars. There has been a resurgence of interest in Livy among modern scholars over the last decade. No doubt Livy's fan from Cadiz would have approved of the burgeoning number of books, articles and commentaries on Livy which have appeared recently.

Notes

1 C.S. Kraus and A.J. Woodman, *Latin Historians*, Greece and Rome New Surveys in the Classics 27, Oxford: Oxford University Press, 1997, p. 53, remind us that

though called *Ab Urbe Condita*, 'from the founding of the city', his history actually begins some four hundred years earlier, with the fall of Troy.

2 Some critics think that Livy's original stopping point would have been in Book 120 with the death of Cicero in 43 BC, but he decided to extend his narrative to the events of 9 BC in Book 142. See further Kraus and Woodman, *op. cit.*, p. 54.
3 Sallust's departure from politics wasn't voluntary. See Kraus and Woodman, *op. cit.*, pp. 15–16, and A.J. Woodman, *Rhetoric in Classical Historiography*, London and Sydney: Croom Helm, 1988, pp. 73–4.
4 C.S. Kraus, *Livy Ab Vrbe Condita VI*, Greek and Latin Classics, Cambridge: Cambridge University Press, 1994, pp. 1–2.
5 On Livy and Augustus, see Kraus and Woodman, *op. cit.*, pp. 70–4; Kraus, *op. cit.*, pp. 7–9; and M. Toher, 'Augustus and the evolution of Roman historiography', in K.A. Raaflaub and M. Toher, *Between Republic and Empire: Interpretations of Augustus and His Principate*, Berkeley, Los Angeles and Oxford: University of California Press, 1990, pp. 139–54.
6 See further L. Hayne, 'Livy and Pompey', *Latomus*, 49, 1990, pp. 435–42.
7 See Kraus, *op. cit.*, pp. 17–24, and Kraus and Woodman, *op. cit.*, pp. 2–70, on Livy's style.
8 See further P. Stadter, 'The structure of Livy's history', *Historia*, 21, 1972, pp. 287–307.
9 See further T.J. Luce, *Livy: The Composition of His History*, Princeton, NJ: Princeton University Press, 1977, pp. 25–32.
10 See further Woodman, *op. cit.*
11 See Luce, *op. cit.*, pp. 139–84, on Livy's sources.
12 See R. Syme, *Tacitus*, Oxford: Oxford University Press, 1958, pp. 685–6.

See also in this book

Cassius Dio, Herodotus, Polybius, Sallust, Tacitus, Thucydides, Xenophon

Texts, translations and commentaries

The Latin text is available in OCT (6 volumes, as far as *Ab Urbe Condita* 40), Teubner (6 volumes) and Loeb (14 volumes).

As well as the Loeb, there are Penguin translations of *The Early History of Rome* (*Ab Urbe Condita* 1–5) and *The War with Hannibal* (*Ab Urbe Condita* 21–30) by A. De Selincourt, *Rome and Italy* (*Ab Urbe Condita* 6–10) by B. Radice, and *Rome and the Mediterranean* (*Ab Urbe Condita* 31–45) by H. Bettenson; and *Oxford World's Classics* translations *The Rise of Rome* (*Ab Urbe Condita* 1–5) by T.J. Luce; and *Livy: The Dawn of the Roman Empire* (*Books 31–40*) by J.C. Yardley.

There are commentaries on *Ab Urbe Condita* 1–5 by R.M. Ogilvie, on *Ab Urbe Condita* 6–10 by S.P. Oakley, on *Ab Urbe Condita* 31–4 and 35–7 by J. Briscoe, all published by Oxford; on *Ab Urbe Condita* 6 by C.S. Kraus in the

Cambridge Greek and Latin Classics Series; on *Ab Urbe Condita* 21 by P.G. Walsh, published by Bristol University; and on *Ab Urbe Condita* 36–39 and 40 by P.G. Walsh, in the Aris and Phillips Series.

Further reading

Dorey, T.A. (ed.), *Livy*, London: Routledge and Kegan Paul, 1971.

Feldherr, A., *Spectacle and Society in Livy's History*, Berkeley, Los Angeles and London: University of California Press, 1998.

Jaeger, M., *Livy's Written Rome*, Ann Arbor, MI: University of Michigan Press, 1997.

Kraus, C.S. and Woodman, A.J., *Latin Historians*, Greece and Rome New Surveys in the Classics 27, Oxford: Oxford University Press, 1997.

Luce, T.J., *Livy: The Composition of His History*, Princeton, NJ: Princeton University Press, 1977.

Walsh, P.G., *Livy: His Historical Aims and Methods*, Cambridge: Cambridge University Press, 1961.

Woodman, A.J., *Rhetoric in Classical Historiography*, London and Sydney: Croom Helm, 1988.

PROPERTIUS

More than a thousand years before the medieval troubadours placed a beloved woman on a pedestal and so invented 'chivalry', Propertius presented himself as the slave of his mistress and thereby subverted conventional Roman notions of the relationship between the genders and the nature of power. A crucial difference between the first century BC and the twelfth century AD, however, was the development between those times of an 'ethic of humility' (the idea that there might be something morally and spiritually ennobling in self-abasement), which would have been barely comprehensible to a Roman of the time of Augustus and Propertius. To such a reader, an erotic relationship in which a man is enslaved and so loses that 'autarky' (control of himself) which was – officially – thought so important, is more shocking and paradoxical than it might seem today.

Sextus Propertius was a native of the Umbrian town of Asisium (Assisi), north of Rome, where he was born sometime between 54 and 47 BC. Like all talented provincials, he was educated in Rome and settled there, probably until his death sometime after 16 BC. His family were equestrian, rich and important enough to start their son on a conventional legal and political career in Rome, which led not in fact up the normal ladder but to a poetic career which brought him into the circle of Maecenas, the right-hand man of Augustus and influential patron of the arts. The frequently repeated story that Propertius' family suffered the reduction of their estate in the land confiscations which Octavian (Augustus) ordered in 41–40 BC may well be true; it is played upon by Propertius in poem 4.1, probably both in order to connect himself with that paradigm for the life of the poet, Virgil (who suffered similarly), and to make a poetic statement of Callimachean littleness.

Propertius left four books of poems in elegiac couplets: alternating lines of hexameters (six metrical feet) and pentameters (five). The vast majority of the poems involve an 'I' – a first-person speaker who 'opens his soul' to the reader and directs her/his point of view on the rest of the elegiac world. In the criticism of some past ages, that 'I' would have been seen as unproblematically equivalent to the real Sextus Propertius; today, most people would agree that the suffering lover who speaks in the poems is a construct created by (and through) the poet. It is now, however, the extent and nature of the gap between the persona ('Propertius') and the poet (Propertius) which is a matter for critical debate. By contrast with epic and tragedy, elegy is a subjective genre in which attention is focused almost exclusively on the thoughts, feelings, views and actions of one person, all other things being seen through this lens; even the contemporary lyric of Horace (which is also a 'personal' genre) doesn't achieve the concentrated display of a self for which elegy successfully strives. If we say this is a 'pose', we mean not that it is false and insincere, but that it is a particular poetic choice of style and manner, which may be as real or as unreal as that of any other style of writing.

'Sincerity' has, indeed, been something of a bugbear in the history of responses to the elegiac poets, partly because the poems of Propertius are, in their themes (*topoi*) and images, so similar to those of Tibullus and Ovid in the same genre, partly because Propertius, like the other elegists, is as interested in poetics as he is in erotics. To the Romantic tradition of reading poetry, which still has powerful traces in modern reading practices, that self-conscious artistry is incompatible with sincerity and hence with true poetic force. Ancient poets, however, and this applies well to Propertius, didn't see a tension between emotional self-revelation and poetic self-consciousness as odd or irreconcilable.

The object of Propertius' devotion is a woman he calls 'Cynthia'. The story told by Apuleius in the second century AD, that this is a pseudonym for a Roman lady called Hostia, is as likely to be a product of his imagination as an accurate historical record. The name is indeed almost certainly Propertius' invention, in the tradition of Catullus' mistress Lesbia (thought to have been Clodia) and Gallus' Lycoris (whose name is twice removed, since it is a pseudonym for Cytheris, itself a stage-name invented by the real Volumnia). 'Cynthia' is the feminine form of 'Cynthius', a cult-title of the god Apollo, who played a crucial role in the Callimachean tradition in directing the poet towards the right type of poetry and inspiring his best efforts. By calling his beloved 'Cynthia', Propertius has made her into his muse, the inspiration of his best efforts; into his first and best critic, the 'learned girl' who is imagined as reading the poems; into a statement of his artistic allegiance to Callimachean poetry; and perhaps also into poetry itself. Cynthia can be seen as an embodiment of Propertius' artistic material – his poetry – however much or little she might also be a real woman. The opening word of Book 1 – 'Cynthia' – sets it up. In antiquity, it was common for poems to be known by their opening word (or words); the first book has always been called the 'Cynthia Monobiblos'. Cynthia, then, is the name of the poetry book.[1] Since in poem 1.3 she is compared to a famous statue (probably the *Sleeping Ariadne* now in the Vatican museum) and a series of paintings, since throughout the *corpus* she is an image lovingly created with a few strokes, since even her supposedly negative aspects of 'cruelty', 'infidelity' and 'venality' are part of the poet's dream, it seems to many of us that she is a work of art and a construct of the text. That in no way undermines Propertius' sincerity, although it may change its nature.

However real or unreal Cynthia may be, the question of her social status will always be raised. Views differ: she is most often called a 'courtesan', which means a high-class prostitute whose services involved not only sex but entertainment and companionship, and whose payment might be less directly monetary than the few coins given to what was called a *scortum* (a 'common prostitute'). Such a courtesan is usually a freedwoman, and therefore of a status where she might marry a citizen, but not one of the highest class. At the other end of the social possibilities, Cynthia can be seen as a married woman, of 'middle' or even aristocratic class, whose behaviour is as decadent as our images of Republican and Imperial Rome can invent. Alongside this second category is the possibility that Cynthia might be a widow or (less plausibly) an unmarried citizen girl. The question will often interest, but it is unknowable and perhaps not very important, for love poetry isn't in the business of making socially real distinctions; rather, its aim is to create hints of barriers and half-glimpsed situations in which the lover may display his sufferings, and occasionally his joys.

Barriers, literal or metaphorical, are likely to figure prominently in any love poetry. In elegy, they take their paradigmatic form in the situation of the 'locked-out lover'. There is even a word for this situation: the *paraclausithyron* is the song performed by a lover who arrives at his mistress's house, perhaps drunk from a party, and finds himself excluded. He bewails his lot, begs for entry, calls the stars to witness, and so forth – all in vain. Eventually he gives up, often leaving a garland or some other token on the threshold to signify his love and his suffering. The poems which take this form aren't in fact all that many. (Propertius' most explicit example is 1.16, an amusing variant in which the lover's song is quoted – and thus framed – within the self-righteous complaint of a very respectable Roman door, who objects to being made into the focus of this deranged behaviour.) They are, however, paradigmatic for the situation of the elegist, whose love is a passion of longing, hopeless despite occasional moments of joyous reception, and concentrated on the display of the loving subject's hopes and fears, in particular his desire for literal and metaphorical entry into the girl's heart, home and body.

As Ovid, the master of erotic behaviour, knew, continual suffering, however poetic, will pall eventually. Propertius has his moments of ecstatic joy, presented in poems like 1.8b (which may be integral with 1.8a), when Cynthia has decided not to leave after all, or 2.14 and 2.15, in which a night of love with Cynthia has brought him to a state bordering on divinity. But the fulfilment of desire stimulates greater desire, for the elegiac world takes on and makes its own a notion of love which was prevalent in antiquity – that it is a magic spell.

The notion of love as magic is part of a whole nexus of images which Propertius and the other elegists used to explore the loving subject's emotions. Here, they are both using and subverting traditional Roman ideas about love. According to these, while *sex* was an unproblematical Good Thing, *love* was another matter altogether. Love was a madness, a disease, something which caused normally sensible men to lose their self-control, without which they couldn't really be men. Love even made men a bit like women. (Hence the paradox that the lover is effeminate.) Propertius took on this belief – and gloried in it. He is probably responsible for developing the most prevalent and most influential manifestation of the loss of autarky in love: the conceit of the lover as slave (*seruitium amoris*, the slavery of love). The image is wide-ranging, slipping through various levels of literalness and metaphor. One may see in it four broad categories, which also overlap and interact: the lover performs servile tasks in order to please and so win his mistress; the lover is willing to undergo servile torture in order to prove his love; the lover feels chained to the beloved as if to a mistress of slaves; the lover feels the pains (and desires) of love *as if* they were the torturous punishments of slaves. Literal or metaphorical, willing or unwilling, the lover becomes a slave because he cannot help it, because he has lost himself in his love. The ultimate loss of self is in death, and Propertius is among the most forceful ancient exponents of the 'love and death' motif.[2] In a strange and powerful poem towards the end of his *corpus* (4.7), Propertius imagines the now-dead Cynthia returning to him in a ghostly mixture of desire and erotic threat.

Rome in 20s BC was dominated by one man, Augustus, so much so that no work of culture from that time can be free from his influence. The supposedly personal poetry of Propertius was concerned with issues which were highly charged in Augustan society – war, sex, lifestyles of work and leisure, and poetry itself. Exactly how Propertius came to terms with the Augustan situation is a matter for debate, in part because the ambiguity of his language opens his work to a range of interpretations.[3] One view is to see him as initially independent and opposed to the Augustan regime, but becoming more reconciled or compromised as he grew older and the regime hardened. Some of the poems of Book 4 encourage this belief, when they purport to turn away from erotic themes in order to concentrate on patriotic ones, although other critics judge that these poems themselves are signs that Propertius would not and could not write to the order of Augustus.

Whether or not Augustus, through the agency of Maecenas, actively sought a celebratory epic from all the best poets, it suited the poets of the day to claim that such a request had been made, but – they were sorry, it was too much, they were not worthy of such great and elevated themes – they refused. This refusal is known as the *recusatio* and functions as both a political and a poetic statement of intent. While the grand refusal might offer compliments to the emperor by the back door, more often (particularly with the elegists) its effect is to belittle Augustus by making his 'greatness' into an embodiment of the bombast which was fundamentally opposed to the 'true greatness' of Callimachean littleness. In poem 3.3, Propertius plays a complicated intertextual game, moving back through Ennius to Callimachus (and so to Hesiod), to invoke that most influential of all passages of Greek literature: Callimachus' conversation with Apollo in the opening of his *Aetia*. It was historical epic which Propertius had been dreaming of writing (he claims) and from which Apollo and the muse Calliope direct him back to the elegiac pure stream (sea shore, little boat, little chariot in an untouched meadow – all Roman-Callimachean images) and the traditions of Callimachus and Philetas.[4] Historical epic, and by implication praise of Augustus, is rejected.

Likewise in 2.1 the refusal to write epic in praise of Augustus is bound up in the advancement of the poetic ideals of Callimachus, for Augustan politics and Callimachean poetics are intricately bound by being constructed as opposites in Propertius' poetry. The climax of that poem is a phrase through which Propertius opposes the life of elegiac love to the 'patriotic' demands of the regime: 'it is a praiseworthy thing to die in love' (2.1.47). This is the opposite of Horace's famous dictum that 'it is sweet and fitting to die for one's country' (*Odes* 3.2.13). For Propertius, the life of elegiac love has become a living metaphor for the espousal of Callimachean poetics.

Notes

1 See M. Wyke, 'Written women: Propertius' *scripta puella*', *Journal of Roman Studies*, 77, 1987, pp. 47–61.
2 One recent major study of Propertius is entirely devoted to his involvement in the eros of death (T.D. Papanghelis, *Propertius: A Hellenistic Poet on Love and Death*, Cambridge: Cambridge University Press, 1987).
3 A classic example of ambiguity is the juxtaposition of poems 3.4 and 3.5, a panegyric on (the divine) Augustus' military achievements with a celebration of Love as the god of peace.
4 Philetas was a fourth-century BC poet, whose work was influential over Hellenistic and Latin poetry, but now only exists in a few fragments.

See also in this book

Callimachus, Catullus, Horace, Ovid, Sulpicia

Texts, translations and commentaries

The poems are available in the standard editions (OCT, Teubner, Loeb, Penguin, World's Classics), all fairly recent except for the OCT (1963), which awaits improvement.

The most convenient commentary suitable for a non-specialist audience is that of W.A. Camps, originally 1961–7 but reprinted with further notes in 1985 by Bristol Classical Press. An Aris and Phillips edition of Book 1 was published in 2001.

Further reading

Green, E., *The Erotics of Domination*, Baltimore, MD: Johns Hopkins University Press, 1998.

Hubbard, M., *Propertius*, London: Duckworth, 1974.

Kennedy, D.F., *The Arts of Love: Five Studies in the Discourse of Roman Love Elegy*, Cambridge: Cambridge University Press, 1993.

Stahl, H.P., *Propertius: 'Love' and 'War'. Individual and State under Augustus*, Berkeley, CA, and London: University of California Press, 1985.

Sullivan, J.P., *Propertius: A Critical Introduction*, Cambridge: Cambridge University Press, 1976.

Veyne, P., *Roman Erotic Elegy: Love, Poetry and the West*, Chicago, IL: University of Chicago Press, 1988.

Wyke, M., *The Roman Mistress: Gender, Politics, Love Poetry, Reception*, Oxford: Oxford University Press, forthcoming.

OVID

In Umberto Eco's *The Name of the Rose*, a post-modern novel set in medieval Italy, an older monk responds to the question of his junior, 'Have you ever been in love?', by saying: 'Many times – Virgil, Ovid … '. Many ages have been in love with Ovid, perhaps because 'Ovid' is as fluid and flexible as a character in his own *Metamorphoses*. He is the darling of the post-modern critical world, both in academia and in literary circles, as the recent *Tales from Ovid* by Ted Hughes bears witness; and also of the medieval troubadours and monastic scribes. In between, Shakespeare and the other giants of early modern English literature would also have subscribed to the view that *Naso magister erat* ('Ovid was master').

And who tells us that? Ovid himself (*Ars Amatoria* 2.744). Of all the ancient Greek and Roman poets, Ovid is the one who tells us most about himself (see *Tristia* 4.10). But we must be wary of the seductive power of his poetic autobiography, which makes us feel like he is giving us the details straight, because Ovid never does anything straight. Still, for what it's worth, here is the brief sketch. Publius Ovidius Naso was born on 20 March 43 BC, at Sulmo in the Abruzzi region of Italy, into an equestrian family. His father paid for a good Roman education for Ovid and his brother, both of whom started out on traditional civic careers. Ovid soon took against this option, however, and devoted himself entirely to poetry. It was an exceptionally rich time for Roman poetry, and after the deaths of Virgil and Tibullus in 19 BC, of Propertius in or soon after 16 BC, and of Horace in 8 BC, Ovid became the leading literary figure of the Roman world. His own world was turned upside down, however, when in AD 8 he incurred the displeasure of Augustus in some manner and was sent into exile (or, strictly speaking, relegation – which didn't involve the loss of property and citizenship) to Tomis on the shores of the Black Sea, where he died in AD 16 or 17. The reason for his exile is one of the great mysteries of the Roman world, to which he adds a great deal of smoke and not much fire by talking about it incessantly but uninformatively from exile. He says it was caused by a 'song' and an 'error'. The song was the *Ars Amatoria*; he hints that the error was some kind of complicity in a palace scandal, although he suggests that it was something he innocently saw, rather than did. But who knows? The poet is in control of the dissemination of information, tempting us with hints of biographical details, playing with issues of knowledge and power.[1]

Ovid's poetic output was large. The story begins with the elegiac *Amores*, in which the speaker (constructed as 'Ovid himself') celebrates his successes and – more often – bewails his failures in love, while exploring the avenues of the erotic discourse of contemporary Rome and of Roman love poetry. About the same time come the *Heroides*, letters from legendary heroines to their absent lovers, which are remarkable for their concentration on the 'woman's voice', with Ovid the ventriloquist hiding his own voice under the frameless epistolary form. Then Ovid gets his own persona back with a vengeance, and moves up a notch into didactic, with the *Ars Amatoria* ('Art of Love') and *Remedia Amoris* ('Cures for Love'). Still using the elegiac metre and elegiac conventions, he takes on the pose of Professor of Love to teach readers how to be good lovers (and bad citizens). After elegy and didactic, the next step was obviously epic, but how could so flippant, so playful, so subversive a poet as Ovid scale these poetic heights and challenge Virgil's *Aeneid*? The answer was the *Metamorphoses*, an epic poem (in a sense) in fifteen books of hexameter verse, on the highly self-referential theme of changing forms. It is tempting to put a paragraph break here, to show that with the *Metamorphoses* we have reached the watershed, but I ask you to note that Ovid always puts the book divisions in his epic in odd, disruptive and challenging places.

Be that as it may, at around the same time (approximately the first decade of the new era), Ovid put his hand to a different kind of didactic and a different kind of 'national' poem (epic is, in the Augustan period, necessarily 'national' and 'political', even when it refuses to be so): a poem in elegiac couplets on the Roman calendar, the *Fasti*. The poet is now a kind of antiquarian investigator, gathering information about Roman cults and myths to explain Roman religious practices. He only got half way through the year, however. The exile almost certainly did interrupt the work, but the claim that he couldn't continue in exile for lack of a decent library and stimulating colleagues may well be a rhetorical pose. It is certainly provocative that he breaks off just before the two big Julian months, July and August. The remaining years in Tomis are taken up with the 'exile poetry': five books of *Tristia*, four of *Epistulae ex Ponto*, and the spectacular invective poem *Ibis*. Ostensibly, many of these poems beg for forgiveness and the chance to return to Rome, but subliminally they continue Ovid's battle with political authority and defence of his poetic position.

As well as various bits and pieces and works spuriously attributed to Ovid, here was also a tragedy, *Medea*, the loss of which is made particularly tantalising by the comment of Quintilian that

> Ovid's *Medea* seems to me to show how much that man could have excelled if he had preferred to control his intellect rather than to indulge it.
>
> (*Training in Oratory* 10.1.98)

But restraint wasn't exactly Ovid's style. (Or at least not his pose – his diction and versification are actually extremely neat, and could be called restrained.) This has annoyed some critics, especially in his own day and in the nineteenth and early twentieth centuries, but has delighted many more.

Ovid offers a paradigmatic case for reading poets' lives in-and-from their work. He talks about himself incessantly, but he will never quite let on what 'himself' is, and what its relation might be to the various levels of poetic and erotic persona, or artistic character/creation within his work. Or indeed outside it: Ovid's life as a poet is constructed out of interaction with the lives and poetry of his great predecessors, especially Virgil. A simple way to see this is the manner in which the sequence from *Amores* to *Ars Amatoria* to *Metamorphoses* maps onto that from *Eclogues* to *Georgics* to *Aeneid*. A poetic life of 'stealing from Virgil' is not, however, the life of a plagiarist: rather, we might see Ovid's work as imbued with an aesthetics of repetition – differently. This is how he engages with and makes a virtue out of the 'anxiety of influence',[2] which (creatively) afflicts all poets, especially those of the Roman culture which so highly values 'the ways of our ancestors'.

A possible way of seeing this 'compulsion to repeat', mixed up in the artistic playfulness about the poet's life, is to look at the story of the two editions of the *Amores*. The official line is that the love poems were first published in five books, then re-edited, with some removed and others added, and republished as three books, in pretty much the version we have now. Ovid tells us this himself in the opening epigram, with the self-deprecating joke that at least it makes our job as readers lighter. Okay, but what is at stake in *starting out* your poetic career by telling everyone it is already (and was always already) a repetition? Especially when at least some readers would remember that Callimachus (Hellenistic guru of Roman poets) re-edited and republished his *Aetia*. So Ovid's repetition repeats that of Callimachus.

The aesthetics of repetition is brought to a high art by Ovid, both intertextually and intratextually. Virgil, Horace, Propertius, Lucretius and others stalk his verses; the content of the *Amores* 'repeats' the elegiac world of Propertius and Tibullus, and then the *Ars Amatoria* 'repeats' the *Amores*; in the *Heroides* self-repetition becomes a programmatic symbol for (and enactment of) the feminine voice of the abandoned heroine; it does so again, differently, in the (problematically) feminised voice of the poet 'abandoned' in exile. But repetition is always different. Let's look at an easy example.

One of the most famous lines in the whole of Latin poetry is the opening of the *Aeneid*: 'arms and the man I sing' (*arma uirumque cano*). When Ovid starts to write, he cannot resist repeating that *arma*: the first poem of the *Amores* opens *arma graui numero* ('arms in serious metre'; notice that *numero* echoes *cano* as well, while *graui* is chiasmatic[3] with *uirumque*). He says that he was going to write an epic (*arma uirumque*) in continuous hexameters, but Cupid stole a foot from his second line, thus turning it into a pentameter and changing his epic poem into elegiac couplets. But formally, generically, it always already was – and the opening is a repetition (with a difference) also of the opening of Propertius' first book: *Cynthia prima suis miserum me cepit ocellis* ('Cynthia was the first to capture with her eyes my unhappy self'). 'Cynthia' has been replaced by *arma*, elegy by epic, but the epic weapons will turn out to be reappropriated for the elegiac erotic world, for the *arma* of Aeneas and of Ovid are also sexual, phallic symbols.[4] In case we missed the point here, Ovid reminds us of it in exile. When he wants to claim that all poets write about sex, so Augustus shouldn't be angry with him for the *Ars Amatoria*, he says that 'even that lucky author of your *Aeneid* took *arma uirumque* into the bed of Dido – and that's everyone's favourite bit of the epic' (*Tristia* 2. 533–6; I paraphrase somewhat). The *arma* in the bed of Dido are undoubtedly sexual weapons. So not only has Ovid rewritten the *arma* of the *Aeneid* for his *Amores*, but he has even rewritten Virgil's *arma* for its own context, and in the context of its contemporary reception.

Despite Ovid's claim that all poets write about sex, however, what Augustus objected to in Ovid's poetry wasn't obscenity. Although the entire Ovidian corpus is pervasively sexy, it is not at all obscene by Roman standards. So what was Augustus' problem with it? I would say it was the consistent refusal to take authority seriously, combined with a general irreverence and slipperiness about Rome, the army, politics, Augustus, Augustan monuments, Augustan laws and everything else. In the *Ars Amatoria*, it is also specifically the didactic form: this is a poem written under the shadow of Virgil's *Georgics*, which teach the reader how to be a good citizen under the sign of learning how to be a good farmer. Likewise, Ovid's poem teaches the reader how to be a 'bad' citizen under the sign of learning how to be a good lover. Since Augustus had staked a significant part of his authority on his attempts to legislate sexual morality, targeting particularly adultery, Ovid's manual for successful adultery is highly political and highly subversive.

But although the *Ars Amatoria* is the poem officially designated as the *carmen* which caused the poet's exile, interesting cases can be made for the politically subversive nature of all the other works as well. Somehow, even in his flattery, Ovid seems to challenge us to read what he says as parody. One example is the apotheoses of Julius Caesar and of Augustus at the climax (is it?) of the *Metamorphoses*. Since the poem claims to perform the annals of changing forms from the beginning of time down to Ovid's own day, the culmination of (its) history in the projected deification of Augustus seems like pretty good propaganda for the emperor. The trouble is that it is so heavily problematised by its context that the 'praise' looks like 'parody': Augustus' deification is subject to the same fictionalisation as pervades the whole poem; in any case, it is capped by the apotheosis of Ovid himself, whose work 'cannot be destroyed by the anger of Jupiter'; moreover, that 'Jupiter' who has misbehaved and been made fun of throughout the *Metamorphoses* looks all too like the emperor himself.[5] Flattery-we-don't-believe becomes one of the driving forces of the exile poetry. It doesn't surprise me that neither Augustus nor Tiberius after him let Ovid back, except perhaps that by doing so they could have shut him up.[6]

I just referred to the fictionality of the *Metamorphoses*. The point raises a crucial recurrent theme in the Ovidian *corpus*, that of the interactions of art and nature. Ovid, like Oscar Wilde (to whom he has often been compared), was a great prophet of the doctrine of *art*ificiality, celebrating the power of art and the positive value of artfulness. This isn't to say that he wasn't interested in 'human nature' – on the contrary – but that his poetry gives us a strong sense of the way that 'nature' is constructed through 'art', as in poetry so in life. In the amatory poetry, we can see this in the interplay between love as, on the one hand, a conventionalised ritual, a poetic game and a skill to be taught, and on the other hand as the greatest power of nature, an overwhelming force to be reckoned with and something we all know anyway. In the sexiest of all poems, *Amores* 1.5, the poet describes a love scene in which he draws a veil over the crucial moment of consummation with the words: *cetera quis nescit?* ('who doesn't know the rest?'). In the *Metamorphoses*, the very categories of art and nature are subject to deconstruction. Ancient art theory had a great deal to say about the power of art to imitate nature; Ovid turns this round in his description of the grotto in which the goddess Diana was seen naked by Actaeon: *simulauerat artem/ingenio natura suo* ('nature by her own *ingenium* [intellect/skill/ innate ability] had imitated art', *Metamorphoses* 3.158–9).

Probably the best-known story of art and nature which Ovid tells is that of Pygmalion and his statue, a story which has inspired the Burne-Jones series of paintings and the George Bernard Shaw play *Pygmalion*, among many other artefacts. In Ovid's version, Pygmalion is a sculptor and a misogynist, who has turned against all of womankind because he was offended by the behaviour of the Propoetides, the first prostitutes. (It is worth remembering that the Propoetides were forced into prostitution by Venus for rejecting her, and were then turned to stone in recognition of their hard hearts – they can't win either way.) Pygmalion creates a beautiful statue of a girl, on whom he lavishes erotic attention. When he prays to Venus for a wife 'like' his ivory maiden, the goddess, no fool, answers the prayer by bringing the statue to life. As Shaw well saw, this is a story of man's love for his own creation and his own creative power, and his desire for a woman who will be totally under his control. Ovid uses the story of Pygmalion to reflect not only on the male artistic process, but also on the nature of (male) constructions of women. The beloved of elegy is a work of art like Pygmalion's statue (for statuesque descriptions of girls, see *Amores* 1.7.52 and particularly Propertius 1.3). As such, the Pygmalion story relates to a wider issue which is crucial to the *Metamorphoses*, and indeed to the rest of Ovid's poetry: the construction of identity.

What remains stable in a world of changing forms? Well, sometimes there is a continuity in metamorphosis in which the final form plays out an aspect of the character which was latently present before the change. The double-sexed Hermaphroditus (*Metamorphoses* 4.285–388) was originally a boy – or should we say 'he' was 'originally two people, a boy and a nymph'? Hermaphroditus was out on a quest for novelty when he came across a lovely pool. The nymph of the pool desired him, but he rejected her, and instead jumped into her pool for a swim (overcome with desire for the water – itself obviously a symbol of the nymph). Salmacis, the nymph, jumped in after him and 'raped' him, with the result that the two of them fused into one, in a grotesque but telling parody of the lover's desire for physical union (entertainingly expressed in the myth in Plato's *Symposium* of the original double form of people). But the 'one' they become is both man and woman and neither – yet somehow it is still clearly 'Hermaphroditus'. His final state is a continuation of his original condition, clearly signalled not only in his name (child of Hermes and Aphrodite) but also in his ambivalent status as a young man on the edge of sexual maturity.[7]

What changed? What stayed the same? Ovid's strength isn't so much in the answers he gives as the questions he raises. Another famous story of the instability of identity and the difficulties of gender-difference that it involves is that of Echo and Narcissus (*Metamorphoses* 3.344–510). Echo was a nymph who could only repeat what she heard, never initiate. She fell in love with Narcissus, a beautiful boy of whom it was prophesied that he would do well as long as, paradoxically, he never came to know himself. The reference is to the Delphic maxim 'know thyself'. But Narcissus rejected Echo and sat down by a pool, where the face of a beautiful boy caused him to fall in love in his turn. The boy, of course, was himself. Narcissus wasted away with love, and turned into a flower. Echo wasted away with love, and turned into nothing but an echoing voice. In some sense, they both become what they always were.

Other tales tell the story of the self, stability and change still more disturbingly. Actaeon (*Metamorphoses* 3.138–252) is a hunter punished, for seeing the goddess Diana bathing, by being turned into a stag and torn to pieces by his own hounds. As the 'sport' climaxes, Actaeon is fully aware of his innate humanity and his stag-form. He can hear his companions calling out to him to come and watch, when in fact it is himself that they are watching being torn to pieces. The acuteness of his self-awareness in his last moments not only arouses pity for the victim but also enhances the sense of human vulnerability that these confident young men ignore.

Stability is constantly offered and denied in the poetry of Ovid, and in his poetics. One of the most outrageous games that Ovid plays in the *Metamorphoses* with his readers, the Roman establishment, and with literary critics ancient and modern, is the question of 'unity'. An epic is meant to be unified, with a kind of symbolic wholeness which is more than a matter of simply being a coherent story or on a single topic. Ovid, however, constantly both proclaims and denies the possibility of finding some kind of unified structure in his work. One of the ways he does this is through the complexities of narrative voice. The epic narrator is generically expected to produce a single voice, and a largely objective and hardly visible one, channelling the epic truths from the gods through the Muses. Ovid, by contrast, both splits up and highlights his epic voice. He imposes himself on the narrative, as a big Super-Narrator mirrored in a plethora of images of the artist within the poem, and in a whole range of internal narrators, sometimes two or three levels deep. The effect of this is labyrinthine, and offers a bewildering challenge to our learnt modes of reading and expectations of epic.

Sometimes we can see relatively simply links between internal narrator and the story narrated, for example in the Pygmalion story mentioned above. The episode is told by Orpheus, who tries to comfort himself for the loss of his wife, Eurydice, whom he had won back from the Underworld only to lose her again on the shores of light because he couldn't resist looking back. As a result, he rejects women, 'invents' pederasty and sings songs of (mostly pathological) love. (And then eventually gets torn to pieces by irate women – but that's another story ... .) If we are tempted to get romantic about the Pygmalion story, we would do well to remember the context of its narration. Likewise, it makes a difference to the Hermaphroditus story that it is told by one of a group of girls, the daughters of Minyas, who reject the rites of Bacchus (they are too respectable for them!) and instead wile away their time on their very proper wool-work and their very improper stories.

One could get lost forever in the maze of Ovidian narrative. I would just like to mention one particular effect of this concentration on narrativity and the status of narrators in the *Metamorphoses*, which is to contribute to the powerful but tricksy poetic persona of Ovid. Throughout his work questions like this are at issue: who speaks? by what authority? what is at stake in speaking? who can no longer speak? what is the relationship between speaker and poet? between poet and man? man and Rome? And so on. Is the poet in exile still the elegiac lover who played the field and taught others to do the same? Or has he turned into one of his own *Heroides*?

Notes

1 For a discussion of possible interpretations of the exile, see J.C. Thibault, *The Mystery of Ovid's Exile*, Berkeley, CA: University of California Press, 1964.
2 H. Bloom, *The Anxiety of Influence: A Theory of Poetry*, New York: Oxford University Press, 2nd edn, 1997 (1st edn, 1973).
3 'Chiasmus' is a stylistic feature following the pattern ABBA.
4 See the excellent discussion of this opening poem and its sexual innuendo in D.F. Kennedy, *The Arts of Love: Five Studies in the Discourse of Roman Love Elegy*, Cambridge: Cambridge University Press, 1993, pp. 58–63.
5 This isn't the only way of reading the ending of the *Metamorphoses*. See P.R. Hardie, 'Questions of authority: The invention of tradition in Ovid *Metamorphoses* 15', in T. Habinek and A. Schiesaro (eds), *The Roman Cultural Revolution*, Cambridge: Cambridge University Press, pp. 182–98, and A. Barchiesi, 'Endgames: Ovid's *Metamorphoses* 15 and *Fasti* 6', in D.H. Roberts, F.M. Dunn and D.P. Fowler (eds), *Classical Closure: Reading the End in Greek and Latin Literature*, Princeton, NJ: Princeton University Press, 1997, pp. 181–208.
6 See S. Casali, '*quaerenti plura legendum*: On the necessity of "reading more" in Ovid's exile poetry', *Ramus*, 26, 1997, pp. 80–112, and the other essays in that volume.
7 See L. Barkan, *The Gods Made Flesh: Metamorphosis and the Pursuit of Paganism*, New Haven, CT, and London: Yale University Press, 1986, on continuity in metamorphosis; G. Nugent, 'The sex which is not one: De-constructing Ovid's Hermaphrodite', *Differences*, 2.1, 1990, pp. 160–85, on Hermaphroditus.

See also in this book

Callimachus, Catullus, Lucan, Propertius, Statius, Sulpicia, Virgil

Texts, translations and commentaries

There are OCT editions of the amatory works and the exile poetry, but as yet not of the *Metamorphoses* or *Fasti*, nor the *Heroides*. There are up-to-date Teubners of *Metamorphoses*, *Fasti* and both exilic collections. The Loeb series is complete. The *Metamorphoses* exists in Penguin (prose) and World's Classics (verse), while a World's Classics edition of the *Fasti* was published in 2001, following the 2000 Penguin translation. The amatory poetry exists in both standard translations.

In Cambridge Greek and Latin Classics, there are editions of *Metamorphoses* 13, *Fasti* 4, a selection of single *Heroides*, and the double *Heroides*.

There is a major edition and commentary in four volumes on the *Amores* by J.C. McKeown (Leeds: Francis Cairns Publications), of which three volumes have appeared to date (1987, 1989, 1998). There is also an Aris and Phillips edition of *Amores 2* by J. Booth.

On the *Ars Amatoria*, there is an edition with commentary on Book 1 by
A.S. Hollis (Oxford University Press, paperback edn, 1989) and a
forthcoming Cambridge commentary on Book 3 by R. Gibson.

On the *Metamorphoses*, there are W.S. Anderson's *Ovid's Metamorphoses: Books 1–5* and *Books 6–10* (Norman, OK: University of Oklahoma
Press, 1997 and 1972 respectively); and A.S. Hollis' *Ovid Metamorphoses 8*
(Oxford: Oxford University Press, 1983). There is an Aris and Phillips
version now of the whole poem, in four volumes, by D.E. Hill.

Further reading

Ahl, F., *Metaformations: Soundplay and Wordplay in Ovid and Other
Classical Poets*, Ithaca, NY, and London: Cornell University Press, 1985.

Allen, P.L., *The Art of Love: Amatory Fiction from Ovid to the Romance of
the Rose*, Philadelphia, PA: University of Pennsylvania Press, 1992.

Barchiesi, A., *The Poet and the Prince: Ovid and Augustan Discourse*,
Berkeley, CA: University of California Press, 1997.

Galinsky, G.K., *Ovid's 'Metamorphoses': An Introduction to the Basic
Aspects*, Oxford: Basil Blackwell, 1975.

Mack, S., *Ovid*, New Haven, CT, and London: Yale University Press
(Hermes Books), 1988.

Myerowitz, M., *Ovid's Games of Love*, Detroit, MI: Wayne State University
Press, 1985.

Newlands, C.E., *Playing with Time: Ovid and the Fasti*, Ithaca, NY, and
London: Cornell University Press, 1995.

Solodow, J., *The World of Ovid's Metamorphoses*, Chapel Hill, NC:
University of North Carolina Press, 1988.

Syme, R., *History in Ovid*, Oxford: Oxford University Press, 1978.

Verducci, F., *Ovid's Toyshop of the Heart: Epistulae Heroidum*, Princeton,
NJ: Princeton University Press, 1985.

Wheeler, S., *A Discourse of Wonders: Audience and Performance in Ovid's
Metamorphoses*, Philadelphia, PA: University of Pennsylvania Press, 1999.

Williams, G.D., *Banished Voices: Readings in Ovid's Exile Poetry*, Cambridge: Cambridge University Press, 1994.

SULPICIA

It is too easy to forget what great swathes of ancient culture are lost
to us, for the voices of the poor, the marginalised, slaves and women
are almost entirely drowned by the trumpet of patriarchy emanating
from the ancient world. For this reason, the snippets that do exist are
especially precious. We have therefore decided to include Sulpicia in
the list of 'Fifty Key Classical Authors', even though doing so
requires the exclusion of writers who would in general be considered
more important (and, at some level, rightly so). Six poems (or just
possibly eight), around forty lines in total – it isn't much on which to
build a position as a 'Key Author', and yet the story is an important

one not only for the history of ancient culture, but also for the history of the reading of ancient culture.

If we start from the assumption that current modern theories are broadly right, we will say that Sulpicia was the daughter of Servius Sulpicius Rufus, a patrician of wealth and prestige, himself the son of a jurist by the same name who was consul in 51 BC. Her uncle, under whose control she seems at some time to have lived, was Gaius Valerius Messalla Corvinus, an important statesman and patron of the arts, most notably of the Augustan elegiac poet Tibullus. This Sulpicia loved a man whom she calls Cerinthus – and, in the 20s BC, dared to write about it.[1]

If we start from the manuscript tradition, we get a story like this. The corpus of poems circulating in antiquity under the name of Tibullus contains two books of poems by the man himself and another group (sometimes presented as Book 3, sometimes divided into Books 3 and 4) spuriously attributed to him, but in reality to be assigned to various authors of uncertain date. Eight of these poems speak in the persona of 'Sulpicia'. As long as it was assumed that the author was Tibullus, or indeed another man pretending to be Tibullus, the poems stood a chance of being seen as artful and skilful manipulations of elegiac situations and erotic voices (even if early critics wouldn't exactly have phrased it like that). But in 1838 a German scholar, Otto Gruppe, first put forward the theory that the author might be a woman. (Only since 1871 has 'she' been the daughter of Servius Sulpicius Rufus.) Overnight – I exaggerate slightly – s/he turned from being an artist to being the embodiment of natural simplicity.[2] Before we get too excited about celebrating the voice of a Roman woman, we ought at least to remember that the attribution of these poems to a real live girl (a 'crying talking sleeping walking living doll', as Cliff Richard said) stems from a chauvinistic reading of her artlessness. With that caveat, I shall suggest a reading of the poems as artful expressions of a woman's voice – by a woman. Whatever the truth of the poems' attribution (that is, the question of who wrote them), a woman as desiring subject (not desired object) is a radical departure from the norms of traditional elegy.

The first poem ([Tibullus] 3.13) looks remarkably like a programmatic introduction to this little collection. 'At last love has come', she begins, 'and here I am writing about it' (I paraphrase). Issues of public and private (that great paradox of love poetry), of saying and not saying, of telling and reading, are all hinted at in five elegiac couplets of declaration of love. This is love poetry which no-one must read before the beloved (8), and yet also which other less experienced women might use as a discourse of (their own) sexuality (5–6). The language of erotics and poetics is as skilfully intertwined as we see anywhere, but mixed in also is an element of social construction which we could read as distinctively feminine. The opening lines say this:

> At last love has come, for which there would be more notoriety to me in having covered it up with shame, than there would be for having exposed it to another.[3]

The language is working on three levels here: social, in so far as the issue is to do with the shame surrounding the sexuality of an aristocratic Roman woman, which is the last thing that should ever be talked about; sexual, for the language in which the discussion of overing and uncovering the secrets of an affair is couched is also that of erotic behaviour; and poetic, for the issues of *fama* – both (ill-) repute and literary fame – are crucial to the public persona of the poet, especially the elegist who thrives on notoriety.

Likewise, in the final couplet, Sulpicia celebrates her pleasure in having sinned. This too is both poetic and social. On one level, it answers the male elegists' programmatic preference for *otium* ('leisure') rather than the 'proper' business of a Roman Man, although a concern with shame (*pudor*) and sinning (*peccare*) is rather stronger than the male elegist's enjoyment of his *nequitia* ('naughtiness'). On the social level, however, the final couplet also constitutes an outspoken opposition to Roman patriarchy (whether Messalla or the male elegist) in its very enactment – the speaking of personal emotional and sexual pleasure by a woman.

This question of control is picked up again in the second poem, in which Sulpicia complains that her uncle is planning to take her off to the country for a time, which will mean that she will be away from the city and Cerinthus on her birthday. Not only is there a telling, if economically expressed, opposition here to the Tibullan naïve celebration of love in the countryside, but also – in its very enactment – the complaint is an act of defiance against patriarchal power. The fact that it also *constructs* that patriarchal power is unfortunate, but inevitable. The next poem, a celebration of the repeal of Messalla's plan, might be read as a sign that Sulpicia has been more successful in opposing Roman *mores* than her male counterparts usually are. This *might* lead us to reflect that power relations work on an axis of class as well as of gender. It should also remind us that this is poetry, and there is an intertextual relationship here with the poem of Propertius in which he bemoans the Augustan marriage laws and then celebrates their failure (Propertius 2.7) and with the various paired poems in Propertius and Ovid.[4]

Class is at issue again in the fourth poem, in which Sulpicia haughtily complains about her beloved's infidelity with a slave girl. The complaint is typically elegiac, but there is a brilliant twist on the usual *topos* of 'slavery of love' when Sulpicia takes advantage of her father's name to destabilise the carefully constructed patrician superiority of her pose. She is, after all, *Serui filia* – 'the daughter of Sulpicius Servius Rufus', 'the daughter of a slave'.

Another elegiac *topos* is cleverly inverted in the penultimate poem, where the sick beloved speaks for herself. But the last poem introduces something that seems to have no clear parallel in male-authored elegy. Sulpicia apologises for the stupidest thing she has ever done in her life – that yesterday she ran away from her beloved, because she wanted to hide her passion. A brilliant piece of the writing of realism (I don't mean 'realistic writing'), hinting at a story that makes the reader desire to know more, to fill in the gaps. It also offers a cleverly closural answer to the opening discussion (3.13.1–2) of hiding and exposing. With this the cycle stops.

In addition to the six poems generally now thought to be the work of an Augustan Sulpicia, there is a group in the same collection which also deal with the Sulpicia story, and which are referred to as the 'Amicus poems'. These five elegies ([Tibullus] 3.8–12) consist of three in the voice of a male 'friend' who speaks for and about Sulpicia and Cerinthus, interspersed with two (3.9, 3.11) in the voice of Sulpicia herself. Although they are usually thought to be the work of a male poet, there are some critics who believe that poems 9 and 11 might also be the 'genuine article' – a woman's voice. Whatever the truth, it is a matter of great interest to literary and cultural studies from a feminist perspective that issues of voice and authority (the capacity of being an author) should be so contested and problematised by this odd collection of elegiacs.

Finally, a word about Tibullus himself. Although described approvingly as *tersus atque elegans* by Quintilian, Tibullus is perhaps now the least popular of the three great Augustan elegists (see PROPERTIUS, OVID). His elegies, sixteen poems in all, are mostly constructed around a network of themes rather than concentrating on exploring one in depth. Favourite issues are the interactions of fantasy and reality, of town and country, of war and peace. The persona Tibullus constructs for the lover-poet is a gentle, rustic, pious one – or so he would like it to be. The picture is problematised by the necessities of war, the fear of death (and its delight), the power of money and venality to corrupt paradise. One poem presents the lover benignly looking on as his beloved picks fruit from the farm for his dear friend and honoured guest Messalla (1.5.31–2). But it is a picture with the seeds of its own undoing sown within it, for the beloved is also constructed according to the mode of elegy, and we are meant to think that she might spoil that lovely dream. In fact faithful, pious Tibullus has three beloveds in his short *corpus*: Delia (the feminine form of Delius, the cult-title for Apollo), Nemesis (whose name tells it all) and Marathus, a beloved boy whose relationship with the speaker offers a rare development of homoerotic sentiment in Roman elegy. Tibullus died in the same year as Virgil.

Notes

1 Not everyone agrees with the identification of Sulpicia as a woman. See N. Holzberg, 'Four poets and a poetess, or a portrait of the poet as a young man? Thoughts on Book 3 of the *Corpus Tibullianum*', *The Classical Journal*, 94, 1999, pp. 169–91.
2 K.F. Smith, *The Elegies of Albius Tibullus: The Corpus Tibullianum*, Darmstadt: Wissenschaftliche Buchgesellschaft, 1964 (originally published in 1913), p. 80: 'this slip of a girl has that rarest of all gifts, the gift of straightforward simplicity'.
3 Sulpicia's syntax isn't easy to understand, no doubt partly because we have so little of it. But it once spawned a minor industry in attempts to reconstruct a specifically feminine way of using Latin grammar (N.J. Lowe, 'Sulpicia's syntax', *Classical Quarterly*, 38, 1988, pp. 193–205).
4 See, for example, Ovid *Amores* 1.11 and 1.12, Propertius 1.8a and b.

See also in this book

Ovid, Propertius

Texts, translations and commentaries

The text of Sulpicia is usually presented with that of Tibullus, for example in the OCT, although not all editions of Tibullus include the spurious poems of the *corpus Tibullianum*. There is a Loeb edition. The volume of Tibullus' poems by G. Lee, with introduction, text, translation and notes (Leeds: Francis Cairns Publications), didn't include the non-Tibullan works in its first edition (1975), but was revised in 1990 with the inclusion of Book 3 and therefore Sulpicia.

There is also J.R. Bradley, 'The elegies of Sulpicia: An introduction and commentary', *New England Classical Journal*, 22 (1993).

Further reading

Discussions of Sulpicia have to be found in articles.

Flaschenriem, B., 'Sulpicia and the rhetoric of disclosure', *Classical Philology*, 94, 1999, pp. 36–54.

Hallett, J.P., 'Women as same and other in Classical Roman elite', *Helios*, 16.1, 1989, pp. 59–78.

Hinds, S., 'The poetess and the reader: Further steps toward Sulpicia', *Hermathena*, 143, 1987, pp. 29–46.

Keith, A., '*Tandem uenit amor*: A Roman woman speaks of love', in J.P. Hallett and M. Skinner (eds), *Roman Sexualities*, Princeton, NJ: Princeton University Press, 1997, pp. 295–310.

Parker, H.N., 'Sulpicia, the *Auctor de Sulpicia* and the authorship of 3.9 and 3.11 of the *Corpus Tibullianum*', *Helios*, 21.1, 1994, pp. 39–62.

Santirocco, M.S., 'Sulpicia reconsidered', *Classical Journal*, 74, 1979, pp. 229–39.

Standard books on Tibullus include:

Bright, D.F., *Haec mihi fingebam: Tibullus in His World*, Leiden: Brill, 1978.

Cairns, F., *Tibullus: A Hellenistic Poet at Rome*, Cambridge: Cambridge University Press, 1979.

Lee-Stecum, P., *Powerplay in Tibullus: Reading Elegies Book One*, Cambridge: Cambridge University Press, 1998.

NERONIAN
AND FLAVIAN

SENECA THE YOUNGER

Seneca has provoked extreme reactions in ancient and modern critics. Vespasian's professor of rhetoric, Quintilian, squirms uncomfortably, postponing for as long as possible his discussion of Seneca because, he claims, people wrongly thought that he hated the man. This, presumably, wouldn't have mattered if Quintilian had been ready to contradict this opinion by complimenting Seneca unreservedly, but this he cannot do. Despite some nice opening remarks, Quintilian goes for the kill: 'his style is mostly corrupt and extremely dangerous, since it overflows with attractive vices' (*Training in Oratory* 10.1.129). Moreover, Quintilian proposes that Seneca's greatest fans are boys rather than learned men, thereby implying that Seneca's style is flashy and shallow.

This backlash against Seneca during the self-consciously austere era of the emperor Vespasian is understandable. His style was, after all, inextricably bound up with Nero's flamboyant court. Nor was Quintilian Seneca's only ancient critic. Aulus Gellius disapproves of his 'common and vulgar' language (*Attic Nights* 12.2.1), while Fronto attacks him using an eloquent metaphor:

> There certainly are some skilful and weighty sayings in his books. Yet little pieces of silver plate are from time to time found in sewers. Should we therefore undertake to clean out the sewers?

> *(De Orationibus* 3)

Yet tastes change or, more precisely, move in cycles. Seneca became more popular among Christian authors, who appreciated the moralising element of his work. So Minucius Felix in the third century AD wrote the *Octavius*, a dialogue between a pagan, Caecilius Natalis, and a Christian, Octavius; both style and content reveal debts to Seneca. There is also the anonymous author of the spurious *Correspondence between Seneca and St Paul*, a collection of letters intended partly to substantiate the belief that the two men were friends.[1] Petrarch accepted the correspondence as genuine, but Erasmus, who edited Seneca's works, rejected the letters.

Of course, Seneca's sententious style proved the perfect hunting ground for those who compiled anthologies of maxims, and we have several such collections (*Monita, Senecae Proverbia*). How Seneca himself would have reacted is open to speculation. He once advised Lucilius:

> Put aside that hope that you can get a taste of the greatest men's wisdom through epitomes. You should look at their complete works and study them as a whole.
>
> (*Moral Epistles* 33.5)[2]

One problem with these collections of excerpts is that they can suggest that an author was better known than he really was. Even so, some authors quote fairly substantially from Seneca's works, which suggests a reasonably good knowledge of the Senecan *corpus*: in the twelfth century AD both Abelard and Héloïse quote from Seneca's *Moral Epistles*.[3] Ross comments that Abelard 'goes out of his way to show his admiration for Seneca'.[4] Some writers knew not just Seneca's works, but also the criticisms raised against them. So John of Salisbury defends Seneca against the charges brought by Quintilian (*Polycratus* 8.13). At the University of Piacenza in the fourteenth century, there was even a Professor of Seneca.

However, it was during the Elizabethan and Jacobean eras that Seneca really came into his own. Seneca's tragedies superseded their Greek models, which were less accessible to a community who knew Latin much better than Greek. The tragedies soon served as a model for contemporary dramatists.[5] As Boyle has observed,

> in Kyd's *The Spanish Tragedy*, Shakespeare's *Titus Andronicus* and *Richard III*, Marlowe's *Edward II*, Tourneur/Middleton's *The Revenger's Tragedy* and several plays of Marston, Senecan lines make a telling re-appearance.[6]

Yet this creative interaction subsided during the Restoration and the eighteenth century, and there are signs of impatience in the remarks of Coleridge:

> You may get a motto for every sect or line of thought or religion from Seneca – yet nothing is ever thought out in him.[7]

In the first few decades of the twentieth century, Seneca's tragedies were a particular bone of contention between T.S. Eliot and Ezra Pound. The former wrote two essays attempting to disentangle analysis of Seneca's work from exploration of its influence on Elizabethan drama. Pound was unconvinced and saw

Seneca's writings as symptomatic of a nation 'losing a grip of its empire and of itself'.[8] Yet Pound's condemnation of Seneca didn't prevail and, in 1966, Herington published an important article in which he commented on 'the superb speakability of Seneca's verse'.[9] Only two years later, in 1968, Ted Hughes wrote an adaption of Seneca's *Oedipus*, directed by Peter Brook at the National Theatre in London. This play was revived in April 1998 at the Northcott Theatre in Exeter.

Seneca the Younger, born in Corduba between 4 BC and AD 1, was perhaps the most successful and prolific representative of a group of authors from Spain (including Lucan, Martial, Columella and Quintilian) whose work dominated the Roman literary scene of the first century AD. His father was Seneca the Elder (*c*. 50 BC–*c*. AD 40), who wrote a lost history of Rome, as well as the partially surviving *Controversiae* and *Suasoriae* which enable us to glimpse some techniques of composition used in the declamation schools, which were often blamed for a decline in the quality of Latin literature after the Augustan era.

Quite an engaging picture of Seneca the Elder emerges from these works. In the *Controuersiae*, which are dedicated to his two sons, he reminisces about the extraordinary capacity of his memory when he was younger, claiming that at one time had 2,000 names been recited to him, he would have been able to repeat them in the same order (*Controuersiae* 1 preface 2). The cases themselves involve a combination of colourful historical, mythical and imaginary scenarios, such as in *Suasoria* 3, where Agamemnon deliberates whether to sacrifice Iphigenia, or *Controuersia* 7.5, where a five-year-old boy accuses his stepmother's lover, a *procurator*, of murdering his father. Seneca the Elder offers soundbites, both good and bad, used by the various declaimers in this case. For instance, he praises Licinius Nepos' strategy over the stepmother's lovebite: 'That is no wound – it is the bite of a playful lover' (*Controuersia* 7.5.10).

However, Seneca the Elder can also be critical, especially if a declaimer learns an *exemplum* by heart but then applies it inappropriately. So, in this case, Musa, speaking for the son, draws an analogy with the story of Croesus' son in Herodotus, saying of the boy:

> Although he had been silent for more than five years, in the face of danger to his father, the mute boy broke through the natural impediments to his voice.

> (*Controuersia* 7.5.13)

Seneca the Elder is impatient since the declaimer uses the analogy of Croesus' son indiscriminately, regardless of whether it is appropriate to the case.

To grow up with such a father must have been stimulating. Seneca the Younger certainly heard some of these extraordinary fabricated cases as a boy, and no doubt began to create his own pithy and attention-grabbing *sententiae* under his father's guidance. Like many of his contemporaries, Seneca was educated in Rome, learning from the declamation schools and from various different philosophers, particularly Stoics. Among his tutors were Papirius Fabianus, whose style Seneca defends in *Moral Epistle* 100 as being written for the mind rather than for the ear, and Attalus, whom Seneca often quotes (as at *Moral Epistle* 63.5–6). He also attended the lectures of the Pythagorean philosopher Sotion, under whose influence he experimented with vegetarianism, which he abandoned after a year when his father intervened (*Moral Epistle* 108.17–23). At some point, Seneca became ill and went to Egypt to recuperate under the care of his aunt Helvia, the wife of C. Galerius, the prefect of Egypt.

After successfully escaping a shipwreck which killed his uncle (*To Helvia, on Consolation* 19), Seneca returned to Rome in AD 31 and started a career in politics and law. Yet his life was marked by extreme twists of good and bad luck, during which his Stoicism must have proved comforting, and apparently abstract passages in his works, such as the choral ode on the mutability of fortune (*Thyestes* 546–622), may partly have been inspired by real experiences. In AD 39 Seneca offended the emperor Caligula by eloquently pleading a case in the Senate, and as a result was condemned to death. However, he was spared thanks to an unnamed woman, who claimed that Seneca had consumption and would die soon anyway (Cassius Dio *Roman History* 59.19).

That was a narrow escape, but Seneca's luck ran out in AD 41 when the emperor Claudius banished him to Corsica on a charge of adultery with Julia, Claudius' niece. Cassius Dio suggests that Seneca was merely a scapegoat chosen by Messalina, who, angry that her husband Claudius was spending time with the beautiful Julia, fabricated charges of adultery to eliminate her rival (Cassius Dio *Roman History* 60.8). The fact that Claudius intervened to change the penalty from death to banishment may substantiate the notion that Seneca was an innocent victim in this domestic drama.

At any rate, Seneca spent almost a decade mouldering on Corsica. There are some anonymous epigrams in the *Anthologia*

Latina which some critics have attributed to Seneca. Corsica is presented as a menacing place:

> Barbarous Corsica is shut in by sheer cliffs. It is wild and vast with deserted places on all sides. The autumn does not draw forth fruit, nor does the summer draw forth corn …

(Epigram 3.1–3)

This description bears a striking resemblance to Ovid's *Epistulae ex Ponto* 1.3.5ff., which is typical of Seneca's general stylistic debt to Ovid in his writings.[10]

Just as Seneca was cast down by one imperial wife, he rose to prominence again through another. In AD 49 Claudius' new wife, Agrippina the Younger, had Seneca recalled to Rome where, like some latterday Aristotle, he became tutor to her son Nero. Suetonius claims that on the very next night, Seneca dreamed that his new pupil was really Caligula (*Nero* 7), a worrying omen. Suetonius often records appropriate dreams, and this one is perhaps too good to be true. Seneca was now locked into a relationship with Nero which he would only escape by his (untimely) death. When Nero became emperor in AD 54, Seneca became his political adviser.[11] Tacitus records with disapproval that Seneca composed the speech which Nero delivered at Claudius' funeral, calling him the first emperor to need borrowed eloquence (*Annals* 13.2).

In AD 59 Nero decided to eliminate his oppressive mother and deployed Seneca to write the letter to the Senate accusing her of being involved in a conspiracy and informing them that she had committed suicide. Since most people knew that Nero had been actively trying to murder his mother for some time, this connivance damaged Seneca's reputation (Tacitus *Annals* 14.11.3). Contemporaries and later critics thought that Seneca was a hypocrite. There seemed to be such a glaring discrepancy between the wholesome message of Seneca's philosophical writings and the sordid reality of his life, so inextricably bound up with Nero. Tacitus recreates the words of one critic, Suillius Rufus: 'By which philosophy, by which precepts of the philosophers had Seneca procured three hundred million sesterces during four years of imperial friendship?' (*Annals* 13.42.2–4).[12] In a typical manner, Tacitus removes some of the sting from this outburst by revealing subsequently that Suillius too had collaborated with Nero, but mud has continued to stick to Seneca ever since. In his defence, we can say that Seneca did offer to return much of his property to Nero (Tacitus *Annals* 14.54.2). Seneca, isolated and miserable, tried (unsuccessfully) to gain permission to extricate himself from politics. Despite Nero's refusal, Seneca withdrew anyway, eating nothing but fresh fruit and drinking nothing but running water for fear of being poisoned by the emperor's agents (Tacitus *Annals* 15.45.3). If we remember that Nero may have collaborated with his mother in poisoning Claudius with a mushroom, then Seneca's fears may be justified.

In the end, Seneca died, not by poison, but by enforced suicide in AD 65, after Nero accused him of being involved in the Pisonian conspiracy. Tacitus' dramatic description of the suicide echoes Stoic principles in an exemplary way and testifies to the enthusiasm for *exitus* literature during the first and second centuries AD.[13] The passage (*Annals* 15.60–4) may be an instance of (Tacitus') art imitating (Seneca's) life imitating (Plato's) art imitating (Socrates') life: Seneca himself may perhaps have modelled his suicide on the death of Socrates. The scene was famously painted in 1612–13 by Rubens, who shows Seneca, surrounded by Nero's soldiers, standing in a bath of water while a doctor cuts his veins and a loyal disciple records his final words (Alte Pinakothek, Munich, Germany).

Seneca was an extremely versatile writer. There are ten surviving ethical prose treatises: *On Providence, On the Constancy of the Wise Man, On Anger, To Marcia, on Consolation, On the Happy Life, On Leisure, On the Tranquillity of the Mind, On the Brevity of Life, To Polybius, on Consolation* and *To Helvia, on Consolation*; as well as other prose works: *On Clemency*, to Nero; *On Benefits*, to Aebutius Liberalis; *Natural Questions*, dedicated to Lucilius; and, in his final years, *Moral Epistles*, also addressed to his pupil Lucilius.[14] Seneca also wrote one satire in a mixture of prose and verse, the *Apocolocyntosis* (*Pumpkinification*), which mocked the deification of the emperor Claudius. Finally there are the eight tragedies based on Greek myths with a distinctly Roman twist: *Hercules, Troades, Phoenissae, Medea, Phaedra, Oedipus, Agamemnon* and *Thyestes*.

If we read Seneca's tragedies through the filter of Greek tragedy, then we may be disappointed or just puzzled. It seems extraordinary that the same basic myths could generate the plays of both Aeschylus and Seneca, but of course genres develop and change. The gulf between Seneca's plays and those produced in Athens is accentuated by the fragmentary state of the Republican tragedies of Ennius, Naevius, Pacuvius and Accius. Even Ovid's acclaimed *Medea* unfortunately hasn't survived. So how and why does Senecan tragedy differ from the Greek model? If one reads Euripides'

Hippolytus and Seneca's *Phaedra*, various differences immediately become apparent. Where Euripides starts and finishes his play with the appearance of Aphrodite and Artemis, Seneca dispenses with the divine machinery and constructs a world where gods have little impact. Instead, Seneca's drama begins with an anapaestic prologue delivered by Hippolytus and ends with his distraught father Theseus trying to reassemble his son's fragmented body, the only direct physical contact between father and son. Gone is Euripides' powerful scene where Hippolytus forgives Theseus and dies in his arms. Stoicism pervades these plays, as flawed heroes and heroines confront (usually unsuccessfully) terrifying forces in a world where the balance between *furor* and *ratio* has slipped out of kelter.

There is also the question of language. Seneca boils down language to its bare essentials, forming jarring and antithetical sentences driven by paradox and black humour. Such is his desire to startle that he often disregards what a character might reasonably be expected to say in a given situation. One line in particular exemplifies Seneca's technique. As the distraught Theseus gathers pieces of his son's body, he says: 'Which part of you it is I cannot tell, but part of you it is' (*quae pars tui sit dubito; sed pars est tui*; *Phaedra* 1267). Coffey and Mayer propose that this is 'arguably the worst line in Senecan drama'[15] and one can see why they might think this. If Theseus is comforted by picking up part of Hippolytus' fragmented body, this must increase our horror at a world in which this can constitute solace. The idea that a father could even articulate such a sentiment (with the repetition of *pars ... tui*) may strain the scene's dramatic credibility. We can contrast the moment where Euripides' Agaue finally realises that she is holding the decapitated head of her son Pentheus (*Bacchae* 1280ff.). Disjointed questions are all she can manage initially; there is no word play.[16]

Another crucial difference between the *Hippolytus* and *Phaedra* is that Seneca suspends the action of his play while his characters utter long digressions on common rhetorical themes which evoke the declamation schools rather than the world of the play. So the nurse addresses Hippolytus in a long speech urging him to act like a young man and indulge in love (*Phaedra* 435–82). Hippolytus responds with another rhetorical set-piece contrasting the wholesome countryside and the morally corrupt city (*Phaedra* 483–564). It feels as if the characters are speaking at, rather than to, each other, but perhaps Seneca's audience, steeped in the culture of the declamation schools, might have found such techniques less disturbing than we do today.

There are certainly other speeches which owe something to the declamatory schools, such as when Thyestes praises the simple life of the poor man (*Thyestes* 446–70). Although such speeches may seem generic, they do repay a closer examination. Thyestes gradually shifts from praising poverty to denouncing luxury (using anaphora to express what the poor man does *not* do), but goes into such extraordinary detail that his disapproval seems insincere. With some relish, Thyestes describes a wood swaying on a palace's roof and steaming indoor pools (cf. Seneca *Moral Epistles* 122.8). It looks as if he might soon succumb to the temptation of power offered to him by his brother Atreus. So, although we can say that the passage has been influenced by the declamation schools (for example, see the remarks of Seneca the Younger's teacher Papirius Fabianus on poverty; Seneca the Elder *Controuersia* 2.1.13), dramatic context and characterisation are still important.

One central issue differentiates Senecan drama from Greek tragedy, namely the question of performance. The Athenian dramatists wrote plays for performance at particular civic festivals before a large audience, but Seneca's tragedies may not have been performed in a theatre at all during his lifetime. Pompey was the first to build a permanent theatre in Rome in 55 BC, but under the principate recitation of new works, including plays, became popular. So Ovid, despite his *Medea*, claims that he never wrote anything for the theatre (*Tristia* 5.7.27) and Tacitus refers to Curiatius Maternus' recitation of his tragedy *Cato* (*Dialogus* 2.1).

This doesn't mean either that Seneca's plays were unstageable or that they are devoid of devices which create the illusion of a staged drama, but they do differ from their Greek counterparts: Seneca's tragedies didn't have to compete directly with other plays, nor were they performed as part of a trilogy. Of course, Roman audiences under the principate did enjoy spectacular performances in the amphitheatre, and mimes remained popular. One story records an incident which took place during the performance of a mime, *Laureolus*, when the stage was mistakenly flooded with blood (Suetonius *Caligula* 57.4). Seneca himself refers to the way in which 'the whole theatre would resound' when the people applauded a fine sentiment, even when uttered in the context of a mime (*Moral Epistles* 108.8). His own tragedies, however, were probably not exposed to an audience on this scale.

It is strange that a Stoic philosopher should have bothered to write these tragedies at all, but they do contain themes which reflect concerns that Seneca explores more extensively in his prose works.

So the ideas presented in *On Anger* are given further substance during, for instance, Atreus' furious speech (*Thyestes* 267–86). In addition, in the *Hercules* Seneca explores more deeply the character of Hercules, who appears in his prose works as a model of the Stoic *sapiens* (*On Benefits* 1.13.3). Boyle comments on the striking ending of the *Hercules* whereby the hero decides not to kill himself because he wants to prevent his father from committing suicide.[17] As Seneca made a Stoic friend observe: 'It is a great thing to die honourably, wisely and bravely' (*Moral Epistles* 77.6). If Hercules had killed himself at this moment, then he wouldn't have achieved this. We can therefore read the unusual ending of the *Hercules* in a Stoic light.

Seneca often makes his moralising more palatable for his pupil Lucilius by using some creative similes and metaphors. As he says,

> I think that comparisons are necessary, not for the same reason which makes them necessary for the poets, but in order that they may serve as props to our feebleness, to bring both speaker and listener face to face with the subject under discussion.

> (*Moral Epistles* 59.6)

Even in a work such as *Natural Questions* on natural phenomena, Seneca deploys some unexpectedly colourful material. So, when discussing mirrors, he includes a long moralising digression about the notorious Hostius Quadra, who surrounded his bedroom with mirrors to enhance his sex life (*Natural Questions* 1.16). Elsewhere Seneca's imagery is less salacious but equally forceful. So, when discussing the problems of an aging body, he uses an elaborate simile of a leaking ship:

> Just as in a ship which drags along bilge-water, the first and the second holes can be stopped, but when many holes begin to open and let in water, no aid can be brought to the gaping hull.

> (*Moral Epistles* 30.2)

The brief comparison communicates the dilemma well.

The theme of seafaring crops up in other letters too. Seneca describes a short journey between Puteoli and Naples on which he became seasick: when the helmsman refused to dock the boat, since there was no harbour, Seneca explains that he jumped overboard and swam for land, comparing himself wryly with Odysseus (*Moral Epistles* 53.1–4). Having seized our attention with this dramatic opening, he moves neatly from bodily to spiritual diseases, which can be eased by studying philosophy. This is typical. Seneca uses both poetic images and direct quotes from the poets (especially Virgil) in order to make his philosophical and ethical points more forcefully. Throughout the letters to Lucilius, Seneca presents an engaging (and sometimes flawed) persona, which draws us into his discussions and makes us warm to him. After his long discussion on how to face old age and death, Seneca ends with a joke for Lucilius: 'I ought to fear that you will hate this long letter worse than death itself; so I shall stop' (*Moral Epistles* 30.18). Whatever the contradictions of Seneca's troubled life, his literary persona in the prose works is forceful, reassuring and charming.

Notes

1 See *Acts* 18:12–16 for the idea that Paul was protected at Corinth by Seneca's brother Gallio.
2 This is a salutary concept for our readers, who shouldn't see this book as a substitute for reading the works of the ancient authors themselves.
3 Héloïse *Letter* 1 quotes from *Moral Epistle* 40.1, Héloïse *Letter* 3 from *Moral Epistle* 24.1 and Abelard *Letter* 7 from *Moral Epistle* 5.4.
4 G.M. Ross, 'Seneca's philosophical influence', in C.D.N. Costa (ed.), *Seneca*, London and Boston, MA: Routledge and Kegan Paul, 1974, p. 35.
5 See G.K. Hunter, 'Seneca and English tragedy', in C.D.N. Costa, *op. cit.*, pp. 166–204.
6 A.J. Boyle, *Tragic Seneca: An Essay in the Theatrical Tradition*, London and New York: Routledge, 1997, p. 143.
7 S.T. Coleridge, *Table Talk II*, *Collected Works*, vol. 12, London: Routledge and Kegan Paul, 1969, p. 171.
8 E. Pound, *ABC of Reading*, London and New York: Routledge, 1934, p. 34.
9 J. Herington, 'Senecan tragedy', *Arion*, 5, 1966, pp. 422–71.
10 See further J.-M. Claassen, *Displaced Persons: The Literature of Exile from Cicero to Boethius*, London: Duckworth, 1999, pp. 241–4.
11 See M. Griffin, *Seneca: A Philosopher in Politics*, Oxford: Oxford University Press, 1976, pp. 67–128, on Seneca as Nero's minister.
12 See Griffin, *op. cit.*, pp. 286–314, on Seneca combining philosophy and wealth.
13 See Griffin, *op. cit.*, pp. 367–88, on Seneca's suicide.
14 See D.A. Russell, 'Letters to Lucilius', in C.D.N. Costa, *op. cit.*, pp. 70–95.
15 M. Coffey and R. Mayer, *Seneca: Phaedra*, Greek and Latin Classics, Cambridge: Cambridge University Press, 1990, p. 195.

16 Unfortunately, there is a lacuna at *Bacchae* 1329ff., where Agaue lays out Pentheus' body for burial.

17 Boyle, *op. cit.*, p. 109.

See also in this book

Cicero, Ennius, Euripides, Ovid, Pliny the Younger, Tacitus

Texts, translations and commentaries

The Latin text is available in OCT and Teubner (though neither publishes the whole *corpus*), and in Loeb (10 volumes).

Apart from the Loeb translation, there are Penguin translations of *Four Tragedies and Octavia* by E.F. Watling and of *Letters from a Stoic* by R. Campbell, and Cornell University Press translations of *Phaedra* and *Medea* by F. Ahl.

There is a commentary on *Apocolocyntosis* by P.T. Eden and on *Phaedra* by M. Coffey and R. Mayer in the Cambridge Greek and Latin Classics Series; on *Medea* by H. Hine, on *Four Dialogues* (that is, *To Helvia, on Consolation, On the Constancy of the Wise Man, On the Happy Life* and *On the Tranquillity of the Mind*) and on *Letters: A Selection* (that is, 7, 12, 24, 47, 54, 56, 57, 78, 79, 83, 88, 90, 92, 104, 110, 114 and 122) by C.D.N. Costa in the Aris and Phillips Series; on *Thyestes* by R.J. Tarrant in the American Philological Association Series; on *Troades* by E. Fantham (published by Princeton University Press) and by A.J. Boyle (published by Francis Cairns Publications); on *Hercules Furens* by J.G. Fitch (published by Cornell University Press); on the *Medea* by C.D.N. Costa (published by Oxford University Press); and on the *Agamemnon* by R.J. Tarrant (published by Cambridge University Press).

Further reading

Boyle, A.J., *Tragic Seneca: An Essay in the Theatrical Tradition*, London and New York: Routledge, 1997.

Griffin, M., *Seneca: A Philosopher in Politics*, Oxford: Oxford University Press, 1976.

Harrison (ed.) *Seneca in Performance*, London: Duckworth, 2000.

Herington, J. 'Senecan tragedy', *Arion*, 5, 1966, pp. 422–71.

Hunter, G.K., 'Seneca and English tragedy', in C.D.N. Costa (ed.), *Seneca*, London and Boston, MA: Routledge and Kegan Paul, 1974, pp. 166–204.

Miola, R.S., *Shakespeare and Classical Tragedy: The Influence of Seneca*, Oxford: Oxford University Press, 1992.

Ross, G.M., 'Seneca's philosophical influence', in C.D.N. Costa (ed.), *Seneca*, London and Boston, MA: Routledge and Kegan Paul, 1974, pp. 116–65.

Russell, D.A., 'Letters to Lucilius', in C.D.N. Costa (ed.), *Seneca*, London and Boston, MA: Routledge and Kegan Paul, 1974, pp. 70–95.

PETRONIUS

You might not think that a set of fragments of Latin prose,
interspersed with verse which presents itself as doggerel, of uncertain
date, authorship, title, genre and scope, and of frivolous content,
would be considered the text of a 'Key Classical Author'. Such is
Classics. And such is both the oddity and the popularity of the
Satyricon of Petronius and of his characters, the naïve narrator
Encolpius (who has trouble with the god Priapus) and the rich
freedman dinner-host Trimalchio (who has trouble with Roman
austerity), that Petronius' position is secured. The work in question
is conventionally called the *Satyricon*, although *Satyrica* ('things to
do with satyrs') is more accurate. (*Satyricon* is probably a Greek
genitive plural, with *libri*, 'books', understood.) We don't even know
for certain how to categorise the work: is it one of the earliest novels?
or a type of satire in prose mixed with verse (known as 'Menippean
satire')? Still, there is no doubt that the *Satyricon* has had
considerable influence over the later development of the novel,
particularly the picaresque.

Despite the lack of firm evidence, scholars today generally agree
that the author of the *Satyricon* is the Gaius (or Titus) Petronius
whose death on the orders of Nero is recorded by Tacitus. The date,
then, must be the early 60s AD (since the novel possibly includes
allusions to Lucan's *Pharsalia*) and before 66, since that is when
Gaius Petronius died. Tacitus' story comes in a catalogue of deaths
of upper-class Romans (*Annals* 16.16–18), in which he stresses not
only the bloodshed but also the impotence and passivity of the
victims, whose loss of traditional Roman autarky is, for Tacitus, one
of the worst features of the empire. Petronius' turn comes just after
Lucan's father Annaeus Mela, who, like many imperial victims,
opened his veins to die. So did Petronius.

The odd thing about Petronius was that having done so he bound
them up again and had dinner before dying, indulging in light poetry
and engaging conversation, so that he might take ownership, so to
speak, of his own death and thereby salvage some independence
from Nero, while refusing (on the other hand) to follow the Stoic
'good death' tradition. He caps his independent death by sending to
Nero not a sycophantic farewell, in the manner of others who hoped
to protect their families by doing so, but a list detailing all of Nero's
sexual adventures, with names attached. Petronius then broke his
signet ring, so that it couldn't be used in forgery. Tacitus' account
portrays a man of contrasts, in some ways admirable, in others

deplorable. Petronius is presented as a man who had raised decadence to an art, which earned him his position as Nero's *elegantiae arbiter* ('professor of sophistication'; *Annals* 16.18) before his fall from imperial grace. But he was also, in Tacitus' account, an able administrator, and the pro-Republican historian seems to admire the sophisticated novelist's gestures of defiance, while deploring his frivolity and decadence.[1]

The text that has come down to us has had a very chequered history. It suffered from the ancient fashion for preserving excerpts of large works, which meant that it was, in a sense, deliberately fragmented, although this process was probably also what assured the survival of what does remain. Different parts circulated separately, were lost and found, and were only gathered into the selection we now have and published in 1669.[2] The fragmentary state of the work, which breaks off and restarts many times within the 'text' we have, makes for difficult reading: it is like watching a soap opera but missing a random selection of episodes, including the first and the last several, and missing the beginnings and ends of some you do see. Indeed, we don't know the overall size of the work. Some scholars think that what we have is fragments from Books 14–16; if so, the original must have been huge, perhaps twenty-four books on the model of the Homeric epic poems.

It would be fun to entertain the possibility that the text we have is all there ever was, since Petronius is so playful with narrative traditions and so defiant in refusing conventions, including literary ones. The opening scene of the extant novel, *in medias res* with the hero expounding his views on oratory, literature and artfulness in general, would make a fine, ironic, playful programmatic introduction, since discussions of literature and other forms of artfulness form a recurrent motif in the extant novel, which opens in a school of rhetoric (with Professor Agamemnon!) and has a substantial section in an art gallery. There is no historical justification for such a possibility, however, and the fragmentary circulation of the text in late antiquity would tell against it, as does the existence of fragments of uncertain position. If the original was the monster-work which the scholars suggest, then our interpretations of apparently important themes might be somewhat askew.

The hero of the novel is a young man named Encolpius, educated and 'of good family', but poor (14, 81, 133), who travels around having various adventures and making a living from crime and on his wits – only *just* a living, since he suffers a series of disasters. Encolpius is also naïve and vulnerable without being despicable, for all the outrages he perpetrates and suffers. He is accompanied most of the time by a beautiful young boy-slave called Giton, whom he probably stole from Tryphaena before our fragments begin, with whom there is an embarrassing meeting on board ship towards the end of the extant novel. Various other characters become companions, and generally rivals for the affections of Giton. In the extant novel, the first of these is Ascyltus, whose speaking name (as all names do in the novel) indicates that he doesn't have Encolpius' problems with sexual potency. Ascyltus means 'unwearied': on one occasion, he is caught naked in the baths and roundly applauded for the size of his genitals. Indeed, Eumolpus ('good-singer': who is about to take over Ascyltus' role as companion and rival) actually recognises him as 'unwearied' in said bath-scene before knowing his name (92).

The homosexual relationship is an inversion, in some sense a parody, of the romantic, heterosexual relationship around which the traditional 'serious' Greek novel (sometimes called the 'idealistic' novel; see LONGUS) was based. In the serious version, the lovers are generally separated and undergo all sorts of trials, particularly to their chastity, before finally being reunited in very respectable marriage. The relationship of Encolpius and Giton is a complete contrast: they are rarely separated, and only then when Giton – to Encolpius' amazement – deliberately chooses his rival Ascyltus (80); neither is faithful; neither turns out to be the long lost son of rich and respectable citizens (unless there is something of that nature hiding in the lost parts of the work, but more likely it would be a parody of recognition); and in particular their relationship is directed towards the barren pursuit of pleasure, not towards marriage and procreation, and it often fails to achieve that pleasure. The entire novel is a celebration of 'negative' sexuality.

In the novel as we have it, Encolpius first of all takes up with the teacher of rhetoric called Agamemnon (he has an assistant called Menelaus) and it is through him that Encolpius, Ascyltus and Giton secure the invitation to dinner with Trimalchio, which produces the most famous section of the novel, detailing the freedman's gross extravagance (he chastises a slave for picking up a plate that has been dropped – it must be thrown away), boasting self-love and macabre obsession with his own death ('pretend I'm dead: play something nice', 78). Before that, however, the heroes are forced to undergo 'purification' from their crime of interrupting the rites of Priapus. Encolpius' persecution by the ithyphallic god is presumably the cause of his many sexual troubles, including his serial impotence.

Priapus' anger is a parody of a narrative *topos*, such as the anger of Poseidon against Odysseus, or of Juno against Aeneas. It also inverts the protection of a god which the hero enjoys in the 'serious' novel (and in epic). In their punishment at the hands of Quartilla and her slaves, there is a fine line, as often in the *Satyricon*, between sensuous luxury and sexual torments: are they guests or victims? After the dinner at Trimalchio's, Ascyltus and Encolpius fight, and Giton chooses Ascyltus. Alone, Encolpius wanders into an art gallery (83; another parody of the idealistic novel, which often began with a painting, as in Longus' *Daphnis and Chloe* and Achilles Tatius' *Leucippe and Clitophon*), where he meets the poet Eumolpus. This puzzling character is both a figure of fun, in that everyone hates his poetry, and also, for the remainder of our text, the foremost manipulator of art and artifice – and words – in the novel.

Giton returns to Encolpius, only to fall victim to the sexual interest of Eumolpus. Encolpius' attempted suicide incites Giton to snatch a razor (94), slit his throat and fall down dead ... only to rise a few seconds later, when it is discovered that it was a blunt practice-knife that he took.[3] This is a parody of the *topos* in the idealistic novel of the false death, in which the most horrific scenes of death (usually of the female beloved) turn out, often much later, to have been misleading. After a general free-for-all, Encolpius and Giton board a ship with Eumolpus – only to discover that it belongs to Lichas (from whom they fled much earlier in the narrative), together with Giton's owner Tryphaena. They are disguised by Eumolpus, but Lichas recognises Encolpius by the shape of his penis (105), having been warned by Priapus. Eventually there is general recognition, during which Eumolpus tells the salacious story of the widow of Ephesus (111–12), but then a storm shipwrecks them – another parody, both of the novel and of epic (114). Lichas is killed. The heroes find themselves near Croton, a city of legacy-hunters and the rich and childless on whom the legacy-hunters prey. Eumolpus proposes posing as such a person, with the others as his slaves. It is at Croton (128) that Encolpius has his bout of impotence, when confronted with the beautiful Circe. After various other sexual adventures, the fragments start to peter out. It looks as if Encolpius gets his potency back and Eumolpus tells everyone that people will inherit from him if they eat his dead body.

I have spoken of parody, but this isn't simply a matter of joking inversion of a genre (the 'idealistic' novel) which takes itself very seriously. Rather, the *Satyricon* is involved in a complex web of intertextuality, with other genres, most notably epic (especially the

Odyssey), as well as prose fiction; it isn't only the novel itself which is tied up with other literatures, but even its hero – for Encolpius is constantly being tempted to put himself into the position of epic hero, elegiac lover or whatever pose suits the moment. Both text and narrator have delusions of grandeur, but (perhaps) only the text (the author, if you prefer) is an ironist. Encolpius' self-image and Petronius' representation of it constitute a celebration of artificiality, in a work where nothing is quite what it seems, not even your dinner. Trimalchio has a lot of fun tricking his guests with food jokingly dressed up. We are meant (I suppose) to laugh at his un-Roman vulgarity and ostentation in not letting food be food, but the artificiality is part of the novel – and our poor naïve hero Encolpius never gets the joke, until a kindly neighbour explains it to him.

Still, Encolpius knows his epic better than does Trimalchio, who makes a whole series of howlers in his attempts to show off his knowledge of epic and tragic myth (the Cyclops tore out Ulysses' eye, 48; Cassandra killing her children, 52; Hannibal captured Troy, 50; even his own garbled version of the Trojan cycle, 59). Encolpius knows his Homer and his Virgil (and Lucan). That is why he can tell (105) that Lichas' unusual means of recognition is much more remarkable than (but also a replay of) the nurse's recognition of Odysseus by his scar (*Odyssey* 19); why he knows he is meant to have sex with a woman called Circe (from the *Odyssey*), since at this point he is using the sobriquet 'Polyaenus', used by Homer of Odysseus; why he gets shipwrecked and escapes like Odysseus from the Cyclops under the ram. 'Let's imagine we've entered the Cylcops' cave', says Eumolpus as the opening gambit to help them think of their escape from the ship (101). These characters use literature as a way of confronting reality. Our heroes play out epic scenes all over the place, although they sometimes backfire. When Encolpius, Ascyltus and Giton are attempting to escape from Trimalchio's house (72), they are startled by the barking of a dog, which causes Ascyltus and Encolpius to end up in the fish pond. Now it is Giton's turn to play the epic hero: he throws bits of food, saved from the banquet, to the dog and thereby pacifies it. In this, he is replaying the actions of Aeneas on his way down to the Underworld, who threw Cerberus, monstrous guard dog of Hell, a magic sop which sent him to sleep. But our heroes are trying to get out of Hell, not into it. And the way is barred, so that they have to return to the labyrinth (73) as failed Theseuses to face the Minotaur of Trimalchio. Eventually they find their way home using Giton's chalk marks (79).

Parody, then; but is this satire? The extant fragments offer us a fine selection of traditional satirists' butts, from the sexual pervert to the legacy-hunter, and of traditional tirade, such as the golden oldie about how things aren't what they used to be. But, unlike in Horace, Persius or Juvenal, there is no apparent 'moral voice', only an ironic amoral one. Perhaps a contribution to the answer lies in seeing the work as Menippean satire, grown to monstrous proportions, with the lack of moralising voice stemming from the difference between narrative and monologue. It could be that the novel seeks to satirise something (which *could* be the very decadence it portrays) simply by displaying it, but there must be a fine line between satire and celebration.

And, a related question, where is Nero in all this? Is he in the audience or is he the butt of the jokes? It could be that the work was written for the court, just as a bit of fun. It could be, however, that the work was written in the first place for a small private audience, with Nero pilloried. Critics have often been tempted to see something of Nero in the figure of Trimalchio. It could hardly be a straight allegory, but there are a number of points of contact, particularly with the notorious dining rooms of Nero's Golden House. Whether or not there is a specific connection with Nero, Trimalchio is clearly a tyrant in his own home, in his arbitrary decisions (kind as well as, more often, cruel) and his obsessive self-importance. For whatever reason, Nero wasn't amused. Tacitus tells us (*Annals* 16.18) that Nero's anger with Petronius stemmed from an alleged friendship with Scaevinus, an enemy of Nero's. To many scholars it is a distressing fact that Tacitus' account doesn't mention the *Satyricon* at all.[4]

Notes

1 For a view of Petronius as an 'aesthetic dissident' who despised Nero for artistic reasons, see V. Rudich, *Political Dissidence under Nero: The Price of Dissimulation*, London: Routledge, 1993.

2 See P.G. Walsh, *Petronius: Satyricon*, Oxford: Oxford University Press, 1996, esp. p. xxxvi n. 54.

3 On people killing themselves with razors, see R. Ash, *Ordering Anarchy: Armies and Leaders in Tacitus' Histories*, London: Duckworth, 1999, p. 88.

4 The connection between Tacitus' Petronius and the author of *Satyricon* isn't quite as weak as this makes it sound. For one thing, the manuscripts give the author as 'Petronius Arbiter', which is clearly an allusion to Nero's pet name for Petronius, as recorded by Tacitus. Of

course, the scribes could be making the same mistake as we are, but in fact few people actually doubt that both Petroniuses are the same man.

See also in this book

Apuleius, Longus

Texts, translations and commentaries

There is no OCT, but there is a Teubner edition by K. Mueller (1995).

There is a Penguin translation, along with the *Apocolocyntosis* of Seneca, by J.P Sullivan (1986) and a Loeb with the same bedmate, this time by M. Heseltine (revised by E.H. Warmington, 1969). The World's Classics volume by P.G. Walsh is very good. First published in hardback by Oxford University Press in 1996, it was reissued as a World's Classic (current printing, 1999).

Further reading

Connors, C.M., *Petronius the Poet: Verse and Literary Tradition in the Satyricon*, Cambridge: Cambridge University Press, 1998.

Conte, G.B., *The Hidden Author: An Interpretation of Petronius' Satyricon*, Berkeley and Los Angeles, CA: University of California Press, 1996.

Panayotakis, C., *Theatrum Arbitri: Theatrical Elements in the Satyrica of Petronius*, Leiden: Brill, 1995.

Slater, N.W., *Reading Petronius*, Baltimore, MD, and London: Johns Hopkins University Press, 1990.

Walsh, P.G., *The Roman Novel: The 'Satyricon' of Petronius and the 'Metamorphoses' of Apuleius*, Cambridge: Cambridge University Press, 1970.

QUINTILIAN

Quintilian is perhaps most widely known for his intriguing comments about ancient authors in Book 10 of his *Training in Oratory*. Yet, as Fantham reminds us, Quintilian is here

> directing students to the classical authors as models for oratory; so he emphasises especially genres, authors, and aspects of those authors which were suited for imitation.[1]

In general, he certainly deserves closer scrutiny than is granted to him by those who raid his work for punchy soundbites about other authors. He survived the turbulent reigns of some difficult emperors,

living and working close to the centre of power at a time when
Roman literary culture was undergoing some far-reaching changes.

Quintilian (*c.* AD 35–*c.* 96) was born in Spain and, together with
Columella, Seneca the Younger, Lucan and Martial, was part of a
blossoming literary culture among writers of Spanish origin in the
first century AD. His home town, Calagurris near the River Ebro,
was once famous for its resistance to Pompey in 76 BC (Sallust
Histories 3.86–7; Valerius Maximus *Memorable Deeds and Sayings*
7.6 ext. 3) and it had also provided Julius Caesar and Augustus with
bodyguards (Suetonius *Augustus* 49.1). Nevertheless, Quintilian only
mentions Spain once in his writings (*Training in Oratory* 1.5.57) and
even then, as Syme says, 'it is with the curious affectation of not
knowing much about a certain word'.[2]

After leaving Spain as a boy, Quintilian went to Rome where his
teachers were the witty and patriotic Domitius Afer, and (perhaps)
the colourful Remmius Palaemon. Quintilian preserves some of the
former's jokes (*Training in Oratory* 6.3.32, 6.3.54, 6.3.68, 6.3.81,
6.3.84–5, 6.3.92–3), while Suetonius calls the latter

> a woman's home-bred slave, who learned the trade of
> weaving first (they say) and then learned his letters while
> accompanying his mistress's son to school.
>
> (*On the Grammarians* 23)

The question of whether Quintilian was *really* taught by the
disreputable Palaemon is disputed. Our only source for this detail
is a scholiast commenting on Juvenal (*Satire* 6.452), but Quintilian
himself simply mentions Palaemon as a contemporary (*Training in
Oratory* 1.4.20).

After Quintilian had completed his education, he returned to
Spain and lived quietly, practising law, until Galba (the elderly
governor of Hispania Tarraconensis) was proclaimed emperor in
AD 68. Galba brought Quintilian with him to Rome in an entourage
of high-ranking Spaniards, but the situation changed dramatically
on 15 January AD 69 when the elderly emperor was beheaded.
Quintilian, unlike many others, survived the civil wars and stayed on
in Rome to become a successful teacher of rhetoric.

One of his most famous pupils was Pliny the Younger, who
affectionately recalls an anecdote from Quintilian about Domitius
Afer being interrupted by noises in the courtroom while pleading
(*Letters* 2.14.10–11). Pliny's enjoyment of his schooling suggests that

Quintilian was a talented teacher. So too does the fact that Vespasian took the unusual step of making Quintilian a professor of rhetoric; he even paid him a salary of 100,000 sesterces from his own funds (Suetonius *Vespasian* 18). As a conspicuously non-aristocratic man himself, Vespasian may have felt drawn to this talented orator from the provinces, whose literary tastes diverged from the more decadent and epigrammatic style of those writing under Nero, particularly Seneca the Younger. During the Flavian period, there was an intellectual backlash against what many saw as the literary excesses of the Neronian era. Since the frugal Vespasian self-consciously defined himself as being the very antithesis of Nero, Quintilian's hostile attitude towards Neronian literature (which presumably pre-dated the *Training in Oratory*) probably met with the emperor's approval.

One example of close co-operation between the emperor and the orator is Quintilian's defence of Queen Berenice (*Training in Oratory* 4.1.19), who was not only the mistress of Vespasian's son Titus, but who had also supported Vespasian financially during his rise to power (Tacitus *Histories* 2.81.2). From this and from other cases, Quintilian grew rich – so much so that Juvenal alludes to the pleasant estates procured by the orator and suggests that, unlike most other teachers of rhetoric, Quintilian was a lucky man (*Satire* 7.186–90).

Quintilian himself may have taken a rather different view of the course of his life, particularly after both of his two sons and his wife died in quick succession (*Training in Oratory* 6 pr. 1–13). Nor can it have been easy for him when in about AD 90 he was entrusted with the education of Flavius Clemens' two sons, who had been selected by the emperor Domitian as heirs to the principate (*Training in Oratory* 4 pr. 2, 6 pr. 1). Clemens, who was the husband of Domitian's niece, was so grateful that he obtained the prestigious rights of an ex-consul for Quintilian. The rhetorician was clearly not going to be allowed to enjoy a peaceful retirement. Certainly it wasn't an easy time to be close to the heart of power. An abortive rebellion of Saturninus in Upper Germany in AD 89 had left Domitian worried about the future, and many high-profile deaths during this period are recorded. The chief vestal Cornelia was buried alive late in AD 89 on a charge of incest (Pliny *Letter* 4.11), the rhetorician Maternus was executed in AD 91 for reciting an exercise against tyranny (Dio 67.12), and Pliny's friend Helvidius Priscus was executed because Domitian thought that this man had criticised him through a farce about Paris and Oenone (Suetonius *Domitian* 10.4).

It was against this turbulent backdrop that Quintilian, over a period of about two years, wrote his final work, the *Training in Oratory*, which was a study in twelve books of an orator's development from birth to the peak of his career. This subject matter might at first seem relatively uncontroversial, but in fact it would have been difficult to write such a work in the AD 90s without confronting some potentially dangerous questions. What is the role of an orator in a society where the emperor's influence can potentially filter into all areas of social and professional interaction, including the law courts and the schools of rhetoric? For what sort of a career is an orator preparing, once he has left the relatively safe environment of the declamation schools? Does a competent orator necessarily have to be a good man?

The uncomfortable atmosphere in which Quintilian was writing is perhaps reflected in specific passages. For example, Quintilian discusses the rhetorical figure known as *schema*, in which hidden meaning is embedded in a word or phrase, and notes the different circumstances in which it might be useful:

> one is if speaking openly is not safe enough, another is if it is unbecoming, and a third is when it is applied for the sake of charm and delights more by its novelty and variety than a direct reference would.

> (*Training in Oratory* 9.2.66)

The executions of Maternus and Helvidius Priscus by Domitian perhaps indicate that expertise in a figure of speech such as *schema* could have been useful. Even if they themselves hadn't intended to conceal any sinister meaning in their work, sensitivity to this figure of speech could at least have alerted them to possible misinterpretation of their words by the suspicious Domitian.

Quintilian himself is careful to include passages which flatter the emperor, most notably when calling for inspiration on all the gods and above all on Domitian, 'than whom no other power is more excellent nor more favourable to learning' (*Training in Oratory* 4 pr. 5; cf. 10.1.91–2 and 3.7.9).[3] Here, in a self-conscious manner, Quintilian apologises for not having delivered this invocation at the beginning of his work, which he dedicated to his friend Vitorius Marcellus (who was loyal to Domitian), hoping that it might enhance the education of his son, Geta.

Even so, there are passages which seem particularly suggestive when we consider that they were written under Domitian. For example, Quintilian proposes that the approval of posterity, not of contemporaries, should be sought (*Training in Oratory* 12.2.31) and that it is an orator's duty to defend a man accused of plotting against a tyrant (*Training in Oratory* 12.1.40).[4] Such references don't mean that we should consider Quintilian to be a subversive writer, but they may indicate that by the time Quintilian wrote Book 12, the atmosphere in Rome had become particularly tense.[5] We can gain a sense of perspective from looking at Martial's *Epigrams*, particularly Books 4–9. They were written between AD 89 and 95 and show signs of Martial judiciously adopting a pro-Domitianic role that he would renounce subsequently.

There are some revealing moments about Quintilian's character (or at least about his literary persona) elsewhere in the work. He looks back on his own youth with amusement, recalling his involvement in a sensational case about Naevius Arpinianus, who may or may not have pushed his wife from a window (*Training in Oratory* 7.1.24),[6] and noting ruefully that a youthful desire for fame drove him to get involved. At the same time, he looks back fondly on his past: his affection for his teacher Domitius Afer is shown when Quintilian notes the pathos of seeing him lose his rhetorical powers in old age (*Training in Oratory* 12.11.3). Nor is this a one-way street. There is a nice moment when he fondly refers to his own pupils with a diminutive as 'my dear young men' (*Training in Oratory* 7.3.30) and adds that he will always think of them in this way (even when they are no longer young).[7] This admission seems particularly poignant given the death of his own sons.

Elsewhere we get a sense of Quintilian as a hard-working man, despite his wealth and fame. Even the most eminent orators, he argues, should undertake routine teaching (*Training in Oratory* 2.3.1), and in preparing for a case he claims to have encouraged his clients to talk at length so as to give him a full picture of the situation. He says also that he was careful to study every document conscientiously (*Training in Oratory* 12.8.7–14). Some of Quintilian's most famous sentiments include his belief that women should be educated (*Training in Oratory* 1.1.6) and that corporal punishment for children is undesirable (*Training in Oratory* 1.3.13–14).

Above all, Quintilian wanted contemporary orators to abandon Seneca the Younger and to return to Cicero as a stylistic model. Yet Ciceronian rhetoric was arguably a product of the turbulent political conditions of the Late Republic, which was a stimulus no longer available to those living under the Imperial system. A more pragmatic assessment of contemporary oratory can be found in the mouths of Marcus Aper and Curiatius Maternus from Tacitus' *Dialogus* (*c.* AD 102), although these two are counterbalanced by the Quintilianesque portrait of Vipstanus Messalla, who believed that the decline in modern oratory could be reversed by a return to old-fashioned methods of education. There is perhaps some irony in the fact that the one speech which has survived between Cicero and the writers of Late Imperial panegyric is the *Panegyricus* of Quintilian's pupil Pliny the Younger. This speech was delivered in *c.* AD 100 in gratitude to Trajan for Pliny's election to the consulship and was successful in its own way, but it didn't herald the return of Ciceronian oratory.

Notes

1   E. Fantham, '*Imitatio* and decline: Rhetorical theory and practice in the first century after Christ', *Classical Philology*, 73, 1978, p. 103.
2   R. Syme, *Tacitus*, Oxford: Oxford University Press, 1958, p. 618.
3   On Quintilian and Domitian, see K. Coleman, 'The Emperor Domitian and literature', *Aufstieg und Niedergang der römischen Welt*, II.32.5, 1986, pp. 3108–11.
4   Coleman, *op. cit.*, p. 3111.
5   G. Kennedy, *Quintilian*, New York: Twayne's World Authors, 1969, p. 125.
6   Cf. Tacitus *Annals* 4.22, where the emperor Tiberius gets involved in a similar case involving Plautius Silvanus.
7   M.L. Clarke, 'Quintilian on education', in T.A. Dorey (ed.), *Empire and Aftermath*, London: Routledge and Kegan Paul, 1975, p. 106.

See also in this book

Cicero, Demosthenes, Lysias, Seneca the Younger, Tacitus

Texts, translations and commentaries

The Latin text is available in OCT, Teubner and Loeb.

There is no Penguin or Oxford World's Classics translation, so the Loeb is important. D.A. Russell and M. Winterbottom are producing a revised version of H.E. Butler's Loeb.

There are currently no commentaries on Quintilian in either the Aris and Phillips or the Cambridge Greek and Latin Classics Series, but there are commentaries on *Training in Oratory 1* by F. Colson (published by Cambridge University Press) and on *Training in Oratory 12* by R.G. Austin (published by Oxford University Press).

Further reading

Clarke, M.L., 'Quintilian on education', in T.A. Dorey (ed.), *Empire and Aftermath*, London: Routledge and Kegan Paul, 1975, pp. 98–118.

Coleman, K., 'The Emperor Domitian and literature', *Aufstieg und Niedergang der römischen Welt*, II.32.5, 1986, pp. 3087–115.

Fantham, E., '*Imitatio* and decline: Rhetorical theory and practice in the first century after Christ', *Classical Philology*, 73, 1978, pp. 102–16.

Fantham, E., 'Quintilian on performance: Traditional and personal elements in *Inst.* 11.3', *Phoenix*, 36, 1982, pp. 243–63.

Kennedy, G., *Quintilian*, New York: Twayne's World Authors, 1969.

Winterbottom, M., 'Quintilian and the *Vir Bonus*', *Journal of Roman Studies*, 54, 1964, pp. 90–7.

Winterbottom, M., 'Quintilian and rhetoric', in T.A. Dorey (ed.), *Empire and Aftermath*, London: Routledge and Kegan Paul, 1975, pp. 79–97.

LUCAN

Eighty years after the *Aeneid*, when the Augustan dynasty of the Julio-Claudian emperors had reached its apogee in Nero, Lucan took up from Virgil the epic mantle, together with the Roman story – or rather twisted it inside out and did it terrible violence, which expressed (and participated in) the horrors of civil war and the imperial tyranny which they spawned. Lucan's poem, like its subject, is a horrific, obscene *nefas* ('thing not to be spoken of') – and a magnificent, troubling, puzzling piece of literature which is enjoying a vogue in our pessimistic millennial world.

Lucan lived only twenty-five years. As with Terence, they were years packed tight with literary activity but, unlike the comic dramatist, the epic poet was a young aristocrat. He studied in Athens and began a senatorial career, as well as writing a vast number and range of poetic works, of which only one, an epic poem in ten books, has survived. At first sight, we seem fairly well supplied with ancient testimonies to Lucan's life, including one from his friend the poet Statius (*Silvae* 2.7), but, as ever, much that the ancient sources say needs to be treated with caution. Ancient biographers were inclined to think in patterns: in particular, the lives of poets were often shaped by the lives of previous poets. Sometimes poets probably did shape their lives by reference to literary precedent, but it is almost certainly the case that biographers say things about their subjects which *seem appropriate*, because this is 'the sort of thing known from other poets' or because it is being inferred from the poet's own work, rather than because they know it to be true.[1]

Marcus Annaeus Lucanus was born in Corduba in Spain on 3 November AD 39, the son of Marcus Annaeus Mela. He was thus the nephew of the Younger Seneca, the philosopher and tragedian, and grandson of the rhetorician Seneca the Elder. As a baby, Lucan moved to Rome with his family, where he received an excellent education, including philosophical training from the Stoic Cornutus, who was also the teacher of the satirist Persius. Lucan was made quaestor by Nero, and so entered the Senate, when he was in his early twenties (below the normal age). He enjoyed the emperor's favour at first, and even wrote a panegyric on Nero that was performed at the 'Neronian games' in AD 60.

Soon, however, the imperial friendship was lost: Lucan's works were banned, and he was forbidden to give poetry readings or to engage in the activities of the courts (which were still an important part of public life). The ancient witnesses suggest that Nero was jealous of Lucan's poetic success, for Nero himself was a poet. It is also possible that the subversive elements in Lucan's work pre-date the ban, rather than merely stemming from it. Lucan joined the ill-fated 'conspiracy of Piso' in AD 65: the plan was to assassinate Nero. When it was discovered, Lucan was ordered to commit suicide. On 30 April 65 he obeyed, opening his veins in a bath, according to the ancient sources, and bleeding to death while reciting some verses of his own which relate a soldier's death from loss of blood. The story is suspiciously appropriate, given the obsession in his epic poem with death and particularly with suicide, and also with this kind of display, but it is entirely possible that it was Lucan himself, not just the biographers, who modelled his death on his life and literature. His widow, Polla Argentaria, is said to have celebrated his birthday for many years.

The title of the epic is uncertain: *Pharsalia*, *De Bello Civili* or *Bellum Civile*.[2] Each is appropriate, none exact. The poem relates the events of the civil war between Julius Caesar and Pompey, who is placed more or less on the side of the Senate and the old Republic, from Caesar's crossing of the Rubicon in January 49 BC, through the Battle of Pharsalus in August 48 and the murder of Pompey in Egypt soon after, up to the campaign of Caesar in Egypt in 48–47. The banquet in Alexandria, which takes up much of the final book, is almost the only haven from horrors in the entire epic: it recalls Aeneas at the court of Dido or Odysseus among the Phaeacians, but ironically heralds the endlessness of civil war and the next, unspoken, stage of the story, as does the funeral feast for Hector at the end of the *Iliad*. Lucan's intertextuality offers us highly complex readings.

Lucan's story expounds only a snippet of the civil war (as Homer's *Iliad* tells only a snippet of the Trojan War), but it is magnified to epic greatness. The narrative has a strong epic teleology (although ironically, pessimistically, it is directed towards no proper end) and yet little of the space is taken up with actual story-telling; rather, the poem is driven by a series of magnificent set-pieces. Memorable episodes include the spontaneous fraternisation of enemy troops at Ilerda in Spain (a highly emotive and popular motif, in literature and in life, as the famous episode of the Christmas carols in World War I also attests); the sea battle at Massilia (Marseilles) in which the boats are so tightly packed that it becomes a land battle; the mass suicide of a group of Caesarian soldiers in an impossible position; the march of Cato and his men through the burning desert of Libya and their fight with all manner of snakes and scorpions, in which scientific details and mythological 'fighting the monster' are intertwined; the descriptions of Thessaly and of the source of the Nile; and, perhaps above all, the consultation by Pompey's son Sextus of the witch Erictho, whose unspeakable necromantic rites (described – spoken – at length) resuscitate a corpse and force it to tell Sextus the future (terrible, but misleading). The scene is an imitation and perversion of Virgil's story of Aeneas' visit to the Underworld, in *Aeneid* 6, to consult his father and learn the glorious future of Rome. It may stand as symptomatic of the way Lucan uses and creatively abuses Virgil. As is so often the case, there isn't just one intertext here. Virgil's own *katabasis* (descent to the Underworld) has a long ancestry, including the passage in Homer's *Odyssey* where Odysseus summons the ghost of Tiresias to tell him how to get home. In a sense, Lucan corrects Virgil by going back to the 'purer' Homeric necromancy.

As an epic poem, the *Pharsalia* is necessarily involved in a constant counterpoint with the *Aeneid*. Virgil's mythological epic of the origins of Rome, although set in the distant past, resonated not only with Virgil's own day (the time of Augustus) but also with the future of 'Eternal Rome'. It was this opening which Lucan exploited. The interaction with Virgil is both political and literary: political, since (for all its ambivalences) Lucan's poem is passionately committed to denouncing the imperial 'Augustan lie' (as Matthew Leigh calls it) which he, for his own purposes, reads Virgil as having bought and sold;[3] literary, since Lucan enacts his position as an epic poet by provoking and perverting the *Aeneid* as the epic genre.

Right from the beginning, we can see how Lucan both imitates and defies Virgil. His opening word *bella* ('wars') evokes the *Aeneid*'s opening *arma* ('arms'), and in one word challenges the whole epic: it is much more direct, more violent, even more prosaic.[4] War, endlessly, will be the subject of this poem, but with no divine arms (as for Achilles in the *Iliad* and Aeneas in the *Aeneid*) and no hero: Lucan refuses to follow his version of Virgil's *arma* with any version of the *uirum(que)* ('and the man') that follows in Virgil. Instead the line glosses the wars as 'worse than civil' and sets the tone for the seven-line proem (just like Virgil's) which castigates the wickedness of this war of partners. Having no *uirumque*, the poem has no hero, although both Caesar and Pompey play some Aeneas-like roles. Not even Cato, who certainly does heroic things, can be 'the man' of the poem in the manner of Aeneas. For one thing, his starring moment is delayed until Book 9, in the Libyan desert, and then leads nowhere. By denying the hero-role, Lucan refuses to be Virgil. Invoking *bella* but refusing to match it with *uirumque*, and by the minor variation *canimus* ('we sing' – Latin frequently uses plural for singular) in the second line, echoing the last word of Virgil's opening three words (*arma uirumque cano*, 'arms and the man I sing'), Lucan throws down the intertextual gauntlet. There was 'angry madness' in Virgil's poem: he piously and rhetorically asked could such *furor* exist in the hearts of the gods (*Aeneid* 1.11). In Lucan's poem, however, this force has become a human *furor*, a madness leading Romans to civil war (*Pharsalia* 1.8). In this poem the gods are wicked or don't care or don't exist.

Lucan ends with (and against) Virgil, as he began with him. At least, so it seems. The ending of the poem is one of the most vexed questions in its critical tradition, for it is generally believed that the poem was left unfinished when Lucan died – 'in mid-sentence' as one critic rather romantically and implausibly puts it. This view has been challenged, most recently and powerfully by Masters (1992: 248; see also Ahl 1976: 306–26), but not resolved. Apart from the unreliable ancient witness (it is primarily that from the tenth century), the main reason for thinking that the poem is unfinished is that the tenth book is shorter than others and fizzles out in the middle of Caesar's campaign in Egypt. Moreover, there are only ten books when, by analogy with the *Aeneid*, we might expect twelve (or fifteen under the influence of Ovid's *Metamorphoses*). But what more powerful denial of Augustan teleology could there be than to leave the poem 'unfinished' and refuse, as far as one can without talking forever, to have an ending?

It is not only Virgil who provided intertextual material for Lucan, however. Alongside the provocation of Virgil in the proem, we should notice that Lucan introduces the causes of the war with a strong allusion to the intervening epic poet, Ovid: *fert animus* ('the mind moves me') in 1.67 is a quotation of the opening line of the *Metamorphoses*. (The sentence at 1.67 is also evocative of Lucretius.) It is through Ovid that Lucan entered the topsy-turvy world of resistance to Augustan epic. Important also were the historian Livy and the commentaries on the civil war by Caesar himself. These works are alive in Lucan not just as 'sources' for historical facts, but as intertexts. It is worth noting that the chronological scope of Lucan's poem is very similar to that of Caesar's commentaries. The intertextual relationship between Lucan and the historical Caesar is a counterpart to the troubled opposition-cum-identification between the narrator of the *Pharsalia* and the poetic Caesar: for, despite his violent opposition to Caesar, Lucan-as-narrator shows (worrying?) Caesarian tendencies. And, addressing Caesar as the narrator in this poem often addresses characters, Lucan refers to 'our Pharsalia' (9.985).

But, for all that, the poem shouts its Republicanism from the rooftops. The fight of Roman against Roman, standard against standard, pilum against pilum, is an unspeakable crime which has an even more unspeakable outcome: the victory of one side and the end of 'freedom'. Although Caesar is castigated and his every motive held suspect, and Pompey is celebrated even though he is a shadow of his former self, the conflict is bigger than either. That is why the praise of Pompey increases as he loses ground – it is by losing the civil war and therefore *not* becoming the tyrant he could so easily have been that Pompey remains Republican and therefore admirable. Caesar is despicable not only for himself – for he will ultimately, outside the scope of the poem, fall victim to (the superhero?) Brutus – but also for the new state of affairs which he engendered: the empire.

Where does that leave Nero? In the first book, Lucan claims that if fate could find no other way (very Virgilian, this) to bring Nero's reign to the world than through the civil war, then *nihil, o superi, querimur* ('we do not complain at all, o gods above', 1.37). It is hard not to see this encomium as ironic, since the poem goes on to complain at length. The praise continues with the deification of Nero. But whichever god Nero chooses to be, let him not choose his celestial seat too far to the north or south, since his great weight would tip up the world. Gods are traditionally heavy for their size, but Nero was fat. And making the emperor a god in a poem where the gods are deposed, and where later the poet will berate the practice of imperial deifications ('worshipping ghosts', 7.459), seems hardly calculated to offset the obvious Republicanism of the poem. On the other hand, the *topoi* Lucan employs in his proem are standard elements in panegyric and might have delighted Nero.[5]

The exclusion of the gods is perhaps the obvious way in which Lucan changed the shape of epic. There is no 'divine machinery' in the *Pharsalia*. This isn't simply because the poem is 'realistic': there is, for instance, Erictho's necromancy. Neither is it that the gods are simply ignored, for both characters and narrators constantly cry out to them, usually in anger. Rather it seems that the gods are debased and perverted by civil war, like everything else. Given Lucan's assumed Stoic education, given also the high profile accorded in the poem to the Stoic Cato and also to a number of Stoic notions (such as the power of fate and the positive value of suicide), it is tempting to see the traditional pantheon of Olympian gods replaced by a more sophisticated Stoic theology, moving towards monotheism. But the poem actually gives little encouragement for such a view. Stoic ideas, dogmas and rhetoric, such as providentialism, are there in the poem, but the inevitability of fate is a matter for despair, while the positive value of suicide is as much a matter of pessimistic and macabre fascination with death (*amor mortis*, 'love of death') as it is of Stoic reason and autarky. Many readers have noticed the poem's gladiatorial imagery, which combines the Roman military ethos with a more disturbing, even voyeuristic, obsession with death.[6]

Lucan is very much a 'silver Latin' poet.[7] Features that make critics want to apply the term include the rhetorical flourishes, the long descriptive passages, the baroque and the *sententiae*, which are pithy, pointed, epigrammatic sayings which Lucan likes to use to close off a section and which are eminently quotable. Some of them seem to compress the seething mass of his poem and all its violence, hatred and longing into a few words: *uictrix causa deis placuit, sed uicta Catoni* ('the conquering side pleased the gods, but the conquered [pleased] Cato', 1.128); *non Magni partes sed Magnum in partibus esse* (the Senate made it clear that 'they were not the party of Magnus, but Magnus was in their party', 5.14); *si dominum, Fortuna, dabas, et bella dedisses* (to those born after the battle: 'if you, Fortuna, were giving a master [that is, Caesar], you ought also to have given us war [that is, the chance to fight against domination]', 7.646). 'Silver' also is the Gothic violence of the poem. It may not be comfortable; it may even be compromised and infected by the evil it depicts; but it is undoubtedly effective. At 7.620, in the midst of a catalogue of anonymous and gruesome deaths, a soldier steps on his own entrails. This horrific moment encapsulates civil war: *in sua ... uiscera* ('against their own entrails', 1.3).

Notes

1 See J. Masters, *Poetry and Civil War in Lucan's Bellum Civile*, Cambridge: Cambridge University Press, 1992, also F.M. Ahl, *Lucan: An Introduction*, Ithaca, NY, and London: Cornell University Press, 1976. The ancient witnesses are Statius, Tacitus, Suetonius, Dio Cassius, Vacca (who may be first century AD, but may be as late as the fifth; Ahl 1976: 333–4) and the tenth-century Life. On literary dying, see also SENECA THE YOUNGER.

2 See Ahl, *op. cit.*, pp. 326–32. We will use the title *Pharsalia*, in order to avoid confusion, but the reader should remember that the poem is also known as the 'Civil War' and therefore statements about war apply metaphorically to the poem as well as to the military action.

3 This doesn't mean that Lucan *really* thought the *Aeneid* completely lacking in ambiguity, anxiety or ambivalence about the Augustan regime, or that he denied the existence of those 'further voices' in the poem, but that for the purposes of his literary and political agenda in the *Pharsalia* he can present the *Aeneid* in this monolithic light.

4 It is important to note here that what Lucan is doing with Virgil is similar to (and different from) what Virgil is doing with Homer. Behind Lucan's *bella* is also the *menin* ('wrath') which opens the *Iliad*.

5 For a straightforward discussion, see Braund's excellent introduction to *Lucan: Civil War*, World's Classics Series, Oxford: Oxford University Press, 1992, pp. xiv–xvi.

6 On spectacle, see M. Leigh, *Lucan: Spectacle and Engagement*, Oxford: Oxford University Press, 1997. For an introduction to the Stoicism of Lucan, see Braund, *op. cit.*, pp. xxiii–xxv, who describes Stoicism as 'Lucan's idiom'.

7 The term implies inferiority to the 'Golden' age of Augustan literature. As a result, it doesn't sit comfortably with current critical fashion.

See also in this book

Apollonius Rhodius, Homer, Ovid, Seneca the Younger, Statius, Virgil

Texts, translations and commentaries

The OCT is by the great A.E. Housman (1926), but is now out of print. There is a Teubner by D.R. Shackleton-Bailey (1988).

The World's Classics volume (S.H. Braund, *Lucan: Civil War*, Oxford: Oxford University Press, 1992) is excellent.

There is an Aris and Phillips edition of Book 8 and Cambridge Greek and Latin Classics edition of Book 2.

Further reading

Ahl, F.M., *Lucan: An Introduction*, Ithaca, NY, and London: Cornell University Press, 1976.

Bartsch, S., *Ideology in Cold Blood: A Reading of Lucan's Civil War*, Cambridge, MA: Harvard University Press, 1997.

Hardie, P.R., *The Epic Successors of Virgil: A Study in the Dynamics of a Tradition*, Cambridge: Cambridge University Press, 1993.

Henderson, J.G.W., 'Lucan: The word at war', *Ramus*, 16, 1987, pp. 122–64.

Henderson, J., *Fighting for Rome*, Cambridge: Cambridge University Press, 1998, pp. 165–211.

Leigh, M., *Lucan: Spectacle and Engagement*, Oxford: Oxford University Press, 1997.

Masters, J., *Poetry and Civil War in Lucan's Bellum Civile*, Cambridge: Cambridge University Press, 1992.

MARTIAL

Martial's work has always provoked polarised critical responses. His literary persona embraces paradox, wit, creative intertextuality and verbal dexterity on the one hand, but also displays adulation of emperors, xenophobia, sexism, ageism and (perhaps most notoriously) obscenity. Martial was certainly worried that critics might disapprove and defends himself in the preface by stressing that these are epigrams written for people accustomed to the *Ludi Florales*, games held since 173 BC to honour the goddess Flora, which included the performance of obscene farces.[1] It was not just Martial's contemporaries who found the full range of his epigrams difficult to stomach. Editors through the ages have tended to assemble anthologies of the *Epigrams* to produce whichever sort of 'Martial' might be most acceptable to contemporary tastes. So, for example, when W. Hay (1695–1755) brought out his *Select Epigrams of Martial* (London, 1755), he claimed to have translated 'not all of his epigrams; that would be unpardonable. Many are full of obscenity ... '.[2] Even today there is no translation of all of the epigrams in English conveniently available in paperback.[3]

Reconstructing Martial's life is challenging, largely because so many details come from the epigrams themselves and are therefore subject to artistic distortions, despite their apparent rootedness in 'real life'.[4] Yet Martial, like Catullus and Ovid, certainly makes a point of distinguishing between his poetry and life (*Epigrams* 1.4.8, 11.15.13). Martial was born on 1 March between AD 38 and 41 in Bilbilis in Hispania Tarraconensis, and came to Rome in AD 64 (*Epigram* 10.103.7–9), which was the year in which the great fire which destroyed much of the city broke out. He was initially supported by the family of his fellow Spaniard, Seneca, but was abruptly deprived of this network in AD 65 when Seneca, Lucan and various others killed themselves or were exiled after the abortive conspiracy which aimed to replace Nero with the bland but acceptable Gnaeus Piso. In this context Martial laments the death of Lucan (*Epigram* 7.21) and celebrates his friend Ovidius' decision to follow Maximus Caesonius into exile (*Epigrams* 7.44, 7.45).

The period which followed cannot have been easy: Martial was deprived of his friends and then the empire began to self-destruct. He says very little about the civil wars, apart from celebrating Otho (*Epigram* 6.32) whose effeminate appearance belied a tough personality when facing death. Nor does he dwell on the founder of the Flavian dynasty, Vespasian, whom Tacitus later refers to as the 'special author of strict morals' (*Annals* 3.55). Martial must have been writing poetry with some success, but the first real evidence of his rise to prominence is the publication of his *Book of Spectacles* in AD 80 to celebrate the inauguration of the Flavian amphitheatre (known today as the Colosseum) under Titus. Martial contrasts the tyrannical Nero, whose Golden House dominated the entire city, and the generous Titus, who returned the city to the people, investing it with baths and extraordinary shows in the new amphitheatre (*Book of Spectacles* 2). The arena is presented as the realm where the benign Titus can settle a friendly dispute between factions about which gladiator should be called upon to fight (*Book of Spectacles* 20), show mercy to a 'Leander' (*Book of Spectacles* 25), give the wooden sword symbolising discharge to two gladiators (*Book of Spectacles* 29) and even be supplicated as a god by a pious elephant (*Book of Spectacles* 17). Titus seems to have appreciated Martial's efforts to endow the ephemeral spectacles with immortality through poetry, and rewarded him with the rights of those who had fathered three children (*Epigram* 9.97.5).

Martial's next works came out in the reign of Domitian. The *Guest-Presents* and *Carry-Outs*, descriptions of food and drink and miscellaneous presents, are poems which must be seen in the context of the Saturnalia, the main holiday of the Roman year, which took place in December with presents being exchanged and the normal social hierarchy suspended.[5] Some of these poems continue the pattern of eulogising the current ruler, such as *Guest-Presents* 1 where an analogy is drawn between Domitian and Jupiter. Other poems in the collection are more frivolous, such as *Guest-Presents* 197 on dwarf-mules or *Guest-Presents* 144 on the sponge. There are some interesting social and political details, such as in *Guest-Presents* 96 which describes a type of toby jug modelled on the face of the *nouveau riche* cobbler Vatinius, whose gladiatorial show at Beneventum was attended by Nero in AD 64 (Tacitus *Annals* 15.34). Vatinius was eventually knocked off his pedestal by Curiatius Maternus (Tacitus *Dialogus* 11) and clearly thereafter became a legitimate target for mockery.

However, Martial is best known for the twelve books of epigrams that were published regularly between AD 86 and AD 101. The epigrams are written in different metres, including elegiac couplets, hendecasyllables and scazons, and embrace many different subjects, including funerary notices, dinner parties, the amphitheatre, patronage, physical defects, sexual deviations, praise of the emperor, literary questions, the city of Rome and autobiographical material. Not every book covers all of these subjects to the same degree. For example, Book 5, published perhaps for the Saturnalia of AD 90, contains no indecent epigrams and is uncharacteristically short as a result. Possibly Martial wanted to win favour with Domitian, who had become censor in perpetuity in AD 85, and decided therefore to produce a cleaner book of poetry to please the emperor.[6]

Within books, Martial will sometimes include a sequence of epigrams on the same topic, which he will then scatter throughout the book. So, he writes eight epigrams on the lion and trained hare (1.6, 1.14, 1.22, 1.44, 1.48, 1.51, 1.60, 1.104). Some loose structural links are also created by addressing a number of epigrams to the same person over several books: important addressees include: Flaccus, a poet from Padua; Faustinus, the wealthy owner of several villas; and Martial's namesake, Julius Martialis, a lawyer. Creative juxtaposition is a feature of the collection, as at 1.44–5 where Martial, who has been criticised for repetition, offers a second poem about repetition.[7] Even so, readers familiar with the genre would certainly not have expected to read books of epigrams organised along formal lines and the surprise generated by the varied subject matter in each book is an especially enjoyable aspect of the collection.

Martial uses various techniques to give his epigrams their characteristic sting, including word-play, obscenity, relentless logic, brevity, accentuation of the gulf between appearance and reality, pointed historical or literary allusion, and paradox.[8] Some scholars have tried to fit Martial's poems into analytical schemata of epigrammatic types, but this isn't easy. Individual poems will usually draw on a wide range of techniques and some will gain in power because the individual under attack has already served as a target in previous epigrams. Certainly not all of Martial's epigrams have the trademark sting in the tail. One of the most famous epigrams (*Epigram* 1.49), addressed to Licinianus who is about to return to the Spanish countryside, has a lapidary ending, but no sting, which is made more conspicuous because Horace *Epode* 2, on which Martial modelled this epigram, certainly does have a twist: the money-lender Alfius unexpectedly abandons his retirement to the countryside and decides to continue his career as a money-lender in Rome.

The genre of epigram was seen as being rather humble. Martial boldly chose to make it his speciality, even though so many of his contemporaries (such as Statius, Silius Italicus and Valerius Flaccus) were turning to the lofty genre of epic. Others before Martial had written epigrams in Latin, including Lutatius Catulus (*c.* 150–87 BC), Porcius Licinus (end of second century BC), Helvius Cinna (died 44 BC) and Licinius Calvus (*c.* 82–47 BC), but very little of their work has survived. We do at least have the poems of Catullus (*c.* 84–54 BC); Martial himself claims that he is second only to Catullus (*Epigram* 10.78.16) and elegantly alludes to Catullus' poems on a number of occasions (Catullus 16/Martial *Epigrams* 1.4 and 11.20; Catullus 85/Martial *Epigram* 1.32; Catullus 101/Martial *Epigram* 1.88).[9] Unlike Catullus, however, Martial generally avoids invective against eminent living people, although he happily criticises them once they are dead. So he is delighted that he no longer has to flatter Domitian (*Epigram* 10.72).

Martial tends to work instead with broad stereotypes, such as greedy guests, upstart freedmen, incompetent doctors and heavy drinkers (whether male or female), and in this he was followed by the satirist Juvenal. This technique lent Martial's epigrams a timeless quality that made them an inspiration for much later Elizabethan and Jacobean imitators, such as Sir John Harington and Ben Jonson, who saw analogies for these character-types in their own contemporaries. Martial's work continues to attract translators and imitators in the modern era, including the American poets Dudley Fitts and J.V. Cunningham, the British poet and playwright Tony Harrison, and the British writers Olive and Fiona Pitt-Kethley.[10] Pliny the Younger suggested that, despite Martial's efforts, his *Epigrams* were unlikely to achieve immortality (*Letter* 3.21). Martial, who died in *c.* AD 104, would no doubt have been pleased that we are still actively proving Pliny wrong.

Notes

1   P. Howell, *A Commentary on Book One of the Epigrams of Martial*, London: Athlone, 1980, p. 100.
2   J. P. Sullivan, *Martial the Unexpected Classic*, Cambridge: Cambridge University Press, 1991, p. 299.
3   There is, however, a recently revised Loeb edition in three volumes by D.R. Shackleton-Bailey. In the previous Loeb edition by Ker, anything considered rude was translated into Italian!
4   See Sullivan, *op. cit.*, pp. 1–55, for Martial's life, although there is a tendency in this survey to take details from the epigrams at face value.
5   On the *Book of Spectacles*, *Guest-Presents* and *Carry-Outs*, see Sullivan, *op. cit.*, pp. 6–15.
6   J. Garthwaite, 'Putting a price on praise: Martial's debate with Domitian in Book 5', in F. Grewing (ed.), *Toto Notus in Orbe: Perspectiven der Martial-Interpretation*, Stuttgart: Steiner, 1998, p. 171, suggests that there is a tone of disaffection, if not sarcasm, beneath the apparent humility of Book 5.
7   D. Fowler, 'Martial and the book', *Ramus*, 24, 1995, p. 44.
8   Sullivan, *op. cit.*, pp. 240–9.
9   See Sullivan, *op. cit.*, pp. 95–6, 105 and 114, on Martial's debt to Catullus.
10 See J.P. Sullivan and A.J. Boyle, *Martial in English*, London: Penguin, 1996.

See also in this book

Archilochus, Catullus, Juvenal, Statius

Texts, translations and commentaries

The Latin text is available in OCT, Teubner and Loeb.

Apart from the new Loeb (by D.R. Shackleton-Bailey), there is a Penguin translation by J. Michie of selected epigrams; there is no Oxford World's Classics translation.

There are commentaries by P. Howell on *Epigrams 5* (Aris and Phillips) and *Epigrams 1* (Athlone), and by N. Kay on *Epigrams 11* (Duckworth).

Further reading

Fowler, D., 'Martial and the book', *Ramus*, 24, 1995, pp. 31–58.
Garthwaite, J., 'Putting a price on praise: Martial's debate with Domitian in Book 5', in F. Grewing (ed.), *Toto Notus in Orbe: Perspectiven der Martial-Interpretation*, Stuttgart: Steiner, 1998, pp. 157–72.
Saller, R.P., 'Martial on patronage and literature', *Classical Quarterly*, 33, 1983, pp. 246–57.
Sullivan, J.P., *Martial the Unexpected Classic*, Cambridge: Cambridge University Press, 1991.
Sullivan, J.P. and Boyle, A.J., *Martial in English*, London: Penguin, 1996.

White, P., 'The friends of Martial, Statius and Pliny, and the dispersal of patronage', *Harvard Studies in Classical Philology*, 79, 1975, pp. 40–61.

STATIUS

If Virgil's executors had listened to his final wishes and burned the unfinished *Aeneid*, then the poet Statius would have won fame as the author of our finest surviving example of epic poetry in Latin: the *Thebaid*. Instead posterity has reacted rather suspiciously to Statius, above all because of his unsubtle flattery of the emperor Domitian, particularly in his shorter poems, the *Silvae*. In general, Statius avoids overt criticism of Domitian's regime and any attempt to trace covert disapproval in his epic along the lines of Virgil's 'further voices'[1] is hampered by the tone of his other poetry.

To be fair, Statius himself explicitly advises his epic not to try to match the *Aeneid*, but urges her to 'follow from afar and always worship her steps' (*longe sequere et uestigia semper adora, Thebaid* 12.817). By this formulation, he modestly casts his own poem as a poor cousin to the *Aeneid*, and some critics have certainly taken this assessment at face value. Statius may also be alluding elegantly to a famous scene from Virgil that raises important questions about the status of the *Thebaid*. When Aeneas' wife Creusa leaves Troy with her family, she demurely follows her husband at a distance (*Aeneid* 2.725) before being killed in the chaos.[2] In many ways, this relationship between Aeneas and Creusa can be said to mirror the relationship between the *Aeneid* and the *Thebaid* – except that, unlike Creusa, Statius' poem survived. Where other poets such as Ovid (*Metamorphoses* 15.871–9) had laid bold claims to the immortality which would be generated through their work, Statius' narrative persona is much more modest.[3]

As with so many ancient authors, almost everything that we know about Statius' life comes from what he himself chooses to tell us, above all in the *Silvae* (especially 3.5.22–42, 5.3.209–45). We should therefore be aware that much of this information was originally used to create a poetic persona rather than to provide a convenient source of details for us (cf. the 'autobiographical' Ovid of *Tristia* 4.10).

Statius came from Naples in Magna Graecia, a city steeped in Greek culture that had therefore proved particularly attractive to the philhellene emperor, Nero, as a venue for his singing debut in AD 64 (Tacitus *Annals* 15.33.2). Statius, born at some point between AD 45 and the early AD 50s, might even have seen Nero's performance. In later life Statius was certainly hostile to the 'rabid tyrant' (*Silvae* 2.7.100) who was responsible for the death of his great friend Lucan (*Silvae* 2, preface 26ff.). At the request of Lucan's widow, Polla Argentaria, Statius wrote a birthday poem for his dead friend, most of which is delivered by the Muse Calliope (*Silvae* 2.7; cf. Martial 7.21–3).

Statius had a good literary heritage. His father was a poet and orator, who competed successfully in various Neapolitan festivals before moving to Rome to become a teacher.[4] Statius' father lectured on Greek poetry including Homer, which he translated into Latin prose for his pupils (*Silvae* 5.3.129). It is unclear when Statius' father moved to Rome, although he was already there when civil war broke out in AD 68, and he subsequently wrote a poem about the battle on the Capitol between the Vitellians and the Flavians, which unfortunately hasn't survived (*Silvae* 5.3.203ff.). Rome was the scene of Statius' early public recitations (*Silvae* 5.3.215), although he won his first literary victory in Naples at the games (*Silvae* 5.3.225). In his formative years as a writer, then, Statius certainly 'lived between two different cultures'.[5]

His career as a poet really took off during Domitian's principate. Juvenal describes how people rushed to hear Statius' attractive voice at a recitation of the *Thebaid* and even broke the benches in their excitement at hearing his poetry (*Satire* 7.82–7). This description of 'Beatlemania' in the literary world might initially seem pretty positive but, in a hyperbolic tone, Juvenal casts Statius as a pimp, stirring up the lust of the masses by titillating them with his 'girl', the *Thebaid*, and driven by hunger to sell his 'untouched' *Agaue* (a work which isn't extant) to the pantomime actor Paris. Juvenal was notoriously hostile towards people of Greek extraction in his satires and elsewhere programmatically casts epic as a clapped-out genre (*Satire* 1.1–13), so Statius must have been a tempting target. The fact that Juvenal does all this in hexameter, the metre of epic, makes the attack more pointed.

If we believe the conveniently neat figure (*Thebaid* 12.811–12), Statius spent twelve years writing the twelve books of the *Thebaid*, which was completed in AD 92. He claims (*Silvae* 5.3.233–7) that in the early stages his father helped him to compose the poem, although how pervasive this collaboration really was is impossible to say. The poem in which Statius makes this claim was, after all, a lament written three months after his father's death, so the context demands an emphasis on the dead man's talents and influence.

After Virgil and Lucan, it must have been a tricky business to choose a topic for a potential epic. Was it best to opt for something historical or mythical, or for a combination of the two? Should the framework be Roman or Greek? In the end, Statius selected Greek myth as his subject, specifically the war between the two sons of Oedipus, Polynices and Eteocles, for control of Thebes. The theme of civil war is of course common to both Virgil's *Aeneid* and Lucan's *Pharsalia*, but it was particularly topical for Statius' readers, many of whom had lived through the 'Year of the Four Emperors' in AD 68–9. Conflict between brothers also had a familiar resonance for a Roman audience, since the fraternal strife between Romulus and Remus was central to the early mythology of the city. The subject of brothers had been treated fairly recently by Seneca in his tragedy *Thyestes*, where the dominance of desire for power over fraternal bonds unfolds in a world of disintegrating moral standards, as the terrifying Atreus lures his unsuspecting brother Thyestes to a banquet at which he eats his own children.

For Statius to depict the clash between Polynices and Eteocles was rather bold, given the potential parallels with the brothers Titus and Domitian, whose personal relationship had allegedly been tense. There was always a danger that ancient readers, and especially the sensitive Domitian, might read more into the poem than was actually there. Indeed, we know of one incident where Domitian actually put to death a historian, Hermogenes of Tarsus, for producing a piece of work in which he judged that the parallels between the written word and real life were potentially unflattering (Suetonius *Domitian* 10.1).[6]

Even so, it is difficult to read the epic as a subversive allegory and it may actually reinforce the stability of the Flavian household by demonstrating its opposite. There is also Statius' initial praise of Domitian as a world conqueror and as the kind of man with whom Jupiter might eventually want to share his realm (*Thebaid* 1.17–31). It is possible, perhaps, that this enthusiastic passage is designed to create a distraction from more subversive undercurrents in the body of the poem (as may well be the case with Lucan's praise of Nero at *Pharsalia* 1.33–66), but there are also the flattering poems of the *Silvae* to be taken into account, as well as the crucial fact that, unlike Lucan, Statius didn't fall out with his emperor. However much we would like to enhance Statius' standing by detecting disloyal 'further voices' in his epic, it is difficult to do so convincingly on the available evidence. Perhaps if the *Silvae* hadn't survived, we might have cast Statius as a rather different type of author.

As an epic, the *Thebaid* has much more in common with the second martial half of the *Aeneid* than with the 'Odyssean' first half. True, Polynices is forced to leave the city of his birth, but Thebes, unlike Troy, remains standing and Polynices, unlike Aeneas, doesn't embark on a long journey to found a new city. Instead, he only goes as far as Argos (albeit through a storm which recalls the opening of the *Aeneid*). Here, in the manner of Robin Hood encountering Little John, he fights with the hero Tydeus (*Thebaid* 1.401–81), a fratricide who will in due course become Polynices' firm friend and wage war loyally on his behalf until he is killed in battle (*Thebaid* 8.716–66). At Argos, Polynices and Tydeus are pacified by the elderly king Adrastus, who serves as a kind of Latinus figure and, in accordance with an oracle, presides over the marriage of the new arrivals to his daughters, Argia and Deipyle (*Thebaid* 2.152–305). These weddings, however, are a prelude to war with Eteocles and the Thebans, just as Lavinia's betrothal to Aeneas heralds conflict with Turnus and the Rutulians.

Individual characters and episodes in the *Thebaid* certainly have their counterparts in the second half of the *Aeneid*, although naturally there are sometimes multiple echoes of several Virgilian figures. Statius' beautiful young hero Parthenopaeus, killed poignantly in battle by a Theban warrior called Dryas (*Thebaid* 9.841–907), recalls the doomed Pallas (*Aeneid* 10) and the misguided young Euryalus (*Aeneid* 9).[7] Parthenopaeus' mother Atalanta, who has dreams which seem to foreshadow her son's death, simultaneously recalls both Pallas' father, Evander, and Euryalus' mother, although Statius doesn't narrate Atalanta's grief directly (*Thebaid* 12.805–7). There is also an extended replay of the famous raid on the enemy camp by Nisus and Euryalus (*Aeneid* 9.176–467), when Hopleus and Dymas participate in a night-time attack on the sleeping Thebans (*Thebaid* 10.156–448). Statius makes the connection with the Virgilian model explicit in his coda to the episode: 'Perhaps Euryalus will not spurn your shades as comrades and the glorious Phrygian Nisus will welcome you' (*Thebaid* 10.447–8).

We can also see parallels between Virgil's Mezentius, the Etruscan ally of Turnus, and Statius' Capaneus. Both men are linked by their total disregard for the gods: Mezentius' famous tag is *contemptor diuum* ('the one who spurns the gods', *Aeneid* 7.648), while Capaneus is *superum contemptor* (likewise 'the one who spurns the gods', *Thebaid* 3.602). If anything, however, Capaneus is even more sacrilegious than Mezentius, who at least redeems himself before his death by his futile attempt to kill Aeneas in revenge for his son Lausus' death. Capaneus' death is brought about not by a man, but by Jupiter himself, who hears his mad, blasphemous challenge delivered from the walls of Thebes: 'Come now, Jupiter, with all your flames struggle now against me!' (*Thebaid* 10.904–5). There is only one possible response to be expected from the king of the gods, who duly blasts Capaneus with a thunderbolt. Unlike Mezentius, Capaneus remains larger than life – a man who mocks the gods right to the bitter end.

It wasn't only the *Aeneid* that inspired Statius. The absence of a single hero who dominates the action suggests Lucan's *Pharsalia* as an epic model. In fact, we could go even further and suggest that the tyrannical brother Eteocles' excessive lust for power (which makes him refuse to relinquish control of Thebes in the first place, despite the agreement that the brothers should change places each year) specifically recalls Lucan's energetic Caesar.[8] At the same time there are similarities between Statius' Eteocles and Seneca's Atreus from the *Thyestes*, a play which is drawn on when Mercury brings Laius up from the Underworld at the start of *Thebaid* 2.

While Eteocles, like Lucan's Caesar, is depicted as an isolated figure with no wife to comfort him in times of trouble, the warm relationship between Polynices and his new wife Argia evokes Lucan's moving portrait of Pompey and Cornelia. Argia, however, is allocated a much bigger role in the epic than Lucan's Cornelia, particularly in the final book of the *Thebaid* where she bravely makes her way over the battlefield at night to find her husband's corpse (despite Creon's order that Polynices shouldn't be buried). Argia only finds the body when Juno takes pity on her and asks the moon to provide light, but despite the delay she still beats her defiant sister-in-law Antigone to the spot. There are also quite specific allusions to scenes from Lucan's epic, such as the necromancy conducted by Teiresias and Manto (*Thebaid* 4.406–645) which is partially modelled on Erictho's reanimation of a corpse at the request of Sextus Pompey (*Pharsalia* 6.419–830).[9]

What are the strengths of the *Thebaid* as an epic? For some readers it is Statius' creative use of the traditional devices of epic, such as similes. Many of his interconnected similes involve animals, particularly bulls, snakes, tigers, lions and boars, but there is also nautical and weather imagery. One particularly memorable image compares the enormous Agylleus falling upon Tydeus during a wrestling match with a miner in Spain caught in a rockfall:

> It was just as when a miner in the hills of Spain descends and leaves the day and his life far behind; if the earth that hangs far above him trembles and the broken land gives a sudden roar, he lies crushed inside after the mountain has slipped

and his utterly broken and worn corpse has not restored his
angry spirit to his own stars.

(Thebaid 6.880–5)

There are some delicate touches here, such as the way in which the
miner's spirit is described as indignant even after his body has been
crushed. This may recall the final line of the Aeneid, where Turnus'
spirit is 'indignant' as it flees to the shades below. We can also see
that the dark mine is (appropriately) like the Underworld: when the
miner initially leaves 'the day and his life' behind him, we take this to
mean his daily life in the daylight, but the phrasing is proleptic. His
descent into the mine really does mean that he will leave his life
behind him forever. Unlike the miner, of course, Tydeus survives,
even winning this wrestling bout with Agylleus, but his death is only
deferred until the end of Thebaid 8. This is an epic in which
boundaries are often confused[10] and this simile offers a good
example of that.

For other readers, the attraction of Statius' epic lies in the vivid
depiction of its female characters, which is perhaps unexpected given
the poem's martial nature. The spirited Argia is a much more
rounded character than Virgil's blushing Lavinia, for example, and
her treatment of her sister-in-law Antigone after they have found
Polynices' corpse marks her out as a sensitive and humane
personality even in her grief. Knowing how much Antigone loves
her brother, Argia comforts her by swearing that what Polynices
really wanted was not the throne of Thebes, but to return to his
beloved sister. She suggests without bitterness that, as his wife, she
was always a lesser concern for the dead man than Antigone was
(Thebaid 12.392–408). What matters at this moment isn't the truth,
but the feelings of those left alive, and Argia handles this situation in
an extraordinarily altruistic way, considering her own personal
tragedy. By privileging Polynices' love for his sister in this way, Argia
allows Antigone some comfort. We remember too the poignant
moment at which Polynices almost laid down his weapons in
response to Antigone's moving appeal from the walls (Thebaid
11.363–82) until the fury intervened.

Some critics have considered that the final book is a rather weak
ending to the epic after the brothers have finally killed each other in
the climactic eleventh book. It certainly differentiates the Thebaid
structurally from the Aeneid, with the dominance of the female
characters at the end enriching the narrative and aligning the work
more closely with the end of the Iliad. Argia is, of course, not the

339

only vibrant female character of the work. There is also the extraordinary Hypsipyle, who recounts her misfortunes on Lemnos and her unhappy encounter with Jason and the Argonauts as an inset story which dominates *Thebaid* 5. The fact that this story is focalised through a female voice not only adds variety, but also offers a sharp contrast with the most significant inset story of the *Aeneid* – the account of the fall of Troy as told by Aeneas. Statius reverses the gender roles: Hypsipyle tells her story to the Argive men, whereas Aeneas tells his story to Dido. As if to trigger associations with *Aeneid* 2, in particular the snake which kills Laocoon and his two sons, Statius ends *Thebaid* 5 with a graphic account of the huge snake which kills the baby boy Archemorus, for whom Hypsipyle is responsible.

The *Thebaid* was certainly Statius' finest legacy, but it wasn't his only project. He also wrote shorter poems, the *Silvae*,[11] on a wide variety of different topics, mostly in hexameters: Books 1–3 were published in AD 93 or 94, Book 4 was published in AD 95 and Book 5 appeared after Statius' death (perhaps shortly before the assassination of Domitian in September AD 96). There was also an epic on the German campaigns of Domitian, the *De Bello Germanico*, of which we have only one tiny fragment. Finally, there was his *Achilleid*, which had only progressed as far as the second book when he died, but whose tone is much more playful than that of the more sombre *Thebaid*. The surviving books offer us an engaging picture of the young Achilles hiding in drag among the women of Scyros. All is well until Odysseus tricks Achilles into blowing his cover by including some manly weapons among the jewels and trinkets which he is giving to the women as presents. We can only regret that the rest of this epic was never written.

Notes

1 R.O.A.M. Lyne, *Further Voices in Vergil's Aeneid*, Oxford: Oxford University Press, 1987.
2 Cf. Virgil *Aeneid* 2.753–4 <u>uestigia</u> retro / obseruata <u>sequor</u>.
3 P.R. Hardie, *The Epic Successors of Virgil: A Study in the Dynamics of a Tradition*, Cambridge: Cambridge University Press, 1993, pp. 110–11.
4 A. Hardie, *Statius and the Silvae: Poets, Patrons and Epideixis in the Greco-Roman World*, Liverpool: Francis Cairns Publications, 1983, pp. 6–14, discusses the career of Statius' father.
5 E. Fantham, *Roman Literary Culture*, Princeton, NJ: Princeton University Press, 1996, p. 176.
6 S. Bartsch, *Actors in the Audience: Theatricality and Doublespeak from*

Nero to Hadrian, Cambridge, MA, and London: Harvard University Press, 1994, pp. 88–90.
7 Differences can also be instructive. P. R. Hardie, *op. cit.*, p. 48, says that

> where the Virgilian Pallas had focused the final gathering of epic wrath, Parthenopaeus is the source of a grief that at last brings the two sides together.

8 On Lucan's Caesar as a 'force of nature', see S. Bartsch, *Ideology in Cold Blood: A Reading of Lucan's Civil War*, Cambridge, MA, and London: Harvard University Press, 1997, pp. 62–3.
9 Erictho herself looks back to the *Aeneid* (see P. R. Hardie, *op. cit.*, pp. 76–7).
10 F. Ahl, 'Statius' *Thebaid*: A reconsideration', *Aufstieg und Niedergang der römischen Welt*, II.32.5, 1986, pp. 2898–903.
11 Statius called these poems the *Silvae* ('woods'), a title referring metaphorically to raw material and suggesting the 'profusion and variety of a wood' (Coleman 1988: xxiii). K. Coleman, *Statius Silvae IV*, Oxford: Oxford University Press, 1988, p. xxiv, observes that the title found imitators: 'Ben Jonson published *The Forrest* in 1616 … and in 1640 another miscellaneous collection, *Underwoods*, a title borrowed subsequently by Robert Louis Stevenson'.

See also in this book

Aeschylus, Ennius, Homer, Lucan, Ovid, Virgil

Texts, translations and commentaries

The Latin text is available in OCT, Teubner and Loeb.

Apart from the Loeb, there is an Oxford World's Classics translation by A.D. Melville of the *Thebaid* and, in *Broken Columns: Two Roman Epic Fragments*, a (rather free) translation by D.R. Slavitt of the *Achilleid*.

There are commentaries on *Silvae 4* by K. Coleman (published by Oxford University Press and Bristol Classical Press), on *Thebaid 9* by M. Dewar (published by Oxford University Press) and on *Thebaid 10* by R.D. Williams (published by Brill).

Further reading

Ahl, F., 'Statius' *Thebaid*: A reconsideration', *Aufstieg und Niedergang der römischen Welt*, II.32.5, 1986, pp. 2803–912.
Bartsch, S., *Actors in the Audience: Theatricality and Doublespeak from Nero to Hadrian*, Cambridge, MA, and London: Harvard University Press, 1994.
Bartsch, S., *Ideology in Cold Blood: A Reading of Lucan's Civil War*, Cambridge, MA, and London: Harvard University Press, 1997.
Fantham, E., *Roman Literary Culture*, Princeton, NJ: Princeton University Press, 1996.
Feeney, D.C., *The Gods in Epic*, Oxford: Oxford University Press, 1991.

Hardie, A., *Statius and the Silvae: Poets, Patrons and Epideixis in the Greco-Roman World*, Liverpool: Francis Cairns Publications, 1983.

Hardie, P.R., *The Epic Successors of Virgil: A Study in the Dynamics of a Tradition*, Cambridge: Cambridge University Press, 1993.

Hershkowitz, D., *The Madness of Epic*, Oxford: Oxford University Press, 1998.

Lyne, R.O.A.M., *Further Voices in Vergil's Aeneid*, Oxford: Oxford University Press, 1987.

Vessey, D., *Statius and the Thebaid*, Cambridge: Cambridge University Press, 1973.

TRAJAN AND HADRIAN

PLUTARCH

Plutarch's work has certainly had some striking admirers. Mary Shelley made Frankenstein's monster a devotee of Plutarch's *Parallel Lives* and US President Harry S. Truman is said to have read Plutarch in search of political lessons. Today, Plutarchan studies are thriving on a global level. Unlike many other Classical authors, Plutarch has his own society, the International Plutarch Society, and there is a lively and extensive website devoted to him by the University of Texas.[1] So who was he?

Plutarch (born *c.* AD 50) was a central figure in the renaissance (AD 50–250) of Greek literature and culture under the Roman empire, which is now known as the Second Sophistic. Today we have seventy-eight wide-ranging discussions by Plutarch on various topics, which are known collectively as the *Moralia*, but there are also his sets of paired biographies, the *Parallel Lives*. As with so many Classical authors, not everything has survived. The so-called 'Lamprias catalogue' (an incomplete list of Plutarch's writings which dates from late antiquity) cites 227 different works.

Plutarch came from Chaeronea in Boeotia, where he lived for most of his life. Boeotia could already boast a respectable literary tradition, since both Hesiod and Pindar came from the region. Plutarch takes a particular interest in these two local boys made good, claiming that the gods bestowed honours on Hesiod because of his Muses (*Numa* 4) and noting in Alexander the Great's favour that he spared Pindar's descendants during the destruction of Thebes in 335 BC (*Alexander* 11).

Boeotia had also produced some dynamic military men. One of the first pairs of the *Parallel Lives* included a biography (now lost) of the famous Theban general Epaminondas, who must have particularly appealed to Plutarch's sense of Boeotian identity. Elsewhere Plutarch preserves Epaminondas' vivid description of Boeotia as a 'dance-floor of Ares [that is, war]' (*Marcellus* 21). Plutarch's home town Chaeronea was certainly notorious for military reasons, being the place where Philip of Macedon defeated the Greek army (including the elite Theban band) in 338 BC, which signalled the beginning of the end for the Greek city-states. Plutarch himself thought that before that battle, some divinely ordered twist of fortune was putting an end to the freedom of the Greeks (*Demosthenes* 19).

At the same time, Plutarch gives us a more personal view of Chaeronea, which he wryly claimed he didn't want to leave for fear of making a small place even smaller (*Demosthenes* 2.2). There are frequent references to various local landmarks, such as the tomb of Lysander on the road from Delphi to Chaeronea (*Lysander* 29.3) or to the little river Haemon, which (Plutarch thinks) must be the same as the river Thermodon, referred to in a dire prophecy drawn from the Sibylline books by the Pythian priestess before the Battle of Chaeronea (*Demosthenes* 19). In addition, we have one piece of external evidence of Plutarch's warm relationship with his home town, an inscription from the base of a statue which was found in Chaeronea: 'Philinus dedicated to the gods [this statue of] Plutarch the benefactor'.[2] It seems that Plutarch gave practical help to Chaeronea, as well as enhancing its status through his writings.

Plutarch also travelled extensively, visiting sites and acquiring useful information which would later surface in his writings: at Ravenna Plutarch claims to have seen a statue of Marius (*Marius* 2.1) and in northern Italy, while travelling with his friend the ex-consul Mestrius Florus, he visited the civil war battlefield at Bedriacum (*Otho* 14.2). Plutarch went to many places in Greece and also visited Asia (*Moralia* 501E), but it was Athens which drew him back most often. The Athenians even made him an honorary citizen and enrolled him in the tribe Leontis (*Moralia* 628A). For the last thirty years of his life, Plutarch served as a priest at the Greek sanctuary of Delphi (*Moralia* 792F), where he acquired specialised knowledge. For example, Plutarch says that there was a statue of Aphrodite of the Tomb at Delphi and uses this fact to explain why the Romans sold items for funerals in the precinct of the goddess Libitina (*Moralia* 269B). He also wrote whole essays drawing on his knowledge of Delphi, including *On the Pythia's Prophecies* (*Moralia* 394D–409D) and *On the Delphic E* (*Moralia* 384D–394C). Plutarch died at some point after AD 120.

Although Plutarch lived in Greece, he was also a Roman citizen. One inscription[3] refers to him as Mestrius Plutarch, a name which suggests that he acquired citizenship through friendship with the ex-consul Mestrius Florus. This man was one of a circle of influential Plutarchan contacts which also included Sosius Senecio, to whom the *Parallel Lives* were dedicated. Both of these Romans feature as affable characters in *Table Talk* (*Moralia* 612C–748D), in which dinner guests at the same table included members of Plutarch's family, well-born Greeks and high-ranking Romans.

In many ways, Plutarch was a Janus figure: a Roman citizen who still retained a strong Greek identity, but who could see positive (and negative) qualities in both cultures. So Plutarch valued the stability which came with the Roman imperial system (*Moralia* 317C), but saw the influence of Greek culture on Rome as valuable and (indeed) necessary: 'for the time in which Rome reached its greatest success was the time when it welcomed Greek studies and education' (*Cato the Elder* 23.3).

Elsewhere, Plutarch is sensitive towards different perceptions about Greek culture from within Roman society. When Marcellus first brought back Greek spoils after capturing Syracuse in 212 BC, Plutarch notes that the common people were pleased about the city being adorned with objects which had a Hellenic grace and charm. At the same time, however, Plutarch notes that the older men thought that Marcellus was making the city a potential target for divine envy, since images of the gods were being paraded about in triumphal processions. There is unmistakable exuberance in Marcellus himself, who 'said that he taught the ignorant Romans to honour and admire the beautiful and wonderful creations of Greece' (*Marcellus* 21).[4] This doesn't mean that Plutarch is blind to Greek flaws. When Flamininus liberates Greece from the Macedonians in 196 BC, Plutarch uses internal focalisation to construct the reactions of the Greeks to this momentous event: the unnamed Greek commentators speculate that Greece owed her downfall largely to the self-destructive rivalry which grew up between her own leaders (*Flamininus* 11).

Plutarch's first attempt at writing biography before the *Parallel Lives* was a series about the eight Roman emperors from Augustus to Vitellius, produced probably before AD 96. Unfortunately, only the short lives of *Galba* and *Otho* have survived, although we have some material in the *Moralia* which may originally have appeared in the other lost imperial lives. There is one anecdote about Augustus' harsh treatment of a man called Eros, who bought a champion quail but then roasted and ate the bird. The emperor nailed him to a ship's mast as a punishment (*Moralia* 207B). Plutarch must have found the research for these imperial biographies difficult, since he only learned Latin late in life (*Demosthenes* 2.2–4). He certainly didn't have the advantages of the later imperial biographer, Suetonius, whose post as imperial secretary gave him access to some unique documents and archives about the emperors.

Plutarch's most popular works today are the *Parallel Lives*, biographies of paired subjects, one Greek and one Roman, including in most cases a formal *synkrisis* (comparison) at the end. The purpose of these biographies was predominantly didactic: Plutarch hoped that his readers might imitate examples of good behaviour

(*Pericles* 1–2) and be deterred from doing wrong by seeing instances of bad behaviour (*Demetrius* 1.4–7).

This innovative strategy of pairing Greek and Roman lives was symptomatic of an era when interaction between Greek and Roman cultures was gaining momentum. The *Parallel Lives* appear to have been written early in the second century AD under the more enlightened principates of Trajan (emperor AD 98–117) and Hadrian (emperor AD 117–38). Previously, biographers such as Cornelius Nepos and Varro had certainly written groups of lives centring on men of a particular profession, such as orators, poets or generals, but Plutarch allowed himself the potential for developing vivid and subtle portraits by restricting himself to only two subjects at a time in the *Parallel Lives*, apart from the single double pairing of *Agis and Cleomenes* and *Tiberius and Gaius Gracchus*.

Plutarch wrote twenty-two paired biographies of single individuals and kept his readers engaged throughout by his tremendous powers of description and by his astute eye for detail. As Plutarch famously says:

> Nor is it always the most famous actions which reveal a man's good or bad qualities: a clearer insight into a man's character is often given by a small matter, a word or jest, than by engagements where thousands die ...

> (*Alexander* 1.1–2)

Although Plutarch does sometimes step back from the narrative and analyse his subject's personality, some of the most memorable moments occur when he allows character to emerge from carefully chosen anecdotes. For example, in one story Antony tries to impress Cleopatra on a fishing expedition by getting his assistants to swim underwater and attach to his line fish which had already been caught. Cleopatra pretends to be impressed, but then on the following day gets her own attendant to swim underwater and place a salt fish on Antony's line. This prompts much laughter, but there is a more serious moment: Cleopatra urges Antony to lay aside his fishing rod and to hunt cities, kingdoms and continents instead (*Antony* 29.5–7). Pelling refers here to the 'charm with which Cleopatra turns Antony's discomfiture into a majestic compliment'.[5]

Plutarch's writings rapidly became popular. In the Byzantine era, there were more transcriptions made of Plutarch than of any other ancient author. One scholar, John Tzetzes (died *c.* 1180), after falling on hard times, resigned himself to selling almost all his library, but he refused to part with his Plutarch. The individual who did most to preserve Plutarch's works is undoubtedly Maximus Planudes (c. 1255–1305). In 1294–5, Planudes, who was devoted to Plutarch, assembled a group of scribes to copy most of the *Moralia*, as well as the *Galba* and the *Otho*. The *Parallel Lives* and the remaining essays from the *Moralia* were added to the project in 1296. Without Planudes' determination to gather together the scattered pieces, Plutarch's work wouldn't have survived on the scale it does today.

After that, there was continual interest in Plutarch. In one pervasive but inaccurate medieval tradition, Plutarch was said to have tutored the emperor Trajan, just as Aristotle taught Alexander. There is even a Latin version of a 'letter' supposedly written by Plutarch to Trajan and consisting of a compilation of quotations from the surviving works. During the Renaissance, Plutarch was translated into French by Amyot (*Lives* 1559, *Moralia* 1572) and into English (via the French) by North (*Lives* 1579). Material from Plutarch was also used by William Barker in 1578 to supplement the incomplete text of Appian on the civil wars. Such translations provided crucial inspiration for Shakespeare and Montaigne.

Notes

1 http://www.utexas.edu/depts/classics/chaironeia/
2 W. Dittenberger, *Sylloge Inscriptionum Graecarum³*, Leipzig: Hirzelium, 1915–24, no. 843b.
3 Dittenberger, *op. cit.*, no. 829.
4 For a more dismissive synopsis of Greek artistic talents, see Anchises' famous words at Virgil *Aeneid* 6.847–50.
5 C.B.R. Pelling, *Plutarch: Life of Antony*, Cambridge: Cambridge University Press, 1988, p. 192.

See also in this book

Cicero, Seneca the Younger, Suetonius

Texts, translations and commentaries

The Greek text is available in Teubner and Loeb (*Lives*, 11 volumes; *Moralia*, 16 volumes).

Apart from the Loeb, there are Penguin translations of *The Rise and Fall of Athens*, *The Age of Alexander* and *The Makers of Rome* by I. Scott-Kilvert, *The Fall of the Roman Republic* by R. Warner, *Essays* by R. Waterfield and *On Sparta* by R.J.A. Talbert. There are Oxford World's Classics translations of *Greek Lives* and *Roman Lives* by R. Waterfield.

There are commentaries on *The Life of Antony* by C.B.R. Pelling in the

Cambridge Greek and Latin Classics Series; *The Life of Cicero* by J.L. Moles, *The Malice of Herodotus* by A.J. Bowen, *The Life of Themistocles* by J.L. Marr and the *Lives of Cato and Aristeides* by D. Sansone, all in the Aris and Phillips Series; *Pericles* by P.A. Stadter, published by the University of North Carolina; and *Alexander* by J.R. Hamilton, published by Oxford University Press.

Further reading

Dittenberger, W., *Sylloge Inscriptionum Graecarum*[3], Leipzig: Hirzelium, 1915–24.

Jones, C.P., *Plutarch and Rome*, Oxford: Oxford University Press, 1971.

Mossman, J. (ed.), *Plutarch and His Intellectual World*, London and Swansea: Duckworth and the Classical Press of Wales, 1997.

Pelling, C.B.R., 'Plutarch and Roman politics', in I. Moxon, J.D. Smart and A.J. Woodman (eds), *Past Perspectives: Studies in Greek and Roman Historical Writing*, Cambridge: Cambridge University Press, 1986.

Pelling, C.B.R., 'Is death the end? Closure in Plutarch's *Lives*', in D.H. Roberts, F.M. Dunn and D.P. Fowler (eds), *Classical Closure: Reading the End in Greek and Latin Literature*, Princeton, NJ: Princeton University Press, 1998.

Russell, D.A., *Plutarch*, London: Duckworth, 1973.

Scardigli, B. (ed.), *Essays on Plutarch's Lives*, Oxford: Oxford University Press, 1995.

Stadter, P.A. (ed.), *Plutarch and the Historical Tradition*, London and New York: Routledge, 1992.

Swain, S., *Hellenism and Empire: Language, Classicism and Power in the Greek World AD 50–250*, Oxford: Oxford University Press, 1996.

TACITUS

We are all products of our own times and historians are no exception. The idea that historians' reliability and objectivity require them to be timeless and disengaged from their political situation would be a notion quite alien to the historian Tacitus, as to any ancient historian. Tacitus had a successful political career under a system which he considered degenerate and leaders he considered wicked. Indeed, he tells us himself that he owed the beginning of his career to Vespasian, and its advancement to Titus and also the tyrannical Domitian: the hint is that this is evidence that he doesn't write out of personal enmity (*Histories* 1.1.3). Tacitus hates the emperors, but it is nothing personal.

We are particularly fortunate to possess an account of the first century AD, albeit incomplete, by a near-contemporary historian of astute and informed political sensitivity, considerable reliability and outstanding rhetorical skill. For the modern historian, Tacitus' history of the Roman empire abroad and particularly at home, from the death of Augustus (AD 14) to the death of Domitian (AD 96), is a crucially important source for this fascinating period. For the reader, whether driven by 'historical' or 'literary' interest, the major works offer a magnificent – if bleak – vision of Rome under the early emperors, to which the dramatic narrative and the caustic irony add a novelesque quality.

The details, then, as we know them: Gaius (or Publius) Cornelius Tacitus was born in the mid-50s AD, probably in Gallia Narbonensis, probably to an equestrian family. He studied in Rome, where he was able to acquire the necessary backing to follow a traditional aristocratic career: quaestor in 81 or 82, praetor in 88 (both under Domitian, although Titus was alive until 13 September 81 and so will have been instrumental in Tacitus' early advancement), suffect consul[1] in 97 (under Nerva, but probably as a result of designation by Domitian), governor of the province of Asia in 112 or 113 (under Trajan). An advocate in important trials, a member of a priestly college, possibly also with some military service during his absence from Rome in 89–93 – he did all the right things. His marriage to the daughter of Gnaeus Julius Agricola, to whom he was devoted, is likely to have been a sign of his success as well as the partial cause of it. The date of Tacitus' death is unknown, but he may well have survived into the reign of Hadrian, who succeeded Trajan in 117. The best evidence about Tacitus' life outside his own works comes from the letters of the Younger Pliny, who counts him a friend both personal and political (for example, *Letters* 1.6, 1.20, 2.11, 4.13).

It is a recurring interest in Tacitus to try to understand and explain the nature of contemporary Roman-ness, and in particular to consider how it was possible for good men to follow good Roman careers under tyrannical emperors. It is highly likely that his attitudes were affected by a sense of the communal responsibility of the Senate, and his own part in it, for the 'enslavement' of the Roman people under the emperors. (It is worth remembering that it is the loss of freedom among the small senatorial class, not a generalised democracy, that particularly distresses Tacitus.) He is concerned to explore the morality of power, as it affects both its holders and its victims. Writing under Trajan, Tacitus purports to suggest that his beneficence, and that of his recently dead predecessor Nerva, is in contrast with the villainous emperors described in his narrative: a more subversive, ironical reading might, nonetheless, be appropriated from his work. He promises in the *Histories* to treat the contemporary happier times later, but in fact he turned back after the *Histories* to the earlier period of the Julio-Claudians. Was this one of those stalling promises which was never meant to be fulfilled? Tacitus' ideology, his passion, is senatorial and Republican, but like other senatorial ideologues who looked back to the Golden Age of the Republic, he presents the principate as a necessary evil. Such men might, indeed, have seen it as indicative of the debilitating effects of 'enslavement' that they themselves could only complain, not offer an alternative.

Tacitus' first works are not narrative history. He starts out in biography with a highly encomiastic account of the life of his father-in-law Agricola, the main focus of which is the latter's very considerable contribution to the pacification and government of Britain. The work is, not surprisingly, of particular interest today for the study of Roman Britain. But our hero isn't just a good general; or, rather, his being a good general, also a firm but fair administrator, and a loyal citizen of the Roman government, creates a paradigm for the 'good Roman' flourishing (moderately) under tyranny (in his case Domitian) without being wholly compromised by it. Tacitus often presents great deeds as being accomplished at the edges of the world, whereas at Rome the atmosphere is stifling: when Agricola returns to Rome, he stagnates, because Domitian does not take advantage of his talents.

Tacitus' main interest in barbarians is in how Rome interacts with them, and how they may reflect on and contribute to Roman identity, troubled as it is in these imperial times. He isn't unusual among Romans in rating Western barbarians more highly than Eastern, and indeed there is more than a hint of the noble savage in the heroes of revolts in Germany (Arminius) and Britain (Boudicca). Even if they lost – and in Tacitus' view it was right to beat them into submission – they were worthy opponents, and capable of exposing the weakness and degeneracy of the Romans, although barbarian vices are illustrated as well. The *Germania*, published about the same time as the *Agricola*, is a study (largely derivative) of the land and customs of the Germans. It has been read and appropriated as an unequivocal celebration of the German nation, and, as such, as partly responsible for the horrors of twentieth-century Nazi Germany. The notorious excursus on the Jews in *Histories* 5 also offers a hostage to such a reading. The *Germania* may, however, also be seen as a deeply ambivalent reading of civilisation, barbarism and decadence.

Today the least well known of Tacitus' works is the incomplete *Dialogue on Orators*, which was published probably in 102 (it is dedicated to one of the consuls of that year). It is written in the tradition of Cicero's rhetorical dialogues: fictional conversation, set in the recent past (AD 75 or 77), between historical persons, on technical or philosophical subjects, with a strong political under-current. The characters debate the current state of oratory, bewailing (in time-honoured manner) the decline in education and standards. There is, it seems, no room for and no point in great oratory, now that the risky freedom of the Republic, when there was everything to speak well *for*, is lost (see QUINTILIAN). There may be an irony in this analysis, coming from the pen of a forceful and effective orator, but we shouldn't doubt that there is also a sense in which his ideological point is right.

Neither the *Histories* nor the *Annals* is complete. The *Histories* originally consisted of twelve or fourteen books, covering the period AD 69–96. Of that total, only the beginning survives, the manuscript breaking off (apart from some fragments) in mid-speech part-way through Book 5.[2] Since these four-and-a-half books cover only the years 69–70, the remaining twenty-six years must have been treated more cursorily. This is hardly inappropriate, however, since 69 is the famous 'Year of the Four Emperors', when Galba, Otho and Vitellius each in turn held and lost power, before Vespasian brought an end to that civil war and established the Flavian dynasty. In this short period there were also major upheavals in both West and East, where in the light of subsequent events the Jewish revolt is of particular interest.

The excursus on the history and people of Judaea towards the end of our text is one of the few cases where Tacitus can be shown to be seriously in error, for much of what he says about the Jews is at best garbled, at worst lies. Since the errors are all in his sources, which are mostly Greek, he should be blamed more for failure to consult other more reliable sources (including Jewish ones, which would have been available to him in Greek), than for distorting the facts himself. Tacitus is not so much interested in the Jews for their own sake, as in how they seem totally Other to the Romans. The ethnographic excursus had been part of the ancient historiographic tradition at least since Herodotus, and is paralleled in Sallust (*Jugurtha* 17–19) and Caesar (*Gallic Wars* 6.11–28). Like most ancient historians, Tacitus doesn't tell us much about his sources, but we know that he used earlier historians and also some more primary material, such as the 'minutes' of the Senate, as well as preserved speeches and memoirs of his subjects. For the later periods that he covers, he also used oral accounts from living people.

It was the tradition of Republican historians to recount the 'annals' of the Roman people: the events, that is, of each year in order. It is for this reason that Tacitus begins the *Histories* on 1 January 69 or, as a Roman would put it, in the consulship of Servius Galba (for the second time) and Titus Vinius. After a prologue laying out the programme of death and destruction alleviated by only the tiniest sparks of traditional Roman heroism, Tacitus cunningly moves back to what is in a sense the true starting point of his story: the death of Nero and ascension of Galba in June of the previous year. He makes an astute comment on this important historical moment: it was the end of the Julio-Claudian dynasty and the divulging of a 'great secret', as he calls it, that 'an emperor could be made elsewhere than at Rome' (*Histories* 1.4). The importance of the armies, the provinces and the sheer size of the empire for the future history of imperial rule is brilliantly condensed into half a sentence.

The *Annals* is Tacitus' consummate achievement. The annalistic year-by-year format is the explicit structuring of a narrative of emperors and their various counterpoints: the Senate, the provincial armies, the few good men and true, and the many wicked advisers (both depraved aristocrats and – worse? – freedmen). At times the requirement to recount the events of the year causes the narrative to become disjointed to the point that Tacitus apologises for not being able to follow through a particular issue (4.71); but the effect is deliberate, for the interspersed narration of foreign affairs, whether successful or not, provides a welcome respite and a pointed contrast to the litany of good Romans ruined by the hatred and fear of the emperors, and by the greed and unscrupulousness of the 'informers' who press charges flattering to the emperor and devastating to the victims. The work was originally sixteen or eighteen books long. We still have Books 1–6 (although 5 and 6 are both incomplete), covering the reign of Tiberius, and Books 11–16 (again, with gaps), covering the period 47–66 (part-way through Claudius to part-way through Nero).

What Tacitus would have made of Caligula, whose popular reputation today is one of spectacular viciousness, remains unknown. Perhaps so simple a villain (if so he was) would have been less interesting to the historian than the complexities of Tiberius, Tacitus' 'pet-hate' to whom he nonetheless allows some creditable activity, albeit in a back-handed way. The picture of Tiberius is built up gradually: a man of considerable ability, but deceptive, secretive and vengeful, increasingly showing the cruelty of his true nature as various constraints disappear. Finally there is a reign of terror. At the end, Tiberius is deceptive even about his death: after he has apparently stopped breathing and Gaius (Caligula) is about to claim the throne, Tiberius tricks everyone by suddenly reviving. He meets the fate of tyrants, however, when Macro (his supposedly faithful commander of the Pretorian Guard) casually has him smothered with bedclothes. Tacitus offers an assessment of the emperor's character and significance in an obituary-like passage at *Annals* 6.51, but he could never fully make sense of the man who clearly fascinated and appalled him.

The image Tacitus offers is one of the incremental degeneration of a system. Over-powerful and wicked advisers have always been a problem with autocratic rulers, Tiberius' adviser Sejanus being a spectacular example, but it is with Claudius (remember that the account of Caligula is missing) that we first really see the power of freedmen, women and even slaves taking hold. This power was to become a forceful negative motif in the history and satire of the later empire. With Nero comes another recurring motif: the fresh new hopes soon to be dashed. The young, apparently cultured Nero was a pleasant change after the fumbling old Claudius and was, at first, controlled by advisers of a better sort. But power did its wicked work. His 'Games of Youth' and poetic and athletic pretensions are a fascinating embarrassment to the senatorial historian; his increasing tyranny and terrible crimes (of which matricide – he arranged the death of his mother, the younger Agrippina – seems hardly the worst) are a tragedy for Rome no less than the great fire that subsequently allowed him to do so much rebuilding.

The account of the fire in AD 64 is a brilliant piece of suggestive rhetoric (15.38–41). It is juxtaposed with the story of Nero's homosexual marriage (15.37), in which he, to leave no depths of depravity untried, played the bride's part. The two events are connected with the dry comment: 'whether it [the fire] was accidental or caused by the emperor's criminal act is uncertain – both versions have their supporters' (15.38.1). The hinted implication is both that the fire could actually have been started deliberately on Nero's orders, in order to allow him his ambitious rebuilding (a rumour which has never lost its attraction), and that his other degenerate behaviour might be somehow implicated. The gods could be angry (Tacitus uses them when it suits him) at the depraved 'marriage', and the story is that he took an arsonist's or at least a tragedian's pleasure in the spectacle. The famous 'fiddling' while Rome burned is a perversion of Tacitus' story that Nero went to his private stage and sang of the destruction of Troy (15.39). The story provides a good example of Tacitus' rhetorical technique, which works by gradually building up a suggestive picture out of a range of different rumours, opinions and possibilities, rather than by straightforward statement. There is often a sting in the tail.

It would perhaps not be unfair to call Tacitus a pragmatist who liked to hint at something more radical. Throughout all his major works there is an opposition between the servile flattery undertaken by the majority of senators on the one hand, and brave but ultimately self-destructive and useless displays of opposition on the other. (Between them is the 'middle way' of Agricola and Tacitus himself.) Flattery is a leitmotif: Tacitus even seems, in a sense, to join in the bleak, ironic game. His favourite device of the final clause or element that undermines what came before it works to good effect in this game. At the first meeting of the Senate under Tiberius' principate, for example, Tiberius asks M. Valerius Messalla Messallinus to confirm that he (Tiberius) had not prompted him (Messallinus) to make the flattering suggestion that the oath of allegiance to Tiberius be repeated every year. Messallinus replies that

> it was his own idea – in matters of public importance he intended to use his own judgement and no-one else's, even at the risk of causing offence.

> (*Annals* 1.8)

Tacitus ends his report with a comment: 'this show of independence was the only sort of flattery left'. So Tacitus gets the last strike in the power-game between the new emperor and a Roman aristocrat of outstanding lineage (he is the son of Messalla Corvinus, consul with Octavian in 31 BC).

Just how conscious the Senate is of its degradation is sometimes made clear. At times the competition in flattery seems like a silly, sick joke which the senators play quite openly, while pretending to take themselves seriously. It is a game in which Tiberius too engages, jostling for the position and authority which comes in *refusing* the flattery offered him. After the death of Germanicus (a hugely popular general whom Augustus intended to be heir to Tiberius), Tiberius wrote to the Senate in modest terms, asking for the promotion of his son Drusus. The Senate responded with hackneyed old complimentary proposals, until M. Junius Silanus moved that dating should no longer be by the Republican tradition of the names of consuls, but by those of the tribunes (namely, Drusus). Quintus Haterius capped this by moving that the day's decrees should be engraved on the Senate-house in gold lettering. This embarrassingly un-Roman suggestion was greeted with laughter (*Annals* 3.57). The Senate, we might think, acknowledged a 'point in the game' to Haterius – and despised him.

On the other hand, however, are those few who make a principled stand against the emperors. It is often said, including by Tacitus himself (*Agricola* 42.4), that Tacitus disapproves of the empty martyrdom of the opposers as much as the sycophancy of the flatterers, since their deaths do the state no good and are driven by desire for personal glory. A number of deaths are described in the *Annals* in graphic and honorific terms. Most unequivocally praised, perhaps, is the end of the philosophy-minded Thrasea Paetus, during whose death the manuscript of the *Annals* finally breaks off. He had refused to flatter Nero; he paid the penalty of death; he died as befitted a Roman. I don't see the picture as suggesting we should despise Thrasea. The case of Seneca is more problematic, since he has been an ambivalent figure all along: able and virtuous, but compromised and ultimately failing to control the increasingly depraved Nero. He dies an ideal Stoic death, but it doesn't come easily (the blood will not flow). A noted contrast is the death of Petronius, which must be at least to some extent a parody of the Stoic death. The fact that it is a parody does not, however, destroy the romantic heroism of either the Stoics or Petronius himself. Tacitus' own reaction to the long stream of citizens' deaths in the later years of Nero is that it 'wearies, depresses, and paralyses the mind' (*Annals* 16.16). The emotions aroused towards the victims are a mixture of pity, admiration and disdain.

Notes

1 In the imperial period, several people were elected *consul suffectus* in each year, in order to give more people the honour of being consul. The Republican origin of the practice was that the suffect consul would replace a regular consul who had died in office.
2 It is the German rebel Julius Civilis talking. A Batavian auxiliary captain who has served in the Roman army, Civilis is treated by Tacitus as playing the barbarian, rather than being a real barbarian leader. Cf. *Histories* 4.13.

See also in this book

Cassius Dio, Herodotus, Livy, Polybius, Sallust, Thucydides

Texts, translations and commentaries

There are OCT editions of the *Annals* and the *Histories* by C.D. Fisher (1963), and of the *Opera Minora* (minor works) by R.M. Ogilvie and M. Winterbottom (1975). All the works also exist in Teubner editions.

The Penguin edition of the *Annals* is by M. Grant, dating originally from 1956 but reprinted with new bibliography in 1989. A new translation of the *Annals*, by A.J. Woodman, is expected soon.

W.H. Fyfe's translation of the *Histories* in the World's Classics Series (1997) has a good introduction and notes by D.S. Levene, who also revised the translation.

Aris and Phillips editions are available for *Annals 4*, *Annals 5 and 6* and the *Germania*. In Cambridge Greek and Latin Classics, there is *Annals 4* and an edition of the *Dialogue on Orators*, while an edition of *Histories 1* is in preparation. There is also a translation and commentary on the *Germania* by J. Rives (Oxford University Press, 1999).

Further reading

Ash, R., *Ordering Anarchy: Armies and Leaders in Tacitus' Histories*, London: Duckworth, 1999.
Luce, T.J. and Woodman, A.J. (eds), *Tacitus and the Tacitean Tradition*, Princeton, NJ: Princeton University Press, 1993.
Martin, R., *Tacitus*, Berkeley and Los Angeles, CA: University of California Press, 1981 (reprinted in Bristol Classical Paperbacks, 1994).
Mellor, R., *Tacitus*, London: Routledge, 1993.
O'Gorman, E., *Irony and Misreading in the Annals of Tacitus*, Cambridge: Cambridge University Press, 2000.
Syme, R., *Tacitus*, 2 vols, Oxford: Oxford University Press, 1958.
Syme, R., *Ten Studies in Tacitus*, Oxford: Oxford University Press, 1970.
Woodman, A.J., *Tacitus Reviewed*, Oxford: Oxford University Press, 1998.

PLINY THE YOUNGER

Everyone has a favourite moment from the *Letters* of Pliny the Younger. It might be the temptation to read less favourably than Pliny himself does the moment when the emperor Trajan urges him to spare his voice during the trial at which Pliny makes a speech lasting for five hours (*Letter* 2.11.15). Or it could be the startling image of the woman who throws herself from a villa into Lake Comum with her husband tied to her wrist. Having inspected her husband's ulcerated groin, she concludes that he cannot be cured, decides that suicide is his best option and leads the way herself (*Letter* 6.24). The beautiful backdrop of the lake contrasts drastically with the rather ugly details of the suicide.

However, although it is entertaining to pick out such gems, we need to read Pliny's collection of letters in a more integrated and subtle way. In the opening letter to Septicius Clarus, Pliny claims that he hasn't kept to the original chronological order in which the letters were written, but has arranged them randomly as each one had come to hand. This creates the impression of a collection casually put together, but the reality is that the letters are arranged extremely carefully, with an eye to *variatio* in tone and subject matter, as well as attention to suggestive juxtapositions and the building up of sequences of letters addressed to the same person and scattered over several books.

So, for example, *Letters* 8.10 and 8.11 both tackle the painful topic of his wife's recent miscarriage from very different angles.[1] *Letter* 8.10 is written to a man (Calpurnius Fabatus, the grandfather of Pliny's wife) and in it Pliny blames his inexperienced wife for bringing the miscarriage on herself. There is rather a different tone in *Letter* 8.11, written to a woman (Calpurnia Hispulla, his wife's aunt). Pliny quickly reassures her that his wife is safe, not criticising her at all for the child's loss. The dramatic juxtaposition of these two letters brings sharply into focus the need to handle different addressees appropriately and shows how Pliny has to wear a different mask depending on the identity of the letter's recipient. Fantham observes generally that 'the sheer self-consciousness of these letters, the concern with self-representation, is itself character-istic of this postclassical phase of Roman culture'.[2]

Another way of reading the collection is to examine different letters addressed to the same person. This process is perhaps easier for modern readers, with their convenient editions in book form, than it would have been for ancient readers, with their more ungainly book-rolls. Still, interesting contrasts do emerge. Pliny writes to his friend Clusinius Gallus to argue that we never appreciate the sights that are available on our own doorstep, illustrating his point with a description of Lake Vadimon, near his wife's grandfather's property in Ameria (*Letter* 8.20). The details which he offers are intriguing and include the perfect symmetry of the lake, together with the fact that there are a number of floating islands, all of the same height and buoyancy. He observes engagingly that cattle sometimes wander on to the islands thinking that they are still on the mainland, but react with surprise as they discover that they are soon bobbing around in the middle of a lake. What does Pliny reveal about himself and his correspondent by such a letter? First, he shows his vivid powers of description, which might seem surprising if we think of him primarily as a bureaucrat and an administrator. Second, he demonstrates by the diverting contents of the letter how much he values his friendship with Clusinius Gallus, who, like Pliny himself, otherwise spends his time immersed in more mundane activities. The only other letter to Clusinius Gallus in the collection is *Letter* 4.17, where Pliny replies to his friend's request that he should take charge of the defence of a woman called Corellia, who is involved in a legal case. It is as if Pliny is reminding us that, even within a single friendship, there are many facets to the relationship and that, despite the intrusions of business, life still has the potential to be surprising and delightful, especially when two people share a similar attitude to the world around them.

Pliny wrote ten books of *Letters*. Books 1–9 contain letters composed between AD 99 and 109, addressing a wide range of people, while Book 10 incorporates exchanges between Trajan and Pliny during his service as imperial legate in the province of Bithynia-Pontus in northern Asia Minor. This last book is different from the first nine in that we have the emperor's replies to Pliny's letters, which are on the whole shorter and more concise than the literary letters of *Letters* 1–9.

We know a certain amount about Pliny's life from his writings, although as ever we must be sensitive towards his strategy of self-presentation.[3] Pliny was born Gaius Caecilius Secundus in AD 61 or AD 62 in Comum, a town just south of the Alps, about 350 miles away from Rome. He remained fond of his home town as we can see from *Letter* 1.3, in which he writes to his friend Caninius Rufus: 'How is our darling Comum looking? How is your most lovely suburban villa? How is that colonnade where it is always spring-time?' Pliny's affection for Comum also found expression in practical support: he set up arrangements for a Corinthian bronze statue to be displayed in Comum's Temple of Jupiter (*Letter* 3.6) and offered to sponsor some teachers for his home town so that local boys could be educated more effectively (*Letter* 4.13).

After being adopted by his formidable uncle, Pliny the Elder, whose name he took, Pliny went to Rome where he studied rhetoric under Quintilian and Nicetes Sacerdos (*Letter* 6.6). We know that he tried his hand at writing tragedy, since he casts an amused eye back on these boyish endeavours and is pretty disparaging about his efforts (*Letter* 7.4). As a young man, Pliny went to Syria for his military service, but seems to have had some time on his hands because we know that he became quite friendly with one of the local philosophers, Euphrates (*Letter* 1.10). After returning to Rome, Pliny entered the Senate and began rather a successful law career: in fact he documents one of his most important early cases, where he acted successfully on behalf of

Junius Pastor (*Letter* 1.18). Despite wanting to create the impression in his letters that he was an outspoken and fiercely independent advocate under the oppressive regime of Domitian, Pliny's career flourished, as he became praetor in AD 93 and prefect of the military treasury between *c.* AD 94 and 96. Perhaps even more so than his friend Tacitus, Pliny seems to have been uncomfortable about the fact that he did well under Domitian. One of his regular targets throughout the letters is the dubious prosecutor Marcus Regulus, who had close associations with the dead emperor (*Letters* 1.5, 1.20.14, 2.11.22, 2.20, 4.2, 4.7, 6.2). By attacking Regulus, Pliny may have felt better about himself, but some of his criticisms can seem a little spiteful, such as his complaints that Regulus mourned his son excessively (*Letters* 4.2, 4.7).

It was with Trajan, however, that Pliny developed a particularly productive working relationship. He was awarded a suffect consulship in AD 100 and duly delivered a speech to thank the emperor for this appointment. A revised version of Pliny's speech, the *Panegyricus*, survives, although how closely it reflects the original oration is impossible to determine. Pliny claims that he delivered the speech above all 'so that our emperor's virtues might be recommended to him by true praises' (*Letter* 3.18.2). The optimistic speech is organised around a series of antitheses which cast the dead Domitian as a tyrant and Trajan as an enlightened, hard-working ruler and ideal general.

Of course, there is a danger that the speech might undermine its own message through the simple fact that it is praising a living emperor. Isn't it the case that any emperor, good or bad, will be praised during his own lifetime? Pliny solves this dilemma by suggesting that this praise is different because it is sincere:

> Let us not say the same things in public about the emperor as we did before: for we do not say the same things in private as we did before.

> (*Panegyricus* 2.2)

This is probably why Pliny uses the revealing adjective '*true* praises' to describe the speech in his letter.[4] This was a bold strategy. One only has to look at Tacitus' *Annals* to get a sense of how deeply entrenched the tendency towards *adulatio* of the emperor was among senators. A good illustration is the 'absurd flattery' of Cornelius Dolabella that Tiberius should enter Rome in triumph from Campania after the successful conclusion of the Gallic revolt, even though the emperor hadn't participated directly in crushing it (*Annals* 3.47.3–4).

We can learn more about the relationship between Pliny and Trajan from the tone of the letters which they exchanged when Pliny was imperial legate in Bithynia-Pontus in his final years (AD 111–*c.* AD 113). The problems which Pliny had to address on a daily basis were often fairly mundane and we might be surprised at some of the topics about which he writes to his emperor, especially since letters took time to reach Rome from the provinces. In *Letter* 10.98, for example, Pliny writes to Trajan about his plan to cover over a putrid stream which runs down the central street of the otherwise elegant town of Amastris. In his reply (*Letter* 10.99), Trajan approves of the plan and comments on Pliny's diligence. Other letters are less practical, but just as interesting in elucidating the relationship between emperor and legate: Pliny writes formally to the emperor hoping that he will spend 'both this birthday and many others to come in the happiest way possible' (*Letter* 10.88), and Trajan cordially writes back to acknowledge these good wishes (*Letter* 10.89). Pliny's tone is deferential and reverent, while the emperor's response is polite but perfunctory.

Some critics have detected a note of impatience in some of Trajan's replies to his meticulous legate, who regularly seeks reassurance from the emperor that he is taking the appropriate action. Certainly Trajan's letters are usually only four or five lines long, whereas Pliny often writes at greater length about particular dilemmas. It is also interesting to note the terms in which the two men address one another: Pliny calls Trajan *domine* ('master'), while Trajan often calls Pliny either *mi Secunde* ('my Pliny') or *mi Secunde carissime* ('my dearest Pliny'). One can contrast Pliny's style of addressing the emperor in *Letters* 10 with his earlier outspoken claim about Trajan in the *Panegyricus*: 'we do not speak about a master (*de domino*), but about a parent (*de parente*)' (*Panegyricus* 2.3). No doubt speaking about an emperor is rather different from speaking to him, but Pliny's slightly nervous tone in *Letters* 10 may nudge us to read the optimistic *Panegyricus* in a different light.

Nevertheless, Pliny's desire to communicate with the emperor so meticulously is understandable if we consider that Bithynia had a bad track record with imperial legates. Six of them had been prosecuted upon returning to Rome, and Pliny himself had direct personal experience as a defence lawyer in the most recent cases involving Julius Bassus in AD 102 (*Letters* 4.9, 5.20, 6.29, 10.56, 10.57) and Varenus Rufus in AD 106 (*Letters* 5.20, 6.5, 6.13, 6.29, 7.6,

7.10). His fastidious communications with the emperor may simply have been a practical way to draw a line between himself and his predecessors. At any rate, Pliny's toils in the province concluded without scandal when he died there in *c*. AD 113.

Why was it that, out of all the genres available, Pliny chose to write letters? We know, after all, that he enjoyed writing poetry in his spare time and he mentions, for example, how he wrote hendecasyllables 'in my carriage, in my bath or at dinner' (*Letter* 4.14.2). Perhaps he simply felt more comfortable writing in prose than in verse. Certainly, he points out that after having been hampered by the restrictions of metre, 'we take delight in the freedom of prose' (*Letter* 7.9.14). Still, even within the medium of prose, there were other genres which he could have chosen. His friend Titinius Capito, for example, urged him to write history, but Pliny rejects this possibility because he wants to concentrate on polishing his speeches for publication (*Letter* 5.8). Yet he never completes this task, since the *Panegyricus* is the only speech which we have, and this is rather different from the forensic oratory which he had intended to prepare for publication.

It may be that his uncle's literary legacy restricted the possibilities available to Pliny in seeking his own niche. Pliny the Elder had certainly been both a prolific and an eclectic writer. His works included a practical manual (*Throwing a Javelin from Horseback*), a biography (*The Life of Pomponius Secundus*), twenty books of history on *The German Wars*, a discussion of an orator's training (*The Student*), eight books on *Problems in Language*, thirty-one books of history (*A Continuation of the History of Aufidius Bassus*) and, the only work extant today, thirty-seven books of *Natural History* (*Letter* 3.5.3–6). One can perhaps see why Pliny chose to avoid writing history given his uncle's impressive track record in this genre. If Pliny the Younger wanted to make his mark on the literary world, then he would have to find something different.

The genre of letter-writing was in many ways an inspired choice. It had the advantage of being different from all the genres favoured by his uncle, and it was also a practical project for someone whose daily life usually kept him very busy. To revise one letter at a time for publication was much easier than to polish a monumental and continuous historical narrative. It may also have been that the natural variety imposed on the collection by the different addressees appealed to Pliny. He could thereby provide a series of snapshots of his life from different angles, showing us a complex web of public and private contacts, and casting himself as a patron, poet, advocate, administrator and family man.[5] The medium of the letter also allowed him to polish bite-sized chunks of material which could so easily have been incorporated in a more monumental narrative: he could include letters about natural phenomena, such as his piece about Lake Vadimon (*Letter* 8.20), without embarking on a formal natural history in thirty-seven books, or he could provide Tacitus with an account of the eruption of Mount Vesuvius for the *Histories* (*Letter* 6.16), without finding himself committed to a huge project of his own.

Finally, there was also the fact that in publishing a collection of letters, Pliny was in some sense aligning himself with Cicero, who he claims as his model in literary matters (*Letter* 4.8.4). Much had, of course, changed between the final years of the Republic and the now well-entrenched principate, but the arrival of Trajan as emperor prompted a mood of optimism among writers, as we can see too from Tacitus' *Agricola*. For Pliny to choose a genre which harked back to the Republican past of Cicero may reflect this collective mood of confidence. In addition, Pliny was as ambitious as the next man and wanted to gain a sense of immortality through his writings: in this, he has succeeded.

Notes

1 On Pliny's depiction of his wife, see J.-A. Shelton, 'Pliny the Younger and the ideal wife', *Classica et Medievalia*, 41, 1990, pp. 163–86.
2 E. Fantham, *Roman Literary Culture*, Princeton, NJ: Princeton University Press, 1996, p. 201.
3 N. Rudd, 'Stratagems of vanity: Cicero *Ad Familiares* 5.12 and Pliny's *Letters*', in A.J. Woodman and J. Powell (eds), *Author and Audience in Latin Literature*, Cambridge: Cambridge University Press, 1992.
4 S. Bartsch, *Actors in the Audience: Theatricality and Doublespeak from Nero to Hadrian*, Cambridge, MA, and London: Harvard University Press, 1994, pp. 148–87.
5 A. Riggsby, 'Self and community in the Younger Pliny', *Arethusa*, 31, 1998, pp. 75–97.

See also in this book

Cicero, Seneca the Younger, Tacitus

Texts, translations and commentaries

The Latin text is available in OCT, Teubner and Loeb.
Apart from the Loeb, there is a Penguin translation by B. Radice.
There is a historical commentary on all of the *Letters* by A. Sherwin-White and a commentary on *Correspondence with Trajan from Bithynia* by

W. Williams in the Aris and Phillips Series. R. Gibson is currently working on a Cambridge Greek and Latin Classics edition.

Further reading

Bartsch, S., *Actors in the Audience: Theatricality and Doublespeak from Nero to Hadrian*, Cambridge, MA, and London: Harvard University Press, 1994.

Fantham, E., *Roman Literary Culture*, Princeton, NJ: Princeton University Press, 1996.

Gamberini, F., *Stylistic Theory and Practice in the Younger Pliny*, Hildesheim: Weidmann, 1983.

Hershkowitz, D., 'Pliny the poet', *Greece and Rome*, 42, 1995, pp. 168–81.

Morford, M.P.O., '*Iubes esse liberos*: Pliny's *Panegyricus* and liberty', *American Journal of Philology*, 113, 1992, pp. 575–93.

Riggsby, A., 'Self and community in the Younger Pliny', *Arethusa*, 31, 1998, pp. 75–97.

Rudd, N., 'Stratagems of vanity: Cicero *Ad Familiares* 5.12 and Pliny's *Letters*', in A.J. Woodman and J. Powell (eds), *Author and Audience in Latin Literature*, Cambridge: Cambridge University Press, 1992.

Sherwin-White, A.N., *The Letters of Pliny: A Historical and Social Commentary*, Oxford: Oxford University Press, 1966.

Sherwin-White, A.N., 'Pliny, the man and his *Letters*', *Greece and Rome*, 16, 1969, pp. 76–90.

SUETONIUS

A tabloid Tacitus? The personal, almost intimate nature of biography, and the light, almost gossipy tone of the *Lives of the Caesars* (not to mention the graphically described sexual antics of the subjects) make the label tempting, but it would not, in the end, be a fair assessment of the work of Suetonius. Their projects, like their styles, are quite different, although Suetonius cannot have been unaffected by Tacitus, in whose shadow he lived and has been read ever since. Suetonius was an imperial bureaucrat, and a scholar, an antiquarian and a biographer, rather than a historian.[1]

Gaius Suetonius Tranquillus was born around AD 70, into an equestrian family. There is a possibility that he could have come from north Africa, since an inscription probably honouring him has been found in Hippo Regius (in modern Algeria), but the evidence isn't overwhelming. His father was a military tribune under Otho in the turbulent year 69, but probably soon transferred, along with his legion, to Vespasian. Suetonius grew up in Rome during the Flavian era (the last about which he writes) and studied the usual curriculum of a Roman gentleman. The support of his friend and patron, the

Younger Pliny, was important to him, both for advancement in his career as a court official under Trajan and Hadrian (although Pliny was dead by this time) and for encouragement in his literary endeavours, about which, it seems from one letter of Pliny's (5.10), he was somewhat hesitant.

He must have got over his initial shyness, however, since on the evidence of the *Suda*, a tenth-century encyclopedia, Suetonius was a prolific writer on a vast range of recondite subjects, like the names of seas and rivers, and biographies of famous courtesans. Besides the *Lives of the Caesars*, the only work substantially remaining is garbled parts of the *Lives of Illustrious Men*, primarily literary men. On the bureaucratic side, Suetonius held, besides a number of honorific positions, three posts as a kind of secretary in the imperial service: he was at different times in charge of 'research', the library and the emperor's correspondence.[2] His position in the court would have given him access to a vast resource of archives, which must have proved invaluable for the work of imperial biography. But in AD 122, Suetonius fell from favour and was dismissed, along with his friend and patron the praetorian prefect Septicius Clarus. According to one version (*Scriptores Historiae Augustae, Hadrian* 11.3), he was accused of impropriety (over-intimacy or rudeness) with the emperor's wife. It is sometimes said that the decreasing quality of the individual biographies may suggest that they deteriorated when he lost his access to imperial archives. Other explanations, for example that the material was less stimulating as the century and the principate wore on, or that Suetonius just got fed up with an old project, are just as plausible.[3]

The *Lives*, which survives almost intact, consists of twelve biographies, first of Julius Caesar, and then of the emperors from Augustus to Domitian. They are of vastly different scale and detail, the biographies of the emperors of AD 69 being, like their reigns, short; but there is considerable uniformity of style and there are some repeating patterns – as no doubt there were in the subjects' lives. The work is an important historical source, not only because we have here some material to set beside Tacitus' magisterial account, but also because of the biographer's habit of quoting sources verbatim, including, for example, some letters of Augustus. Such quotation is not the custom of the ancient historian, but is of great interest to the modern.

However much Suetonius may be used by historians today, it is important to remember that ancient biography was a different project from history. Suetonius is not writing 'great man' history; he is describing individual important men. Where history is didactic and morally charged, biography is more directly informative; where Tacitus writes with passion, Suetonius writes with interest; where history offers a narrative of events in order to explain the world, biography assumes we know the general outline of the story and mentions events only in so far as they illuminate the subject. Far from telling us the story of the principate, Suetonius doesn't even tell us the life-story of each emperor: rather, he offers a generalised appraisal of the man and his reign. Most biographies begin with some background information on the emperor's family, parentage, birth and early life. They then consider his activities under a series of headings. Somewhere in the biography will come a physical description of the man. Each biography ends with an account of the subject's death, which in many cases involves violence or the suspicion of it. The division of material by topics is clearest and most explicit in the biography of Augustus, which must rate as one of the best – as well as one of the longest. Since we in fact *do* know the story reasonably well, this arrangement is quite effective. There is no doubt that, from our point of view, Suetonius downplays the importance of some political events, such as the Augustan settlement of 27 BC and the events of 23, to both of which he makes only the slightest reference. He says words to the effect of 'Augustus twice thought of restoring the Republic, but changed his mind' (*Augustus* 28.1). This might be political naïveté; it *might* even be a subtle kind of irony; or it might just reflect a determination not to be drawn away from the individual into politics.

Suetonius aims for a 'warts and all' presentation of his characters, from brutally honest (or just brutal) physical description to a full account of his subject's vices. It would have been hard for Suetonius to write about any emperor closer to his own adult day than Domitian (with whom he in fact ends), for he would have been driven towards either satire or the panegyric which he studiously avoids. Even Augustus, whom he clearly admires, is not just whitewashed. We hear of his adulteries (no terrible crime for an aristocratic male, as long as it was without complications), although of serious crimes only his viciousness during his rise to power is given any extended treatment. Those many of his activities which are recorded with obvious approval aren't described in the manner of eulogy. Part of the reason behind this approach may be Suetonius' apparent intention not to take a line, not to be political. There is nothing here of the interests of peace requiring the enslavement of the Roman people (the ironic kind of comment we get from Tacitus), nor conversely is there any partisanship for the emperors, although Suetonius generally seems to be in favour of the system (see *Augustus* 28).

It is often thought that the earlier accounts are better. They certainly offer us characters who are far more distinctive and exciting. Julius Caesar is presented as an outrageous hero: popular, brilliant, daring, cavalier in moral and legal matters. Only such a man would have crossed the Rubicon. This is the sort of man who is spectacularly successful in battle, because he dares: in one anecdote,

> [he] was crossing the Hellespont in a small ferry-boat, when Lucius Cassius with ten naval vessels approached. Caesar made no attempt to escape but rowed towards the flagship and demanded Cassius' surrender; Cassius gave it and stepped aboard Caesar's craft.

> (*Divus Iulius* 63)

Augustus is quite different. Here Suetonius portrays a man who is cautious, calculating and devastatingly effective, despite his weak health and many early set-backs. Indeed, these obstacles seem to enhance his terrifying success. Towards the end of this long account, Suetonius seems gradually almost to enact the deification which he doesn't explicitly record. He repeats, without comment, the story that Augustus' mother Atia conceived him from the god Apollo in the form of a serpent (*Augustus* 94.4). Various portentous and miraculous stories and dreams also build up the picture of divine power. There is a crescendo of omens portending the death and a description of the funeral in which a senator claims to have seen Augustus' soul rising to heaven from the flames. But instead of recording the deification which the Senate decreed a month after Augustus' death in AD 14, Suetonius ends with a very sober account of the emperor's will.

Forceful rhetoric and subtle colouring are not Suetonius' style. Nonetheless, his biography of Caligula (the emperor Gaius) is peculiarly effective. It begins with a mini-biography of Caligula's father, the popular general Germanicus. The emperor who never was, whom everyone could pretend would have restored the Republic, or would at least have ruled benignly, is set by this means in contrast with a figure whose name is a byword for savagery. Then we move to the boy himself, and his early popularity, in his little army boots from which the nickname 'Caligula' comes. There is a hint for the psychoanalyst in the story that Germanicus and Agrippina had an older son, also called Gaius, who was supremely beautiful and doted on by all his family, but who died and left a sacred memory – hardly conducive to mental ease in an unstable younger brother who was his namesake. Nothing is made of it, however. The account of Caligula's life after the death of his father is brief, with just a few hints at the brutality with which he is associated. (It is common in ancient thought to assume that character changes little. It usually just becomes more or less obvious.) The next section, however, from the moment of Caligula's ascension (following Tiberius), shows us an orgy of public acclaim, of generous and pious acts, and of populist spectacles. Then suddenly: 'So much for the Emperor; the rest of this history must deal with the Monster' (ch. 22). And so he does, cataloguing the horrors perpetrated by a man he shows and openly states to be mad. The contrast is effective and shocking.

The effect is somewhat undermined, however, by the same technique of 'the good then the bad' being used to lesser advantage for some of the later emperors.[4] Perhaps Wallace-Hadrill is right – perhaps Suetonius did get bored.

Notes

1 Syme puts the case rather strongly: 'The *Historiae* of Tacitus no man of the time could ignore. Suetonius decided to write as if that masterpiece did not exist' (Syme 1984: 1258).
2 The three posts are called *a studiis*, *a bibliothecis* and *ab epistulis*. It isn't entirely clear what they entailed, particularly the first. See A. Wallace-Hadrill, *Suetonius: The Scholar and His Caesars*, London: Duckworth, 1983, ch. 4.
3 See Wallace-Hadrill, *op. cit.*, p. 62.
4 See, for example, *Nero* 29–30, *Domitian* 10.

See also in this book

Plutarch, Tacitus

Texts, translations and commentaries

There is a Teubner edition of the *Lives of the Caesars* by M. Ihm (originally 1907), but no current OCT. The other works also exist in Teubner editions. The Loeb edition (2 volumes; originally 1914, but considerably updated in 1997–8) contains, in addition to the *Lives of the Caesars*, the most readable parts of the fragmentary *Lives of Illustrious Men*.

The Penguin translation is by R. Graves. It is important to read the version revised by M. Grant (1979; revised again in 1989 and 1996), not the original 1957 translation. A better bet is the recent World's Classics edition by C. Edwards (2000).

There are commentaries on various individual *Lives*, often with a historical bent. There is an Aris and Phillips edition of the *Lives* of Galba, Otho and Vitellius (D. Shotter), and a Cambridge Greek and Latin Classics edition of *Divine Claudius* (Hurley). On *De Grammaticis et Rhetoribus*, part of the *Lives of Illustrious Men*, there is a good edition with introduction, text, translation and commentary, by R.A. Kaster (Oxford: Oxford University Press, 1995).

Further reading

Baldwin, B., *Suetonius*, Amsterdam: Hakkert, 1983.
Syme, R., 'Biographers of the Caesars', *Roman Papers*, vol. 3 (ed. A. Birley), Oxford: Oxford University Press, 1984, pp. 1250–75.
Wallace-Hadrill, A., *Suetonius: The Scholar and His Caesars*, London: Duckworth, 1983.

JUVENAL

'Bread and circuses': that's all the common people want. The much-quoted phrase was coined by the Roman satirist Juvenal (*Satire* 10.81). He was deploring the recent state of affairs in which the 'once free' Roman people, who in the golden past (of nostalgia) had wielded real power, now only cared about these trivial pleasures, even in the face of momentous events like the murder of Sejanus. (It isn't really 'now', actually, since Sejanus was the right-hand man of Tiberius, a hundred years earlier.) Another of Juvenal's pithy observations is perhaps even more famous in our health-obsessed world: that one should pray for *mens sana in corpore sano* ('a healthy mind in a healthy body', 10.356). The second quotation shows us Juvenal at his most (that is, not very) gentle: much of his work displays such verbal violence that it may seem surprising (or perhaps not) that he was enormously popular with later moralists, in the first Christian centuries and in the early modern period when he was highly influential over the growth of modern satire. Juvenal's satiric programme of savage anger became the driving force of the genre, through the Elizabethan and Jacobean satirists to the present day.

The life-history of Decimus Junius Juvenalis – even the name is uncertain – is almost entirely lost to us.[1] His contemporary, the epigrammatist Martial (7.91, 7.24, 12.18), hailed him as 'eloquent', an epithet which can hardly be denied him, since his work is permeated by the rhetorical training of a well-off Roman. Indeed, it is at least in part the loss of the rhetorical fireworks in any of the modern English translations, together with the loss, perhaps, of sympathy with such fireworks, that has made Juvenal less popular in

schools and universities today than at practically any other time in
his history – except perhaps his own day. Apart from Martial, there
are no contemporary witnesses, and there is no ancient Life, those
that exist being at best very late. What comment there is in the
critical tradition is based mainly on the poems themselves and on the
biographical fallacy which takes hints in the poems as statements
about the poet's life. We can be reasonably sure that Juvenal lived
and worked in Rome, composing his sixteen satires in five books
between about AD 115 and 130. Stories such as an exile under
Domitian and a very late military service are probably inventions.

Juvenal the satirist comes late in the history of this exclusively
Roman genre (Quintilian *Training in Oratory* 10.1.93). There was
nothing which the ancients recognised as a 'genre of satire' in Greek
literature, although there are affinities between Roman satire and the
Greek iambic poets (see ARCHILOCHUS) who had a similarly fierce
reputation, while the Old Comedy of Aristophanes had plenty of
material which is clearly in the same spirit as Roman satire and
which is 'satiric' in the sense we understand the term today. 'Satire',
to the Romans, is a collection of shortish hexameter poems on a
variety of themes, in bantering and sometimes mock-heroic style,
spoken in the first person with a pose of being autobiographical.

Through imitation and irony, Juvenal consciously writes in the
tradition of his predecessors: Lucilius, who produced a powerful and
independent satiric voice in the second century BC; Horace, who
developed a much gentler tone in the Augustan period; and Persius,
who wrote as an angry young man under Nero, alienated from
society, taking comfort only in the superior pleasures of Romano-
Stoic philosophy. Juvenal writes as a ranter. The character who
speaks is one driven by *indignatio* (anger, indignation) at the evils
around him. The voice softens a bit in some of the later poems, but
there is nothing genial about Juvenal, unlike Horace. Different from
Horace also is Juvenal's style. Horace presented his satires as chatty,
unpretentious and barely to be considered poetry, whereas the most
important innovation that Juvenal made to the genre was the
development of a 'grand style', expansive and magnificent.[2] He
combined lowly satire with the greatness of epic and Roman
rhetoric, to create a voice which is at once elevated and self-parodic.

We must not take the speaking voice as equivalent to the 'real'
Juvenal, or even to the poet Juvenal. The satirist, like every other
poet, adopts a persona (a mask), indeed many personae, to speak his
poetry. The poet is somewhat distanced: he may be making fun of
the speaker, as well as of the speaker's target. The moraliser who

speaks is also a racist, homophobic, misogynist bigot whom we both laugh at and, a bit uncomfortably, identify with. It wouldn't be right either, however, to make a straightforward split between poet and persona, for the one will necessarily leak into the other.

Nor must we take the satirist at his word that this is how the world is. The Rome Juvenal shows us – the Rome of the legacy-hunter and the gladiator, the greedy client and the abusive patron, the pimp and the pervert, the hypocrite and the miser, the robber and the leaky garret – certainly existed, but not in quite so concentrated a form as his tirade of vituperation would suggest. Indeed, as Braund has pointed out, you no doubt *could* see all these characters if you stood on a street corner in Rome, but you would have to stand there rather a long time. Moreover, the refined and sophisticated Rome of Juvenal's contemporary Pliny the Younger also really existed. Juvenal's Rome isn't more real than Pliny's, but it is more realistic – in the sense that term often holds – for there is a powerful sense of immediacy in the catalogue of discomforts, from high rents to crowds to foreigners, with which the satirist characterises his Rome. The pose of realism is crucial, but always slightly ironic. The poems are a mishmash of fantasy, history and literature, as well as of reality.

What exactly is Juvenal angry about? Satire is generically a 'mixed bag' (*Satire* 1.86), so any imposition of order onto the farrago of varied elements which constitute the satirist's target must be always already undermined (or rather, a bit of a joke). Greeks, women, wealth, pathics, new rich, Greeks, Jews, other foreigners, hypocrites, perverts, bad friends (both patron and client), emperors (dead ones), other poets and, of course, Greeks: all these and more are attacked. If there is any common thread, it might be that, in many cases, what the satirist bemoans are failings in 'Roman-ness'. He may not know for certain what that is, but he thinks it is a good thing which used to exist in the Republic and probably under Augustus, but doesn't any more.

One of its crucial elements is 'autarky' (control of the self). In the fourth satire, an entertaining epic parody about a huge fish presented to Domitian, the hated emperor is not abused more than the sycophantic sons of Romulus (the Senate) who flock to 'advise' him on how to cook it (and of course to tell him what he wants to hear).[3] Likewise in *Satire* 5, a set-piece about a dinner party, the mean rich host who insults his poor guests with mouldy bread they can hardly get their teeth into is not noticeably worse than the slavish clients who put up with it. The situation described in the satire is a mockery of the grand old institution of *amicitia* (political friendship) which was the backbone of Roman life. But what the satires expose, although the satirist perhaps suppresses it, is that this very impotence is endemic in satire itself. If all these abuses are happening, why aren't we doing something about it? What does satire do but toothlessly rage? Juvenal's rather pathetic-looking climb-down from his daring programme of attacking corruption up to his own day – he confines himself in fact to the dead (1.170–1) – is symptomatic and perhaps symbolic of this powerlessness.

The satires are peopled by many characters whose complaints are deconstructed by their own self-delusions. The client in *Satire* 9, who has been rejected by his patron after unflagging sexual services (to both the patron and his wife), complains to the satirist (playing journalist here) as if he had an unproblematic right to feel aggrieved at his rejection. Juvenal slyly points out that he will expose all of this to the world. Even Umbricius, the 'hero' of *Satire* 3, is hoist with his own petard. This last true Roman is leaving the city because he can't stand its various horrors. In particular, he can't afford it (3.23–4). Rome nowadays is not only full of Greeks (60–1), but is a place where one cannot make an honest living from being a client. The only way to get on, he claims (41ff.), is by bringing yourself to all kinds of crimes, like arranging adultery and complicity in extortion, or lies, like praising an awful book. The target of the satire is undoubtedly the state of things in the venal and wicked city. But Umbricius (a shadow of his former self: *umbra* means 'shade') isn't an uncomplicated mediator of satiric invective. However much the satirist and his implied audience may sympathise with Umbricius' view of Rome, they also see that he is a far-cry from the self-sufficient citizen of Republican myth. The patron–client relationship was never meant to be a way of clients making a living, however honest, and moreover Umbricius says he has *tried* all that flattery, but he isn't any good at it (3.92–3). Umbricius blames the Greeks and everyone else except himself for his own impotent dependency.

If Umbricius is bigoted in his hatred of Greeks and other foreigners, he is outdone by the speaker of *Satire* 2 in his hatred of pathics and by that of *Satire* 6 in his hatred of Roman wives. This latter poem, nearly 700 lines of invective on the horrors of womankind, is a satiric development of a standard rhetorical debating point: Should one marry? The answer is clearly 'no', unless you want to be associated with a disgusting creature who is sick in public or, even worse, gives her opinion on literature! The joke on literature is part of the Juvenalian programme from the beginning: the collection opens with the complaint that he is so fed up with contemporary poetry that he feels he ought to have a chance to bore others for a change. Not infrequently Juvenal will bring a climax (or rather anti-climax) to a crescendo of crimes with an ironic joke about literature, as here. But there is a real misogynistic point too, for the woman is presented as if she actually were throwing up literary criticism in public, so distasteful is the idea of a literary woman.

There is an important point about persona here also. We can say that the ironic undercutting created by the literature joke exposes the absurdity of the speaker's viewpoint. We can say, also, that what is being satirised in this poem is precisely the extremist bigotry that the speaker displays. Many modern readers would find this a more comfortable approach to the poem than a straight reading. We should not, however, allow the device of 'persona' to remove the misogyny of the poem. That way we risk colluding in its attitude even while we try to deny its 'sincerity'.

Just as Horace has his violent moments, so Juvenal has his gentler, more Horatian moments. It is in his fourth book (poems 10–12) that Juvenal comes closest to the style of his genial predecessor, and is most overtly intertextual with him. The blessings of poverty are celebrated in contrast with the extravagance and excesses of wealth, and the dangers to the wealthy. In *Satire* 11, a variation on the dinner party set-piece, there is an invitation to join the poet in simple fare (this is a common *topos*) as was enjoyed by old-fashioned senators who tilled the land, ran the state and fought its wars, all as a seamless whole. The poem is filled with nostalgia for Horatian nostalgia for a lost world of Republican innocence. Since it is addressed to someone whose name, Persicus, suggests Eastern luxury, the poem may have an indirect satiric bite.

In the final book, we are back to ranting, but the tone is now more cynical, perhaps 'older and wiser'. *Satire* 14, about the way immoral behaviour is inherited by children from their parents, could almost be the inspiration for Philip Larkin's famous, despairing poem *This Be The Verse*, which opens: 'They fuck you up, your mum and dad./They may not mean to, but they do.' Similar is poem 8, which abuses degenerate members of grand families for failing the ways of their ancestors. One can imagine many a Roman father saying the same thing. Satire can effectively not only police antisocial behaviour, but also expose the violence of that act of policing.

Notes

1 R. Syme, 'The *patria* of Juvenal', *Roman Papers*, vol. 3 (ed. A.R. Birley), Oxford: Oxford University Press, 1984, pp. 1120–34, esp. p. 1120. Clear discussions can be found in S. Braund's introduction to the Cambridge Greek and Latin Classics edition and in her *Roman Verse Satire* (1992).

2 See Braund, *The Roman Satirists and Their Masks*, Bristol: Bristol Classical Press, 1996, pp. 5–9.

3 With this, we might compare the way in which Tacitus, at around the same time, was trying to show how it was possible for an upright Roman aristocrat to follow a conventional public career and even to prosper under tyrannical emperors, though Tacitus also is full of contempt for flatterers.

See also in this book

Archilochus, Horace, Martial

Texts, translations and commentaries

There is an OCT by W.V. Clausen (1992) in which Juvenal shares space with the Neronian satirist Persius, the omission of whom from this book is my first regret. There is also a Teubner edition by J. Willis (1997).

The Penguin edition is by Peter Green (1967) and the World's Classics version by Niall Rudd (1992).

A substantial commentary is E. Courtney, *A Commentary on the Satires of Juvenal* (London: Athlone, 1980). More accessible is a Cambridge Greek and Latin Classics edition by S. Braund of a selection of *Satires*.

Further reading

Braund, S., *Beyond Anger: A Study of Juvenal's Third Book of Satires*, Cambridge: Cambridge University Press, 1988.

Braund, S., *Roman Verse Satire*, Greece and Rome New Surveys in the Classics 23, Oxford: Oxford University Press for the Classical Association, 1992.

Braund, S., *The Roman Satirists and Their Masks*, Bristol: Bristol Classical Press, 1996.

Henderson, J.G.W., *Figuring Out Roman Nobility: Juvenal's Eighth Satire*, Exeter: Exeter University Press, 1997.

Syme, R., *Roman Papers*, vol. 3 (ed. A.R. Birley), Oxford: Oxford University Press, 1984, chaps 80–1.

(NOT) THE END

LUCIAN

Lucian has won many admirers over the centuries, but perhaps the most prestigious was Erasmus, whose *Praise of Folly* and *Colloquies* interact extensively with the works of this talented writer. It was perhaps the range of Lucian's humour that Erasmus found particularly appealing:

> All the dark humour which men attribute to Momus and all the light they ascribe to Mercury may be found in plenty united in the one Lucian.

> (Erasmus, in the preface to his translation of Lucian's *Alexander*)

Not only Erasmus, but also Thomas More, Rabelais, Voltaire, Henry Fielding and Jules Verne were all influenced by Lucian in various ways.

The cultural background of Lucian was eclectic. He was born in *c.* AD 120 in Samosata, a fortified city on the bank of the river Euphrates in Commagene, which had only been incorporated in the Roman province of Syria in AD 72. Iranian and Greek traditions were blended together in this place, which was also an important commercial centre from where merchants could travel to Persia and to India. Lucian wrote in Greek, but his mother tongue was probably an Aramaic dialect known as Syriac.[1]

If we take at face value what he says in one of his works, Lucian came from a poor family and initially served his apprenticeship as a sculptor with his uncle, until confronted in a dream by two women. One was squalid and masculine (Sculpture), while the other was beautiful and neatly dressed (Education): Lucian claims to have been won over by the latter, who took him on a chariot ride 'from the East all the way round to the West' (*The Dream* 15) so that he could see what he would have missed if he had chosen Sculpture, whose anger at losing her disciple (appropriately enough) makes her turn to stone like Niobe. The device of the significant dream might make us think of Hesiod and Callimachus meeting the Muses in their sleep, but here Lucian creates humour and bathos by polarising the portraits of Sculpture and Education so sharply, in the manner of Xenophon's portrait of Hercules choosing between Virtue and Vice (*Memorabilia* 2.1.21–34).

It seems that the chariot ride with Education reflected real travels undertaken by Lucian in his professional capacity as a rhetorician.[2]

In another work, he depicts personifications of Rhetoric (female) and Dialogue (male) arguing with one another about him. Rhetoric plays the part of the scorned wife and claims that Lucian owes her something for her services:

> On our travels in Greece and in Ionia I do not lay so much emphasis; but when he took a fancy to go to Italy, I crossed the Adriatic with him and finally I journeyed with him as far as Gaul, where I made him rich.

> (*Twice Accused* 27)

Nor is Dialogue himself much happier, because Lucian has taken away his respectable tragic mask and replaced it with a comic one.

From this initial sketch, it might appear that the itinerant Lucian was something of a chameleon. The huge variety of his works would certainly endorse that impression. We have about eighty pieces attributed to him, although not all of these are genuine. About half are in dialogue format, which allows Lucian scope for creative and vivid characterisation of figures ranging from Zeus down to a cobbler called Micyllus. A few of the dialogues are loosely philosophical, including the *Hermotimus*, where a would-be philosopher Hermotimus is questioned by Lycinus about his motives in studying Stoic doctrines until he resolves to give up his pretensions and live the life of an ordinary man. The dialogue still has a humorous edge to it, as when Hermotimus, during his final renunciation of Stoicism, says: 'I can tell you that I would not flinch from drinking hellebore, for the opposite reasons to Chrysippus – to remember their doctrines no more' (*Hermotimus* 86). Elsewhere, Lucian claims that Chrysippus drank hellebore as a cure for madness (*True Histories* 2.18). Another aspect of the *Hermotimus* which proves particularly enjoyable is the well-observed Socratic tone of the discussion, so evocative of Plato's dialogues. In general, literary parody is one of Lucian's great strengths as a writer.

Other dialogues are more overtly comical, such as the four collections of *Dialogues of the Gods*, *Dialogues of the Dead*, *Dialogues of the Sea-Gods* and *Dialogues of the Courtesans*. These are short, punchy pieces which draw their humour from the audience's knowledge of Homer, Hesiod and Theocritus. In spirit they have something in common with modern comedy sketches, in that they often imaginatively pursue a situation beyond its logical or familiar conclusion. As Bracht Branham says of these dialogues,

'[Lucian's] subject is the implicit dimension of tradition, the curious and comic paradoxes the old myths generate if reimagined as literally true'.[3]

So, for example, we are given a conversation between the petulant cyclops, Polyphemus, who has been recently blinded by Odysseus, and Polyphemus' father, Poseidon (*Dialogues of the Sea-Gods* 2). Lucian exploits the format to make Polyphemus appear even more stupid than in *Odyssey* 9. When Poseidon asks his son how Odysseus managed to escape from the cave, he adds: 'I'm sure that he couldn't have moved the rock from the doorway'. Polyphemus replies: 'No, I did that myself', amusingly implying that he was obliging (and foolish) enough to help his enemy to escape. The audience's knowledge of the original text is also exploited. When Polyphemus demurely tells his father that Odysseus used some sweet and pleasant-smelling drug to lull him to sleep, we remember that in the *Odyssey*, it was actually three bowls of wine which the Cyclops guzzled before collapsing in a drunken stupor. Polyphemus is behaving like an evasive teenager who doesn't give the full story to a parent. It is almost as if Poseidon is wryly nudging us to remember the Homeric version when he exclaims: 'How soundly you must have slept, my son, if you didn't jump while he was blinding you!' This dialogue is typical in the techniques Lucian uses to create humour.

The other half of Lucian's extraordinary *corpus* is not in dialogue form. There is *Demonax*, a biography about a contemporary Cypriot philosopher of the same name, which consists largely of Demonax's witty rejoinders and wry observations about people. Jones says that its 'anecdotal style is also a bow to tradition, having its origins in Xenophon's recollections of Socrates'.[4] We also have rhetorical exercises, both genuine and spoof (such as the *Trial of the Consonants*), speeches of praise (likewise including a playful version, *In Praise of the Fly*), letters (such as *How to Write History*), parodies of tragedy (such as *Gout*), *prolaliai* ('preliminary chats', which can describe buildings or paintings and often inspired real painters, particularly during the Renaissance) and novels (such as *Lucius* or *The Ass*).

Perhaps Lucian's best-known piece is the *True Histories*. This is an account of some extraordinary adventures, narrated by Lucian in the first-person singular, after he sails through the Pillars of Hercules with a crew to find out who lives across the ocean. The story moves from their arrival on the moon and their service as mercenaries during a war with the sun, to their time spent in the belly of an enormous whale which swallowed their ship ('a parody of the

Charybdis episode in *Odyssey* 12.431')[5] and finally to their stay on the Island of the Blest. On their travels, they encounter various extraordinary people, such as the pumpkin pirates, who sail around in hollow pumpkins sixty cubits long (*True Histories* 2.37), or the men who float around on their backs using their penises as masts, complete with sails attached (*True Histories* 2.45). At the end of the second book, the narrative closes with a promise of further tales, but these aren't given.

The humour of this work functions on many different levels. Lucian characterises the narrative as a relaxation for students normally immersed in serious works, but at the same time he highlights the fact that it parodies various historians, poets and philosophers, setting up a 'spot the allusion' competition in the prologue. Yet, as Jones emphasises, 'though much of Lucian's humor is literary, the work is not thereby made other-worldly or scholastic'.[6]

Historiography comes in for sustained jokes, the first of which is the reversal of the typical protestation that the narrator is telling the truth:

> Be it understood then, that I am writing about things which I have neither seen nor had anything to do with nor learned from others – which do not in fact exist at all and, in the nature of things, cannot exist at all.

> (*True Histories* 1.4)

The status of autopsy, so important to historians such as Polybius, is also targeted here. Not surprisingly Herodotus becomes a running joke. On a mysterious island, they find a faded inscription in Greek noting that Hercules and Dionysus had come this far, together with two huge footprints in the rock, one a hundred feet long and the other slightly smaller. This recalls Herodotus' description of a mysterious footprint in Scythia: 'They show you a rock with the imprint of Hercules' foot; it looks like a human footprint, but it is three feet long' (*Histories* 4.82). Everything on this journey will be larger than life and this instance sets the pattern for what follows.

There are other jokes at the expense of historiography too, including an ethnographical excursus documenting the habits of the people on the moon (*True Histories* 1.22–6) and a miniature account of a war between the Selenites and Heliots (*True Histories* 1.12–21), complete with a spoof battle narrative. It may be that the details of the war, such as the disputed colonies and the peace treaty, are meant to recall in general terms Thucydides' narrative of the Peloponnesian War. We can also see humour in, for example, Lucian's criticism of Homer for a misleading description of the city on the Island of Dreams (*True Histories* 2.32). Historians often added authority to their narrative voice by condemning their predecessors, whether this involved Polybius attacking Timaeus or Livy attacking Valerius Antias. Yet the context of Lucian's quibble is intrinsically ridiculous. There is humour in his deadpan application of standard historiographical techniques to a place which doesn't even exist, especially when he adds a topographical description.[7]

Lucian also casts himself as Odysseus at various points, and the way in which he sometimes loses members of his crew on the journey recalls the same process in the *Odyssey*. In fact, he even meets Homer and Odysseus on the Island of the Blest (*True Histories* 2.15) and takes the opportunity to ask the poet a series of classic Homeric questions, such as where he came from and whether he wrote the *Odyssey* before the *Iliad*, to which he says 'no' (just as modern scholars have established using philology!). When Lucian is forced to leave the island, Homer writes a hexameter couplet for him, the miniaturised nature of which interacts playfully with the huge scale of the epics. The same sort of game is played when Odysseus (without Penelope's knowledge) entrusts Lucian with a letter for Calypso that boils down in unadorned prose the entire plot of the *Odyssey* and beyond (*True Histories* 2.35).

This highly inventive work inspired subsequent story-tellers, such as the continuators of Rudolf Raspe's *Adventures of Baron Münchausen*, and it remains Lucian's most popular work today. Yet it is only a small part of a hybrid *corpus*, whose diverse nature makes Lucian a difficult figure to categorise. He was certainly a leading light of the revival of Greek literature known as the Second Sophistic; his achievement is particularly impressive if we remember that Greek was not even his mother tongue.

Notes

1 See C.P. Jones, *Culture and Society in Lucian*, Cambridge, MA, and London: Harvard University Press, 1986, pp. 6–7.

2 See J. Hall, *Lucian's Satire*, New York: Arno Press, 1981, pp. 16–44, for Lucian's life and travels.

3 R. Bracht Branham, *Unruly Eloquence: Lucian and the Comedy of Traditions*, Cambridge, MA, and London: Harvard University Press, 1989, p. 143.

4   Jones, *op. cit.*, p. 91.
5   A. Georgiadou and D.H.J. Larmour, 'Lucian and historiography: *De Historia Conscribenda* and *Verae Historiae*', *Aufstieg und Niedergang der römischen Welt*, II.34.2, 1994, p. 1490.
6   Jones, *op. cit.*, p. 54.
7   See Georgiadou and Larmour, *op. cit.*, pp. 1494–1500, for further categories of historiographical joke.

See also in this book

Apuleius, Homer, Polybius, Thucydides, Xenophon

Texts, translations and commentaries

The Greek text is available in OCT (4 volumes) and Loeb (8 volumes).
    There are no Penguin or Oxford World's Classics translations, so the Loeb translation is particularly important.
    There is a commentary on *Lucian: A Selection* (namely, *The Dream, The Judging of the Goddesses, The Assembly of the Gods, The Fisherman, Menippus, On the Death of Peregrinus, On Sacrifices, Zeuxis* and *How to Write History*) by M.D. MacLeod in the Aris and Phillips Series.

Further reading

Anderson, G., *Lucian: Theme and Variation in the Second Sophistic*, Leiden: Brill, 1976.
Baldwin, B., *Studies in Lucian*, Toronto, Ont.: Hakkert, 1973.
Bracht Branham, R., *Unruly Eloquence: Lucian and the Comedy of Traditions*, Cambridge, MA, and London: Harvard University Press, 1989.
Georgiadou, A. and Larmour, D.H.J., 'Lucian and historiography: *De Historia Conscribenda* and *Verae Historiae*', *Aufstieg und Niedergang der römischen Welt*, II.34.2, 1994, pp. 1448–1509.
Hall, J., *Lucian's Satire*, New York: Arno Press, 1981.
Jones, C.P., *Culture and Society in Lucian*, Cambridge, MA, and London: Harvard University Press, 1986.
Robinson, C., *Lucian and His Influence in Europe*, London and Chapel Hill, NC: University of North Carolina Press, 1979.
Swain, S., *Hellenism and Empire: Language, Classicism and Power in the Greek World AD 50–250*, Oxford: Oxford University Press, 1996.

APULEIUS

We are extremely lucky to be able to read Apuleius' novel, the *Metamorphoses* or *Golden Ass*. If it hadn't been for a single manuscript, which was copied in Monte Cassino late in the eleventh century, we would have been left entirely in the dark. So too would various writers and artists who drew inspiration from the text:

Boccaccio adapted some of the adultery stories of *Golden Ass* Book 9 when writing his *Decameron*, Shakespeare in *A Midsummer Night's Dream* drew on Apuleius for his comic character Bottom, and Raphael was inspired by the inset story of Cupid and Psyche when painting the ceiling of the Villa Farnesina in Rome. Particularly over the last thirty years, this sophisticated and hugely enjoyable novel has drawn the attention of modern scholars, especially those interested in narratology and literary theory. There have been regular colloquia held in Groningen by Hofmann to examine all aspects of the ancient novel, which is still a relatively new area of specialisation.

So what do we know about Apuleius? He came from Madauros in North Africa, where he was born in about AD 125, and his mother tongue was probably Punic, though he later lectured in both Latin and Greek (*Florida* 18.38).[1] Having been educated in Carthage, Athens and Rome, he developed interests in philosophy and rhetoric, both of which come to fruition in the *Golden Ass*. His diverse cultural experiences are reflected in the variety of his works, although many are now unfortunately lost. As well as the *Golden Ass*, we have the *Florida*,[2] a collection of twenty-three extracts from his speeches; the *Apologia*,[3] a speech of defence delivered in AD 158/9 against a charge of having used magic to lure a widow called Pudentilla into marriage; and the *De Deo Socratis*,[4] a philosophical monograph about demons that reveals Apuleius' fundamental interest in Plato. Works which have not survived include another novel, the *Hermagoras*; a study of trees, the *De Arboribus*; a treatise on politics, the *De Republica*, whose title evokes Cicero; as well as monographs on music, astronomy and arithmetic.[5] Apuleius died at some point after AD 170.

Apuleius was a polymath (and certainly represents himself as such). The range of his interests recalls only a few previous ancient writers, perhaps Seneca the Younger above all. Indeed, he called another lost work the *Naturales Quaestiones* – a title designed to trigger associations with Seneca. We can see that Apuleius liked to name his own works in such a way as to recall other authors (for example, *De Republica*, *Naturales Quaestiones* and *Metamorphoses*, this last his own title for the novel that is now often known as the *Golden Ass*), which suggests a strong rivalry with previous literary giants. Perhaps as a non-native speaker of Latin, who spent much of his life away from the centre of the empire in Rome, Apuleius felt the need to claim his place in the Roman literary tradition. As we shall see, there are many allusions to earlier Latin authors in the *Golden Ass*, which may project the same message.

The eleven books of the *Golden Ass* follow the adventures of a Greek called Lucius, who lives in Corinth. In a complex and varied narrative, Apuleius often uses the Alexandrian device of the inset story, such a pervasive feature of Ovid's *Metamorphoses*. The structure of the novel is (unevenly) tripartite: Books 1–3 narrate what happens to Lucius before becoming an ass, Books 4–10 relate his experiences as an ass and Book 11 explains his transformation back into human form, through the intervention of Isis, and his initiation into the rites of that goddess.[6]

We first meet Lucius in Book 1, travelling to Hypata in Thessaly on a business trip. On the journey, he encounters two travellers, one of whom tells him about his friend Socrates, who was seduced by an innkeeper called Meroe while travelling through Macedonia on business. Aristomenes (the traveller) and Socrates share a room for the night, but their sleep is interrupted when two old women break into their room. In a violent scene, one of the women, Meroe, appears to kill Socrates and the terrified Aristomenes tries to escape, but is prevented from doing so by the doorkeeper. The next morning it transpires that Socrates is still alive, so the relieved pair leave the inn. Soon, however, Socrates dies on the road of the wound that he sustained on the previous night. So ends the first inset story. Lucius continues his journey to Hypata, where he stays with a man called Milo.

In Book 2 Lucius meets his aunt Byrrhena, who warns him that Milo's wife Pamphile is a dangerous witch. This only serves to stir up Lucius' curiosity, so using a strategy that recalls love elegy, he decides to seduce Pamphile's maid, Photis. After some delay, Lucius is successful. Soon afterwards, Byrrhena invites her nephew for supper, where we hear the inset story of a man Thelyphron, which involves mutilation and necromancy. On the way home, Lucius encounters three figures in the dark and kills them, thinking that they are robbers.

In Book 3 Lucius finds himself hauled up before the magistrates on a murder charge and defends himself in the packed theatre where the trial is held. He becomes particularly worried upon seeing that the whole crowd is laughing after his speech. However, the corpses of the three victims turn out to be wineskins, brought to life by Pamphile, and Lucius has been the victim of a collective practical joke – the centrepiece of the so-called 'Festival of Laughter'. Lucius is more determined than ever to see Pamphile in action and when, a few days later, she turns herself into an owl, Lucius asks Photis to help him to undergo a similar metamorphosis. Unfortunately, she uses the wrong ointment, which turns him into an ass, and before the maid can turn him back into human form by making him chew rose petals, Lucius is captured by robbers, who take him to their mountain lair. So ends the first segment of the tripartite novel.

In Book 4, after various robbers arrive (giving Apuleius the opportunity to create further inset stories), a young girl, Charite, is brought to the lair as a hostage and an old woman distracts her from her troubles with a long tale about Cupid and Psyche. This famous story straddles several books (4.28–6.24) and relates the sufferings of a beautiful young girl, Psyche, at the hands of the jealous Venus. Cast out by her family, Psyche marries Cupid, although he never appears to her in his true form. Her curiosity (aroused by her jealous sisters) eventually prompts her to take a lamp into their bedroom to identify him. As a result, Cupid flies off and Psyche is forced to begin a miserable series of wanderings and tasks for Venus until Jupiter intervenes. The story ends happily when Cupid and Psyche marry properly and give birth to Pleasure. In the rest of Book 6 Lucius escapes briefly with Charite but is recaptured and faces the horrible prospect of having the vengeful robbers sew Charite inside him and leave the pair to die in the sun. In Book 7 a new robber, Haemus the Thracian, arrives and argues that the proposed punishment of the ass and the girl will be a waste of money. Fortunately, it turns out that this man is in fact Charite's bridegroom Tlepolemus, who successfully engineers their escape. Charite wants to reward the ass, but this backfires when Lucius is sent off to an unscrupulous married couple in the countryside who put him to work instead.

In Book 8 a man arrives with the story of Charite's death, and when her servants leave, they take Lucius the ass with them. He is eventually sold to a priest called Philebus, but faces further peril when a cook decides to butcher the ass to replace a haunch of meat which has been stolen by dogs. In Book 9 Lucius avoids the immediate danger by making people think that he is rabid. Four tales of adulterous love affairs are inserted into the rest of this book, during which Lucius is sold first to a baker (9.10) and then to a gardener (9.31). In Book 10 there are further inset stories, including the tale of the lecherous stepmother. Lucius is sold (10.13) to a pastry cook and a chef, who are delighted that he enjoys gourmet food and turn him into something of a local celebrity. As a result an infatuated local woman arranges with his owner that she should spend the night with the ass. A bizarre night of love-making follows. Lucius' owner decides to offer the spectacle to the public, with a condemned woman in the role of the respectable matron. Lucius manages to escape just in time.

In the final section of the novel, Book 11, Lucius prays for deliverance and is confronted with the vision of a lovely goddess, who turns out to be Isis. She tells him of a lavish procession to take place on the following day, which will include a priest carrying a garland of roses. Lucius duly eats the roses which enable him to regain his human form. The delighted Lucius is eventually initiated into the service of Isis in an elaborate ritual and travels to Rome to undergo further initiation rites into the cult of Osiris, the brother and husband of Isis. In a final twist, the identities of Lucius the character and Apuleius the narrator seem to merge, as the suggestively named priest Asinius Marcellus dreams that a man from Madaurus (Apuleius' home town) is being sent to him for initiation (11.27).[7] Thus the novel ends.

The sheer entertainment value of the main narrative is thus overlaid at the end with a more serious message, which prompts us to reconsider the picaresque adventures of Lucius. At the start of the novel, Lucius appears to be rather a flawed character, who seems incapable of learning from experience. Despite hearing the chilling and programmatic tale about Socrates, who is killed in mysterious circumstances by the witch Meroe (1.19), and despite being warned by his aunt Byrrhena that his host's wife Pamphile is a witch (2.5), Lucius cannot suppress his curiosity:[8] 'I am one who desires most passionately to know magic at first-hand' (3.19), as he announces to his lover Photis. Lucius is also firmly rooted in the world of the sensual, taking every opportunity to satisfy his sexual appetite with the obliging Photis. He clearly cannot resist temptation of any sort, even if it means putting himself in danger. So although Photis warns him not to stay late at Byrrhena's dinner party because of some recent murders in the town (2.18), the drunken Lucius has to be prompted by his slave to leave (2.31). When he does get turned into an ass, it feels as if it is his own fault. A different personality in the same situation wouldn't have been tempted to meddle with such dangerous powers.

Yet once he has become an ass, we begin to see him learning from experience. He appears to become ambivalent about sexual desire: not only does he disapprove of Charite's obvious attraction for the 'robber' Haemus (7.10), but he also feels a sense of shame about making love to the condemned woman in public and runs away

(10.35). Even the series of tales about adulterous love affairs in Book 9 projects a message about the perils of infidelity, which pulls against our impression of the hedonistic Lucius in human form.

Certainly, there are times when the ass gives in to pleasure, as when he indulges his desire for choice human food (10.13–17) and when he makes love to the matron (10.20–2). Yet generally he seems more aware of the likely consequences of his actions than when he was in human form. His intense misery has, it seems, started to make him wiser, as he realises what he has lost. As he says in a moment of reflection, '[a]s I recalled the happy state of the old Lucius, now driven to utter degradation, I lowered my head and grieved' (9.13). It is suggestive that when Lucius finally eats the garland of roses which will transform him, Apuleius uses richly hedonistic language: *coroneam ... auido ore susceptam cupidus promissi cupidissime deuoraui* ('I took up the wreath with greedy mouth and, eager for the promised result, I wolfed it down most passionately', 11.13). Such sensual language, just at the moment when Lucius is about to enter a new life of worship and celibacy as a priest of Isis, is pointed. Even the means of his salvation, the garland of roses, had appeared before in a more morally ambiguous context, adorning Photis' breasts as they are about to make love (2.16). Lucius still feels desire, but it is directed at an entirely different end from before.

We are further encouraged to read the double transformation of Lucius in a moral light by the priest who speaks to him after the final metamorphosis:

> Not your birth, not even your position, nor even your fine education has helped you at all; but on the slippery path of headstrong youth you plunged into slavish pleasures and reaped the perverse reward of your unlucky curiosity.
>
> (11.15)

Even the language in which the priest urges him to 'enlist in this holy army, to whose oath of allegiance you were summoned not long ago' (11.15) reminds us of the old Lucius. Previously Lucius and Photis used to speak in military metaphors to fire up their sexual passion (2.16–17), so the priest's recollection of this language in a new context is pointed. By the end of the novel, Lucius has undergone a spiritual as well as a physical metamorphosis, although this has only been triggered by the intervention of Isis, just as Psyche in the inset story is rescued by Jupiter, who eventually takes pity on her.

It is important to stress that the entertaining narrative of the *Golden Ass* never gets weighed down by its moral message, which is only activated in the final book. There are certainly many other issues which the text raises for critics. Apuleius' intertextuality, for instance, would have enhanced the enjoyment of the work for educated readers. Harrison argues that

> it is not an exaggeration to state that the *Metamorphoses* (like Petronius' *Satyricon*) often has a depth of literary allusion which rivals that of the richest Augustan poetry.[9]

One scene which creatively engages with another text is when Lucius, after arriving in Hypata, visits his aunt Byrrhena's house and sees in the atrium a vivid sculpture of the goddess Diana surrounded by hounds, about to bathe in a delightful pool. In the background lurks Actaeon, 'already animal-like, on the point of becoming a stag as he waited for Diana to take her bath' (2.4). The description of sculpture can be constructively compared with Ovid's version of the same myth at *Metamorphoses* 3.138–252. One of the most suggestive differences between the two passages lies in the fact that whereas Ovid's Actaeon is absolved from all blame at the start of the narrative and stumbles upon Diana entirely by accident, Apuleius' Actaeon is gripped by curiosity and leans towards the goddess inquisitively. The depiction of such self-destructive curiosity is particularly pointed given that Lucius' own transformation will be brought about for the same reason: Apuleius' Actaeon and Lucius are their own worst enemies. We might also consider that Ovid's Actaeon-as-stag will be killed by hunting dogs and Apuleius' Lucius will subsequently be attacked by dogs when fleeing with Charite's household (8.17).

Apuleius can also play with various prose genres, including historiography. This is a particularly mischievous target for the author of a creative fiction, given that ancient historians regularly claim to be creating a factually accurate narrative. So, when Apuleius describes the robbers' mountain lair, he does so in terms which recall the standard topographical descriptions from historiography:

> The subject and the occasion itself demand that I lay out a description of the region and that cave which the robbers inhabit, for thus I shall both put my talent to the test and let

you effectively perceive whether in mind and perception I
was the ass that I appeared to be.

(4.6; cf. Sallust Jugurtha 17.1 or Livy 26.42.7)

There may even be a specific echo here of Sallust's description of a
daunting mountain lair near the river Muluccha, the scene of a
daring raid by Marius (*Jugurtha* 92.5–9).[10] There is clearly an
amusingly misplaced grandeur in filtering this description of a lowly
bandit hideout through the impressive set-pieces of ancient
historiography, but this also helps to deepen the character of Lucius.
Since Lucius is acutely aware of the metaphorical association
between the ass and stupidity, he resorts to literary allusion as a
desperate measure to suggest that he isn't as stupid as he looks.

Not even epic is immune, and indeed Harrison proposes that the
Golden Ass 'is particularly concerned with highlighting its similarities with and its differences from epic'.[11] So, at the beginning of
Book 3 Apuleius offers a grandiose description of the sunrise, which
recalls standard epic versions of dawn and successfully trumps his
own depiction of dawn at the start of Book 2:

> No sooner had Aurora begun to ride her horses with their
> crimson trappings across the sky, shaking her rosy arm, than
> I was torn from carefree sleep ...

(3.1)[12]

Even the location of this image at the beginning of Book 3 is
amusing. To start a book with a description of the dawn
misleadingly suggests a conventional attitude towards narrative
structure, but Apuleius will gradually become more Ovidian, as he
makes stories straddle book-divisions and allows the coherence
between sunrise/sunset and beginnings/endings of books to disin-
tegrate. Even his decision to narrate events in eleven books indicates
that he is deliberately pulling against the traditions of epic poets,
who generally use six, twelve, fifteen, eighteen or twenty-four books,
as commentators have noted. One of the few epics which breaks this
pattern is Silius Italicus' *Punica* in seventeen books, but this
exception proves the rule since the author died before he could
finish his work.

Apuleius' *Golden Ass* is undoubtedly brilliantly creative, but we
need to set it in context. In the prologue, Lucius tells us that 'the
romance on which I am embarking is adapted from the Greek' (1.1).

This claim naturally raises questions about originality, since we know from a reference to Photius in the ninth century that an author called Lucius of Patrae wrote the Greek version of the story to which Lucius is made to refer. Some trace of this work remains: the Greek writer Lucian preserves an abridged form of the original called *Lucius* or *The Ass*. Should we therefore knock Apuleius from his pedestal? Scholars suggest that to do so would be hasty. Although the basic outline of the story and some of the main characters are foreshadowed in Lucian's summary, the inset tales (including the central narrative of Cupid and Psyche) and the eleventh book about Isis are almost certainly Apuleius' own creations. The general consensus is that Apuleius has taken the bare skeleton of a short story in Greek and fleshed it out in his own unique fashion. The result is certainly very different from the modern notion of a novel, but it is a work which is winning more and more attention from modern audiences.

Notes

1 See S.J. Harrison, *Apuleius. A Latin Sophist*, Oxford: Oxford University Press, 2000, pp. 1–10, on Apuleius' life.
2 See Harrison, *Apuleius. A Latin Sophist*, pp. 89–135.
3 See Harrison, *Apuleius. A Latin Sophist*, pp. 39–88.
4 See Harrison, *Apuleius. A Latin Sophist*, pp. 136–73.
5 See Harrison, *Apuleius. A Latin Sophist*, pp. 16–36, for the lost works.
6 J. Tatum, *Apuleius and the Golden Ass*, Ithaca, NY, and London: Cornell University Press, 1979, pp. 24–91, discusses the books in order.
7 On this blurring of identities between author and narrator, see further the narratological study of J.J. Winkler, *Auctor and Actor: A Narratological Reading of Apuleius' Golden Ass*, Berkeley, CA: University of California Press, 1985; Harrison, *Apuleius. A Latin Sophist*, pp. 226–35; and R.T. Van Der Paadrt, 'The unmasked "I": Apuleius *Metamorphoses* 11.27', in S.J. Harrison (ed.), *Oxford Readings in the Roman Novel*, Oxford: Oxford University Press, 1999, pp. 237–46.
8 On Lucius' curiosity, see J. DeFilippo, '*Curiositas* and the Platonism of Apuleius' *Golden Ass*', in Harrison, *Oxford Readings in the Roman Novel*, pp. 272–7.
9 Harrison, *Apuleius. A Latin Sophist*, p. 222.
10 See E.D. Finkelpearl, *Metamorphosis of Language in Apuleius: A Study of Allusion in the Novel*, Ann Arbor, MI: University of Michigan Press, 1998, pp. 50–3, for other examples of Apuleius parodying Sallust.
11 Harrison, *Apuleius. A Latin Sophist*, p. 222.
12 See Finkelpearl, *Metamorphosis of Language in Apuleius*, p. 86.

See also in this book

Longus, Lucian, Petronius

Texts, translations and commentaries

The Latin text is available in Teubner and Loeb.

Apart from the new Loeb, there is an Oxford World's Classics translation by P.G. Walsh and a Penguin translation by E.J. Kenney.

There are commentaries on *Golden Ass* 4.28–6.24 (*Apuleius: Cupid and Psyche*) by E.J. Kenney in the Cambridge Greek and Latin Classics Imperial Series; on *Metamorphoses 1* by A. Scobie (published by Hain); and on *Apuleius of Madauros: The Isis Book (Metamorphoses XI)* by J. Gwyn Griffiths (published by Brill).

Further reading

Finkelpearl, E.D., *Metamorphosis of Language in Apuleius: A Study of Allusion in the Novel*, Ann Arbor, MI: University of Michigan Press, 1998.

Hägg, T., *The Novel in Antiquity*, Berkeley and Los Angeles, CA: University of California Press, 1983.

Harrison, S.J. (ed.), *Oxford Readings in the Roman Novel*, Oxford: Oxford University Press, 1999.

Harrison, S.J., *Apuleius. A Latin Sophist*, Oxford: Oxford University Press, 2000.

Hofmann, H. (ed.), *Latin Fiction: The Latin Novel in Context*, London and New York: Routledge, 1999.

Tatum, J., *Apuleius and the Golden Ass*, Ithaca, NY, and London: Cornell University Press, 1979.

Tatum, J. (ed.), *The Search for the Ancient Novel*, Baltimore, MD, and London: Johns Hopkins University Press, 1994.

Walsh, P.G., *The Roman Novel*, Cambridge: Cambridge University Press, 1970.

Winkler, J.J., *Auctor and Actor: A Narratological Reading of Apuleius' Golden Ass*, Berkeley, CA: University of California Press, 1985.

LONGUS

One of Longus' most enthusiastic readers was Goethe, whose passion for the novel *Daphnis and Chloe* is clear from his advice as an old man to Eckermann: 'You should read it anew each year to learn from it over and over again and be influenced by its great beauty'. There is certainly something moving about the fondness of an old man for an idyllic novel with a central romance between two teenagers, frozen in time. Not everybody reacted so favourably. At one stage, Longus' novel was regarded as a lightweight diversion, 'a most sweet and pleasant pastoral romance for ladies' as Thornley suggested in 1657. Critics tended to observe the surface charm of the romance between the naïve rustic adolescents Daphnis and Chloe, and then to dismiss the novel as a banal work that couldn't possibly appeal to a sophisticated readership. Such reluctance to look below the surface fortunately no longer prevails. As Bowie and Harrison comment:

> Now the ancient novel has become one of the hottest properties in town, even if its pursuit is still seen as trivial by the strait-laced.[1]

Longus' *Daphnis and Chloe* is in many ways the least typical of the various Greek novels which survive. There are five central works in this genre. The earliest is probably Chariton of Aphrodisias' *Chaereas and Callirhoe*, a historical novel set in the fourth century BC which was perhaps written in the first century AD, although earlier and later dates have also been suggested. The heroine, Callirhoe, is the daughter of a historical character, the Syracusan general Hermocrates who defeated the Athenians during their expedition to Sicily (415–413 BC), and the hero, Chaereas, is the son of Hermocrates' rival Ariston. Although the two marry despite tensions between their families, they are soon separated after the jealous Chaereas kicks Callirhoe, who seems dead as a result and is placed in a tomb. However, as so often happens in the world of the novel, appearances are deceptive and Callirhoe survives. After a bizarre and sometimes harrowing chain of events, the husband and wife are eventually reunited.[2] Chariton's novel contains allusions to both Homer and Thucydides.

The next novel, written perhaps between AD 100 and 150, is Xenophon of Ephesus' *Ephesian Tale*, about the adventures of a young married couple, Anthia and Habrocomes, who are sent away from Ephesus after a sombre oracle issued by Apollo. After being captured by pirates, the two are separated and undergo various misfortunes before finding one another again. This novel may be an abridged version of a longer original.[3]

Third, there is Achilles Tatius' *Leucippe and Clitophon*, written perhaps at the end of the second century AD and, if surviving papyri are anything to go by, popular with ancient audiences. This novel is (unusually) narrated in the first person by Clitophon, a young man from Tyre, who recounts what happens to him after falling in love with his cousin Leucippe.[4] They elope with one another, but are shipwrecked in Egypt and captured by robbers, which marks the start of a series of escapades and narrow escapes, culminating in their wedding at Byzantium. The novel contains plenty of digressions and quotations from other ancient authors, above all Homer.

Fourth, there is Longus' *Daphnis and Chloe*, written perhaps around AD 200[5] and, as we shall see, emblematic of the revival of Greek literature known as the Second Sophistic. Finally, there is the longest novel, Heliodorus' *Ethiopian Story*, which may have been written in the third century AD. It tells the story of Chariclea, the beautiful white-skinned daughter of the dark-skinned king and queen of Egypt, who is exposed at birth, and Theagenes, a young Thessalian nobleman. We first meet the pair on a beach in Egypt, surrounded by bodies after a shipwreck, but the climax of the novel comes when Chariclea and Theagenes are captured by Ethiopians, who decide to sacrifice them at Meroe. Fortunately, Chariclea's true identity is revealed in time. The pair marry and become priest and priestess of the sun.[6]

As well as these five central novels, we have a number of fragments from lost texts, such as the *Ninus* (one of the earliest Greek novels, perhaps first century BC, but published for modern consumption in 1893), a romance about an Assyrian king Ninus who is in love with his cousin Semiramis, as well as *Metiochus and Parthenope* (first century AD), set in Polycrates' palace on Samos, and Lollianus' *Phoenician Story* (mid-second century AD?), which includes a description of the first sexual experience of a young man Androtimus with a woman called Persis and narrates the dismemberment and roasting of a young boy by robbers.[7]

All of these Greek novels have common themes, although within the basic framework there is huge scope for variety and creativity. The focus is usually on a young couple who fall in love, but whose happiness is threatened by a series of dangers which they sometimes face together, but more frequently have to confront while separated (and searching for one another). Travel around the Mediterranean often features as a unifying device, linking what would otherwise be a succession of detached tales. Despite the difficulties created by short-lived marriages to other people, warfare, amorous rivals and (inevitably) pirates, the idealised love of the couple usually overcomes all obstacles in the end, and marriage (or a happy return to a peaceful married existence in one place) is the result. Within the body of the novel, the author frequently uses direct speech to characterise the protagonists and injects variety by including inset tales. The tone can at times be serious, but there is also scope for comic touches, even parody, and the stories all tend to end happily.

How far does Longus' *Daphnis and Chloe* conform to this broad pattern? One feature which distinguishes Longus from other novelists is that the basic framework of the novel is merged creatively with a pastoral element, which evokes the poetry of Theocritus.[8] Effe refers to 'the bucolization of the novel, or rather the epicization of the bucolic'.[9] The action of Longus' story takes place on Lesbos and, rather than the couple facing trials on their travels, the trouble tends to come to them, which causes a centripetal rather than a centrifugal dynamic within the narrative. This novel is marked by a progressively unsettling clash between the idyllic pastoral world and various corruptions from outside, especially from the urban sphere. Even so, it isn't until the murder of Dorcon and the kidnapping of Daphnis by pirates (1.28) that the arcadian peace is seriously disturbed, although this initial trouble is surprisingly short-lived and Daphnis is quickly rescued (1.31).

Another unusual feature of Longus' text is its relative shortness. The novel's action takes place over four books, whereas there are eight books of Chariton, five books of Xenophon (perhaps an epitome of an original ten), eight books of Achilles Tatius and ten books of Heliodorus. This 'miniaturisation', as it has been called by Bowie,[10] is highly appropriate for a pastoral novel, since it evokes Theocritus' *Idylls* and Virgil's *Eclogues*, both of which operate on an appropriately delicate Callimachean scale. It would perhaps have been incongruous to house this new pastoral novel in the lengthy framework of the traditional novel. Even the inset stories are narrated on rather a delicate scale, never spanning more than a chapter: for example, Daphnis tells a story about a cowgirl who sings of Pan and Pitys (1.27), Lamon tells a story about the origin of pan-pipes (2.34) and Daphnis tells a story about Echo (3.23). We are in a very different world from Apuleius' *Golden Ass*, where the inset story of Cupid and Psyche spans three books (4.28–6.24).

At the very beginning, Longus sets up his novel as an ekphrasis that describes an elegant work of art. In the prologue he explains that, while hunting in Lesbos, he came across a beautiful painting in a sacred grove which depicted

> women giving birth, others dressing the babies, babies exposed, animals suckling them, shepherds adopting them, young people pledging love, a pirates' raid, an enemy attack – and more, much more.[11]

This literary conceit, whereby Longus depicts the painting in words, recalls Virgil's description of the shield in *Aeneid* 8 or Ovid's account of the tapestries of Minerva and Arachne in *Metamorphoses* 6. Longus uses a sophisticated framing device for an apparently simple story, which suggests a creative and dynamic engagement with a literary tradition. There is also a mischievous allusion to Thucydides when Longus playfully calls his work a 'possession for enjoyment' (*Prologue*): that is, a *ktema terpnon* rather than a *ktema es aei* ('possession for all time', Thucydides *Peloponnesian War* 1.22).[12] This allusion is particularly interesting given the close connection which existed between the novel and historiography in the early stages of the genre. Longus also evokes Thucydides when narrating the brief war between the Mytileneans and Methymneans (3.1–2).

In introducing Daphnis and Chloe, Longus uses a motif familiar from tragedy and comedy, whereby both characters are exposed as babies, but are suckled by animals and rescued by simple country people who bring them up as their own. Daphnis is discovered by a goatherd Lamon, while a shepherd called Dryas finds Chloe. The parallel fates of the pair at birth make their subsequent relationship appropriate, or even inevitable, and the device plants the seeds for a predictable escape mechanism later on in the narrative when their true identities are revealed: conveniently, the rescuers carefully gather the crucial tokens of recognition: 'a purple cloak with a gold clasp, and a dagger with an ivory handle' (1.2) for Daphnis and 'a belt threaded with gold, gilded sandals and golden anklets' (1.5) for Chloe. These are clearly no ordinary babies and the tokens duly make their reappearance at the end of the novel (4.19–22, 4.30–1) when the pair's aristocratic identities are revealed to their true parents.

In many ways, Daphnis and Chloe lead charmed lives. Whenever they get into trouble, a benign divinity or a more experienced adult helps them, so that their extraordinary naïveté never causes such severe problems as they would undoubtedly have faced in the real world. So when Daphnis is captured by pirates (1.28), the dying cowherd Dorcon tells Chloe to play on his pipes, since his cows have been trained to respond to the sound. In an engaging scene, the cows, who have been captured together with Daphnis, hear the pipes and stampede to one side of the pirates' ship, which rolls over and tips everyone into the sea. The pirates, who are wearing heavy armour (a symbolic indictment of pillaging and warfare), drown, but Daphnis is brought safely to land by the cows, who are expert swimmers (1.30). Likewise, when Chloe is kidnapped by the

Methymnean soldiers, rather than being raped or taken to the city (which is the worst fate that the naïve Daphnis can imagine at 2.22!), she is saved by divine intervention as Pan appears to the general Bryaxis in a dream and orders him to return Chloe to the shore (2.27).

Even when the pair face less dangerous problems, outside forces intervene with help. One of the novel's most amusing contrivances is the sexual innocence of the virgins Daphnis and Chloe, which means that despite being attracted to one another, they have no clue how to satisfy their lust. They try kissing, taking off their clothes and lying next to each other, as the old man Philetas suggests (2.2–2.7), and they even try copying the sheep and goats as they mate (3.14), but it is no good. A breakthrough is only possible thanks to a sympathetic neighbour's wife, Lycaenion, who decides to kickstart Daphnis' sex life by giving him a practical lesson in the middle of the woods (3.18).[13] On a one-off basis, she plays a benign Mrs Robinson to Daphnis' Benjamin. Inevitably, she is said to come from the town, where the sexual *mores* are traditionally looser than in the countryside. The sexually experienced Lycaenion is even thoughtful enough to point out to Daphnis that love-making with the virgin Chloe might be less straightforward than their own recent tumble in the woods (3.19). As a result, the worried Daphnis postpones mutual sexual gratification with his beloved, and only at the very end of the novel on their marriage night does he put Lycaenion's helpful lessons into practice (4.40).

Longus' depiction of the countryside and its simple inhabitants is peppered with humorous touches, which surely would have appealed to a sophisticated urban readership. So, when the goatherd Lamon brings Daphnis back home to his wife Myrtale, 'she was amazed at the thought of goats producing children' (1.3). Her hopeless misconstrual of the situation is the beginning of a thematic sexual innocence within the countryside that will pervade the novel.

Elsewhere, Longus seems to deconstruct the idea that the unadorned natural beauty which typifies country people is better than its artificial urban counterpart. As children, Daphnis and Chloe are specifically said to be 'more beautiful than country children usually are' (1.7), which raises some familiar questions about nature versus nurture, and after their true identities are revealed, Chloe is dressed up by her future mother-in-law, Cleariste:

> Then you could learn what beauty is like when it is properly
> presented. For when Chloe was dressed and had put her hair

up and washed her face, she seemed so much more beautiful
to everyone that even Daphnis scarcely recognised her.

(4.32)

We might compare Ovid's gentle subversion of rustic simplicity in
describing the rape of the Sabine women at *Ars Amatoria* 1.103–8,
which hints that there is, after all, something to be said for the
refinements of the city.

Can it be that, despite Longus' beautiful evocation of country life
throughout the novel, the city will have the last laugh? Although we
can see a fundamental antithesis between the city and countryside in
the novel, Longus isn't simply endorsing one over the other, but
prompts us to think instead about what each environment
symbolises. After their marriage, Daphnis and Chloe certainly reject
urban sophistication and return to an idyllic pastoral existence
(4.39). They even try to recreate their own childhood experiences
through their two children, who are suckled by a she-goat and a ewe
respectively. However, it becomes clear that as adults they can never
recapture the innocence of their existence as adolescents: the novel
ends with Chloe realising on her wedding night that 'what they had
done in the woods had been nothing but shepherds' games' (4.40).
The countryside as presented in the novel is so closely bound up with
the characterisation of the inexperienced Daphnis and Chloe that we
cannot look at it in isolation. We see that although the adult lovers
can return to the countryside physically, their emotional lives have
developed, so that a return to their former innocence in the
countryside is impossible. They cannot go back – and that is the
point. Such symbolism makes it particularly poignant that Goethe
as an old man felt the desire to return so often to the idyllic world of
Daphnis and Chloe.

Notes

1   E.L. Bowie and S.J. Harrison, 'The romance of the novel', *Journal of Roman Studies*, 83, 1993, p. 159.
2   See further B.P. Reardon, 'Theme, structure and narrative in Chariton', in S.C.R. Swain (ed.), *Oxford Readings in the Greek Novel*, Oxford: Oxford University Press, 1999, pp. 163–88.
3   See further J.P. O'Sullivan, *Xenophon of Ephesus: His Compositional Technique and the Birth of the Novel*, Berlin and New York: Walter De Gruyter, 1995.
4   See further Reardon, 'Achilles Tatius and the *ego*-narrative', in Swain, *op. cit.*, pp. 243–58.

5 Suggested dates for *Daphnis and Chloe* have ranged from the second century to the sixth century AD, but the consensus now is that the work was composed in the late second or early third century AD. See R.L. Hunter, *A Study of Daphnis and Chloe*, Cambridge: Cambridge University Press, 1983, p. 15, and B.D. MacQueen, *Myth, Rhetoric and Fiction: A Reading of Longus' Daphnis and Chloe*, Lincoln, NB, and London: University of Nebraska Press, 1990, p. 189, who places it 'sometime between AD 175 and AD 200'.

6 See further J.J. Winkler, 'The mendacity of Kalasiris and the narrative strategy of Heliodorus' *Aithiopika*', in Swain, *op. cit.*, pp. 286–350.

7 These and other fragmentary novels are conveniently translated in Reardon (ed.), *Collected Ancient Greek Novels*, Berkeley, Los Angeles and London: University of California Press, 1989.

8 L. Cresci, 'Longus the Sophist and the pastoral tradition', in Swain, *op. cit.*, pp. 210–42, discusses this relationship in detail.

9 B. Effe, 'Longus: Towards a History of Bucolic and its Function in the Roman Empire', in Swain, *op. cit.*, pp. 189–209.

10 E.L. Bowie, 'The Greek Novel', in Swain, *op. cit.*, pp. 39–59.

11 Translations are by C. Gill in Reardon, *Collected Ancient Greek Novels*. See Hunter, *op. cit.*, pp. 38–52, and MacQueen, *op. cit.*, pp. 19–30, on the prologue.

12 See Hunter, *op. cit.*, pp. 48–9, and MacQueen, *op. cit.*, pp. 157–9, on Longus and Thucydides.

13 See MacQueen, *op. cit.*, pp. 72–8, on Lycaenion.

See also in this book

Apuleius, Petronius, Theocritus

Texts, translations and commentaries

The Greek text is available in Teubner and Loeb.

Apart from the Loeb, there is a Penguin translation by P. Turner and a University of California translation edited by B.P. Reardon in *Collected Ancient Greek Novels*.

There is a commentary by J.R. Morgan forthcoming in the Aris and Phillips Series.

Further reading

Bowie, E.L. and Harrison, S.J., 'The romance of the novel', *Journal of Roman Studies*, 83, 1993, pp. 159–78.

Hägg, T., *The Novel in Antiquity*, Berkeley and Los Angeles, CA: University of California Press, 1983.

Hunter, R.L., *A Study of Daphnis and Chloe*, Cambridge: Cambridge University Press, 1983.

MacQueen, B.D., *Myth, Rhetoric and Fiction: A Reading of Longus' Daphnis and Chloe*, Lincoln, NB, and London: University of Nebraska Press, 1990.

Morgan, J.R., '*Daphnis and Chloe*: Love's own sweet story', in J.R. Morgan and R. Stoneman (eds), *Greek Fiction: The Greek Novel in Context*, London and New York: Routledge, 1994, pp. 64–79.

Swain, S.C.R. (ed.), *Oxford Readings in the Greek Novel*, Oxford: Oxford University Press, 1999.

Tatum, J. (ed.), *The Search for the Ancient Novel*, Baltimore, MD, and London: Johns Hopkins University Press, 1994.

Winkler, J.J., *The Constraints of Desire: Anthropology of Sex and Gender in Ancient Greece*, London and New York: Routledge, 1990.

CASSIUS DIO

Cassius Dio is an under-rated historian who, together with Arrian of Nicomedia (AD 86–160) and Appian of Alexandria (before AD 100–*c.* 165), ensured that historiography written in Greek flourished during the second and third centuries AD. This is particularly remarkable given that we have no surviving continuous historical narratives written in Latin between Tacitus at the start of the second century AD and Ammianus Marcellinus in the fourth century AD. Those who wrote in Latin during this period seem to have turned their attention instead to biography and epitomised history.

Dio (born *c.* AD 164) originally came from the prosperous city of Nicaea in Bithynia in northern Asia Minor, but he probably moved to Rome as a boy after his father Cassius Apronianus became a senator.[1] Thus Dio, born in the Greek east and brought up in Rome, had a dual intellectual and cultural heritage, which is often reflected in his writing. Following in his father's footsteps, Dio himself entered the Senate under Commodus, gained a praetorship from Pertinax and, probably in about AD 204, was made consul by Septimius Severus.

His career continued to prosper under Severus Alexander, who in quick succession appointed Dio proconsul of Africa (*c.* AD 223), legate of Dalmatia (*c.* AD 224–6) and legate of Upper Pannonia (*c.* AD 226–8). After holding this last post, Dio claims to have special knowledge about the Pannonians, which he suggests makes his account especially reliable (*Roman History* 49.36.4). These different appointments were certainly prestigious, particularly as they were granted by the emperor, but Dio, who was no longer young, was thereby prevented from spending much time either in Italy (in his pleasant villa at Capua) or in his home province of Bithynia. At the end of his life, Dio didn't forget his Eastern roots, although much of his career had been spent serving Rome around the empire. After the notable achievement of a second consulship in AD 229, he retired to

Bithynia to nurse his bad feet (*Roman History* 80.4.2–5.3). The precise date of his death remains unknown.

Dio's historical work, the *Roman History*, was written in Greek on a monumental scale, narrating events from the origins of Rome until AD 229 in eighty books. Both the magnitude and the chronological sweep of the *Roman History* recall Livy rather than Tacitus as a precedent within the genre, although the fact that Dio combined writing with an active public career distinguishes him from Livy. Not all of the *Roman History* is extant: Books 36–55.9 (covering 69–6 BC) are almost intact, but the rest of the text is preserved only in fragments and epitomes.

Dio explains that his inspiration to write history came after receiving a letter of congratulation from Septimius Severus about an earlier work on the dreams and portents which heralded the emperor's rise to power (*Roman History* 72.23.1). On that very night, Dio claims that he dreamed about a divine power who ordered him to write a historical narrative of Severus' accession to the principate, and the success of this work eventually made him decide to compose a broader historical narrative: the *Roman History*. Another dream features as a structural device at the end of the work, as Dio records that a divine power had appeared to Dio and told him to end his narrative with a quote from Homer (*Roman History* 80.5.3). This use of divine inspiration communicated through dreams to explain why Dio wrote history, unusual within the historiographical tradition, is a motif more often associated with poets.[2]

Even so, Dio doesn't pepper his narrative with fantastic elements, saying at one point:

> I consider it to be the chief characteristic of a trained mind to be able to apply rational principles to historical facts, thereby demonstrating the true nature of the facts and also, by co-ordinating the facts, showing the truth of the principles.
>
> (*Roman History* 46.35.1)[3]

Dio worked hard researching his narrative, proudly claiming that he spent ten years conducting historical investigation and twelve years actually writing the narrative up to the death of Severus in AD 211, which was originally supposed to be the end-point (*Roman History* 72.23.5). In this way, Dio tries to generate confidence in the *Roman*

History as a well-crafted historical work, echoing the claims of previous historians writing in Greek: Diodorus Siculus claims to have spent thirty years on his history and Dionysius of Halicarnassus twenty-two years.

Dio's meticulous methods of research and his rejection of the fantastic recall the historiographical precedent of Thucydides. Both stylistically and ideologically, Dio was influenced by Thucydides, from whom he borrows phrases, ideas and techniques, particularly in the speeches. Thus Dio's Fabius Rullus argues against excessive retaliation for a Latin revolt (*Roman History* fr. 36.1) in a way that recalls Thucydides' Diodotus during the Mytilenean debate. Rich observes that

> in much of his work Dio adopts a Thucydidean stance, that of the cynical observer of human affairs, exposing men's pretences and laying bare the realities of power.[4]

Dio's stylistic and intellectual debts to Thucydides are typical of the Greek cultural revival known as the Second Sophistic.

At the same time, Dio owed much to the Roman historiographical tradition. Like Livy, Dio exploited the decade, a grouping of ten books, as an organisational unit for his extensive narrative. Moreover, for chronology the *Roman History* uses the official Roman year dated by consuls as the principal structural device, at least in the surviving books; but, like Tacitus, Dio isn't restricted by this potentially rigid annalistic format. Certainly Dio can organise material along biographical lines when it suits him to do so, and this is particularly convenient when narrating the principate: individual emperors are often both introduced and allowed to depart with separate character sketches which include material taken out of chronological order.[5] Likewise, Dio is prepared to narrate events spanning several years in one continuous segment of narrative, particularly with foreign campaigns (for example, *Roman History* 49.19–33).

In addition, Dio clearly knew Latin: he appears to have read Seneca's *Apocolocyntosis* (60.35.3–4)[6] and laments the fact that he cannot find a direct equivalent for the Latin word *auctoritas* ('authority'), which he transliterates in Greek (*Roman History* 55.3.4–5). He mentions in passing Sallust (*Roman History* 40.63.4) and Livy (*Roman History* 67.12.4), both of whom he had probably read, although the reference in each case is fairly general, and he also consulted Augustus' autobiography on the amount of Caesar's legacy (*Roman History* 44.35.3).[7] It is difficult to reconstruct which sources Dio used, although he tries hard to convince his readers that he had read all the relevant material and shaped his account from a selection of these writers (*Roman History* 1.3.5–8). Ancient historical writers tended to name their sources either when they were faced with contradictory accounts, or when their careful research had unearthed some particularly unusual material. In this respect, therefore, Dio follows the techniques of his predecessors.

In ideological terms, Dio appears to have valued the stability created by the principate and observed pithily that 'Monarchy sounds unpleasant, but it is the most practical form of government under which to live' (*Roman History* 44.1.2). This stance doesn't make him uncritical of incompetent emperors and even Septimius Severus, who inspired Dio to write history, is given a balanced treatment. We are repeatedly offered perspectives on the principate which reflect the senatorial point of view.[8] So, when Commodus (emperor AD 180–92) decapitates an ostrich and brandishes the head at the senators, Dio discreetly hints to his colleagues that they can avoid laughing by chewing on the laurel leaves of their crowns (*Roman History* 72.21.1–2). In his narrative, Dio's judgement on particular emperors often depends on how well or how badly they treated his fellow senators. He also implies that the senators themselves were obliged to conduct themselves responsibly and gives details of Augustus' measures to make sure that they attended meetings of the Senate. In this context, we hear that Augustus' practice of writing up all the names of the senators on a white board still took place in Dio's own day (*Roman History* 55.3.3).

Nor does Dio's general approval of the imperial system lead him to ignore the difficulties of historical inquiry under the principate, when the size of the empire and the secrecy in which important decisions were taken made it difficult to reconstruct events (*Roman History* 53.19).[9] Dio, who spent his professional life working under the emperors, was fascinated by the transition from republic to principate, as is clear from the fact that the *Roman History* devotes much more space to this period than to any other. Historians today especially value Dio's sophisticated and clear narrative of the triumviral era, and passages such as the unusually frank reassessment of Cicero (*Roman History* 38.12) show that Dio can offer us alternative perspectives on leading historical figures of the period. Perhaps Dio's own experiences of confronting turbulent armies in

Pannonia (*Roman History* 80.4) may have sharpened his interest in the triumviral age as a whole.

Dio was the last substantial writer of annalistic history in Greek from the ancient world whose work is at least partly extant. The Byzantine scholar Photius (*c.* AD 810–93) regarded Dio as a much clearer writer than Thucydides and appreciated the subject matter of the *Roman History*, like other educated readers in the Byzantine world who saw their state as a continuation of the Roman empire. Many fragments of the *Roman History* have survived thanks to the efforts of the excerptors who worked for the Emperor Constantine VII Porphyrogenitus (AD 912–50). A useful epitome of Books 36–80 was made in the late eleventh century by John Xiphilinus, who selected episodes from Dio which he regarded as particularly entertaining or enlightening. Moreover, early in the twelfth century John Zonaras wrote an *Epitome of Histories*, which was a universal history documenting events from the creation until AD 1118, and used Dio especially, both for his account of early Roman history from Aeneas' arrival in Italy to 146 BC and for his account of events from Julius Caesar to Nerva.[10]

Notes

1 F.G.B. Millar, *A Study of Cassius Dio*, Oxford: Oxford University Press, 1964, pp. 5–27, discusses Dio's life and career.

2 See J. Marincola, *Authority and Tradition in Ancient Historiography*, Cambridge: Cambridge University Press, 1997, pp. 48–51, on Dio's elaborate description of his call to history, including the various dreams. Pliny the Elder also had a dream which inspired him to write history (Pliny *Letters* 3.5.4).

3 See further Millar, *op. cit.*, p. 45, whose translation this is.

4 J. W. Rich, *Cassius Dio: The Augustan Settlement (Roman History 53–55.9)*, Warminster: Aris and Phillips, 1990, p. 11.

5 See further C.B.R. Pelling, 'Biographical history? Cassius Dio on the early principate', in M.J. Edwards and S.C.R. Swain (eds), *Portraits: Biographical Representation in the Greek and Latin Literature of the Roman Empire*, Oxford: Oxford University Press, 1997, pp. 117–44.

6 See Millar, *op. cit.*, pp. 78–9, for further examples of Dio's acquaintance with Seneca's writings.

7 Millar, *op. cit.*, p. 85, notes that he gets the figure wrong.

8 See A.M. Gowing, *The Triumviral Narratives of Appian and Cassius Dio*, Ann Arbor, MI: University of Michigan Press, 1992, pp. 21–5, on Dio and the Senate.

9 Marincola, *op. cit.*, pp. 88–9, discusses this important passage.

10 See Millar, *op. cit.*, pp. 1–4, on Xiphilinus and Zonaras.

See also in this book

Herodotus, Livy, Sallust, Tacitus, Thucydides, Xenophon

Texts, translations and commentaries

The Greek text is available in Teubner and Loeb (9 volumes), but there is no OCT. There is also an important edition by U.P. Boissevain (5 volumes).

Apart from the Loeb, there is a Penguin translation of *Roman History* 50–6 by I. Scott-Kilvert, but there is no Oxford World's Classics translation.

There is a commentary on *Cassius Dio: The Augustan Settlement (Roman History 53–55.9)* by J. Rich in the Aris and Phillips Series and on *From Republic to Principate. An Historical Commentary on Cassius Dio's Roman History 49–52* by M. Reinhold (published by Scholars Press).

Further reading

Barnes, T.D., 'The composition of Cassius Dio's *Roman History*', *Phoenix*, 38, 1984, pp. 240–55.

Brunt, P.A., 'On historical fragments and epitomes', *Classical Quarterly*, 30, 1980, pp. 477–94.

Gowing, A.M., *The Triumviral Narratives of Appian and Cassius Dio*, Ann Arbor, MI: University of Michigan Press, 1992.

Marincola, J., *Authority and Tradition in Ancient Historiography*, Cambridge: Cambridge University Press, 1997.

Millar, F.G.B., *A Study of Cassius Dio*, Oxford: Oxford University Press, 1964.

Pelling, C.B.R., 'Biographical history? Cassius Dio on the early principate', in M.J. Edwards and S.C.R. Swain (eds), *Portraits: Biographical Representation in the Greek and Latin Literature of the Roman Empire*, Oxford: Oxford University Press, 1997, pp. 117–44.

Rich, J.W., 'Dio and Augustus', in A. Cameron (ed.), *History as Text*, London: Duckworth, 1989, pp. 87–110.

TIMELINE

Literary events

c. 750–700 BC	Homer composes the *Iliad* and the *Odyssey*.
c. 700 BC	Hesiod flourishes.
c. 650–600 BC	Sappho is born on Lesbos.
c. 525 BC	Birth of Aeschylus at Eleusis near Athens.
c. 518 BC	Birth of Pindar at Cynoscephalae near Thebes.
c. 496 BC	Birth of Sophocles at Colonus near Athens.
480s BC	Birth of Herodotus in Halicarnassus in Caria.
	Birth of Euripides in Athens.
c. 460 BC	Birth of Thucydides in Athens.
c. 459–458 BC	Birth of Lysias in Athens.
458 BC	Aeschylus' *Oresteia* is produced in Athens.
c. 456–455 BC	Death of Aeschylus.
c. 450 BC	Birth of Aristophanes in Athens.
post-446 BC	Death of Pindar.
431 BC	Euripides produces *Medea*.
c. 430 BC	Birth of Xenophon at Erchia near Athens.
420s BC	Death of Herodotus.

Historical and political events

753 BC	Traditional date of the foundation of Rome.
594 BC	Solon's legal reforms in Athens.
c. 560–559 BC	Death of Solon.
527 BC	Death of Pisistratus.
508–507 BC	Cleisthenes reforms the Athenian constitution.
490 BC	Greeks defeat the Persians at the Battle of Marathon.
480 BC	Greeks defeat the Persians at the Battle of Salamis.
479 BC	Greeks defeat Persians at Plataea.
469 BC	Birth of Socrates.
460–446 BC	First Peloponnesian War.
431–404 BC	Great Peloponnesian War.
415–413 BC	Sicilian expedition.

Literary events

c. 428 BC	Birth of Plato in Athens.
411 BC	Aristophanes' *Lysistrata* is produced.
409 BC	Sophocles wins a victory with *Philoctetes*.
406 BC	Death of Euripides.
c. 406–405 BC	Death of Sophocles.
405 BC	Aristophanes' *Frogs* is produced.
post-404 BC	Death of Thucydides.
401 BC	Sophocles wins a posthumous victory with *Oedipus at Colonus*.
388 BC	Aristophanes' last extant play, *Wealth*, is produced.
c. 385 BC	Death of Aristophanes. Birth of Demosthenes in Athens.
384 BC	Birth of Aristotle in Stagira in northern Greece.
c. 380 BC	Death of Lysias.
late 350s BC	Death of Xenophon.
351 BC	Demosthenes delivers his *First Philippic*.
347 BC	Death of Plato.
344 BC	Demosthenes delivers his *Second Philippic*.
342–341 BC	Birth of Menander.
341 BC	Demosthenes delivers his *Third Philiooic*.
322 BC	Death of Aristotle. Death of Demosthenes.
c. 320–305 BC	Birth of Callimachus in Cyrene.
c. 300–250 BC	Theocritus flourishes.
c. 293–289 BC	Death of Menander.
239 BC	Birth of Ennius in Rudiae in southern Italy.
c. 205–184 BC	Plautus writes his comedies.

Historical and political events

399 BC	Death of Socrates.
378 BC	Creation of the Second Athenian Confederacy.
371 BC	Thebans defeat Sparta at the Battle of Leuctra.
359–336 BC	Rule of Philip II of Macedon.
336–323 BC	Rule of Alexander the Great.
301 BC	The Macedonian Antigonus the One-Eyed is defeated at the Battle of Ipsus.
271–216 BC	Hieron II rules Syracuse on Sicily.
264–241 BC	First Punic War between Rome and Carthage.

Literary events

c. 200 BC   Birth of Polybius in Megalopolis in Arcadia.

c. 185 BC   Birth of Terence in Carthage.

169 BC   Death of Ennius.

160s BC   Terence writes his comedies.

c. 159 BC   Death of Terence.

118 BC   Death of Polybius.

106 BC   Birth of Cicero in Arpinum in Italy.

100 BC   Birth of Julius Caesar.

mid-90s BC   Birth of Lucretius.

c. 86 BC   Birth of Sallust in Amiternum in central Italy.

c. 84 BC   Birth of Catullus in Verona in northern Italy.

70 BC   Birth of Virgil near Mantua in northern Italy.

65 BC   Birth of Horace in Venusia in southern Italy.

59 BC   Birth of Livy in Padua in northern Italy.

mid-50s BC   Death of Lucretius.

c. 55–48 BC   Birth of Tibullus.

c. 54 BC   Death of Catullus.

c. 54–47 BC   Birth of Propertius in Asisium in central Italy.

c. 50 BC   Birth of Seneca the Elder in Corduba in southern Spain.

44 BC   Assassination of Julius Caesar.

43 BC   Death of Cicero. Birth of Ovid in Sulmo in central Italy.

42–41 BC   Sallust publishes his *Catiline*.

41–40 BC   Sallust publishes his *Jugurtha*.

35 BC   Death of Sallust.

30s BC   Horace writes his *Epodes* (published *c.* 30 BC).

c. 23 BC   Horace publishes Books 1–3 of his *Odes*.

19 BC   Death of Virgil. Death of Tibullus.

Historical and political events

218–201 BC   Second Punic War between Rome and Carthage.

168 BC   Romans defeat Perseus of Macedon at Pydna.

149–146 BC   Third Punic War between Rome and Carthage.

146 BC   Destruction of Carthage by the Romans.

86 BC   Death of Marius.

79 BC   Death of Sulla.

63 BC   Catilinarian conspiracy.

60 BC   Formation of the first triumvirate.

53 BC   Crassus is killed while fighting the Parthians.

48 BC   Julius Caesar defeats Pompey at the Battle of Pharsalus.

44 BC   Assassination of Julius Caesar.

31 BC   Octavian (soon to be Augustus) defeats Antony and Cleopatra at the Battle of Actium.

27 BC   Title of Augustus is awarded to Octavian.

Literary events

17 BC	Horace publishes his *Carmen Saeculare*.
post-16 BC	Death of Propertius.
13 BC	Horace publishes the fourth book of his *Odes*.
8 BC	Death of Horace. Death of Maecenas.
c. 4 BC–AD 1	Birth of Seneca the Younger in Corduba in southern Spain.
1 BC	Ovid publishes Books 1–2 of his *Ars Amatoria*.
pre-AD 8	Ovid publishes his *Metamorphoses*.
AD 8	Ovid is sent into exile.
c. AD 16–17	Death of Ovid in exile.
AD 17	Death of Livy.
c. AD 35	Birth of Quintilian in Calagurris in Spain.
c. AD 38–41	Birth of Martial in Bilbilis in Spain.
AD 39	Birth of Lucan in Corduba in Spain.
c. AD 40	Death of Seneca the Elder.
AD 41–9	Seneca the Younger lives in Corsica in exile.
c. AD 45–50s	Birth of Statius in Neapolis in southern Italy.
AD 50–250	Period of revival of Greek literature known as the Second Sophistic.
c. AD 50	Birth of Plutarch in Chaeroneia in Greece.
mid-AD 50s	Birth of Tacitus, probably in Gallia Narbonensis.
c. AD 61–62	Birth of Pliny the Younger in Comum in northern Italy.
AD 66	Death of Petronius.

Historical and political events

AD 14	Death of Augustus.
AD 14–37	Tiberius' principate.
AD 37–41	Caligula's principate.
AD 41–54	Claudius' principate.
AD 54–68	Nero's principate.
AD 59	Nero murders his mother, Agrippina the Younger.
AD 64	Great fire of Rome.
AD 65	Pisonian conspiracy. Seneca the Younger and Lucan are forced to commit suicide.

Literary events

c. AD 70	Birth of Suetonius, probably in Hippo Regius in northern Africa.
AD 80	Martial publishes his *Book of Spectacles.*
AD 86–101	Martial publishes his *Epigrams.*
c. AD 96	Death of Quintilian. Death of Statius.
AD 98	Tacitus publishes his *Agricola* and *Germania.*
AD 100	Birth of Appian. Pliny the Younger delivers his *Panegyricus.*
c. AD 101–102	Tacitus publishes his *Dialogus.*
c. AD 102	Death of Silius Italicus.
c. AD 104	Death of Martial.
c. AD 113	Death of Pliny the Younger in Bithynia-Pontus.
c. AD 115–130	Juvenal writes his *Satires.*
post-AD 117	Death of Tacitus.
c. AD 120	Birth of Lucian in Samosata in Syria.
post-AD 120	Death of Plutarch.
c. AD 125	Birth of Apuleius in Madauros in North Africa.
c. AD 130	Death of Suetonius.
AD 158–159	Apuleius delivers his *Apologia.*
AD 165	Death of Appian.
c. AD 164	Birth of Cassius Dio in Nicaea in Bithynia.
post-AD 170	Death of Apuleius.
c. AD 200	Longus writes *Daphnis and Chloe.*
post-AD 229	Death of Cassius Dio.

Historical and political events

AD 68–69	Civil wars rage after Nero's suicide ('Year of the Four Emperors').
AD 69–79	Vespasian's principate.
AD 79	Eruption of Mount Vesuvius on Pompeii.
AD 79–81	Titus' principate.
AD 81	Domitian becomes emperor.
AD 96	Assassination of Domitian.
AD 98–117	Trajan's principate.
AD 117–138	Hadrian's principate.
AD 138–161	Antoninus Pius' principate.
AD 161–180	Marcus Aurelius' principate.
AD 180–192	Commodus' principate.
AD 193–211	Septimius Severus' principate.

INDEX

LINGG